FOLK SONG IN ENGLAND

A. L. Lloyd

INTERNATIONAL PUBLISHERS
NEW YORK

SBN (hardback) 7178–0067–9; (paperback) 7178–0278–7
Printed in the United States of America

PREFACE

This is a book for beginners not specialists. For all that, it says some things not said elsewhere. It could hardly fail to, seeing how meagre commentary on English folk song is. Collections abound, but information about who made the songs, and how, and for what purpose, is hard to come by. Cecil Sharp's *English Folk Song: Some Conclusions* remains a solitary beacon and a towering one, but it was lit sixty years ago and its glow is fading. It would be pleasant to think this book you are holding might help *Some Conclusions* to shine clearer, if only by putting a little fat in the fire.

Along with such splendid pioneers as Lucy Broadwood, Vaughan Williams, Hammond, Grainger, Kidson, Cecil Sharp was a founder of the folk song revival in the early years of the century. Fruitful as that revival was, many young people of the time resisted it, suspecting that a 'tradition' was being imposed on them for their own good and against their inclinations. However, within the last twenty years or so a new interest in folk song has arisen, nourished by the former revival, but coming from below now, not imposed from above, affecting a broader section of society, employing a wider repertory, and involving a greater variety of uses and usages than were ever imagined in Sharp's time. It is to the enthusiasts of this second revival, for the most part young people searching for something more sustaining than the mumbled withdrawals or frantic despair of the pops, that this book is chiefly addressed.

The work has its history. In America, late in the Depression and early in the War years, traditional song and its topical imitations were coming into vogue, particularly among young radicals, as a consequence of the stresses of the time, and the rumble of newly-found or newly-made 'people's songs' was rolling towards us across the Atlantic. The Workers' Music Association, that admirable but over-modest organization, sensed that similar enthusiasm might spread in England, and they were eager to help in the re-discovery of our own lower-class traditions. They commissioned me to write a brief social-historical introduction to folk song, titled: *The Singing Englishman*. It was put together mainly in barrack-rooms, away from reference-works, in between tank-gunnery courses. It wasn't a good book, but people were kind to it perhaps because it was the only one of its sort: like the okapi, not much to look at but cherished as unique.

The W.M.A.'s presage was justified; the folk song revival swept in, and against all pessimistic forecasts the enthusiasm endured through the years. *The Singing Englishman* went out of print and out of date. People still asked for it, but I did not want to see it reprinted, nor did I feel that mere revision could make it adequate for current needs. So it was proposed that I should write a new book 'based on' the old one; and here it is.

I suppose what is newest in this book is the picture it offers of the continuity of folk song, from the 'classic' rural forms, through the urban industrial forms (those queer amalgams of the collective–folkloric and the individual–'literary'), into that as yet vaguely-charted territory that lies between folklore proper and the realm of the commercial hit, an otherworld into which traditional songs in their resurrected form seem to integrate themselves quite happily, changed in function but still widely sung, listened to, and carried around in the head with love.

I offer a bow to the Workers' Music Association who promoted this work and generously joined the publishers in helping to feed my family while I wrote it. A bow also to the Arts Council who floated me a 'maintenance grant' out of the blue, all the more delightful for being unsolicited. My third bow is to my publishers who waited with patience and heart-breaking forbearance for me to finish this long, long overdue book. Away then, pages; do your best: I have done mine.

A. L. L.

Greenwich,
July 1967.

ACKNOWLEDGEMENTS

For the most part, the makers and bearers of our folk songs were anonymous amateurs who earned their living, meagre as it often was, in other ways than entertainment. By the same token, such educated men as were interested in the songs had little thought of exploiting their curiosity for gain. Folk song was seen as an embellishment, perhaps as a heritage, seldom as a commodity. Now, things are rather changed. From being neglected, if not derided, folk song enjoys wide esteem, and becomes a means of financial reward and commercial success. No harm in that, when it means that lyrics thought dead are brought back to eager life, and through mass diffusion a valuable form of human expression becomes once again part of the cultural baggage of millions. No harm at all, except that inevitably when products of such vague uncertified origin come into the market-place, proprietary rights may be claimed by hucksters with very slender title, and the use of a kind of song which should be free to all is hindered. Fortunately, such restrictive practices are relatively rare, and it is the pleasant duty of the author and publishers of the present volume to record their gratitude to the many singers, collectors, editors, publishers and institutions that so readily and courteously allowed us to reproduce songs in their possession, or which they were initially responsible for bringing to public attention.

Without question, a venture such as the present one could not have been embarked on without the kind aid of the English Folk Dance and Song Society, who allowed material gathered by various collectors including Miss Lucy Broadwood, Miss A. G. Gilchrist, Miss Bertha Bidder, Percy Grainger, George B. Gardiner, Walter Ford and E. T. Sweeting, to be reproduced from their invaluable *Journal*, and were willingly helpful in a variety of ways. Then, we are particularly indebted to Dr. Maud Karpeles who, as Cecil Sharp's executor, freely permitted the use of many items from his unsurpassed collection, and likewise to Mrs. Ursula Vaughan Williams for allowing us to use a number of important pieces from the collections of Ralph Vaughan Williams and H. E. D. Hammond.

We acknowledge similar obligations to Peter Kennedy, Ken

Stubbs, A. E. Green and W. B. Toyn for songs of their collecting, also to John Pandrich ('Johnny Handle') and Keith Roberts, for miners' songs made by themselves. Among many singers drawn upon, we are particularly grateful to the late Jack Elliott of Birtley and his son John, and to the late Ted Howard of Barry. Thanks are also due to the following publishers who kindly allowed us to print songs from the collections named below: Novello and Company: Cecil J. Sharp, *English Folk Songs* (*Centenary Edition*), 1959; Cecil J. Sharp (ed.), *English County Folk Songs*, 1961. J. B. Cramer and Company: L. E. Broadwood, *English County Songs*, 1893. Charles Taphouse and Son: F. Kidson, *Traditional Tunes*, 1891. Acknowledgment is also owed to Schott and Company for a song collected by Percy Grainger, to the Oxford University Press for a sea shanty notated by Cecil Sharp, to Messrs. J. Curwen and Sons for a fragment of a shanty collected by R. R. Terry, and to the Mitchell Library, Glasgow, for permission to reproduce from the collection of Frank Kidson.

Finally, we express our gratitude to Dr. Ray Edwards for his vigilant help with the proofs, and to Mr. James P. Homer who drew all the tunes.

A. L. L.

CONTENTS

I

THE FOUNDATIONS OF FOLK SONG

We hear of a village in the Antilles inhabited chiefly by women. The men have to seek work in the nearest town. Any messages the women want to pass to their men they confide to a tree. 'Why do you talk to that tree?' asked the visiting folklorist. 'Because we're poor', the women answered. 'If we were rich we'd use the telephone.'

The mother of folklore is poverty, and our little Caribbean parable illustrates the force exerted by economics on the peculiar ways of common people. Obvious? So one would think; yet many folklorists would hesitate to admit the importance of material means in conditioning the kind of culture that is the object of their study. That hours, wages and conditions have anything to do with what and how a man sings is an abhorrent idea to them. Part of their shyness, which at times becomes a nervous derision, arises because their minds are vague about the meaning of the word 'folk', a gawky term suggesting English condescension or German soulfulness, but so far without a handy synonym.

What are we to understand by 'folk'?[1] A whole nation, with or without minorities? A single class (the lower class)? A section of that class (country workers)? In those parts of Western Europe and America where class distinctions, though real enough, are rather blurred, some people, specialists as well as amateurs, have taken 'folk' to mean the nation, all classes, upper, lower, urban, rural, regardless of social, historical or spiritual differences. This was the view of German romantics of the time of Goethe and Herder and with modifications it has gone in and out of fashion several times since (in America at the moment it is rather 'in'). It is a permissible view in the attenuated sense that we are all bearers of some sort of folklore, if only in the form of the dirty story, apparently an indestructible type of oral 'literature'. The trouble is, such a prospect extends too easily to a boundless panorama going beyond all reasonable definition, so that in the field of song for instance any piece that has passed widely into public circulation is identified as 'folk', especially if one can pretend it somehow expresses part of the essential character of the nation. Thus, Silcher and Heine's "Die Lorelei" is exhibited as folk song, likewise "The bonnie banks o' Loch Lomond" (words and tune by a Victorian aristocrat, Lady John Scott), Stephen Foster's "Old folks at home", and more recently, with even slenderer title, Bob Dylan's "Blowin' in the wind". To say nothing of Pottier and Degeyter's "Internationale". By this time we are not far from the vague contours suggested by Louis Armstrong's* dreary axiom: 'All music's folk music: leastways I never heard of no horse making it.'

Against this broad and hardly manageable 'popular' view of folk song as national song is set the restricted picture offered by several scientists of musical folklore who follow Bartók in considering the term 'folk song' to be synonymous with peasant song, and who maintain that no other part of the nation but working farmers and farm labourers are the true shapers and bearers of traditional verse and melody.

It is worth considering how Bartók came to this opinion for his conclusions are paralleled by those of Cecil Sharp, though Sharp's are by no means so firmly based. As a very young man Bartók was among those who thought that national music and folk music were one and the same. In 1896, while he was still in his teens, Hungary celebrated its millennium in a fever of nationalism that lasted for several years. Kodály has described the time. Everything was to be Hungarian not Austro-German: Hungarian words of command in the army, a Hungarian coat of arms on every post-office, a Hungarian anthem to replace Haydn's Hapsburg hymn. The young Bartók wore Hungarian costume, then back in fashion, even on the concert platform. In his search for a Hungarian style of composition freed from German influence he was attracted to the *verbunkos* idiom of the gypsy orchestras imagining, as Liszt had, that this was folk stuff; whereas in fact the repertory of the gypsy bands is principally made up of fanciful treatments of tunes composed from the mid-nineteenth century onward by educated amateurs of aristocratic or bourgeois birth; and though this kind of light popular air is often taken for Hungarian folk song, the

---

* If it *is* Armstrong's. Various authors are credited.

real thing is vastly different as Bartók discovered when he set off with his long-horned Edison recording machine to collect peasant songs in the Szekely-Hungarian villages of Transylvania. He felt himself back in the Middle Ages, and the impression was even stronger in the neighbouring villages inhabited by Rumanians. He has described what he found: no railways, often no roads, pack-horses everywhere, settlements occupied entirely by illiterates, men who have never moved out of their birth-place except perhaps for military service or appearance at a court of law, a world where every object of daily use was made in the home, and people lived on what they themselves grew, made their clothes and blankets from wool that they had shorn, spun and woven, carved their own chairs and beds, hardly used money at all, and had only the frailest contact with the commerce and arts of the towns.* He discovered there a submerged world of vigorous music essentially different in many respects from music of learned origin, and it was this kind of melody that he chose to isolate as the genus: folk music.

All very well for Bartók in the Balkans! Meanwhile, in that same year, 1907, at the other end of Europe, and in quite different circumstances, Cecil Sharp was likewise forming an opinion of folk song as the product of a 'primitive' social category living apart from the world of towns and education, with its own ways and standards and works of art that dwindle as the society itself shrinks before the advance of modernism. For Sharp, folk song was 'song created by the common people', and he explains that by 'common people' he means 'the non-educated . . . the unlettered whose faculties have undergone no formal training whatsoever, and who have never been brought into close enough contact with educated persons to be influenced by them'. At one time, he suggests, these 'common people' comprised a large part of the population but now form 'an exceedingly small class . . . and are to be found only in

* Among Rumanian songs collected by Bartók is the complaint of a jilted girl: 'May God punish you by making you eat bread bought with money!' Bartók commented (in a letter to József Szigeti, January 30, 1944): 'Bread bought with money! American town-dwellers wouldn't understand that . . . but the peasant who has a little land grows wheat and makes his own bread. He never buys it unless the hail has destroyed his crop. And then where's he to get money from?'

those country districts which, by reason of their remoteness, have escaped the infection of modern ideas'. In his view, the terms 'peasant song' or 'country song' are synonymous with 'folk song' as opposed to urban or art song, although 'strictly speaking, the real antithesis is not between the music of the town and that of the country, but between that which is the product of the spontaneous and intuitive exercise of untrained faculties, and that which is due to the conscious and intentional use of faculties which have been especially cultivated and developed for the purpose'.[2]

Now, it is true that early in the century when Sharp was cycling along the lanes of the West Country in search of songs, class differences were clearer than they are now and a wide gulf separated the pen-and-ink man from the man with bowyangs of binder-twine. But a whole class, in Western Europe, in England, in Somerset moreover, entirely shut away from and uninfluenced by the world of the educated élite, surely that has not existed since the Middle Ages, if then? Were Sharp's countrymen quite out of the orbit of newspapers, railways, pillar-boxes, medical prescriptions, lightning conductors, fit-up theatres, romantic novels, *Hymns A. & M.*, to name but a few factors that might break down old 'primitive' ideas and replace them with modern ones, including some directly in the service of squire and stockbroker?

Let there be no mistake, Sharp was England's most diligent and responsive folk song collector, by continental standards our only great one, a concise and original thinker and a diligent field-worker, who recorded—almost entirely by mere hand-notation, alas!—nearly five thousand songs and tunes in all. He was a Socialist with a ready sympathy for working people and a keen recognition of their qualities; yet his was an ideology of primitive romanticism with a vengeance. The vengeance, though it would be unkind to lay its responsibility only at Sharp's door, is that after three-quarters of a century of tune-collecting and nearly two hundred years of text-study, we are still without a definition of folk song that really fits our local conditions.

In that, we are not unique. Folklore definitions vary from country to country, epoch to epoch, scholar to scholar. The

American *Standard Dictionary of Folklore and Mythology* alone offers twenty-one of them. All concur that folklore is developed and transmitted by 'the people', but neither dictionaries nor professors agree on a meaning of the term that would be the same everywhere, leading Arnold Van Gennep to remark: 'What's the good of worrying about where folklore begins and ends when we don't even know what characterizes it?' Out of his vast experience, the best the great Belgian folklorist could suggest is that the difficulty is lessened by the kind of intuition scientists acquire through practice, so that just as a numismatist can tell true coins from false by their rough or soapy feel, the folklore specialist may 'instinctively' distinguish the authentic folk creation from, say, the vaudeville song sung in the same company.

Fortunately, intuition is not all that is left to us. Still, if musical folklore is a science, experience shows that it is subject to sudden caprices and its delineation is very hard to fix. In 1954, after long discussion, the International Folk Music Council adopted this definition:

> Folk music is the product of a musical tradition that has been evolved through the process of oral transmission. The factors that shape the tradition are: (i) continuity which links the present with the past; (ii) variation which springs from the creative impulse of the individual or the group; and (iii) selection by the community, which determines the form or forms in which the music survives.
>
> The term can be applied to music that has been evolved from rudimentary beginnings by a community uninfluenced by popular and art music and it can likewise be applied to music which has originated with an individual composer and has subsequently been absorbed into the unwritten living tradition of a community.
>
> The term does not cover composed popular music that has been taken over ready-made by a community and remains unchanged, for it is the re-fashioning and re-creation of the music by the community that gives it its folk character.[3]

The definition derives from a formula set out with classical clarity by Sharp nearly half a century earlier in *English Folk*

Song: Some Conclusions. Continuity of tradition, as he saw it, is founded on the astonishingly retentive memory of the 'unlettered' and their capacity to pass on accurately the songs they have heard. Indeed, says Sharp, 'the traditional singer . . . regards it as a matter of honour to pass on the tradition as nearly as possible as he received it', and he recalls the blind and aged Somerset singer who sang him eleven verses of "Robin Hood and the Tanner" that correspond almost word for word with a blackletter broadside in the Bodleian library, from the collection of the quarrelsome antiquarian Anthony Wood who died in 1695.

The matter of retentive memory affects the words more than the tunes. Against that stability and seeming to contradict it is the factor of *variation*, the tendency of singers constantly to alter melodic phrases in the course of their song. If Sharp's old Robin Hood singer, Henry Larcombe of Hazelbury Plucknett, kept the words rather firmly fixed, he certainly did not do so with the tune. Each time Sharp asked him to repeat a phrase he sang it differently, providing a set of most ingenious and handsome variations.*

Selection implies the working of the community's choice on the songs set before them. If the piece seems beautiful and significant to them, they may take it up and pass it on among themselves. If it appeals to the individual only, if in manner, emotion, and moral it is too personal, too exclusive, too sharp a departure from the line of continuity, the song does not pass into traditional currency but dies on the singer's lips.

So the definition allows that in its natural state a folk song is poetry and music perpetuated by mouth-to-mouth transmission not by print; it is founded on certain inflexible principles but subject to personal variation; its acceptance and survival depends on how well it accords with the tastes, views and experience of the community. As we shall see, there are points to quibble about, but the formulation is valuable for its clear suggestion of the vital dialectic of folk song creation, that

---

* The 'folkloric' tendency to reproduce the words unaltered while treating the tune with great freedom is seen in extreme form in the modern jazz singers' way with 'standards' of the type of, say, "My blue heaven", where the text is sung word for word as printed but the tune is extemporized upon, to the point of re-composition.

is, the perpetual struggle for synthesis between the collective and the individual, between tradition and innovation, between what is received from the community and what is supplied out of personal fantasy, in short, the blending of continuity and variation.

At this point I rest on my typewriter and think how abstract the matter of folk song definition is, and how boring for all but those dogged scholars who dart into argument with voices sharpened, glasses glinting, using their conference-papers as batons in a Tweedledum-Tweedledee fight, with never a notion that their science more than most should be all of a piece with life, or that the materials of their study come directly from the dreams, hopes, glories and despairs, guffaws and night-whispers of such people as the old potato-lifter who cried to the pitiless sun: 'Oh, were you never on hire yourself?' or that other woman in another field who broke off her song to seize the folklorist by the coat-lapels, exclaiming in rapture: 'Isn't it beautiful?'

Deep at the root, there is no essential difference between folk music and art music; they are varied blossoms from the same stock, grown to serve a similar purpose, if destined for different tables. Originally they spring from the same area of man's mind; their divergence is a matter of history, of social and cultural stratification. Traditionally, art music is a diversion for the educated classes, while folk music is one of the most intimate, reassuring and embellishing possessions of the poor (and in large tracts of the world they have been robbed even of that). To comprehend it the folklorist must understand what it means to the people who carry it in their minds and mouths. That calls for sympathy without conde-scension, and an ability to step over the gulfs separating class from class, both qualities in short supply among scholars though some improvement shows. The killing-bottle and pins of academic method can give us only partial data. One after-noon in a sombre room of the Ethnographical Museum in Budapest a well-known folklorist, colleague of Bartók and Kodály, played his visitor a recording of a Csango-Magyar ballad singer from Moldavia. Her song was tragic and she performed it with a fine contained passion, in a way that showed she was totally immersed in the sense of the song. The visitor remarked on the poignant quality of the rendition and the learned professor gave him a sharp look and said: 'Surely by now you know that the sound of folk music is meaningless? It's not until we have it down in precise notation and can see what's happening inside the mould of the melody that it comes to have any significance at all.' For him, what the song meant to the singer was irrelevant; that it brought her almost to tears was a detail not worth enquiring into; the woman was a mere accessory and her heart, mind, voice were superfluities, unnecessary to take into account; pitch and duration were all that mattered. He was a man for Kelvin's principle: What we measure can be understood.

The value of objectivity is not in dispute; but the wilful disengagement that modern Russians deride as 'obyektivizm' is a stumbling-block in the path of folklorists. Far more worthy is the approach of the admirable American folk song scholar Samuel P. Bayard, who says: 'the very thing which forces us to wish to know everything without flinching about our people—the very thing which forces us to intensive and so far as possible objective studies, the very thing which makes us clear-headed at evaluating—is the deep loving regard which we have'.

Amen, though 'deep loving regard' on its own is by no means enough. So Sharp's friend Charles Marson, a Christian Socialist vicar with unusually keen sympathy for his flock, was forced to declare: 'The folk-song is like the duck-billed platypus in this particular, you can live for years within a few yards of it and never suspect its existence.' He confessed that eight years of constant residence in the small village of Hambridge, in Somerset, had left him 'in Stygian ignorance of the wealth of Art which that village contained. Only one song, and that by chance, had fallen upon his untouched ears.' Yet hundreds of songs turned up there and in surrounding villages once Sharp got to work. Surprising? Not at all. Till recently, working people have generally hidden their most precious cultural possessions from the master, the squire, the parson. 'Intimacy with a peasant may go a long way and yet stop short of his songs', says Sharp. So contact between collector and singer tended to be rather less than candid because, however civil, each approached the other gingerly across a social chasm. Notably in England where folk song collecting has been traditionally regarded as an amiable pastime for country curates and maiden ladies on bicycles, and folk song itself was thought of as an ingenuous affair of springtime innocence or clodhopper humour smelling of times past. So, with more pluck than discretion, Miss Laura Smith visited Tyneside boarding-houses in the 1880s in search of sailors' songs. Her harvest was scanty and pallid, partly because, as Captain Whall says: 'If a lady goes round sailors' boarding-houses and attempts to copy down the words and music of Shanties from the men, she is bound to fail. First, sailors are shy with ladies. Secondly, few of the songs have words which a seaman would care to sing to a lady in cold blood.' The diligent Hereford folklorist Ella Leather, a colonel's wife, was prepared to go and work as a hop-picker but even so she found it hard to get to the heart of the gypsies and didikais she toiled alongside. Though they were friendly enough and willing to part with carols and polite lyrical songs, they seem to have kept their more intimate songs to themselves, to judge by what we now know of the repertory of 'travellers'. Lucy Broadwood, noting songs from the Horsham bellringer Henry Burstow remarks that many items in his repertory 'which by their titles promised to be amongst the very oldest ballads, were considered by him to be unfit for ladies' ears, and, as he could not detach the tunes from the words, the airs unfortunately remain unnoted'. But the difficulty is not so much a matter of sex as of social difference. Old Mr. Grantham the Sussex carter 'knew a many songs which he wouldn't sing even to a gentleman', saying: 'They be outway rude.' Commonly, the bourgeois collector anticipates deviousness in the countryman's mind, and the countryman suspects the motives of the bourgeois (how often, in pre-War Eastern Europe, the folklorist was taken for a tax-inspector in disguise!). Such tenuous contact, lack of mutual confidence, downright misunderstanding, has severely restricted folklore study in the past and inhibited the search into such matters as the origin of songs. Any experienced folk song collector has at some time met the singer who produces a version of a well-known venerable piece with the comment: 'I made that one up myself': or who says: 'Here's one for you that's older than Jesus Christ', and it turns out to be a music hall song from the days of Albert Chevalier.

The difficulty has been general. Some years ago in Rumania a wedding party was crossing a frozen river when the ice broke and several of the cortège were drowned. A ballad on the disaster spread rapidly through the district. It ended with the words actually used by the bride's mother lamenting at the water's edge: 'Oh, my daughter, in your lovely shoes the frogs will lay their eggs.' Two years later folklorists visited the locality and tried to establish who had made the song. Authorship was claimed by some whose claim turned out to be baseless; others indicated 'authors' who denied participation. Constantin Brailoiu, reporting this, gives other examples. In 1938 a village was half-destroyed by flood. The king visited the victims and distributed relief. Again, a new ballad sprang up immediately. This time the folklorists descended on the neighbourhood more promptly. Only two people claimed authorship, a shepherd and a young woman, one of the star singers of the village. Behind their backs they accused each other of lying; confronted, they remained obstinately silent. The young woman admitted to receiving the help of friends, but their testimony was so vague that the mystery of authorship remained unsolved.

Things have changed a bit in the last few years. In some parts of Europe, and particularly in the folkloristically-rich South-east, the general democratic trend has set a different pattern in what Americans like to call the 'collector-informant context'. A Balkan collective-farm peasant is no longer daunted by the man in the collar and tie, any more than a Durham miner by the fellow from the B.B.C. The increase of working class self-confidence offers new, more favourable conditions for discovering the full physiology of musical folklore, blood, flesh and wounds, and not merely its anatomy. Other novel factors help, including the invention of the tape-recorder, an easily-carried unfussy tool that, far from intimidating as the cumbersome old cylinder recording-machine did in Bartók's day, arouses the singer's curiosity and easily satisfies his dear and general wish to hear his own voice played back. Nowadays it may happen that the informant knows more about tape-recorders than the collector does, and is able to give him operational advice. Recently I had the pleasure of hearing a blind singer from a hill-farm in North Carolina lucidly lecturing an unhandy collector on the phenomenon of pre-echo on magnetic tape. The folklorist, humbled, lost his superiority and the 'collector-informant context' could not have been more propitious. We may be looking forward to the time when the singer will not only sing the song and supply its documentation, but will gallantly set up the microphones for the recording as well!

No doubt in the past it was the folklorists's lack of truly intimate contact with his singers that made him see them as noble rustic savages, not only unlettered but never brought into touch with the educated world. Yet even a century and a half ago many of the finest Scottish ballad informants were among the best-educated, if self-educated, members of their community (quite apart from the celebrated Mrs. Brown of Falkland who gave to Walter Scott and Robert Jamieson nearly forty ballads out of her mother's family tradition; she was a professor's daughter). And Thomas Hardy's village musicians—fictional, true, but convincing—were they sunk in analphabetic darkness when they trod the snowy roads that night, listening to the far-off bark of foxes during the pauses in their sober discourse on the matter of brass, reeds and percussion, a discourse that ended with the slogans: 'Strings for ever!' and 'Clar'nets was death!'? They remind us that many of the old village church-gallery musicians, folk-singing farm-workers among them, were readers not only of letterpress but of music-notation as well. In our own time we hear of fine Irish country singers who are no strangers to the story of the *Iliad* or the works of Ovid. Possibly Europe's richest area for folk song is Bulgaria where the peasant tradition for book-learning is long, deep and passionate. In Rumania, where illiteracy was indeed very common until recently, the best informants are often those with the strongest urge to education, such as the outstanding North Transylvanian singer Maria Precup, who, interviewed in 1957, told the folklorist that she

owed the singular perfection of her vocal style to the fact that
her father, one of the few readers in his village, had early
impressed on her that 'Man is the emperor of the animals',
so that when she was herding in the upland forests with the
other girls, unlike her companions she had no fear of bears or
other beasts, and would not hesitate to raise her voice till the
mountains echoed with the intricate coloratura songs of her
locality. In the British Isles a large number of traditional songs
are preserved by travelling people, whether gypsies, didikais
or those disobligingly referred to as 'tinkers' (who are secondhand car dealers nowadays, as like as not), and as these live
rather on the margin of society it might be thought that here
was support for the view that folk song belongs to the
unlettered. Well, 'travellers' are culturally more conservative
than house-dwellers, but even among the folk on the road it is
usually the best educated, the book- and newspaper-readers,
the alert and progressive thinkers, who provide the most
important, most coherent songs. From the entirely unlettered
traveller one is more likely to get broken-down melodies and
garbled texts. Far from illiteracy being, as some have pre-
tended, almost a *sine qua non* of the authentic folklore condition,
at least where ballads are concerned it is probably a negative
factor, as the experienced American collector Phillips Barry
maintained.*

Whatever the case elsewhere, in England folk song is the
musical and poetic expression of the fantasy of the lower
classes—and by no means exclusively the country workers. In
the main the songs are evolved by labouring people to suit their
ways and conditions of life, and they reflect the aspirations that
rise from those ways and conditions. In the process of creating
this fund of song, economic conditions are more decisive than
any relative distance from formal culture, book education and
the like, for our experience shows that, as elsewhere, the most
inventive bearers of English folk song are likely to be the

---

* A handful of collectors—five to be exact—recovered versions of 72 Child
ballads in the relatively small and literate states of Maine and Vermont, against
a total of 69 for the entire South, with a battalion of collectors, a vast population,
and an illiteracy rate about four times higher. In Barry's opinion: 'No greater
mistake was ever made than to suppose that ballads survive best among the most
illiterate and ignorant.'

liveliest-minded, best-informed of their community, but among the poorest.

Nor should we overlook the economic factor in such matters as anonymity. By some definitions, a folk song must be anonymous or it isn't a folk song. Sharp, among others, thought so. But what does that tell us? Nothing essential, except that either the original of the song is extremely ancient or, more likely, its first author was too poor for his name to be thought worth preserving. Borrowings, reminiscences, variations on existing stuff play a great part in the composition of folk music—and of art music too, for that matter. The fact that a folk song spends its life mainly in passing from mouth to mouth means that it undergoes a number of alterations for better or worse, and of certain songs it is true to say, as Constantin Brailoiu did (and Bartók used his remark as a motto for his important study on the methods and aims of folk music collecting): 'A folk tune really exists only at the moment when it is sung or played and it only lives by the will of its performer and in the manner that he wants. Creation and performance are intermingled here to an extent unknown in musical practice based on writing or print.' This is especially true of the very fluid and highly varied musics of Mediterranean and eastern Europe and the Orient. Not that western art music is at all exempt from the ephemeral. There are differences in detail between the performances of a Palm Court fiddler, a Menuhin and a Heifetz 'accurately' playing the same printed piece, and therein lies the beauty and majesty of great interpretations. The differences would show clearly enough if the artists' performances were notated with full attention to the smallest nuance and deviation, as happens sometimes with folk music transcriptions. If the concert musician never really plays what is written, still less does the folk singer reproduce precisely what he has received. In the case of English folk music, Brailoiu's remark holds to a greater extent than with art music though to a lesser extent than with the traditional eastern musics. Some of our tunes are no doubt of great antiquity and are the product of infinite variation on some Ur-model from the old old world. But there is no need to go back to Adam; not all our folk songs alter vastly, the words less than the tunes, and an original form—or if you prefer, an *established* form—may often be discerned without much trouble.

To take one example from hundreds, "The dark-eyed sailor" has repeatedly turned up in tradition in more or less identical shape. Pretty surely it had a single author. If one day we find the author's name—and it is not impossible, for all the collected versions derive ultimately from a Catnach broadside of the late 1830s—does "The dark-eyed sailor" at that moment cease to be a folk song?

The Soviet folklorist Yury Sokolov reminds us that anonymity is not a factor that essentially distinguishes folklore from the bookish arts, because generally speaking it is only since the beginning of the capitalist era that men have been much concerned to secure for themselves, in their own name, the works of their creative genius. In feudal times writers, musicians, painters, architects often did not aspire to perpetuate their names. But most of our folk songs have evolved since then, under conditions of capitalism and in times when middle class and aristocratic writers and composers were keenly signing their works with a view to earning money and fame, the humble folk song maker, with no thought of exploiting his work commercially, has been content—or been obliged—to remain unknown, nameless. Of course, the professional folk minstrel, whether he was a Central Asian *ashug* or one of the occupational heirs of the bardic tradition that lingered on in the Gaelic world till the start of the nineteenth century, was interested in securing his proper 'credits'. Just so in our own day, and not only in U.S.A., authentic folk singers moving into the orbit of professionalism as recording or radio artists or performers in concert halls and night clubs or on the university circuit are beginning to claim author's rights on 'their' works (whether they created them or merely carry them); they are acting in self-defence against the folk song collector who may be brisk in trying to secure the copyright for himself. This is a new aspect of the 'collector-informant context' that had not shown itself in Cecil Sharp's day. Then it seemed natural enough that the collector with the clean collar had the rights and the singer with the choker had none. And so down through the ages; whether he was merely the bearer or actually the author of the song the low-class singer has remained faceless. The famous anonymity of folk song is, in the main, an economic and social accident.*

If the importance of illiteracy as a condition of musical folklore has been exaggerated, if the anonymity of folk song is mostly a matter of chance, what about orality? In all parts of the world it is generally agreed that in its natural state folk song is transmitted by word of mouth; in consequence a song does not circulate in a fixed form but undergoes changes from place to place, singer to singer, performance to performance even, and these changes are the signs of its folkish-ness and, some would say, the source of its virtues. That is so, probably orality is a most important characteristic of folk song and we have every right to speak of the grandeurs of oral tradition. Nevertheless, the mouth-to-mouth process is not the only means by which the songs, especially the words, have been passed on. First, whenever singers could write, they have inclined to commit songs to paper as an aid to memory, and folk song collectors all over Europe are familiar with 'family song books' containing manuscript copies of texts preserved often for several generations. Secondly, and this is more important, ballad-sheets and broadsides were printed and distributed in large quantity for something like four hundred years. In the third place, it is likely that our traditional singers have not remained entirely untouched by the effect of printed folk song collections prepared by educated men. There is nothing surprising in this, it happens even among illiterate performers. Unlettered singers of the massive Jugoslav epics studied by Milman Parry have been known to derive their texts from versions collected by Vuk Karadžić in the opening years of the nineteenth century and circulated in 'national song' books.

---

* It is interesting that in present-day eastern Europe, folklore begins to emerge from the state of anonymity. Great pains are taken to trace the makers of songs, and recent peasant paintings, carvings, pottery, needlework displayed in exhibitions or reproduced in print are nowadays usually credited to the individual who created them, however deeply traditional the style may be, and however socially humble the maker. In the West there is a similar tendency but to nothing like the same extent. Some seem to have the feeling that a peasant pot is less of a peasant pot if you can name the potter.

Rural gypsy minstrels in Rumania, masters of the epic art, have sung into microphones 'their' version of ballads that, on examination, turn out to be versions collected—and doubtless revised—by the poet Vasile Alecsandri, and published in his *Poesii populare ale Românilor* in 1866. In such cases, presumably, literate members of the community have dictated the texts to the singers. No doubt, the influence of printed collections has been greater on Scottish singers than on English, because Scottish collections have been abundant over a longer period, and have circulated widely in a land where villagers, crofters and farm-hands have long been busy readers. From the time of Alan Ramsay's *Scots Songs* (1718–19) and *Tea-Table Miscellany* (1724) onward, formal song collections passed briskly from hand to hand in country as well as town, among folk singers as well as drawing room performers. In England it is not impossible that the compilations of Ritson, John Bell the Tynesider, Dixon and others, had some effect on folk singers of the past, as the versions of more modern collectors have had on the surviving traditional singers of our time.

Without question, however, the greatest influence of print on folk song comes from the broadsides. It is a work that went on for centuries. A sequence of Robin Hood ballads was published by Wynken de Worde 'in or about 1495' says William Chappell, though others put the date some ten years later. Beginning in the mid-sixteenth century, broadside printers were required by law to register their ballads with the Stationers' Company. Not all did so, but as a recent writer points out: 'the Company's registers give us a representative survey of popular street ballads from 1557 to 1709'.[4] For that period there are more than three thousand entries. These were mostly 'blackletter' ballads printed on folio sheets in engaging but clumsy Gothic type. An exuberant bibliographer of popular literature, Gershon Legman, remarks: 'These stall-ballads of the sixteenth and seventeenth centuries, with their woodcut-illustrated horrors, hangings, and other attractive marvels, were the combined murder-mysteries and comic books' of the time. They were fashionable with all classes and we read of young sparks of the universities forming collections and swapping duplicates with fellow enthusiasts like schoolboys with stamps. Samuel Pepys, we know, was among the well-born zealots. He bought the collection of a great antiquary, John Selden, and added many specimens of his own to the number of 1,800 ballads which are now an important part of the Pepysian Library in Cambridge. By no means all the blackletter texts were the words of enduring folk songs, nor were they all by lower class writers, nor destined for labouring people. Besides squibs to the general approval such as "The Lancashire Cuckold: or the Country-Parish Clerk betray'd by a Conjurer's Inchanted Chamber-pot, To the Tune of, Fond Boy, &c.", there were also "Verses in the manner of Mr. P–pe", or "Mr. C–ll–y C–bb–r Answered", of little enough interest to ballad-singing cobblers and ploughboys.

The eighteenth century saw some change. With the coming of newspapers containing accounts of foreign wars, Stock Exchange dealings, society scandals, the broadside ceased to interest the 'polite' classes and became more and more exclusively associated with farmhands and farriers, milkmaids and muckmen. And if at first the loss of a part of their custom meant that the broadside printers issued fewer song-sheets during the eighteenth century, they made up for it with the vast flood of printed folk song texts released during the first two-thirds of the nineteenth century from London publishers such as the Pitts family of Seven Dials (rowdy old Mother Pitts was a former bumboat woman of Portsmouth) and their bitter rival James Catnach, Batchelor of Moorfields, Henry Such of the Borough, and from a number of provincial printers among whom we find the names of Marshall of Newcastle, Harkness of Preston, Bebbington of Manchester at the foot of hundreds of folk song and ballad texts firmly fixed in the traditional repertory. The output was enormous, one London publisher alone advertising 'upwards of five thousand different sorts of ballads'. Several of these were produced in massive run-offs. For instance the broadside containing the text of the ballad of the murder of Maria Marten in the Red Barn, sung by the 'street screamers' to variants of the handsome carol tune "Come all ye faithful Christians", sold 1,650,000 copies according to Henry Mayhew who seems to have got his information from the publishers (Charles Hindley, historian of the Catnach Press, puts the figure at half a million lower). Nor is this example singular; the estimated sale of "The Sorrowful Lamentation and Last Farewell of J. B. Rush" runs to two and a half million copies, a figure which, if hard to accept, at least suggests magnitude. However, for all its huge circulation, the ballad of the seducer of Emily Sandford and the murderer of old Squire Jermy did not last as well in the folk singer's mouth as did the song of the Red Barn crime.

Some specialists would try to keep the broadside ballads and songs entirely separate from the rest of folk song, and to consider them as a category apart. In fact the two kinds are as mingled as Psyche's seeds, and probably the majority of our 'folk songs proper' appeared on stall leaflets at one time or another, in this version or that. The broadside ballad-maker as a rule was no artist, no poet, but a craftsman of sorts, a humble journalist in verse who, for a shilling, would turn out a ballad on a subject as readily as his cobbler cousin would sole a pair of shoes. He might provide a song based on news of actual events, small or large, local or international. Or he might invent a romantic story of love, crime, battle or trickery, and make his ballad out of that, like a present-day author of pulp magazine fiction. Or he might take a song already current in the countryside and re-furbish it a little for publication (sometimes a song would undergo this process three or four times, and so circulate in a number of different printed forms, each deriving from one broadside version or the other). James Catnach, who set up as a printer of street literature in Monmouth Court, Seven Dials, in 1814, is said to have paid men to collect ballads from singers in country taverns, and probably other publishers did similarly. Also, according to Charles Hindley, Catnach 'at one time kept a fiddler on the premises, and . . . he used to sit receiving ballad-writers and singers, and judging of the merits of any production which was brought to him, by having it sung then and there to some popular air played by his own fiddler, and so that the ballad-singer should be enabled to start at once, not only with the new song, but also the tune to which it was adapted'.

If occasionally the broadside ballad composers successfully made pieces in something very like the true laconically dramatic style of folk verse, it must be understood that by no means all the broadside texts passed into traditional currency. For instance the countless Sorrowful Lamentations of hanged men did not become anchored in tradition as some of the earlier crime ballads did, perhaps because the song-sheets bearing these effusions are of late appearance and the texts, in consequence, turgidly literary—if not always very literate— and hard for the folk tradition to absorb despite the sturdiness of its digestive system. Sorrowful Lamentation broadsides were unknown before 1820 when the law was passed that allowed a reasonable term between trial and execution. 'Before that', a London chaunter told Henry Mayhew, 'there wasn't no time for a Lamentation; sentence o' Friday and scraggin' o' Monday. So we only had the Life, Trial and Execution' (these usually in the form of prose accounts).

More relevant to our argument than these 'ballads on a subject' are the hundreds of songs lying deep in the tradition, the 'classical' pieces of folk song, that were issued by the street-paper press. To take but one London broadside printer, whose business lingered on into the first decade of the twentieth century, we find in the lists of Henry Parker Such of 123, Union Street, The Borough, such songs as "The foggy dew", "The trees they do grow high", "Seventeen come Sunday", "Rinordine", "Sylvie the female highwayman", "The Blackwater side", "The saucy sailor", "Brennan on the moor", "The three butchers", "The dark-eyed sailor", "The bold fisherman", "Young Riley", "Blow the candles out", and a large number of other songs reckoned among the lyrical masterpieces of the common Muse. For centuries sheets bearing the texts of such songs, and also of 'big' ballads of the order of "The outlandish knight", "Lord Bateman", "Lord Thomas and fair Eleanor", "Barbara Allan", "The demon lover", "The grey cock", were widely on sale in the towns and countryside, at cheap stationers' stalls or along with ribbons, thread and fake jewellery in the packs of door-to-door pedlars. 'Chaunters' sang and sold their songs on street corners, at factory gates, on country fairgrounds, in markets, at prize-fights, on race-courses, at executions, anywhere a crowd might gather. They sang alone or with a company of mates including a 'running patterer' to provide

comic or doleful commentary as each ballad unfolded, and in
the mid-nineteenth century when Henry Mayhew was com-
piling his pungent documents of the condition of street-folk it
was usual for the chaunters to accompany themselves on the
fiddle (the 'dead dull doleful heavy hums' of the hurdy-gurdy
were also to be heard in London's streets but by then the
instrument was very rare).

In early days in country inns song-sheets were pasted up on
fireplace surrounds and high bench-ends for the benefit of
carters, ploughmen and others, and Walton the angler gives
us an idyllic picture of the alehouse, 'lavender in the window
and twenty ballads stuck about the wall'. Milkmaids would
paper the walls of byres and dairies with broadsides, and learn
off the ballads as they milked and churned, until the next coat
of whitewash made ground for a new batch of lyrics. The
sailor ocean-bound would paste underside the lid of his sea-
chest new songs to try out on his shipmates in the fo'c'sle. In
London, so Mayhew's chaunters told him, the Ratcliffe Highway, thronged with rough men and rowdy girls, was always a
lovely pitch. In very poor districts it was not unusual for two
families to club together to buy a penny ballad-sheet, and one
street-singer tells how, having trailed through a poverty-
stricken village and sold but one copy of a song, he retraced
his steps and peered through an uncurtained cottage window
at a crowd of villagers, young and old, listening spellbound as
an elderly man recited the ballad off the sheet by the light of a
flickering fire. What they were listening to, what gripped their
imagination was the execrable ballad of Rush's last farewell,
and what matter of that? At another time or elsewhere it
might have been *Little Musgrave* or the tale of Odysseus's crew.
No doubt the old school of folklorists with their ready mind
for aesthetic value-judgements might regret that in nineteenth
century Norfolk it had to be a gallows song written for a
shilling by some pot-poet of Seven Dials, but there, romance
is one thing and the plight of deprived folk is another. It was a
hardy plant that could keep its blossoms from going sour in the
rigours of lower-class Victorian England. Also it is an old story
that the tastes of folk and folklorist are not always one and the
same. The printed stall-ballad texts cannot compare for

grandeur with the best oral versions of the same songs, but that is no reason for the scientist to ignore them. It is a poor folklorist who is not also in part a sociologist, and the sociologist in us must ask why we should be interested in folk poems of a certain quality (to our way of thinking), and not in other versions that may (to us) seem short of beauty but nevertheless reach a vast public and are accepted with pleasure, and even passion.

When we consider the great distribution of printed folk song texts among our town proletariat during the nineteenth century (even if the élite of industrial workers, in the South at least, came to look down on the broadsides, and even if the flood of stall ballads had slackened to a trickle by the end of the century) we cannot avoid the impression that it was a deafness based on romantic prejudice that caused the great collectors such as Baring-Gould, Sharp, Hammond, the indomitable Miss Broadwood, to hold so firmly to the view that folk song was by its very nature rural, entirely an affair of heaths and hedgerows, chilterns and champaigns. So they maintained, though only a few years previously evidence of town participation and to some extent even town leadership in the diffusion of folk song had been obvious on all sides, and that, as we shall see when we come to consider the ballads of industry, the urban proletariat was active in creating its own folk songs besides learning ready-made ones off penny sheets; indeed, the actual *creation* of folk song survived better in the mining and mill areas than in the rural districts. It is tempting sometimes to sentimentalize the matter and to make oneself believe that our folk songs were by definition and in essence of the countryside, solely the property of simple noble Hodge in corduroy and smock-frock, toiling over the clods with a sharp eye for the bumble-bee on the sunflower, and a keen ear for the musical pitch of a sickle-blade on crooked wheat or a hammer on a distant anvil. Well, our folk songs do belong to the countryside in part, and in large part, but do not let us lose sight of Mayhew's 'street screamers' coming out of Fortey's shop with their bundles of newly-reprinted copies of "The banks of sweet Dundee" or "The bold Princess Royal" (among sheets of "Jim along Josey", "The mistletoe bough" and "A new song on the bloomer costume"). They belong to the march of mountebank and vagrant musicians who since the Middle Ages had carried their art through the outskirts of town into the countryside and back into town again; denounced in the fourteenth century, a time of Lollardry and labour troubles, as a class beyond hope of salvation like whores and epileptics; in Elizabeth's time, when harassed authority saw no end to the growing number of vagrant poor, running the risk of being whipped bloody and 'burnt through the gristle of the right ear with a hot iron the compass of an inch about' (this for the first offence of singing or playing in the street without a licence; for the third conviction, death); and finally in Victorian times suffering under the batons of the policemen who patrolled the Ratcliffe Highway, always in pairs for safety. Despite the chivvying, these itinerant singers were all the time planting new songs in the ears of their listeners, and at least from the sixteenth century onward they reported back to the print-shops what had caught their fancy while on their perambulations. The chaunters were not merely active spreaders of folk song, but were also, in a practical sense, among the earliest collectors of it.

Are we dwelling too long on a kind of low-class song that Francis James Child had called 'veritable dunghills in which, only after a great deal of sickening grubbing, one finds a very moderate jewel'? Perhaps; but like Phillips Barry, we see these stabilized texts not as *contaminated* tradition but rather as *reinforced* tradition. In considering the real life of folk song, to discount the broadsides because they are often short on poetry is dilettantish; it is as if a zoologist would ignore warthogs because they are not pretty. In any case, some emphasis is forced on us because writers in the past have stressed so heavily that whatever folk song is or is not, it is essentially an oral affair whose intrinsic character derives from the peculiarities of mouth-to-ear-to-mouth transmission. Well, that is only true in part. We see that in thousands, indeed millions, of instances the words of folk songs reached their singers by way of print. And not only the words. The existence of manuscript tune-books shows that the melodies too had a certain written currency from quite early days, especially among tune-swapping fiddlers. It would be interesting to know the rate of musical literacy among the lower classes in the decisive folk song period between 1550 and 1850. We might find that at many moments it was a good deal higher than in the present day. It is worth recalling that during the nine years spanned by her husband's diary, Mrs. Pepys had four maids, one after the other, and all, likewise Pepys' own servant-boy, seem to have been sight-readers and singers. Two of the girls, Mary Ashwell and Mary Mercer played the 'harpsichon' and the boy, Tom Edwards, the lute.* Chappell remarks how easy it was, in the seventeenth century to find servants who could play and sing, and he refers us to dramatists of the time who, as in Shirley's *Court Secret*, commonly attribute to the servants in their plays the ability to read music fluently. Even the rough women of the underworld, such as the notorious Mary Frith, nicknamed Moll Cutpurse, might be credited with this accomplishment. In Middleton's comedy *The Roaring Girl* (1611), based on the harridan's early adventures, Moll is asked whether she can play any music, and she replies: 'At first sight, sir'. It would be strange to find such a question casually put, and such an answer received, in a modern television play of crime in the slums. Nevertheless, generally in the past the melodies were handed on orally, as most tunes still are today, for even in highly industrialized societies the majority of people are musically illiterate.

Though orality cannot be considered an *essential* condition of musical folklore, it remains of great importance because by whatever means the songs were learnt, once acquired they began to lead a life quite independent of ink and paper and to receive the buffets and benefits that are a natural consequence of the transit from one forgetful or fanciful singer to another. But very often we find a song circulating widely in almost identical versions, sets of "The Banks of Claudy", say, turning up in Sussex and Scotland, Virginia, U.S.A., and Victoria, Australia, practically word-for-word the same, and we have to

* Pepys sometimes bought sheet-music for Mary Ashwell on his way home from the office. As for young Tom, he seems to have been as devoted to his instrument as any modern guitar-playing folknik, to the point of taking it to bed with him. In Pepys' diary-entry for October 25, 1664, we read: 'My boy could not sleep, but wakes about four o'clock in the morning and in his bed laying playing on his lute till daylight, and it seems did the like last night till twelve o'clock.'

B

presume that these versions have probably come from, and been more or less fixed by, some printed original on a broadside or in a popular songster.

In Britain, print has been a normal condition for folk song texts ever since the sixteenth century. Normal too has been the busy traffic of words and tunes between town and country, not merely by means of street and fairground singers, but also by travelling showmen, fit-up theatre companies, pleasure garden singers and the like. A simple example: the "Green Bushes" song exists in several variants but the dominant form of it, still common in many parts of England, Scotland and Ireland, is the version spread by theatre companies travelling with Buckstone's play *The Green Bushes* written in 1845. And if domestic servants and other workers from the countryside brought rural song into town houses and market-places, they took town versions of songs back home with them to add to the repertory of the villages. So broad is the road between town and country, the great wonder is that English folk melody remained so distinct from the tunes of what is called fine art music (as if the folk arts were never 'fine'). Many of our traditional tunes are conventional enough by the standards of ordinary musical theory, but many more offer features of scale, rhythm, metre and such, that are quite unlike those found in the domain of art music. The early editors were often thrown into confusion, faced with a tonal language contrary to the one they had been taught; they imagined the singers were singing out of tune, and felt it their duty to 'correct' the notations, for instance, to reduce them to standard major or minor shape, before putting them before the public. Cecil Sharp, Ralph Vaughan Williams and Percy Grainger, were among the first in England with a sensitive appreciation of the modal and rhythmic character of traditional song, and even they were baffled by some of its features. Their contemporaries were often quite in the dark, and sometimes for peculiar reasons. An early member of the Folk Song Society, confronted with some of Sharp's notations, said: 'These must be wrong. Nobody's going to tell me that an uneducated singer sings correctly in the dorian mode when, as often as not, even our trained musicians don't know what the dorian is!' Finally, we may remember the great difficulties that composers have met when trying to provide accompaniment to the folk tunes of these islands. Haydn and Beethoven made a hash of it, that we know, but we have heard results just as unsuccessful from modern composers working within the relaxed rules of contemporary music and so, one would think, better equipped to grapple with the actualities of folk melody in all its oddities.

They are not really oddities at all. We only think them so because we live in a literate civilization whose artistic conventions have become more and more inflexible and we ourselves have grown increasingly unreceptive towards other conventions. The notion that Western urban civilization is superior to all others and that European art music is the only kind worth considering, dies hard. Not long before his death, Sir Thomas Beecham began a radio talk with the words: 'I suppose in my lifetime I've conducted all the world's great music', a bold remark to make in the hearing of, say, Indian musicians. For all the efforts of the advanced composers of our century to expand the frame of music, the technique and aesthetic of Western musical art is dominated by an utterly instrumental ideal, a piano-tuner's ideal, the mechanically-tempered scale, and any departure from it we call "out of tune". Now, the good-style folk singer loves to play about with the pitch and duration of his notes, and his deliberately off-centre intonations are as repugnant to the 'concert ear' as the subtleties of Oriental music. Then too, our conventions of harmony have driven us to sacrifice one by one all fine points of mode and have reduced us to a meagre couple of scales, major and minor, and any other series is—or was until recently—either quaint or disturbing. Also, for us, rhythm is either binary or ternary, nothing more, with the result that our ears have become so wooden that often we are unable to grasp the movement of music from such areas as the Balkans where infants sing accurately and at great pace tunes like the following (from a book of Bulgarian children's folk songs compiled by Raina Katsarova and others in 1947):

Ko·-le-dar-che   ko-le-dva-lo, Hei, ko-le-do, moi ko-le-do,

Even Erich von Hornbostel, the great pioneer of ethno-musicology, found 'it is hard to free oneself from the fetters of convention, and one falls too often into the error of taking the foundations of European (art) music for the foundations of music in general, and so using a false yardstick. The ideas of major and minor are so rooted in our minds, and our reasoning rests on them to such an extent, that we can only cast off these ideas with difficulty.' Hence the kind of deafness that falls on European townspeople, including many composers, when faced with the deeper specimens of their own folk culture.*

I do not propose to dwell long on the special musical charac-teristics of English folk song. Sharp and others have done so very well, in the light of the musical understanding of half-a-century or so ago. Since then, ideas of music-notation and tune-analysis have become more sensitive and have moved into territories of rare atmosphere requiring guides with special equipment that I, for one, do not possess. Let us be content here with a few map-markings.

Generally, as usual in Europe, English folk tunes are rather economical in their compass, though not so frugal as in the Balkans. Our melodies usually lie within comfortable reach of the human voice. We have a few airs that stretch up to an octave and a half, even more, but one's first suspicion is that these may be borrowings from Ireland where melodies easily run to luxuriance. Most commonly our tunes range about an octave, but some, presumed to be archaic, are far narrower in compass.

The most primitive tunes in Europe are very tightly res-tricted in range—two tones within the compass of a second, three within the compass of a third.† Usually, melodies of such tiny ambitus belong to folk ritual music, to lullabies, or to the self-made repertory of children. A tune from Cheshire, attached

* Nearly always, where a composer has been attracted to folk music at all, it is to the modified kind of folk melody that has been most influenced by, and lies closest to, conventional art music; often such melodies are the least representative of the true folk tradition. Rimsky Korsakov, curiously enough, was one of the few to recognize this, but he was never artist enough to turn this realization to profitable use. Who else did, apart from Bartók and perhaps Janáček?

† Songs on a single note, literally monotonous, are not unknown. See for example, Vasil Stoin's North Bulgarian collection *Ot Timok do Vita* (Sofia, 1928), No. 196, but such instances are rare.

to the Hallowe'en ritual of begging food for the returning dead, is typical:

A soul! a soul! a soul – cake!   Please, good mis-sus, a soul – cake!

An ap-ple, a pear, a plum or a cher-ry, A-ny good thing to make us all mer-ry,

One for Pe - ter, two for Paul, three for Him who loved us all.

The scale here is the trichord *la-si-do*. The little excursion up to *re* in the third bar does not alter this; it is a kind of aberration that a singer is likely to correct in subsequent repetitions of the phrase. Outside the children's repertory of street game-songs these three-note tunes are uncommon in Western Europe. We call them trichordal melodies. It is usual nowadays to describe scales using consecutive tones by the suffix '-chordal' while scales with gaps or, better description, skips are labelled '-tonic'. So a melody using three notes to the octave, such as a Boy Scout bugle-tune or an Argentine *bahuala*, is called *tritonic*. Tunes using four tones within the range of a 4th are *tetra-chordal*, five-note tunes confined within a 5th are *pentachordal*, while five-note tunes covering an octave are called *pentatonic*. Pentachordal tunes, particularly those whose tone-row corresponds to the lower half of the minor scale are not uncommon in English folk melody. A gaol song collected by H. E. D. Hammond in a Dorset workhouse illustrates the type:

At eight o'—clock our skilly comes in, Some-times thick and some-times thin

And if one word we chance to say, It's bread and wa-ter all next day.

To me Hip! Fol the day, Hip! Fol the day, To me Hip! Fol the day, Fol the di-gee, O!

It would be wrong to take the restricted scale of tunes like the above, or for instance the well-known "Keys of Heaven" in Sharp's *Folk Songs from Somerset*, vol. III, as incomplete portions of an octave scale. The scale of a folk tune is the series of notes used, the tone-row and no more, its actuality not its possibilities.

Various pentatonic (five notes to the octave) scales, with or (more often) without semitones, occur in pretty well all parts of the world. Two are particularly important in western folk music. One is do-re-mi-sol-la, the scale of "Auld lang syne" as it happens; the other is la-do-re-mi-sol which has exerted notable influence on old Hungarian music, but like other pentatonics it is liable to crop up anywhere. Although they abound in Ireland and Scotland, pure pentatonic tunes are rather rare among the records of English song, yet they may once have been commoner in the mouths of our singers. Here is an example, a Robin Hood ballad noted by Vaughan Williams (again in a workhouse) at Billericay, Essex, in 1904. The singer, Mr. Denny, called it: "Robing Wood and the pedlar":

In several of our tunes with six or seven notes to the octave, called hexatonic and heptatonic respectively, one or two of the tones are so weak, and the run of some of the phrases so strongly like those in five-tone melodies that we have to reckon that these were in fact really pentatonic airs whose scale-gaps have been lightly filled in by inessential notes. Folklorists call these inessential notes *pien* tones, borrowing the term from Chinese theory. In the course of a song's life, these piens may come to have a little more weight and the song emerges in the guise of a full-fledged seven-note composition. A glance through any reliable collection of English folk songs shows a great number of tunes marked by phrases of whole tones mixed with thirds, characteristic of pentatonism. Here is a close variant of our Example 4 above. It was notated by Vaughan Williams in 1906, but in his manuscript notebook there is no trace of either its text or title, so we do not know whether it too carried Robin Hood words. It would be classified as a heptatonic tune in the Re or 'dorian' mode, but with Mr. Denny's version in mind, its pentatonic skeleton shows clearly.

Hexatonic tunes, particularly with the sixth step missing and the seventh weak are common enough in the English repertory. Versions of the following ballad tune obtained by Cecil Sharp in Somerset (it is in his manuscript collection) have frequently turned up during the course of this century, attached to various texts.

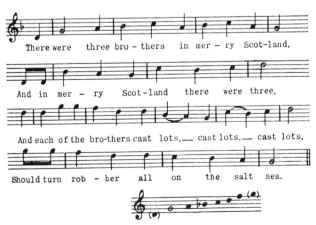

In English folk music, the heptatonic (seven-note) scales are the most numerous and important. Since they are not always well-understood, particularly by young enthusiasts in the folk music clubs, we may deal with them rather less sketchily than we have treated the scales so far. During the nineteenth century when musicians were becoming sharply aware of the differences between conventional music and folk music, it became common to apply the medieval names of the church music modes to the heptatonic folk scales. So if you played on the piano, using the white keys only, the octave scale beginning on D, you were said to produce the dorian mode. If you played from E to E, still on the white keys, that was the phrygian. Beginning on F you got the lydian, on G the mixolydian, on A the aeolian, on C the ionian (whose tones correspond to our ordinary major, though in folk song the scale's behaviour may not be what we expect of the standard major). Nowadays, to get away from the vagueness of the Greek names, to remove the church-music associations, and to come nearer to a more precise characterization of these scales, it is becoming customary to give them sol-fa names—Re-mode for dorian, Mi-, Fa-, Sol-, La-, Do- for the others respectively (if the Si-mode, which churchmen call locrian, occurs in our folk song, it has hardly been noticed).

All these scales or modes are transposable into any key; their personality is determined simply by the way the tones and semitones are disposed. If we bring the modes to a common keynote, say C, we get a clearer view of their character, ranging from the Fa-mode with one sharp (the fourth step) to the Mi-mode with four flats, (the second, third, sixth and seventh) like this:

C	D	E	F♯	G	A	B	C	= Fa ('lydian') mode
C	D	E	F	G	A	B	C	= Do ('ionian') mode
C	D	E	F	G	A	B♭	C	= Sol ('mixolydian') mode
C	D	E♭	F	G	A	B♭	C	= Re ('dorian') mode
C	D	E♭	F	G	A♭	B♭	C	= La ('aeolian') mode
C	D♭	E♭	F	G	A♭	B♭	C	= Mi ('phrygian') mode.

Fully expressed, the Fa-mode is very rare in our folk song. Sharp only knew one tune in this scale, the often-quoted

"James MacDonald", a lurid murder ballad he got from a gipsy. Yet the distinguishing feature of the Fa-mode, the augmented fourth or tritone, colours phrase after phrase in many 'mixolydian' tunes in which it extends from the third step to a whole tone below the tonic. The start of a rather bawdy song, "The long peggin' awl" recorded from the Norfolk singer Harry Cox, illustrates the feature:

The beginning of a soldier's song collected by Cecil Sharp from a 96-year-old Somerset singer vividly shows the engaging Fa-tetrachord both up and down between F and B:

Explaining the scarcity of melodies in the Fa ('lydian') mode, Sharp puts it down to a sensitive aversion folk singers have for the 'harsh effect of the tritone'. Well, conventional musicians do feel the tritone to be un-vocal, and medieval theorists called it the 'diabolus in musica', yet in some parts of the world, Central Slovakia for instance, singers love the Fa-mode better than any other; and in English song its characteristics are so common—tunes such as the well-known "Green bushes" in Sharp's *Folk Songs from Somerset* abound in lydian inflections—that it is possible many of our so-called mixolydian tunes were once based on *fa* not *sol*. Indeed it has been suggested that the 'rare' Fa-mode may formerly have been the European peasant scale *par excellence*, the *agricolae dictus* that Guido d'Arezzo wrote of in the eleventh century.* Incidentally, that tritone

* Affection for the Fa-mode is long-standing. A flute found at Ur in Chaldaea, dating from 2700 B.C., plays in this scale.

*B

effect is particularly common in Ireland. Did it come to us across the Irish Sea? For centuries we have been swapping whole songs or bits of folk melody and verse with the Irish. Such circumstances as the settlement of English smallholders—many of them soldiers with pay in arrears—on confiscated Irish farmland following the fierce Cromwellian subjugation or, more important, the constant come-and-go of Irish labourers seeking work in England, have meant that the two folk song traditions have acted deeply upon each other. That interaction was helped by the vogue of Irish melody in fashionable and popular circles from Elizabethan to Victorian times, and by the imposition of the English language on Ireland from the seventeenth century onward which converted much Irish melody from a dependence on Gaelic metre to a reliance on less elaborate English shapes. The picking work of determining what is Irish in English song, what is English in Irish song, awaits its scholar-Griselda, who must be an objective Griselda too. No doubt she will find that in song as in other matters the English have taken more than they gave but have given more than they get credit for. The Fa-mode does crop up in the distinctive music dialect of north-east England, where the most characteristic tunes are influenced by the peculiarities of the Northumbrian small-pipes, and by the limitations of the older models of that delectable instrument whose chanter, until the early years of the nineteenth century, was restricted to a tone-row of one major octave, sometimes lacking the seventh step. Considerations of fingering as well as of tonal restraint have meant that many small-pipe tunes, whether originally created on the instrument or merely adapted for it, show odd leaps and curious chord-shifts. When these tunes become songs, the result is sometimes quite 'un-vocal' yet full of delightful surprises. The Northumbrian musician W. G. Whittaker tells of a German scholar, confronted with typical north-eastern tunes who said: 'Do you really tell me that the peasants in your district sing these songs?' When asked why he doubted it, the German went on: 'If your peasants can sing such songs they must be the most musical race in the world.' Whittaker's reply was: 'Who told you they weren't?' A version of the old "Bonny pit laddie" tune stresses the 'lydian' sharp fourth repeatedly in its second strain (incidentally, probably half the known Northumbrian pipe-tunes avoid ending on the tonic; this example concludes, rather unusually, on the seventh):

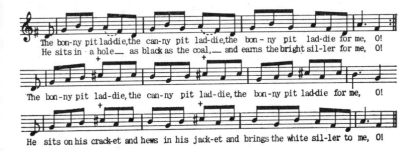

The bon-ny pit lad-die, the can-ny pit lad-die, the bon-ny pit lad-die for me, O!
He sits in a hole—— as black as the coal,—— and earns the bright sil-ler for me, O!

The bon-ny pit lad-die, the can-ny pit lad-die, the bon-ny pit lad-die for me, O!

He sits on his crack-et and hews in his jack-et and brings the white sil-ler to me, O!

The commonest mode for our folk tunes is the major, 'ionian' or Do-mode, and a good half of our collected melodies are in this scale. We hardly need dwell on the tunes in this familiar scale, but it is worth remembering that these are not necessarily less ancient than those in other modes. In England, the 'modern' major seems to have established its importance earlier than on the Continent. Popular musicians, itinerant minstrels for example, had long been specially fond of it, and on that account the theorists of church music looked down on it as the 'modus lascivus' or wanton mode. But despite their strictures, the major scale had already penetrated the world of English composed music by the thirteenth century, and it may well be that its appearance is one of the first signs of national character in our music, and that the early budding of artistic nationalism is connected with a growth of English self-confidence consequent on the emancipation and increasing power of a new social element in feudal life, an individualistic, enterprising merchant class, doggedly insular by cosmopolitan medieval standards, whose fortunes largely derived from new developments in the wool trade and cloth manufacture. There can be little doubt that the precocious growth of secular high art music in the major helped to reinforce this tonality in our folk songs. And if the scale is a common one, some of the tunes employing it are made with such fantasy that it is hard to imagine how their makers arrived at them. Here is one whose

bold curves and surprising intervals delighted Sharp, though
he never published it in any of his popular collections.

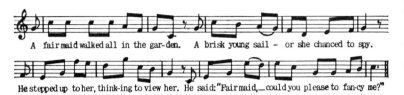

A fair maid walked all in the gar-den.   A brisk young sail - or she chanced to spy.

He stepped up to her, think-ing to view her. He said: "Fair maid,—could you please to fan-cy me?"

Next to the major, the commonest modes of English folk
song are those of Sol, Re and La. The Sol-mode ('mixolydian')
is like the major, but with a flattened seventh step. In the
British Isles, tunes in this mode often have a glorious stride to
them. Here is a specimen whose words concern the fate of
Napoleon. Frank Kidson the Yorkshire collector suspected
that 'all these ballads having Napoleon for their hero (in both
senses of the word) have emanated from an Irish source or from
that large party of Englishmen who, originally holding the
opinions of Thomas Paine, drifted, themselves and their
successors, into Chartists'. Which does not explain why nearly
all our songs of Napoleon are carried by particularly grand
Sol-mode tunes. This example, "The grand conversation on
Napoleon", was noted by Vaughan Williams from an important singer, Henry Burstow of Horsham, Sussex:

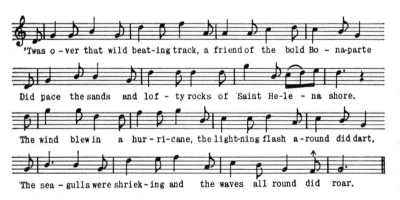

'Twas o - ver that wild beat-ing track, a friend of the bold Bo - na-parte

Did pace the sands and lof - ty rocks of Saint He-le - na shore.

The wind blew in   a hur - ri-cane, the light-ning flash a-round did dart,

'The sea - gulls were shriek-ing and   the waves all round did roar.

Among many beautiful Re-mode ('dorian') tunes hidden in
Cecil Sharp's manuscript collection and so far unpublished

either in the folk song *Journal* or in any piano-set collection is the following, notated in Gloucestershire from a gipsy woman in 1921. Its text is a version of the well-known "Died for love". It is a handy example, for not only is it handsome and characteristic in form but it obligingly sets out the Re-scale for us, step by step, in its second phrase, providing the beginner with a useful mnemonic:

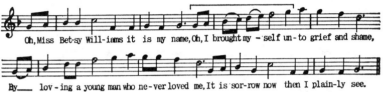

Oh, Miss Bet-sy Will-iams it is my name, Oh, I brought my – self un-to grief and shame,

By___ lov - ing a young man who ne-ver loved me, It is sor-row now then I plain-ly see.

In *English Folk Song: Some Conclusions* Sharp enumerated what he believed were the characteristics of English traditional tunes. According to him, they are built on non-harmonic principles (made by people who had not harmony in mind, they abound in devices that make harmonization difficult); they do not modulate, or hardly ever; they prefer the dorian, aeolian and mixolydian modes (using medieval terminology) though their tonality is sometimes vague; they often contain bars of irregular length; they show a prevalence of five- and seven-time measures (an odd statement: five-time is common enough in English song but as a structural feature, and not merely as an effect of rubato, seven-time is very rare); they make frequent use of wide intervals, and constantly use certain melodic figures such as an ascending scale passage of four quavers or semiquavers connecting tonic and dominant, especially at the start of a phrase. To illustrate this latter feature, and to provide a good specimen of a La-mode tune, overleaf is a melody collected by Vaughan Williams from a Norfolk fisherman named Anderson, of King's Lynn. Other tunes in this book are transposed to end on G, but this one sails a bit high so it is more convenient to have it ending a third lower. Incidentally, the tune carries an engaging text concerning the encounter between a daunting robber and an amiable but resolute sailor.

Persuasive as Sharp's 'conclusions' seem, we are not a great deal the wiser about what makes English song different from

anyone else's because so many of the peculiar characteristics
he had hoped to isolate are not really peculiar at all, but are

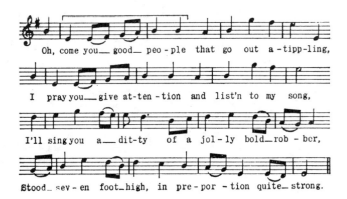

Oh, come you_ good_ peo-ple that go out a-tipp-ling,

I pray you_ give at-ten-tion and list'n to my song,

I'll sing you a_ dit-ty of a jol-ly bold_ rob-ber,

Stood_ sev-en foot_ high, in pre-por-tion quite_ strong.

shared by many other peoples. For instance, the opening
formula of our robber song above is known also in Iceland, in
a ballad about King Pepin of France and his daughter Oluva:

Go — da skemm-tun gjö-ra skal,   thars jeg geng i dans...   *etc.*

It was familiar in Spain as long ago as 1500, as this rather
saucy song from Barbieri's *Cancionero musical* shows:

Si   ha-brá en es-te bal-dés   man-gas pa-ra to-das tres,

Tres mo-zas de a-que-sta vi-lla, tres mo-zas de a-que-sta vi-lla

De-so-lla-ban u-na p...   pa-ra man-gas a to-das tres.

Some Moravian-Slovak love songs begin similarly. The words
of this one would have a familiar ring to many English folk
singers: 'The thunder rolls in the raging sky; it's pouring with

rain. Open your door for me, love, so I know I haven't come to you in vain':

Hro - my bi-jú,___ bú - ri-jú sa   ne-be--sa,

O - te - vri né,   mo - ja mi-la,   le - jė - sa,

O - te - vri né,   mo - ja mi-la,   nech já___ vim,

Ja nech já k vam___ po - da-re-mné   ne cho - dim.

Such examples could be multiplied on and on. Here is a final instance of this 'typically English' opening phrase, from Poland this time, a spring ritual dance-song for girls, to remind us how deceptive such elements are and how delicate a matter it is to isolate specific national characteristics in melody.

Ro - si się ro - si,   by - lic -ka   po wsi...

Similar illustrations, and not limited to Europe only, could be drawn to show the international character of all the elements that Sharp singled out as particularly English. He is not alone in his difficulties, for other musical folklorists, with the advantage of more modern method, have done no better in the hard task of defining the peculiarities of their national music. Bartók and Kodály, after years of patient analysis, presented a definition of the basic stratum of Hungarian folk song that depends on three points—pentatonic scales, terrace-like construction, descending melodic slope. 'Their definition would be clearer,' says Constantin Brailoiu, 'if it did not apply equally well to the music of certain American Indians as well as the Papuans, to say nothing of another theory that the descending slope is characteristic of any primitive melody'.

The vagueness comes from an excess of formalism, from too literal an approach. For instance, in the matter of modes. As our examples show, the modal structure of many tunes is clear enough; but others are in mixed modes, and often it is quite unsatisfactory merely to take the notes that occur in a melody, arrange them in a scale order and say: 'This is a Re-mode, this a Sol-mode tune.' With that, you may have said nothing essential about the tonality of the piece. 'The phrygian mode', says Sharp, 'occurs but rarely in English folk song. I do not think that more than half a dozen English folk airs in that mode have been recorded.' Indeed it is the fact that the Mi-series, which is so common in Spain and which provides practically the sole cadential formula for songs in many Balkan villages (in parts of Transylvania for example) does not seem to have been found attractive by our singers. We do not know why, and it would be interesting to find out. As it is, the few alleged Mi-mode songs that we do possess do not sound very 'phrygian' at all because the flattened second degree, the distinctive note of the Mi-scale, is so weak in all of them, its value is merely nominal and it offers nothing in the way of coloration. At the same time, in view of the rarity of this scale among English singers, it is rather odd that it should attach itself to two or three apparently quite distinct melodies carrying the well-known "Trees they do grow high—Young but growing" words. Here is one of the famous Mi-mode tunes to this tenderly expressed tragedy of child-marriage. The points that distinguish

As I—— was a-walk-ing by yon-der-church wall,

I saw four and twen-ty young men—— a-play-ing at—— the ball;

I ask-ed for my own true love, But they would-n't let——him come,

For they said the boy was young, but a-grow-ing.——

it as 'phrygian' are marked. You will see they do not offer strong evidence of the tune's character.

A kind of fetishism attaches to the matter of folk song modes, especially among younger students and relative newcomers to the urban revival of traditional music. The question: 'What mode is that tune in?' has rather replaced the pointless old enquiry: 'What county does that song come from?' or the even drearier 'What is the Child number of that ballad?' The modal problem is certainly more vital than questions of catalogue (which is something for English Literature) or locality (the same song is likely to turn up in Cumberland or Kent, Durham or Devon; it is evidence of the mobility of our population, not much else). But our great pioneers including Sharp and Vaughan Williams, both of whom had marvellous sense for understanding modal tunes, did not always help by their habit of mechanically placing the notes of a melody in a row and then fastening a label marked 'dorian', 'mixolydian' or even vaguer 'pentatonic'. A great many of our tunes are of simple tonality and a simple label suffices, but there is a multitude of pieces that do not lend themselves to generalized treatment. For example, some melodies are in two layers whose halves require separate description. Here is the splendid little "Crabfish" tune that Mrs. Overd sang to Cecil Sharp 'very excitedly and at breakneck speed . . . punctuating the rhythm of the refrain with blows of her fist upon the table at which she was sitting.' 'The tune is in the mixolydian mode', says Sharp, and so it is in a way, yet that tells us almost nothing about a song whose melody-stanza is essentially a tetrachord based, in terms of solmization, on d = *la*, and whose refrain which surely enough ends on *sol* is only 'mixolydian' by the skin of its teeth, for its third and fourth steps could hardly be feebler. The tune is not a typical mixolydian but a product of two separate systems.

There was a lit-tle man and he had a lit-tle wife, And he loved her as dear as he loved his life,

Mash-a row dow dow dow, did-dle all the day, Mash-a row dow dow dow, did-dle all the day.

Theory made in the ill-aired study is one thing; practice in the blowy fields may be otherwise. Our folk singers do not always utter their songs in a way that suits the folklorists' labels. We have, for instance, other scales besides the major, the modes with Greek names, and the semitoneless pentatonics. The Hungarian Lajos Vargyas was delighted to find among our melodies a scale rare in the West but frequently met with in Moravia, Hungary and Rumania. Sharp had noticed this scale and understandably was baffled by it, for it does not fit accepted theory. Which shows, as Vargyas says, that 'actual life offers much richer treasures than can be inferred theoretically'. The scale is g-a-b-c-d-e flat-f (taking g as keynote) as in this version of "The saucy sailor", reported at the end of the nineteenth century as a favourite song among factory girls in the East End of London, though we may suspect they used a more conventional tune than this one which Sharp found in Somerset:

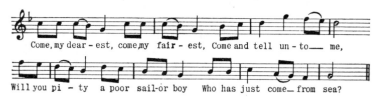

Come, my dear - est, come, my fair - est, Come and tell un - to— me,

Will you pi - ty a poor sail-or boy Who has just come— from sea?

We know so little about the psychology of folk singers, or any other kind of musicians for that matter, where their art is concerned, and we are not sure why certain scale-intervals are vague in the performer's mind, though plenty of theories are offered. Ethnographers and folklorists in many parts of the world have noticed that the intonation of the third step of the scale is likely to fluctuate in the course of one and the same song. Bartók remarked this in Hungary particularly in the area south and west of the Danube; he named it the 'Transdanubian third'. Negro jazz pianists in the United States are often unsure whether they want a major or minor third, so they play the two notes together and call the resulting dissonance the 'blue third'. This kind of unsteady intonation is extremely common in English folk song. It affects not only the third but also the seventh step (less frequently the sixth too). Sometimes these fluctuations occur at different points in the melody as it proceeds from strophe to strophe; at other times the process is fixed and the alterations occur at the same point in the melody every time. The result of this common practice is to play havoc with the accepted notion of modal behaviour but at the same time it is so prevalent that Percy Grainger, playing back his phonograph recordings, concluded that his singers seldom kept strictly to any 'standard' mode and indeed were likely to vary the scale in different performances of the same song. In short they did not seem to him to be singing in different and distinct modes, mixolydian, dorian, aeolian, and he suggested that in fact all English folk songs derive from 'one single loosely-knit modal folk song scale' in which the third, seventh and, more rarely, sixth steps are unstable and appear now flattened, now sharpened. A striking example of the variability of the third and seventh is provided us by the handsome "Fanny Blair" tune noted by Sharp in Somerset. The singer's words were a terrible jumble, and Sharp, taking lines from other sources, produced a text of his own in which Fanny Blair appears as an eighteen-year-old accusing a young man of robbery. Versions have since come to light, including one from the back of a whaling-ship's log-book, from which it is clear that Miss Blair's age was in fact eleven, and that her accusation —apparently false and malicious—was one of sexual assault.*

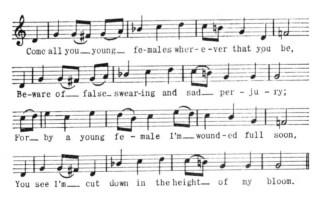

Come all you — young — fe-males wher - e -ver that you be,

Be-ware of — false — swear-ing and sad — per - ju - ry;

For — by a young fe - male I'm — wound-ed full soon,

You see I'm — cut down in the height — of my bloom.

* The nymphet is a rare figure in our folk song, yet Fanny Blair is not alone; in the ballad of "Leesome Brand" is another sister to Lolita. 'This lady was scarce eleven years old / When on her love she was right bold. / She was scarce up to my right knee / When oft in bed with men, I'm told.'

In Britain, folk song seems to show more tonal peculiarities than is usual in north-western Europe. In Germany and the Netherlands and over much of Scandinavia bourgeois music has heavily affected folk song, and the secrets and surprises have gone from most of the tunes and what has generally remained is amiable but obvious. In France country music and town music have long lain so close together that it has been said: 'French folk song was made in Paris.' All the same, as Brailoiu reminds us, the fact that it took Chopin and the alert Mme. Viardot some hours to transcribe a few phrases of Berrichon bagpipe music warns us that even relatively recently the French countryside harboured melodies that had, in George Sand's words, 'a strangeness that seems atrocious and is perhaps magnificent'.[5]

Still, pieces of essential savagery are rare in French tradition, as in any other west European one, and some folklorists pursuing the phantom of out-and-out authenticity, scorning to take refuge in idealistic definitions that do not square with facts, and feeling that folk song is not the pure primitive affair they would like it to be, are reduced to a pessimism that is near despair. So in France Davenson has declared: 'To find an art that is one hundred per cent "folk", it is necessary to seek it in a savage primitive society without an upper class.' Such as the Celts, he suggests, before the first century A.D., because 'from that time on the French people became civilized, possessing a real élite'; that is, they ceased to have a folk music in a 'pure state'. Now, putting aside the fact that the Franks, some five hundred years later, might have been just as satisfactory as runners in the primitive stakes, and disregarding for the time being the dubious proposition that folk song belongs rightly to a society not divided into classes*—and anyway, were the Celts two thousand years ago without a ruling class or a culture

---

* Probably the reverse is true, and what we call folk music as distinct from art music is only imaginable in a society divided in classes, with the leisured few separate from the labouring crowd. Folk song then is a product of civilization, it emerges out of primitive communal song and differentiates itself by ceasing to express the aspirations of society as a whole and by devoting itself to uttering the hopes and fantasies of the lower classes. Many of our older ballads, born of communities obstinately clinging to vestiges of clan culture, represent a halfway stage in the process.

of the warrior-élite separate from that of the peasants?—we see that the quest for pure 'authentic' folk song may lead the scholar into a remote landscape with a mirage on every horizon, a chimera in each shadow.

The heart of the problem lies in the question: how is a folk song made up? The question is the most captivating, most bothersome in all folklore, and we do well to approach it with the humility of ignorance. Is the folk song created in the first instance by a single talented individual like any other poem or musical work? Or is it the product of a collective, a community such as the 'dancing throng' beloved of romantic ballad-scholars in the nineteenth century? Or are we to believe with Laszlo Lajtha in 'the total absence of any author' because through the years and across the landscape so many mouths have varied and re-shaped the song? Or is it the fact, as the Germans Hoffmann-Kreyer and Hans Naumann suggested, that the lower classes are imaginatively so sterile that they can create nothing for themselves but merely take over the songs of the upper classes after the gentry have finished with them?

The proposition of Naumann and his fellows is that song, like all other kinds of art, evolves among the educated classes and filters downward through the layers of society until it comes to rest among the lowest classes, where it lingers on as folk song which is merely the vague and sometimes distorted echo of a once-fashionable musical and poetic culture. Even Naumann, whose arrogant hypothesis is dignified by the title of *Rezeptionstheorie*, had to realize that when one had extracted the items that the folk had 'received' from educated sources, there remained a small irreducible fund of song that had to be considered as 'pure folk', the product of *die primitive Gemeinschaftskultur* (primitive communal culture). The important category, however, was that of *abgesunkenes Kulturgut*, of a comedown cultural heritage, and the theory is strengthened by the fact that songs written by Provencal troubadours eight hundred years ago survive among Catalan peasants, that German scholars led by John Meier have been able to trace the bookish origins of several hundreds of their folk songs, and that in France the influence of aristocratic and bourgeois music and poetry on traditional song is so marked that Patrice Coirault was of the opinion that, while any song might *become* a folk song, none was so in the first instance. Finally, there is the view of Davenson that 'left to themselves, folk singers would never have reached such heights, as we see from the work songs and the cries of shepherds and ox-drivers, which never rise above the lower forms of primitive and spontaneous art.' A lofty view when one considers that these so-called primitive pieces, the Mississippi field hollers, the work-chants of Portland quarrymen, the waulking songs of Hebridean cloth-makers, the closest-bound to the common folk both in function and performance, are generally by no means the most simple and obvious, musically speaking (try to notate them!). Their alleged inferiority resides in the fact that they happen to accord least with the sacred canons of conventional musical art.

The defects of the 'receptionist' view are partly due to its excessively black and white delineation, its lack of dialectic, its failure to appreciate the processes of give-and-take. The traffic between the arts of different social classes proceeds in both directions. At the development stages of great class periods, folk music has always served as a stimulus, and at the same time the folk traditions have never been the fixed monolithic structures that some purists would have us believe. On the contrary, styles of folk music have constantly changed, down the ages, according to changes in the fate of the labouring people who carried that music. Folk-art traditions do not stand still any more than fine-art traditions do, which is one reason why the romantic chasers of the 'authentic' in folk song so often find themselves pursuing a will-o'-the-wisp. Bence Szabolcsi, the Hungarian musicologist, reminds us that the great periods in the history of European music when rich cultures sprang from folk music styles have always indicated a rise or advance of the often hardly visible masses, of the submerged layers of the population, as happened in the fifteenth century at the time of the Reformation when the choral art of Europe was reborn under folk song influence; it happened in the eighteenth century, on the eve of the French Revolution, when French and Italian popular music, comic opera and such, brought about a significant change in style that led through

Haydn and Mozart to Beethoven; it happened again in the nineteenth and twentieth centuries when movements of national independence and social progress brought important new styles of music developed under the influence of folk song (and it is worth remembering that if nationalism was the motive force for Erkel, Dvořák and Smetana, Mussorgsky was more interested in the emancipation of serfs than in hurrah patriotism, and there is some connection between the rise of British Socialism and the enthusiasm with which Sharp and eventually Vaughan Williams set about their work). 'The movement of society', says Szabolcsi, 'looms in the background of all these renewals. The rise of a new group, in each case a temporary or permanent alliance with the masses of people heaving beneath them, accounts for the intervention of folk music in these epochs.' And as the life of the common people is changed, however slowly, through the movement of society, so their folk music alters too, and in part that alteration is effected by taking over, or taking back, elements from upper class music. Hearing the baroque improvisations of a good modern Irish bagpiper, who can doubt the influence of seventeenth and eighteenth century classicism on the music of the Irish countryside? And if we wonder how it came there, we have only to read the accounts of blind itinerant harpers to find that some of them were as familiar with the works of Corelli, Vivaldi and Handel as they were with the dance-tunes and slow airs of the villages. Likewise, many English lyrical folk tunes, especially those carrying idyllic country texts, have a formal classical movement, a sweet stateliness that does not derive from any particular learned composition but from the prevailing musical climate at the time of their formation.

That process of give-and-take-back is an old one. It was already operating at the very birth of English folk song: that is, of folk song as we readiest recognize it today. About the embryo stage of our songs there is much that is mysterious and speculative (after all, if we go back only a thousand years, we are already in musical prehistory). But if our knowledge is shadowy, some outlines emerge. As European society moved out of the stage of collective clan culture and, early or late, took the road towards feudalism, song too began to change its form. Probably our ancient repertory consisted in the main of a few melody formulas endlessly varied, sung collectively, often in shanty-style with choral refrains. The earliest of these were constructed on a descending slope, perhaps because the singer's voice tends to drop as his breath runs out. We still have a few of this primitively-constructed descending-line tunes, though they are no longer common, such as the hauling shanty "Won't you go my way?"

In primitive Europe nearly every song was performed for a particular occasion or purpose, notably for seasonal magic-making, for social ceremonial, and for work. On the other hand, most melodies were 'unspecified', that is, the same tune might serve for a midwinter ritual, a funeral lament, or a hauling job. But with the emergence of a clearly stratified class society, with a new relationship of the individual to the community (for instance, the agricultural serfs and tenant farmers of early feudal times led more isolated and indivi-dualized lives than did the old clan groups and slave gangs) a different sort of song began to show itself: solo song, strophic, arch-shaped, regular in rhythm, not tied to a specific occasion or purpose but suitable for singing whenever the mood took the singer. In short, the embryo of the kind of folk song we are most familiar with now.

Its development was slow and laborious, but nevertheless it had become a powerful though not yet dominant type in our lower-class songs, whether of countryman or townsman, peasant or artisan, serf or small shopkeeper, by the end of the fourteenth century. It was precisely at this time of social tension when feudalism was in crisis, when the rising merchant class was threatening the power of the barons, and the peasants were becoming conscious of the plight of their own class and

were beginning to perceive their importance in the land, that
our present lyrical folk style, both of texts and melodies, came
into being. It is undeniable that the newly-evolved folk song
owed much to stuff from France. As early as the twelfth
century the songs of castle and manor in northern France
began already to spread their influence abroad,* notably the
chansons de toile and the *caroles*. The *chansons de toile* were sung by
ladies at their needlework or weaving, and many of them
concerned the amorous adventures of pretty women with such
names as Belle Yolande or Belle Eglantine. Doubtless these
'cloth songs' were in fact aristocratic and romantic rework-
ings of the kind of pieces that peasant girls chanted during
their evening working-bees for spinning, embroidery and the
like, as they still do today in Balkan villages (in Bulgaria the
largest category of lyrical songs is associated with the *sedenki* or
working-bees). The *caroles*, courtly dance-songs, were likewise
folk stuff re-fashioned. In this case they were originally compositions attached to the pagan ceremonial rites of the agricultural year, with the fertility references softened into amorous
allusion to suit more sophisticated tastes. All over western
Europe such songs, and the aristocratic love songs of Provence
that came after them brought to the rigours of the Middle Ages
a thawing breeze, a flash of blossom, a sweet ring of lyricism that
affected not only the educated poets and musicians but also the
nameless masters of the unwritten arts, the lower class creators
who made the songs for kitchen-boys and horse-grooms,
scullery-maids and goose-pluckers, ploughmen and wood-
cutters and outlaws of the forest. Even the commonplace 'As
I roved out' opening of so many English folk songs can be
traced to a standard incipit of courtly *chansons d'aventure* of
twelfth century France. But all this is simply part of the give-
and-take between the lyrical arts of different classes, the
acknowledgment of a debt to folk song that continued to be
contracted not only by Tudor polyphonists with their pieces

* The influence of French song spread at least as far as Hungary, as is shown
by Lajos Vargyas's interesting studies published under the general title of
'Kutatások a népballada középkori történetében' or 'Forschungen zur Geschichte
der Volksballade im Mittelalter' in *Ethnographia* (Budapest, 1960, 1962) and *Acta
Ethnographica* (Budapest, 1960, 1961), and 'Les analogies hongroises avec les chants
"Guillaneu"' in *Studia Musicologica* (Budapest, 1962).

based on tavern songs and market cries, but also by the harpsi-chordists of the time of Scarlatti, Bach and Couperin (all those bagpipe imitations, for example), and the enormous fascination that folk music had for so many composers between the eighteen-eighties and nineteen-forties.

There are general influences then, class to class, that are reciprocal. And beyond the general is the particular: in some cases actual songs, the words and the tune, created by trained poets and musicians and current among the ruling classes of the era of feudalism and growing capitalism did indeed seep down from the upper layers of society to the 'uneducated mass of the people', especially in Western Europe and perhaps most of all in France and Germany (in Gaelic Ireland too, but here as later in India it was often a form of colonial persecution that drove the cultured songmakers into obscure villages and merged their lives with those of the lower classes). But the view that this is the sole, essential or most powerful creative source of folk song, the view that denies the existence of an original lower-class fund of song whether rural or urban, the view that the common people have no power to create their own lyrical goods but can only receive, appropriate and conserve, seems to us nowadays haughty and vainglorious. It is no surprise that Naumann's views were endorsed by Nazi thinkers, devoted as they were to the notion of a high-horsed élite leading a passive and obedient mass. No surprise either that Soviet folklorists have described the Rezeptionstheorie as 'typical of bourgeois science in the era of decaying capitalism'.

The notion still lingers in the minds of some intellectuals in Britain though in fact it never had much hold on the thinking of our musical folklorists. Among reputable English specialists, Rodney Gallop is almost alone when he declares:

'I have no great belief in the creative originality of the folk. "All folk cultures", I would say with Padraic Colum, "are the popularizations of something that was once aristo-cratic—music, poetry, costume, dance." . . . Tappert, in his *Wandernde Melodien* has put the matter in a nutshell. "The folk", he writes, "cannot compose; it never creates . . . it selects." Nevertheless, since it selects only what it finds congenial, its choice expresses a racial spirit no less for its lack of originality.'[6]

Now, whatever the case with other West European traditions, in the English folk song repertory precious few tunes are found that seem to be re-makes of compositions by educated musicians of the past. A small number entered the tradition from the playhouses of the seventeenth and eighteenth centuries, but few took firm hold on the singers' fancy; the flow of song-traffic was busier in the other direction, from cottage and workshop to stage. A picturesque and odd example of middle-class composition catching on among folk singers seems to be offered by the melody to which "The foggy dew" is most commonly sung in East Anglia, where the song lives vigorously. This is not the tune, possibly of Dutch extraction, that Benjamin Britten used in his piano setting. It is a pentatonic melody:

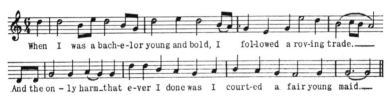

When I was a bach-e-lor young and bold, I fol-lowed a rov-ing trade.____

And the on - ly harm_that e-ver I done was I court-ed a fair young maid.___

It is quite clear that this melody corresponds to the second half of the well-known "Banks and braes o' bonny Doon" tune. The origin of that tune is something of a mystery and the authorship-claims of an Irish countess and a Scottish baroness have been advanced. William Chappell, always something of an expansionist in matters of melody, was sure the tune was English, but his ground is shaky. Robert Burns' account seems feasible, that an Edinburgh gentleman, James Miller, some time in the 1780s it seems, had expressed a wish to write a 'Scots air'. His friend the organist Stephen Clarke, who later harmonized the airs for Johnson's *Scots Musical Museum* where the tune appeared, had playfully suggested that to create a Scots tune all one had to do was to limit oneself to the black notes of the keyboard. Miller employed this simple pentatonic control, and "Ye banks and braes" resulted. If the story is correct and the tune is indeed of educated origin, it is in turn a mechanical imitation of a musical system foreign to educated composers of the time, but entirely at home to folk musicians. But even if we are to admit such pieces as *abgesunkenes Kulturgut*, the fact remains that the body of tunes making up the weightiest and most influential part of our traditional repertory, the tunes that occur most often and in the greatest number of variants are, so far as we can tell, independent of any aristocratic or bourgeois art song. Samuel Bayard, who knows more about British melody than any of us, remarks: 'The fact is that thus far not a single well-known air of our *common* (i.e. dominating) repertory has ever been traced definitely to any known composition of a trained musical artist.'[7] And furthermore: 'any theory that holds our folk tunes, *as organized, individual pieces of music*, to be merely borrowed court or theatre tunes of the past, signally fails to solve one problem or answer one question of importance' concerning English folk song.

Likewise, Vaughan Williams, in his *National Music*, remarks: 'The notion that folk music is a degenerate version of what we call composed music dies hard . . . if folk song were only half-remembered relics of the composed music of past centuries, should we not be able to settle the matter by going to our museums and looking through the old printed music? We shall find there nothing remotely resembling the traditional song of our country except, of course, such things as the deliberate transcriptions of the popular melodies in the *Fitzwilliam Virginal Book*.'

From France—from André Schaeffner, I think—comes a dry observation whose epigrammatic glitter does not conceal its scorn: 'If the folk took their songs from art composers, where did they get their pentatonism? From Debussy?' Schaeffner reminds us that the theory has its parallel in the world of comparative musicology where some specialists see in primitive music the bastardized and reduced relics of music from superior civilizations. It is rather as if the astonishing dreamlike and terrifying masks of Alaskan Eskimos are seen as the humble descendants of Japanese theatre masks, instead of being recognized as their magnificent ancestors.

Naumann was of the ranks of pen-and-ink folklorists whose

thought was founded on experience in the library without benefit of the cottage kitchen, hop-field or four-ale bar. He had no contact with folk singers or the makers of folk song. The discipline of folklore has suffered much from the ideas of scholars who at heart dislike the materials they are working with almost as much as they dislike the bearers of that material whom, if ever they meet them, they find disconcerting, baffling, embarrassing. In parenthesis, and because he is often misunderstood by young enthusiasts of the present urban folk song revival, it is worth remarking that Cecil Sharp was by no means of this kind. A vivid and characteristic story concerns his first meeting with a singer who gave him many fine songs including "The unquiet grave", "Geordie", "The false bride", "Bruton town", "The banks of green willow" as well as the venerable and indecorous "Crabfish" song that seems to have been amusing European audiences at least since about 1400 when its story first appears in a collection of Italian joking-tales (possibly it came from the Levant).

Sharp had been told that his singer lived in a poor street in Langport inhabited by 'bad people'.

She was out when he first called upon her, but was said to be at the public house round the corner. As he approached the public house he saw a group of women standing outside and chatting. 'Is Mrs. Overd here?' he asked. 'That's my name,' an elderly woman replied, 'and what do you want of me?' Sharp explained that he was hunting for old songs and hoped that she would sing him some; whereupon without any warning she flung her arms around his waist and danced him round and round with the utmost vigour, shouting, 'Lor, girls, here's my beau come at last.' In the middle of this terpsichorean display Sharp heard a shocked exclamation, 'But surely that is Mr. Sharp', and looking round he saw the vicar, with whom he was staying, and the vicar's daughter, both gazing with horror on the scene. When asked what he did, Sharp said: 'Oh, I shouted to them to go away, and they went.'[8]

To return from this aside (irrelevant? agreeable though) to the problem of the ability of the labouring people to create their own songs, we have suggested that social differences have made it hard for the conventional folklorist to obtain a fine assessment of matters affecting the inner life of people called 'humble'. The adjective itself is a condescending one and condescension seems common enough in the ethnographer facing the Bambuti pygmy and not less in the folklorist facing the Negro sharecropper, the Szekely shepherd or the Somerset stone-breaker. However amiable and sympathetic, the intellectual looks down from the pinnacle of his western, white, or bourgeois superiority, and from such heights the view may be distant and far from pin-sharp. Consider Béla Bartók. Here was a compassionate man, a convinced democrat, often attacked by middle-class Hungarian critics for his 'infatuation' with the despised peasantry. He had immense experience of working among peasants, for more or less single-handed he recorded 3,700 Hungarian melodies, 3,500 Rumanian, 3,200 Slovak, as well as some hundreds of Ruthenian, Yugoslav, Bulgarian, Arabic and Turkish pieces. He was convinced that on its small scale, peasant song could be 'as perfect as the grandest masterpieces of musical art' such as the works of Bach and Mozart. So at first sight there is some enigma in his statement that 'Whether peasants are individually capable of inventing quite new tunes is open to doubt. We have no data to go on. And the way in which the peasant's musical instinct asserts itself encourages no such view.'[9]

Can it be that the ghost of some haughty old Habsburg prejudice still lurked even in so sympathetic and daring a mind as Bartók's? He recognized clearly the disposition of peasants to vary and re-make the songs current in ther community; he appreciated the remarkable talent that the gifted performers might bring to the art of variation; but he may have underestimated the peasants' capacity for a certain measure of original individual composition. If the Hungarian folk song repertory consists entirely of variants of an original stock, who created that stock if not peasants and herdsmen? Bartók leaves the impression that a small store of tunes came into being (by immaculate conception?) which successive generations of singers have altered, embellished and extemporized upon, so that we have an impression of thousands of different melodies that are in fact all brothers, sons and cousins of a handful of tune families. A fair enough picture, as far as it goes. One of Bartók's devoted colleagues, Laszlo Lajtha, put it this way: 'Folk music is an art of variation *par excellence*. It produces new songs by the process of variation. It is the feeling for variation and spontaneity that assures the strength, the capacity to evolve, the very life of folk music. And that life manifests itself for as long as the folk song keeps its malleability and its ductility.' A clear enough statement that no folklorist would quarrel with. But is it the whole story?

Of course, Lajtha is speaking of melody. Now, we know that folk singers are capable of making new poems; and the use of traditional commonplaces so that hands are almost bound to be lilywhite, cheeks are like the roses red, the outlaw's men are merry, guineas are bright, ships and brothers commonly three, does not affect the poems' claim to originality. And if 'the folk' can make new poems, why not new tunes? Melody is harder to compose than verse, no doubt, but that is not to say it is impossible for a Transdanubian tractor driver or a Durham coalface worker to make an original tune on the strength of his own musical tradition. Nevertheless it is true that folk music is saturated with variation, whether variation during actual performance or variation from one performance to another. Many singers, and instrumentalists to an even greater degree, more or less alter their tune strophe after strophe, and scorn (or are unable, or consider it irrelevant) to perform the piece today in exactly the same way as they rendered it yesterday. In this respect, jazz players resemble folk musicians. Vincent d'Indy at the beginning of the twentieth century prophesied that 'the variation form has a great future', and indeed since Debussy, Webern, Messiaen, it has again become fashionable among the most modern composers. But the variation form also has a great past, not merely in the fixed way of Bach and Beethoven, but in more fluid and extemporized ways too. So the Roman choirs of Palestrina's time considered the stately parts set out on their music sheets merely as a scheme, a naked body that it was their duty to clothe with all manner of *ad lib* ornaments (the result must have been rather like a vocal version of the web of sound produced by a fanciful gipsy orchestra); so the castrati of late baroque opera, the Senesinos, Caffarellis, Farinellis, reckoned to perform their bravura pieces in a different manner night after night, giving their audiences as many ornamental variations of the same tune as, two hundred years later, the Armstrongs, Gillespies and Parkers gave to jazz fans; so too the keyboard players of Mozart's day were expected to improvize their own cadenzas instead of, as now, buying them already printed out in full, a kind of don't-do-it-yourself kit. Musically, the lower classes in the West have remained in this variative state, and, modest as they are, the improvized alterations noted from the Henry Larcombes and Mrs. Overds testify to the power of this art to revivify and embellish the music, no less eloquently than the astonishing extemporizations of Irish fiddlers, Balkan bagpipers or, for that matter, the art-music instrumentalists of the Oriental world (for though it may shock some of our musicologists to realize it, only a minute part of the world's population is affected by music fixed in writing and print).

Here for instance are a few of the ways in which old Mr. Larcombe sang the opening phrase of successive verses of "Robin Hood and the Tanner". Sharp made the notations by ear without the controlling help of sound-recording, so they are only skeletal and do not allow for such small details, important in the process of variation, as deviation from the 'exact' height or duration of notes, irregularities of speed, the placing of barely perceptible ornaments, and the sundry ways the folk singer has of passing from note to note by means of scoops, slides, hovers and such.

Similarly here are some variations used by Mrs. Overd of Langport in singing the final phrase of the "Bruton Town" tune. Sharp says: 'These variations were not attached to particular verses, though Mrs. Overd never sang the ballad to me without introducing all four of them.'

In Sharp's view, singers of the Larcombe and Overd kind are rather exceptional in their feeling for pregnant phrase-variation. Nevertheless, not dissimilar variations are shown in detailed notations from other singers including some whom Percy Grainger recorded on phonograph cylinders as early as 1904.*

In the *Journal of the Folk-Song Society* for 1908, Grainger published a number of transcriptions taken from his recordings and notated in as fine detail as his ear and his command of our system of musical handwriting allowed. Only listening to the actual sound can give an adequate impression of traditional performances of this kind; nevertheless Grainger's transcriptions do sketch for us a notion of those freedoms of rhythm, intonation and ornament that are often hard for good musicians to notate and seemingly impossible for concert singers to reproduce. Those varied departures from

---

* It is a brave passage in the history of folklore science, the story of the pioneers of sound-recording in the field. Dr. Walter Fewkes made phonogram recordings among North American Indians in 1889. By 1897 an enterprising Russian schoolteacher, Evgeniya Lineva, was demonstrating the importance of the phonograph in capturing the polyphonic songs of the Great Russian countryside. By 1904 Grainger, by 1906 Bartók, had accepted the idea of sound recording almost as a *sine qua non* of folk song collecting.

the general run of the tune, the off-centre notes, the vagaries of rhythm have less to do with the singer's inexactitude than with the nature and aims of his performance. Particularly since the invention of the tape-recorder, and with refinements in the skill of notating folk tunes that we owe to Bartók, Brailoiu and their successors, we have much ampler and more precise data to go by regarding the way of the singer with his song. Faced with evidence of constant variation in successive stanzas or successive performances of the same song, Bertrand Bronson suggests that even if the folk singers are not capable of creating entirely new and original tunes at will, their capacity for variation constitutes a 'power of miniature invention', and he proceeds: 'Moreover, what they have in their minds is not a note-for-note accuracy of a written tune; but rather an ideal melody, or melodic idea, which is responsive to the momentary dictates of feeling or verbal necessity.' Well put. The English folk singer of that sort is, in a humble way, in the position of the Oriental musician who has in mind a given *raga* (if he is an Indian) or *maqam* (if he is an Arab) which is but a tune-pattern, a melody formula, based on one or other modal scale and having certain stereotyped, more or less obligatory moments and passages, but otherwise allowing great freedom of treatment. In short, the *maqam* is a kind of skeleton or, better, scaffolding of melody which the musician, observing certain rules, is able to fill in for himself according to his fantasy and the mood of the moment.

For westerners, the clearest most familiar example of the *maqam* principle is provided by the Blues, always the same yet always different, a well-known well-worn frame apt for any extemporization, baffling to strangers, and listened to by fans not simply as a tune but as a traditional exercise at once achingly familiar and arrestingly fresh.* The Blues is an

---

* An outstanding European example of the *maqam* type is the *doina* (Bartók called it *hora lunga*), a decorated lyrical recitative kind of melody once thought to be a Rumanian speciality, which now turns out to be spread over a vast territory stretching from Albania to Tibet, from North Africa to Cambodia, possibly having Persia as its ancient centre or source of diffusion. The modern international spread of jazz and the Blues had its parallel in ancient times, it seems!

In Britain, a most striking illustration of *maqam*-style composition is provided by the pibroch of the Scottish highlands.

extreme example, but in some measure all folk tunes in their natural state, unfixed by print or other control, nourished by constant variation, having no single 'authentic' form but somewhat altering from singer to singer and even from verse to verse, are made on the *maqam* principle, with its balance of constraint with freedom, fixed model with fluid treatment, communal taste with individual fantasy, traditional constancy with novel creative moments, sameness with difference. The extent to which that principle operates varies from tradition to tradition, from singer to singer. In Europe we find Mediterranean and Balkan performers are more given to embroidery and extemporization than their northern counterparts. And in all traditions some performers treat their tunes in inventive and imaginative ways while others passively reproduce them more or less exactly as they receive them. Modern folk singers on the road to stylization and decadence reduce their alterations to a minimum, tending to sing each successive verse of a song in the same way, even the ornaments cropping up at the identical spot, strophe after strophe, regular as clockwork or the 8.30 train.

The idea that somehow all folk music performers are on the same footing, and that folk song is something produced as naturally as a bird sings on the bough, is a myth. Traditional performers no less than the performers of fine-art music show varying degrees of skill, talent, taste and imagination. Some are expert musical hands and acknowledged as such by their neighbours, while others are mere novices nobody wants to listen to. Moreover, in traditions in full flower, training counts for much, and the admired singers will practise over and again to perfect their art. An Irish street-singer, removed to crowded quarters in a London tenement, complained to me: 'This is doing my singing no good. There's nowhere I can get out of everybody's way so I can find the *places* in my songs.'

Our consideration of the great importance of variation, of what some modern scholars choose (fancifully?) to call 'the *maqam* spirit', arises, you may recall, from Bartók's statement that it is doubtful whether the folk can create original songs but what they certainly do is to alter what they have got. Astigmatism and uncharity are not in Bartók's make-up, but when he denies that his peasants are capable of inventing quite new tunes he seems to leave too much out of account. One could say the same of Bach or Mozart, at a pinch. Apart from the fact that a folk song is a more communal and fluid, less personal and fixed affair than an art song, does it start life in a way vastly different from the manner in which formal compositions are born? Kodály has something relevant to say, in an essay published in 1941: 'In folk music, a new transcription, a variation, is produced by the singer on each occasion. An essential trait of folk song is this power of unconditional ownership; but this used to exist also in high art—Shakespeare, Bach, Handel. At first it seems that the mode of production is entirely different: here we have a process of individual creation, there a slow variation of existing material leading to a new work through tiny changes. But let us look closer at musical history. Do compositions of such individual character, showing no likeness to anything already in existence, spring from the heads of composers like Minerva from the head of Jupiter? The early works of the great masters are often mere imitations, scarcely different from the compositions of their predecessors; only gradually do individual tones develop. A new type of folk song develops from existing forms by slow variation, but hardly at slower pace than that discernible in art music.'[10] Thus Kodály reminds us that Palestrina and Lassus, Bach and Handel used countless borrowed themes, while eighty per cent of Mozart's tunes occurred also in the music of his contemporaries. And Bence Szabolcsi, pursuing this line of thought, stresses that, like folk musicians, art composers are also working with recurring tune models whether they realize it or not. 'Definite types of thinking and expression, certain turns and formulas, assert themselves in the taste of a period, the style of an epoch. He who avoids them denies his age and renounces intelligibility. . . . All creative talents seem to vary a fundamental idea throughout a whole lifetime.'[11]

It is not only in the inventive performance of the individual folk singer that the 'maqam spirit' shows itself, it is also in the way the collective, the community, works on the song. When Gorky says: 'the collective power of common people has created deathless values in poetic creation', he is making no windy utterance but a statement of folklore fact. The individual creation, or creation-by-variation if you will, is only effective if the song-maker is expressing the thoughts and feelings of his community, for only then is his song taken up by his neighbours and passed into general currency. Among creators of folk song the desire to explore the obscure margins of private experience is always less than the wish to impose individual order on common experience. So before he starts composing, the maker is affected by the outlook and aspirations of his community; in short, each folk song at its inception is at least partly a product of social determinism. But social determinism is not the only factor in the life of the song because after it has come into being a multitude of other singers are likely to get to work on it, altering it about, de-composing and re-composing it, producing sometimes richer sometimes poorer versions of the original; now deepening the emotional and ideological content, now making it more shallow; now bringing the tune into sad decay, now re-creating and renewing it happily. In a flourishing folk tradition, work on an already-created song never ceases. There is nothing private or exclusive about a folk song; it is the most public and communal form of music and poetry imaginable. In their inception the words and tunes are socially determined, and throughout their life they are subject to endless collective elaboration. Understand, 'collective elaboration' in this sense does not mean that a group of ploughmen or pitmen sit around in committee to alter the song; it means that in the course of the song's life various moments arise when individuals make their changes, perhaps to suit transplantation into a new locality or a fresh social circumstance. In Van Gennep's words, folk creation is 'the act of a single individual whose product is subsequently modified by other individuals who come in contact with it'. It is a collective art displayed by individuals. A single person expresses an idea acceptable by his community, and the community, in the form of a sequence of individuals joins in re-creating and adapting the work over the years and across the counties.

What does that mean? It means that a song may be born into a tradition that fits a certain society; but as that society changes, as the folk change, the song may change too. A folk song tradition is not a fixed and immutable affair, and the word 'authenticity', favourite among amateurs of folk music, is one to use with caution. Traditionalists are always disturbed by the appearance of novelties on the folklore scene, but in any living tradition novelties are constantly emerging, often in tiny almost imperceptible details that accumulate over long periods of time and suddenly, when the social moment is ripe, come together to result in a change that may be drastic.

Rumanian folklore provides a dramatic illustration of this process. (Must I apologize for taking examples from such far-away parts? Well-preserved and flourishing traditions yield clearer illustration than traditions in a state of dilapidation like so many in the West). On the eve of World War I, Bartók visited a group of villages in Padureni, an isolated region of western Transylvania. He recorded several hundred songs there and noted that generally the repertories of the various villages were so small that often neighbouring villages did not know each other's songs, the tunes were of limited, even primitive character, mostly restricted to the lower half of the minor scale, the words not divided into verses but consisting mainly of a single line sung three times to a three-lined melody. The rhythms were very square, the tunes were hardly orna-mented at all; Bartók's impression was that there had been no new creation for several centuries.

About forty years later a group of Rumanian folklorists visited the same district, armed with Bartók's recordings and notes. They re-recorded some of his original singers, now old men and women, and also other singers, middle-aged and young. All told, they collected about a thousand songs, and by contrasting their material with Bartók's they were able to draw conclusions about the fate of local tradition within forty years.

They found the tradition had greatly altered since Bartók's day. First, they found that singing was much more common than Bartók had reported. The songs, including several re-corded by Bartók, now had a far wider compass, many of them extending to an octave. Four-lined melodies, with at least two different textlines, were now the rule. As for ornamentation, the singing-style of the middle-aged inhabitants (sons and daughters of Bartók's informants, many of them) showed a fantastically rich embellishment. The songs were now grand, spacious, flowery, meandering, rather dreamy and reflective, quite different from the recordings of forty years before.

Not only had the old songs altered and become melodically more developed; the folklorists also found an abundance of newly-made songs, especially among the younger generation that had grown up during the 1940s and early '50s. The songs of these youngsters differed again from those of their parents. Instead of being slow, free, flowery and reflective, the home-made songs of the post-War generation showed themselves little-ornamented, four-square in shape, rather wide in compass, of great rhythmic impetuosity, sung in excited energetic fashion often by unison couples or trios standing arm in arm with neck outthrust, and generally with an optimistic air.

It seems then that in this rather remote and deeply tradi-tional area, the folk songs, after perhaps centuries of tiny variation and minute change, took a sudden qualitative leap towards the creation not only of fresh tunes but of a quite new melody-style, that nevertheless contained a fertilizing germ of the old style. What happened to bring about the change? Apparently in the inter-War period there was some expansion of the village economy with improved agricultural methods and such; the opening of bus routes brought the Padureni villages into contact with the culture of surrounding districts and the change was intensified and given a new direction with the establishing of the Communist government after the Second World War when the young villagers in particular became filled with a sense of purpose that their parents had often lacked, passivity was replaced by initiative, apathy by elation, humility by a sense of self-importance. At the same time as new material perspectives came in view, the cultural horizon of the villages widened too, through schools, films, radio and such. The local song tradition proved robust enough to receive all kinds of new nourishment and to digest it satisfactorily. Only a moribund tradition is *dominated* by the past; a living tradition is constantly sprouting new leaves on old wood and sometimes quite suddenly the bush is ablaze with blossom of a novel shade.

Let us not be deceived by that vegetable metaphor. New

songs do not just arise inevitably in the natural course of events; they are a product of work, of the imaginative effort of individuals, farm-hands, factory-hands, sensitive to the ways and conditions of the life they share with their neighbours. The creation of folk song is no more 'natural' than the creation of art music and poetry; it is an entirely conscious affair as Phillips Barry realized when, perhaps impatient with his colleagues who felt it enough to study the ballad with never a thought for the ballad-singer, he wanted it to be cried from the house-tops that a folk singer is a personality, an individual and most of all a creative artist. 'In the name of good science and good sense,' he appealed, 'let us have done once and for all with calling folk song and folk balladry artless'. A work is not artless simply because, once it originates, it is liable to endless variation, to constant change of colour as it passes from mouth to mouth down the years and across the landscape until the community's faculty of improvization dwindles and fails.

Let us consider quite hypothetically how a folk song may arise and what course its life may follow. We will suppose a man is ploughing a field. The work is dull, and he is upset over his girl's behaviour. For diversion and comfort he begins to make a song. He may take a ready-made tune just as it is, or he may adapt it; he may review in his mind a number of melodies and choose from them a phrase here, a phrase there; or he may make a tune that seems to him wholly new, though in the nature of things it is likely to be comprised mainly of old elements to which he has added a modest personal contribution. To this tune he sets his poem, probably likewise made up of old elements redeployed, with additions from his own experience. Some time later, in the kitchen when there is company, or in the little pub on Saturday night when it is too crowded for darts or bumblepuppy, he tries out his song. It may be too poor or too private to be attractive, nobody takes it up, it dies on the singer's lips. On the other hand it may be an apt statement of a common emotional experience and may correspond nicely to the climate of the time, and at least one of the listeners likes the song well enough to want to take it into his own repertory. On the way home from cottage or pub this second person runs the song over in his head. Parts of it have slipped his memory, so he fills in the blanks for himself. Other parts he does not like so well, so he sets his own fantasy to work. By the time he is ready to sing the song it is already somewhat different from the original.

Perhaps a carter carries it into the next county and introduces it to a new community. The song spreads from mouth to mouth, place to place, parent to child, age to age, and so enters the vast reservoir of the collective memory. There it will lead a capricious life of fluctuating fortune. It may divide into countless variants, some close to the original, some so far-removed as to constitute virtually new songs. At times it will be circulating in the liveliest way; at other times it will almost disappear, at least temporarily gone out of fashion, no longer corresponding to the psychological need of the time. Perhaps other variants more in tune with the spirit of the era may chase the 'original' right out of the folklore circuit. But let us presume that, in some of its forms, our song goes on being sung more or less as the ploughman first put it together. At some stage perhaps a broadside ballad seller hears the song, likes it and reports it to a publisher who prepares and issues his printed version which begins to circulate alongside the oral sets. The printed version itself undergoes some alterations in the course of passing from singer to singer, but the text on the ballad-sheet is likely to have special prestige—deserved or not—and very many singers are likely to go on singing the song more or less as printed, that is, the text becomes partly fixed even if the tune goes on varying in detail. At some stage, perhaps at the peak of the song's life—it may be centuries after the ploughman first brooded on his sweetheart's caprices and produced his ballad or it may be within a decade or two—at some stage then, a single version becomes dominant. Other variants of the song go on circulating and fluctuating, improved by one singer, ruined by another; but one version establishes itself above all others. This version may or may not be one that has appeared in printed form, but it is found to be entirely memorable and satisfactory by a large number of singers. Unlike its more pliant brothers it seems to be almost impervious to change and where modifications in its words or tune do occur they are

C*

of the slightest. And so matters stand until times change so much that eventually the song comes to have no meaning and withers away, or else the whole repertory falls into dilapidation and passes mainly into the keeping of broken singers with vague memories and poor command of their art and the agony of the old tradition commences. Even so, the life of the song may not be over, for it may rise again in quite novel circumstances, in industrial cities, carried by a new order of semi-professional singers, spread to some extent by print, gramophone and radio but still subject to the working of oral conveyance. And if, in this 'second existence', the milieu and circumstances of performance have changed and the song moves more impetuously and the rhythm is more regular and the melody less fanciful and accompanying instruments are providing a harmony that used not to be there, still the function of the piece may not have altered much from the time the ploughman first shyly tried it out on his friends. By now, however, the academic folklorist is likely to have washed his hands of the whole affair.

Our example is hypothetical, but feasible. However, the true life story of a folk song's composition may be more surprising and its distribution simpler. As an instance, let us take a modern example because its footprints are easily traceable. The ballad called "Floyd Collins" appears in sundry American folk song collections from the Southern Appalachians (Mellinger Edward Henry) to Michigan (Emelyn E. Gardner and Geraldine J. Chickering) and on various 'field-recorded' discs in the Library of Congress's Archive of American Folk Song. The ballad-story is based on an actual tragedy that provided the subject of an ambitious novel and a memorable film. In 1925, Floyd Collins was exploring a Kentucky cave when the walls fell in and buried him. Rescue gangs worked six days and nights to free him, but he died as they reached him. A ballad sprang up about the incident and seems to have spread rapidly through Kentucky, Virginia, Tennessee and North Carolina. We read of a printer in the Kentucky mountains reporting he did 'moughty well with the song-ballit of Floyd Collins', selling the text on a crudely-printed leaflet to wandering fiddlers who in turn hawked them among the crowd outside the Court house on court day. According to Gardner and Chickering, Collins's family, 'which before the tragedy had belonged to the poorer farming class, became comfortably well-to-do from the proceeds of . . . this song and from the toll which they inaugurated, charging sightseers fifty cents each to view the scene of the catastrophe'. D. K. Wilgus, the best authority on modern American country music says: 'According to the "mystic" principles of folksong composition and dissemination . . . "The Death of Floyd Collins" should have sprung up about 1925 in the vicinity of Horse Cave, Kentucky, and have spread and changed in the performances of a succession of folksingers in time and space. In point of fact the idea of the song was conceived in the mind of Polk C. Brockman, a record distributor and talent scout, as he sat in the Aragon Hotel in Jacksonville, Florida.'[12] It seems that Brockman was connected with a company interested in issuing records for the rural market whose tastes favoured the kind of folk and near-folk music performed by country professionals—whether medicine-show performers, vaudeville musicians, or the part-timers who provided fiddle music for settlement dances. Brockman felt that the Floyd Collins tragedy, which had attracted national attention, would be a good subject for a saleable song, and he commissioned Andrew Jenkins, a blind minstrel, preacher and faith-healer, to make the ballad. That done, the composition was given to a country musician, Fiddlin' John Carson, who made the first recording. Later the song was recorded by a more generally popular singer, Vernon Dalhart, and through him it achieved wide distribution, so that, says Wilgus, though 'there are local variants and adaptations . . . "The Death of Floyd Collins" as now recovered is generally the Dalhart rendition'. The dissemination of the song is by a process similar to that of broadside ballads, with the gramophone record replacing the printed leaflet. The crucial question is whether Andrew Jenkins may be considered as a folk composer. Opinions would differ but Wilgus's view is that 'in terms of his sources, his forms, and the acceptance of his material, I don't think we can deny him the title'.

An even later example, through which blows a more classical air, comes from Gaelic Scotland. In 1963 a dealer bought horses on the island of Berneray, in the Outer Hebrides. To get them to the nearby larger island of North Uist he made them swim after his small boat. The Berneray folk gathered to watch the scene and were moved by the sight of so many white horses on the white sands ready to plunge into the sea. They asked one of their company, a noted song-maker, to make a ballad on the incident. At first she did not think she could, but they prevailed on her to go back to her croft and sit alone while she reflected. By the evening, she was ready with her song, which has now firmly entered the local repertory, and begins to assume its varieties.

Whether a melody is an original composition or somebody's re-fashioning of a ready-made piece hardly matters in folk song. If it appeals to a number of people, the composition or variant will start spreading and undergoing alteration, adapted perhaps to a whole variety of texts. Some tunes lend themselves more readily than others to extensive variation, and of course some singers have a more fanciful way than others with their songs. In any folk singer's repertory one is likely to find a whole number of tunes that the singer believes to be separate melodies but which are in fact variants of each other, melodies whose strong points—cadences particularly—have resisted change but whose weak points have accepted perhaps drastic alteration. The fact that these songs are basically similar encourages the singer to combine and merge them, consciously or involuntarily, in the course of performance. In that way, certain tunes give rise to enormous families, and just as some say there are five basic dirty stories and all other such anecdotes are variants of these, so some specialists will have it that there is a specific number of British tune families (ten? forty? a hundred?) embracing the common folk song repertory of these islands. Doubtless this is over-simplification. All the same, the folk are masters at making much of little; in folk song nothing gets thrown away; a melody comes into being and the possibilities for its exploitation are quickly perceived and acted on. The one tune becomes bent to serve a dozen moods, a score of texts.

Let us take, for illustration, the good tune much used in both England and Ireland, sometimes called "Dives and Lazarus",

or "Come all you faithful (or 'worthy') Christian men", and
generally known in Ireland as "The star of the County Down",
after a popular recording of the tune by John McCormack.
Sharp found it 'one of the most common, the most characteristic, . . . the most beautiful of English folk airs'. William Chappell printed a set of it in the second (1859) volume of his
Popular Music of the Olden Time, saying: 'This is the tune of
many songs. If the reader should meet any half-a-dozen men
perambulating the streets of London together, and singing, the
probabilities are great that they sing to this tune. Sometimes
the men are dressed like sailors; at other times they look like
workmen out of employment. I recollect hearing the tune at
Kilburn, full forty years ago, and have, with tolerable annual
regularity, ever since. I regret never having stopped to hear
the words.'

If this tune was indeed the one 'most frequently heard
in the streets of London in the mouths of men seeking employment', it was also vastly spread in the countryside in countless
transformations, as an instrumental air or attached to a
variety of texts including "John Barleycorn".

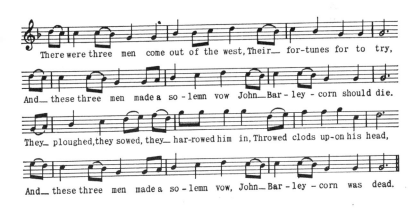

Mr Whitby, the sexton of Tilney All Saints, Norfolk, sang
this version to Vaughan Williams as a setting of "The murder
of Maria Marten":

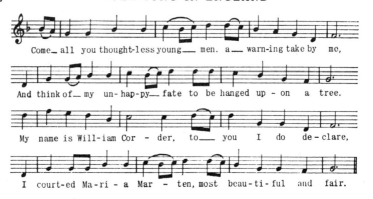

Come_ all you thought-less young__ men. a__ warn-ing take by me,

And think of_ my un- hap-py__ fate to be hanged up - on a tree.

My name is Will-iam Cor - der, to__ you I do de - clare,

I court-ed Ma-ri - a Mar - ten, most beau-ti-ful and fair.

The same tune was adapted to the transportation ballad of "Van Diemen's Land", sometimes called "The gallant poachers". The penal settlement of Van Diemen's Land (Tasmania) received its first convicts in 1804, its last in 1835, so the ballad-text was made between those dates.

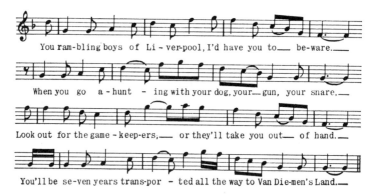

You ram-bling boys of Li - ver-pool, I'd have you to__ be-ware.__

When you go a - hunt - ing with your dog, your__ gun, your snare,__

Look out for the game - keep-ers,__ or they'll take you out__ of hand.__

You'll be se-ven years trans-por - ted all the way to Van Die-men's Land.__

In all our tradition it would be hard to find a tune more extensively used, more ingeniously re-created. The well-known "Jolly miller" (Beethoven harmonized it) is its bluntest, most banal form, but the untampered traditional sets are far finer. Its countless variants fall into two main classes, the one with its cadences on the keynote and the flat seventh, as above, the other having its middle cadence on the fifth or its inversion (with the final cadence on the tonic as usual). An imaginative re-working of this latter form carries the tale of the miller's apprentice who makes a girl pregnant and, being pressed to marry her, murders her and throws her battered body in the river. A broadside of this was published at the end of the seventeenth century, in 44 verses, called "The Berkshire tragedy, or the Wittam miller". Pared down to a more reasonable length, the song has continued to curdle the blood of simple listeners till today, under some such title as "The prentice boy". The ballad probably derived its hold from the contrast between the violence of the tragedy and the pitiful despair of the young murderer, and the re-made Lazarus tune, dramatic and plangent, carries the words well.

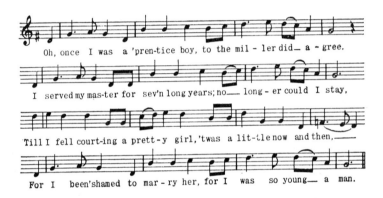

Oh, once I was a 'pren-tice boy, to the mil - ler did— a - gree.

I served my mas-ter for sev'n long years; no— long - er could I stay,

Till I fell court-ing a prett-y girl, 'twas a lit-tle now and then,——

For I been'shamed to mar - ry her, for I was so young— a man.

More far-fetched, and on the way to becoming a separate tune, is the variant below, a well-loved, much-used air (some singers employ it for the "Van Diemen's Land" words) that retains the fourteen-syllable (8 + 6) metre of the 'standard' models of the tune, and uses the keynote-fifth cadences, but transforms the content of the tune-lines from A A B A to A B B A which some authorities believe to be more modern. Our variant shows a change of mode too, from Re to Sol, which comes simply by changing the 'dorian' minor third into a 'mixolydian' major one. It would not be easy to isolate the elements that establish this tune firmly as a cousin or half-brother of "Lazarus". Nevertheless the family resemblance is there, as when an artist over-paints and alters an old portrait but the ingrained basic design shows unmistakably through. This version carries the words of the rousing sailor song, "Rounding the Horn".

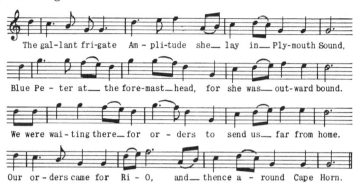

The gal-lant fri-gate Am-pli-tude she— lay in— Ply-mouth Sound,

Blue Pe-ter at— the fore-mast—head, for she was— out-ward bound.

We were wai-ting there— for or-ders to send us— far from home.

Our or-ders came for Ri-o, and— thence a-round Cape Horn.

It is often suggested that one-strain tunes are more ancient than two-strain airs. Alexander Keith, for instance, the editor of Greig's *Last Leaves of Traditional Ballads and Ballad Airs*, was convinced that the one-strain versions of the ballad tunes are the correct original forms, and that the presence of a second strain shows the hand of some later reviser attempting 'to work up the original simplicity of the tunes into a semblance of art music'. The matter is not so simple. If a tune has only one strain it may be a sign of age, but it may also be a sign of senility. Experienced collectors know how often old singers with failing memories provide only half a tune, whether the first half or the second, repeating just the one strain over and again. Sometimes this process has happy results. It comes as something of a surprise to realize that one of the jewels of the English folk song repertory, the "Brigg Fair" tune, is merely a 'decadent' version of the latter half of the common "Lazarus" air we have been dealing with, as we readily see if we compare it with lines 3 and 4 of the "Maria Marten" variant.

It was on the fifth of Au-gust, the wea-ther hot and fair,—

Un-to Brigg Fair I did re-pair, for love I was in-clined.

The "Dives and Lazarus" tune-family is one of those that are widely and more or less evenly spread in these islands, one of that network of melodies extending from the Scottish north-east to the west of England and throughout Ireland, even penetrating the Gaeltacht. Such tunes incline to sound English in England, Irish in Ireland, Scots in the mouth of a Lothian harvester or a Buckie trawlerman. Remarking this, Samuel Bayard emphasizes how impossible it often is to ascertain in which country the parent-tune of a family was composed. 'When a tune-version travelled from one British region or nation to another, it was naturally re-created in the musical style of the region which adopted it. We can often reasonably infer that a given version of some widespread air is Irish or Scottish, for example, but we cannot therefore claim that the air itself was of Scots or Irish origin. The presence of Irish mannerisms in a melody current in midland England, then, indicates only that this version of the melody was presumably evolved in, and brought from Ireland; but it does not allow us to claim that the tune first arose there.'[13]

Bold spirits may declare that the parent-tune of the "Lazarus" family is as Irish as Paddy's pig, and they may be right, though the Scots know it as "Gilderoy", and the Welsh have many songs to it, including "O lachgan wyf o Gymre bach", so we cannot be sure of its birthplace. What we know is, its various sets are as common in the English countryside as in Ireland. For the matter of that, many would consider as English of the English the famous tune of "Searching for lambs", yet this too is but the sprig of a tree whose roots extend south to Somerset, west to Galway, north at least to Northumberland and perhaps, as a psalm tune anyway, into the Scottish lowlands. It is known in Wales as a hymn tune, "Dorcas", and its Northumbrian reincarnation strongly recalls the version of "The false young man" that Sharp collected at the Appalachian settlement of White Rock, Virginia in 1918. Here is the "Searching for lambs" melody in the company of a few of its numerous relatives—a set of the ballad of "The mermaid" found in Hampshire, Vaughan Williams's notation of a psalm tune sung at Dunstan, Northumberland, and an Irish version of the well-known "Sprig of

thyme", a parabolic homily on sexual conduct, from Ballinalee,
Co. Longford.

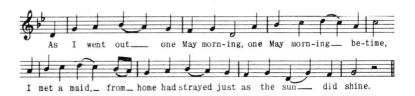

As I went out___ one May morn-ing, one May morn-ing___ be-time,

I met a maid,___ from___ home had strayed just as the sun___ did shine.

One night as I lay on___ my bed, I lay so___ fast a-sleep,

When the thought___ of my true love came run-ning to my head,

And poor sail - ors that sail___ on the deep.

The Lord of life___ my shep-herd is, He makes me down___ to lie,___

In pas-tures green He feed - eth me, And the qui - et wa - ters by.___

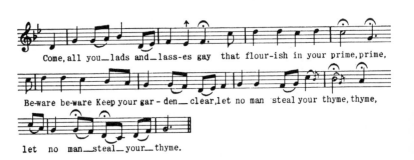

Come, all you___lads and___lass-es gay that flour-ish in your prime, prime,

Be-ware be-ware Keep your gar - den___ clear, let no man steal your thyme, thyme,

let no man___steal___your___thyme.

With singer after singer adding his modifications, minimal or tremendous, to his tunes as he sings them, it is clear that the distinction between performance and composition is of the vaguest. All the same quite new tunes do emerge from time to time and several folk traditions acknowledge individual song creators, and remember when specific songs were made, as in the case of Blind Raftery of Mayo, or Larry Gorman the logger songmaker of the American North-east, or Tommy Armstrong the Durham mine-balladeer (though in fact all these were more remarkable as makers of texts than of tunes).

The folk singer never seems to have paid much heed to a matter that some modern folk song enthusiasts attach importance to, namely the interdependence of tune and words in the sacrosanct sense of one melody for one poem. He would use variants, or even identical sets, of the same air to carry a sordid crime ballad, a lively song of sea adventure, a rustic idyll, a tender love complaint. To vary the psychological climate he would not as a rule put drama and pathos into his voice (though in fact the 'showman' singer is not such a rarity in tradition as some make out); more likely he would convey the mood of the song by a small alteration of pace, a slight change of vocal timbre, an almost imperceptible pressing or lightening of rhythm, and by nuances of ornament that our folklorists, with the exception of Percy Grainger, have consistently neglected in their transcriptions; more's the pity.

Not only did folk tunes move from poem to poem and district to district, but also from country to country. It is a fascinating pursuit, to track a melody across a whole continent and observe its constant variation as it establishes itself in one country after another, taking on features reflecting the peculiarities of whatever peoples it happens to be residing among. A sort of patriotic mysticism inhibits this study to some extent. The notion is still prevalent that a folk tune must be the sacred property of a given country, that its source must reside in 'the melodious soul of the nation', that—to quote a recent German scholar—it has specific ethnic qualities that reveal themselves in 'that mysterious something like a golden aura round holy images'. A less lyrical view shows us that in fact all over Europe folk tunes are likely to be a mixture of common international traits and individual national characteristics. That is, the synthesis between the collective and the individual within a national folk song tradition is repeated on an international scale in the synthesis between melody forms that are shared by various countries and the specific national idiosyncrasies that are brought to bear on those forms.

Like other European countries, England has profited from the common fund of continental melody. To what extent, we do not know; that field of research is still in its infancy though as early as 1865 the German scholar Tappert was discussing the habits of wandering tunes. By what means do melodies wander? How does it happen that what seem to be variants of a single tune turn up in a Rumanian funeral lament, a Hungarian love song, a Dutch hymn, a Spanish ballad, and a highwayman song sung by an elderly couple whom Vaughan Williams met one autumn day when bicycling in Sussex? Such curiosities are not necessarily mere coincidence. They may be melodies that in the course of many centuries have spread out from a single source and, perhaps on account of some peculiar firmness in their architecture, have remained fairly constant and recognizable in shape though taking on new details and serving new functions in the various lands of their adoption. There are many ways by which such tunes may be carried. On the continent, pastoral peoples sometimes drifted with their flocks across an enormous stretch of territory (for instance, Transylvanian shepherds were ranging as far west as northern Moravia, as far east as Crimea and the Caucasus, up to relatively modern times) and it is notorious that music plays a peculiarly important part in the life of shepherds. Soldiers brought home a certain number of tunes from foreign wars, though possibly the extent of this is not large, seeing that other booty was more generally in mind. Walloons settled in the Tokay district of north-east Hungary, speaking both French and Hungarian, used to take waggon-trains loaded with wine into Poland. In settlement after settlement along the route across Slovakia and over the Carpathians to Krakow, the journey would be livened with drinking and singing, in which the local folk would join, sampling the wine and adding to the jollification. What songs and ballads did these bilingual wine-trading peasants carry back and forth, and adapt, and pass on not only eastward but also to their cousins in the West, so that ultimately perhaps some of the themes and melodies may have floated across the Channel to us?

The vagrant scholars of the Middle Ages, some of them rowdy young men changing their universities all the time, drifting from Paris or Salamanca across to Prague and up to Oxford, were also busy traffickers in songs. Sometimes the lyrics were the equivalent of the modern rugger club song-text, but the fact that they were acquired in foreign parts was no hindrance to their circulation among students using Latin as a *lingua franca*. The tunes were likely to be the town hits of the time, adapted folk airs or popular-style compositions of a shapeliness quite new in music. But no doubt the principal tune-carriers were the professional minstrels of the Middle Ages, of whatever class, whether their patrons were aristocrats or the back-street inhabitants of towns or the grinning crowds at a country fair. Some of these followed their occupation within a narrow radius of action, more or less tied to a single locality. Others would roam widely, the courtly musicians, as Walter Salmen reminds us, being equally at home in a Scottish baron's fortified farmhouse or an Austrian duke's castle in Vienna or the palace of the King of Catalonia, while their poorer colleagues went on the pilgrim excursion boats to Santiago de Compostela and heard the music of Galician bagpipers, or at the great six-weeks' fair at Leipzig learned from a Polish fiddler a tune he had picked up at last year's fair in Novgorod. A German account of 1552 tells of the fairground meeting of four wanderers from England, Italy, Denmark and Turkey; it was by such means that oriental instruments, Mediterranean dances, mid-European melodies were helped to spread northward. The same musician would know what audiences and earnings were like in London, Milan, Nuremberg and Reval in Esthonia. In 1192, King Bela III of Hungary sent one of his minstrels to Paris *ad discendam melodiam* to pick up tunes and polish his technique. Each year, from 1483 onward, Richard III used to bring minstrels over from Bavaria and Austria, five at a time, armed with *laissez-passer* letters to facilitate their journey to and fro via Calais. Just as the minstrels were of all classes and kinds, noblemen or jugglers' sons, property-owners or beggars, scholars or illiterates, virtuosi or strummers, so their repertory too was varied according to their audiences, whether of court or countryside. The minstrels were bearers of the most cultivated and the most primitive music, the general supra-national tunes of the medieval towns and the special local traditions of isolated rural communities, highly-stylized music for the festivities of wealthy merchants and wild stuff for the pagan round-dances of the peasantry, stiff flattering battle-ballads for the aristocratic heavy cavalry, lively subversive outlaw songs for the low-born bowmen.

So perhaps after all it is not surprising that variants of many medieval tunes crop up among the folk melodies of a wide variety of peoples. As a famous instance, we find the 'grandchildren' of a fifteenth century Burgundian dance, "Le petit roysin", scattered as folk songs all over Europe and reappearing time and again in the English countryside. The tune is a four-liner, regularly-phrased, built on a compact architectonic skeleton, with the first and last lines ending on the tonic and the second line-end (the important main caesura that, as Bartók says, divides the tune into question and answer) cadencing on the fifth above the keynote. Walter Salmen[14] astutely notes that on this kind of scaffolding a minstrel group could not only improvise polyphonic dance music of any required length, but could also introduce without difficulty special rhythmical or tonal effects to suit a whole variety of foreign audiences, for travelled minstrels were often masters of several musical 'languages', being able to play in the manner of Spain and Scotland, Holland and Hungary, even Kiev and Constantinople.

Here is the "Petit roysin" tune, which may have been circulating for some time already before its appearance in the Burgundian manuscript of *c.* 1470:

And here are a few transformations of the melody-outline, varied in sundry ways as a medieval German hymn, a Spanish ballad from Salamanca, a new-style 'come-all-ye'-like Hungarian song from the neighbourhood of Lake Balaton (the words of its single verse are erotically symbolic: 'Early in the morning I went to the spring. I set my bucket down on the path. The local outlaw came that way, trod on it, and it broke under him'), and finally as one of the best-known English love-songs, the lament called "Died for love" which a famous folk singer, Joseph Taylor, sang into Percy Grainger's phonograph at Brigg, Lincolnshire, in 1906. (Incidentally, and for good measure, another of the avatars of "Le petit roysin" is the little Moravian tune we quote as Ex. 16.)[15]

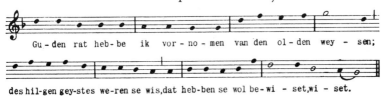

Gu-den rat heb-be ik vor-no-men van den ol-den wey - sen;

des hil-gen gey-stes we-ren se wis,dat heb-ben se wol be-wi - set,wi - set.

Tris-tes nue-vas,tris-tes nue-vas___

Se can-ta-ban en Se-vi-lla.___

Se ha ca-sa-do el Con-de Al - ba___

Con da - ma de gran va-lí - a.___

Reg-gel korín ki-me-gyek a kút-ra, Le-te-szem a zsaj-ta-rom az út-ra

Ar-ra ment a var-me-gye haj-du-ja Be-le-lé-pett, el-tö-rot a-lat-ta

I wish my ba-by it é was born,   Ly-in' smi-lin on___ its fa-ther's knee,

And_ I was dead and in my grave,__ And green_grass growin' all o - ver me.

Our English folk songs then must be considered as part of a general European complex; only gradually, over slow centuries, did they take on their peculiar national and class character. When the embryo of present day folk song began to form in the matrix of medieval Europe, it had as its immediate ancestors the rudimentary solo lyrical song of the *coloni*—tenant farmers of the Roman Empire—and the communal and hardly differentiated work songs and cult songs of the barbarian tribesmen. On the margin of the pedigree, only faintly indicated, is the epic song of the military balladeers, the scops and saga singers paid to recite the exploits of some 'beefy illiterate burner, giver of rings', and the shorter, livelier, more formal song of the professional entertainers, the *joculatores*, who thronged the highways of Europe for some centuries after the chaos of the barbarian invasions closed the theatres of the Roman Empire and turned the great number of its stage musicians into vagrants.

The story of the birth of European folk song hardly concerns us here. It has been admirably reconstructed by the Hungarian musicologist János Maróthy,[16] who has traced the historical processes by which, in the course of a thousand years or so, European folk song changed from the 'non-specified', 'variative', collectively performed music characteristic of tribal culture to the arch-shaped solo song typical of peasants, with its metrical rhythm, well-organized melody lines, and—ultimately—strophic form (by Maróthy's implication, 'non-specified' music is that which is closely bound to some action, whether work, hunting, fighting, or a stylization of these in dance or ritual; 'variative' song is based on the perpetual variation of small melodic motifs or formulas, rather than on the relatively unchanged repetition of larger melodic units, such as prevail in the modern European 'song-proper').

If Maróthy is correct in pointing to the *colonus* (who was quite likely to be a German, Frankish or British ex-soldier of the Imperial Army) as representative of that uniformly levelled, exploited class of agricultural producers who laid the foundations of European folk song, it is hard to resist drawing some musical parallel—with due allowances—between the smallholder of Rome's decline and the Negro tenant farmer in post-bellum America, who came out of slavery with a repertory of communal work-songs and spirituals, and gradually in his novel solitary state, with its joys and anxieties, created for himself his own solo songs of personal emotion, cast in new, more evolved forms—such as the Blues—because his expanding lyrical horizon demanded it, because he wanted to assert his new-felt individuality. So in antiquity the small tenant farmer or serf, detached from his tribal or military community for the first time, making his own way—as far as the master allowed—and raising his voice in field or hut without answer from a group, evolved his solo individual songs, at first probably free-rhythmed and variative (like Bartók's *hora lunga*?), but gradually more metrical, shapely, song-properish. The music of the 'barbarian' tribes in the Dark Ages was already somewhat affected by the new forms that emerged with the early feudalism of Rome, and the dialectical interplay between the communal music of the clans and the relatively individual music of the *coloni* created a more developed kind of melody during the period between the collapse of Rome and the emergence of medieval feudalism.

Slowly, the function of lower class music began to change, and the forms with it. Performances became less exclusively tied to occasion, to ritual or to practical purpose. Songs reflecting reality in more oblique ways, or even made simply for entertainment, became of greater importance in the peasant repertory. Tunes became more 'specified' too, that is, the all-purpose melodies that formerly served just as readily for putting babies to sleep as for lamenting the dead or rousing a rabble of warriors, began to be changed into—or were replaced by—tunes attached to a specific type of text or even to a particular poem (this process is not complete even in our own day; often the same tune will carry wildly different words and serve startlingly diverse ends). Like the social forms, the musical forms became more tightly organized. The long wavering lines of 'endless melody' typical of clan culture, and still lingering in Gaelic music, were gradually replaced in England by a compact symmetrical structure. The women and girls of the eleventh century who sang of the exploits of Hereward the Saxon in their dance, no doubt used the leader-chorus pattern typical of tribal times (it still survives in frozen form in the litanies of the Christian church) but by that time the tunes were likely to be metrical and already quite neatly strophic in form. The give-and-take between common folk and occupational musicians altered too. Whereas in clan societies the interaction had been between, say, the collective eve-of-battle dance song and the free-style solo melody of bardic and scop tradition, in feudal England the altered and novel set of economic relations meant that the rural song of the ploughman affected, and was affected by, the well-defined neatly architected forms of town art music. If "Searching for lambs" has any connection with the wool trade, as has been humourlessly suggested, it is not so much through its text as through its elegantly shaped tune, just of the kind that owes its form to the mingling of the art of the peasantry and the art of the townsfolk. Such mergers and takeovers began early in England because our bourgeois merchant class developed early, whose lower members, tanners, millers, small cloth-makers and such, made a handy bridge between the two class cultures, and this occurred notably where the textile industry spread liveliest into country districts, as in East Anglia, Yorkshire, and the southern Cotswolds.

The story of the development of the 'classic' type of traditional song and its hitherto-neglected extension in the industrial folk song of modern times, is the subject of our study in the chapters to come.

II

THE SONGS OF
CEREMONY AND OCCASION

'Well, ploughman, how do you do your work?'

'Oh sir, I work very hard. I go out in the dawning, driving the oxen to the field and I yoke them to the plough. Be the winter never so stark, I dare not stay at home for fear of my lord; but every day I must plough a full acre or more, after having yoked the oxen and fastened share and coulter to the plough.'

'Have you any mate?'

'I have a boy, who drives the oxen with a goad, who is now hoarse from cold and shouting.'

'Well, well, it is very hard work?'

'Yes, indeed it is very hard work, because I am not free.'

From Aelfric's *Colloquium*, this thousand-year-old piece of reportage. The medieval peasant lived hard, serving his time on the baronial and monastic estates. The way he lived, his isolation, his illiteracy, his social inferiority, meant that he retained certain ways of thought and expression from a time when there was a relatively small degree of class development, a time before the clan patriarch had become an aristocratic landlord in alliance with the lords of the church lands. We know little of what he sang because the chroniclers generally thought his lyrical productions unworthy of report. A handful of sung charms have come to us, without tunes. They show that Christian though he might be, the ploughman walked his furrow in company of far more ancient gods than the abbot preached. So, at the first sod broken, he would set under it a cake baked of various kinds of meal, and sing:

> Earth, Earth, Earth, O Mother Earth!
> May the All-wielder, the Everlord grant you
> acres a-waxing, upwards a-growing,
> pregnant with corn and plenteous in power,
> whole hosts of grain shafts and of shining plants!

Blossoms of broad barley,
waxing of white wheat ears,
harvest of the whole land.

Then, his head jumbled with pagan gods and Christian saints like any voodoo or shango believer nowadays, he would grip his plough handles again, and urge on his oxen with a long-drawn melodious 'yu-yu-yu' cry that, we are told, became a peasant dance-cry, was taken into the towns, elevated in social rank, and made into the kind of wordless melisma of Gregorian chant called, onomatopoeically, *ju-bilus*.

In the monasteries, little ink was spent in describing the thoughts, feelings and still less the songs of the ploughman; but we know that when absolute feudalism began to crack, when farm-leases and money-wages began to replace the old servile system, the commoner's horizon started to enlarge. John Ball had rung the bell, and John Nameless, John the Miller (who ground small, small, small) and their fellows had taken up cudgels to chastise the hated tax-fixer 'Hob the Robber' and his like, in the peasant insurrections. By the end of the fourteenth century, serfdom had practically disappeared. The majority of commoners were free peasant small-holders, and the rural wage-labourers mostly peasants working in their spare time on the large estates or, in certain cases, a special class of regular wage-workers who were also peasant farmers in a small way since besides their wages they had their little allotments, as well as having access to the common land on which to pasture their cattle, gather their firewood, and such. As the community of bondsmen grew into a society of individuals, ways of looking at the world began to alter. As the folk changed, the songs changed with them. The free-rambling tunes took on clearer, more formal shape; the bare wintry themes of the Dark Ages began to blossom; though under the blossom the boughs remained the same, for if in the cottages or out in the churchyards, where medieval villagers liked to dance,* the new songs were full of bird and flower images and

---

* Churchyard dances, originally intended to honour and pacify the dead, were constantly being condemned in the thirteenth century and subsequently, and the Lincolnshire monk Robert Manning, in his account of the Dancers of Kolbigk

loving frivolity, in plough-furrows and harvest-rows and in the village streets at critical seasons of the year the sorcery songs persisted.

Indeed, survivals of agricultural magic-making abound in our folk song even today though—and perhaps this is the fate of the sacred—as the old meaning becomes unclear what was once ritualistic is likely to change into broad comedy, as with the randy animal-guiser song of the "Derby ram", concerning a beast of gigantic, not to say cosmic, attributes, a song that is the lyrical equivalent of those phallophoric dances that survive in farming ceremonies in Europe, intended to celebrate and stimulate the powers of reproduction in plants, animals and men, a song that nowadays survives mainly as a bawdy anthem for beery students or soldiers coming home on leave. Other pieces, formerly ceremonial, become harmless social entertainments, such as the community song of "The herrin's head", whose earliest connections were probably with that central agrarian rite involving a sacrifice, human or other, at some critical time of the farming calendar, aimed at the regeneration of natural forces. In its most explicit form, the ritual involved the leader of the community, considered as the incarnation of a god, being put to death after reigning for a prescribed period, and dismembered. His various parts were distributed and eaten as a charm that passed on his divine qualities. The notion survives today in Christian sacrament, wafer and wine swallowed in token of the body and blood of the sacrificed king. The reason behind the ritual is the constant anxiety of the primitive mind that the useful natural forces around him may wear out unless they are regenerated. If it is imagined that the creation of the world involved the violent death of a giant from whose body the plants grew and livestock and

(1303), begins his poem: 'Carols, wrestlings or summer games, / Whosoever haunteth any such shames / In church other in churchyard, / Of sacrilege he may be afeard.' At North Berwick in 1590, a gathering of so-called witches 'to the number of seven score persons' danced 'endlong the kirkyard' to the music of the jew's harp, with the witchmaster John Fian, masked, leading the ring-dance. In the seventeenth century, John Aubrey noted that village youths and girls in Herefordshire were in the habit of dancing in the churchyards on all holidays, and in his *British Goblins* (1881) Sikes reports the same custom maintained in Wales till late in the nineteenth century.

humans sprang, then the object of the human sacrifice is to re-enact the drama of creation all over again, in order to start the cycle of seeding, growth and harvest afresh and with new vigour. That seems to have been the theory in places where these agricultural ceremonies presumably began, in Egypt, Syria, Mesopotamia. As the ceremonies spread through the world, many communities acquired only scraps of the original scenario, and they made their own alterations. Seemingly quite early on in Europe, substitutes were found for the sacrifice—the real king was replaced by a mock-king (prisoner of war or slave) and he in turn was replaced by a symbolic deputy such as the wren 'king of the birds' or the herring 'king of the sea'. Hence the surrealistic catalogue that Durham miners today bawl over their beer-mugs in the pit-village pub, a list of magic effects that once had to do with the creation of the cosmos, and that in the course of long centuries has lapsed into burlesque.

What'll I do wi' me harrin's heid?
Oh, what'll I do wi' me harrin's heid?

> We'll mak 'em into loaves o' breid,
> Harrin's heid, loaves o' breid,
> An' aal manner o' things.
> Of aal the fish that live in the sea,
> The harrin is the one for me.
> How are ye the day, how are ye the day,
> How are ye the day, me hinny o?

The song is cumulative, like so many old ritual pieces. The hope was that the magic would stick better if the incantation was repeated. So nowadays the final run of it is:

> What'll I do wi' me harrin's scales,
> Oh, what'll I do wi' me harrin's scales?
> We'll mak them into a ship that sails.
> > Harrin's scales, a ship that sails,
> > Harrin's belly, a lass caaled Nelly,
> > Harrin's guts, a pair o' byuts, (boots)
> > Harrin's fins, needles and pins,
> > Harrin's eyes, puddens and pies,
> > Harrin's heid, loaves of breid,
> > And aal manner o' things.
> Of aal the fish that live in the sea,
> The harrin is the one for me.
> How are ye the day, how are ye the day,
> How are ye the day, me hinny o?

It is in the nature of folklore that material once vital and momentous lapses into absurdity or childishness as it loses its ancient meaning. So for instance the legends that terrified and inspired communities of fierce hunters and warriors become harmless nursery tales for children (though often something of the old savagery lingers, to the discomfort of child-psychologists). In the seemingly nonsensical jumble of the "Harrin's heid" there is no longer any trace of the fear and triumph, remorse and relief that attended the bloody ritual in ancient times, though anyone hearing the song sung by communities that have kept it alive cannot fail to be impressed with the power it still retains even in its altered and dilapidated state in the smoky atmosphere of a folk song club. What some call 'folk memory' is very obstinate when it comes to transmitting the associations surrounding certain songs. We see this with a similar anthem of the partition and sharing of the body of a royal sacrifice, in this case the king of the birds, the wren. The well-known "Cutty wren" or "Hunting the wren" is often thought of as an amiable nursery piece, yet when it was recorded from an old shepherd of Adderbury West, near Banbury, he banged the floor with his stick on the accented notes and stamped violently at the end of the verses, saying that to stamp was the right way and reminded of old times. What memories of ancient defiance are preserved in this kind of performance it would be hard to say, but we know that the wren-hunting song was attached to a pagan midwinter ritual of the kind that Church and authority fulminated vainly against—particularly in the rebellious period at the end of the Middle Ages when adherence to the forms of the Old Religion was taken to be evidence of subversion, and its partisans were violently persecuted in consequence.

The agrarian ritual songs, dances and plays have always held special fascination for folklorists because, while they are not the most ancient religious accompaniments, they are very coherent in ensemble, and tell us a great deal not only about the origins of poetry, music and drama but also about man's groping towards an understanding of the world about him and the loam under his feet. At the same time, the matter has been studied so idealistically, with such dazzled concentration on sun-myths and such dark brooding over the pagan soul, that the scholar sometimes forgets that behind the myths and the ceremonials and the songs attached to them lies nothing more obscure, nothing less realistic, than the yearly round of work in the fields, and the perpetual anxiety over yield and increase and a full flour-bin. Behind the conventional folklore calendar of seasons and solstices and mystical moments disguised as Christmas, Easter, St. John's Day, All Souls, there is the economic reality of the farming year, with its ancient customs that fall into two main cycles—one set of rites accompanying the preparation (October to February) and augmentation

(March to June) of the crops, and a second set of rites accompanying the harvest (end of summer, beginning of autumn).

A remarkable number of folk ritual songs have survived in twentieth century England, due not so much to any mystical connection as to their close relation to the work-processes and the economic life of men. Naturally, in the course of time many of the songs have altered in the wake of the transformation of social conditions and working ways, but some of the original content shows through however mistily, and in some cases the tunes also retain a primitive shape that seems to have changed but little over a vast perspective of time.

Especially the festivals of midwinter offer a variety of customs with musical accompaniment, such as animal-guising with such songs as "The Derby ram" and "Poor old horse" to cheer on the capering roisterer, masked and wearing beast-skins or, more likely, a bit of old carpet—a relic not merely of times when the food animal was worshipped as a god, but of even remoter days when Stone Age hunters first put on animal hides as a camouflage when stalking their quarry.* Another powerful midwinter ceremonial is reflected in the mumming plays that nowadays take place towards ploughing time and in our countryside are usually limited to a display of the combat, death and resurrection of heroes, though at one time they were elaborate affairs involving graphic pantomimes of birth, courtship, marriage, the whole cycle of life. The plays appear only in fragmentary and distorted form in modern England, but the classic scenario surviving in the Balkans gives us the Hero (bridegroom), Maid (bride), Enemy (rival) and Doctor, with a host of subsidiaries (Old Man, Old Woman, Baby, etc.). Hero and Enemy fight over the Maid. Hero is killed but is revived by the Doctor. Hero and Maid are united with a good deal of phallic flourish doubtless representing some hierogamy, perhaps the marriage of the

* The famous Abbots Bromley horn dancers were once midwinter creatures who perambulated the countryside with a good deal of obscene horseplay on Twelfth Day. The shift of their season to September occurred in fairly recent times, probably in the same period, *c.* 1893, when the local parson put a check on the phallophoric displays, and his wife sacrificed the vicarage curtains to make the prototype of the present costumes worn by the dancers, tame ghosts of their old wild and ribald selves.

D

sky god and earth goddess. In England, the combat and 'cure' or resurrection are still strong elements, but the bridal part has all but disappeared, though something of its gross humour still shows in the animal-guising capers.

Behind the rough jokes, the buffoonery of the quack Doctor with his revitalizing medicine-bottle, the obscene horse-play around the man-woman Bride (who at times showed a cow's tail under 'her' starched petticoat, a misplaced version of the phallus-on-a-pulley worn by some Rumanian *caluş* dancers), behind all this was a serious intention, for these were once pieces of sympathetic magic to perform at the season when the soil was being prepared, when it seemed the vitalizing sun might disappear, the moon not rise, the plants not ever show green again, and there was urgent need to demonstrate the act of regeneration and revival to the sun, to the earth and to the anxious community watching the ritual. At this critical season everything had to be done to dispel the dark fear that the universe might collapse, and to ensure a share of luck for the coming year. How altered the old observances are! A blow-out of turkey and Christmas pudding is all that is left to us of the collective orgies that once accompanied the mystique of agriculture at the critical seasons.

Of all surviving customs of this time, probably the most important is the door-to-door singing of carols by variously formed parties, whether of children or youths, grown men or mixed groups, roisterers or pious folk, accompanying characters in disguise or not. Of these, probably the young men, roisterers with animal guisers, represent the earliest carol singers from a period long before Christianity, when the luck-visitors going the rounds of the village sang—usually in antiphon—either bracing hero-epics or songs invoking food in plenty and the increase of livestock as a spell against the ox-hunger of ancient winter days. All over Europe, the carols, especially the older ones, tend to carry some kind of repetitive refrain, and it is probable that, when they were not marching along in military fashion, it was common for carollers to dance as they sang (the very word 'carol', of French origin, is said to derive from the Greek *khoros*, a ring-dance, the same word that lies behind the Rumanian and Israeli *hora*).

What was the object of these animal dances, hero plays, musical luck-visits and other rites, most of them considered diabolical by the Church, and some thought downright abominable (such as the mating of young married couples in the furrows at seed-time, a custom known in ancient China, familiar in Hellenic tradition, and recently persisting not merely in Greece and southern Italy but also in the uplands of Missouri and Arkansas according to the Ozark folklorist Vance Randolph)? What lay behind the sacred scenarios enacted at every critical season of the agricultural year? The aim was simply to master nature more fully. Our remote ancestors lived precariously mainly because their technical equipment was poor. Their knowledge and tools were barely enough to ensure that they and their comrades had enough to eat. Nature was a mystery, and sacred because a mystery, and to transform it required more than an axe and a digging-stick. It also required an effort of will. Magic was simply a psychical technique to make up for some of the deficiencies in physical technique. Magic was a necessity, and up to a point it worked. Consider the nomad hunters of our own day, living relics of the prehistoric past, such as the pygmy elephant-chasers of the northern Congo. Elephant meat is their favourite food, but their little spears are poor weapons with which to procure it. Their technique is hazardous: to dart under the elephant, stab upwards, and spring clear. On the eve of the hunt they perform magic-making ceremonies—accompanied by a sweet polyphonic yodelling that is a musical ethnographer's delight— to ensure success in the chase. With their confidence bolstered by ceremony, who can doubt that, when the pygmies face their elephant next morning, they are more efficient providers, that the illusory technique of magic has worked its effect on the real technique of the little hunter and helped him to handle his miserable weapon more effectively? That is magic at its simplest, directest level. Clearly, if the pygmies used high-powered rifles or ate canned food such ceremonies of assurance would not be required.

The later magics of agricultural peoples are far more complex and abstract. The ancient world of wandering hunters, with its gods and myths, died slow and hard over thousands of years, doomed by the advance of husbandry and the completely new kind of civilization resulting from it. When man decided to cease his drifting, abandon his nomad freedoms, and bind himself to the soil, his decision brought psychological repercussions as great as the material ones. Modern society, with its technical advances towards the conquest of time and space, is living in a state of spiritual crisis that some consider novel in intensity. Yet the discovery and development of agriculture, and the social and psychological upheaval caused by the changeover from a wandering to a settled life, when man was no longer content to passively snatch at whatever grew wild, but instead began his active intervention in the mystery of the rebirth of plant life, violating the Earth-Mother, affronting the divinities who lived in the locality before it was cleared, consciously setting himself to the hazardous task of actually dominating the sacred forces of nature, all that must have provoked a crisis in man's mind, a state compounded of anxiety, remorse, hope and aspiration, bad dreams and good, of a magnitude hard for modern minds to grasp. Elaborate myths and startling cults grew around the agricultural gods, and many of the ancient intuitions of the agricultural mentality linger on. Other evidences beside our folk songs show that some of the old conflicts are still only partly resolved.

Dread of hunger is the source of many folk customs and songs, and the sacrifices, ritual feasting, festivals of fire and light that celebrated the passing of the winter solstice and the advent of the season of seed-sowing and new beginnings, had so firm a grip on the hearts of the people that the Church was impelled to take over the 'satanic' celebration—as it did with so many critical moments of the agricultural calendar—and to sanctify the magical period, high season of the supernatural *ancien régime*, by naming December 25th as the birth-day of Jesus; but this transfer of the diabolical to the sacred was never completely effected and roistering carols of wassailing still survive as happy reminders of the luck-perambulations of unchristian ceremony, with such melodies as the one recorded from grand old Phil Tanner before he died in a Gower workhouse in 1947, and with verses like the following:

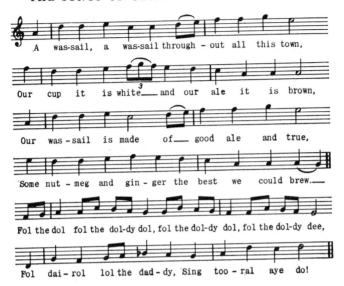

A wassail, a wassail throughout all this town,
Our cup it is white and our ale it is brown,
Our wassail is made of good ale and true,
Some nutmeg and ginger, the best we could brew,
    Fol the dol, fol the doldy dol, fol the doldy
        dol, fol the doldy dee,
    Fol the dairol, fol the daddy, sing tooral-aye-do!

Our wassail is made with an elderberry bough,
And so my good neighbour we'll drink unto thou.
Besides all on earth, you'll have apples in store,
Pray let us come in for it's cold by the door.

We hope that your apple-trees prosper and bear
So we may have cider when we call next year,
And where you've one barrel I hope you'll have ten,
So we can have cider when we call again.

There's master and mistress sit down by the fire,
While we poor wassailers do wait in the mire,
So you pretty maid with your silverheaded pin,
Please open the door and let us come in.

We know by the moon that we are not too soon,
We know by the sky that we are not too high,
We know by the stars that we are not too far,
And we know by the ground that we are within sound.

Here's we jolly wassail boys growin' weary and cold,
Drop a small bit of silver into our old bowl,
And if we're alive for another New Year,
Perhaps we may call and see who do live here.

Here is another set of wassailing verses, in which the old
magical invocation of abundance and fertility shows even
clearer. The begging motive in songs of this kind is important,
not gratuitous, for it is simply a recollection of the sacrificial
offerings that were thought obligatory if the magic was to do
its work. We call such pieces *quête* songs, using a French word
with a handy sense of quest, begging, or collecting.

Here we come a-wassailing among the leaves so green.
Here we come a-wandering so fairly to be seen.
   Now is winter-time, strangers travel far and near,
   And we wish you and send you a happy New Year.

We hope that all your barley will prosper fine and grow,
So that you'll have plenty and a bit more to bestow.
   We hope your wethers they grow fat and likewise all your
     ewes,
   And where they had one lamb we hope they will have two.

Bud and blossom, bud and blossom, bud and bloom and bear,
So we may have plenty and cider all next year.
   Hatfuls and in capfuls and bushel-bags and all,
   And the cider running out of every gutter-hole.

Down here in the muddy lane there sits an old red fox,
Starving and a-shivering and licking his old chops.
   Bring us out your table and spread it if you please,
   And give us hungry wassailers a bit of bread and cheese.

I've a little purse and it's made of leather skin.
A little silver sixpence would line it well within.
  Now is winter-time, strangers travel far and near,
  And we wish you and send you a happy New Year.

Though ancient Gaelic Ireland is outside the frame of our study, it is hard to resist the sweet half-pagan, half-Christian jumble present in a song ascribed to St. Bridget (herself held by some to be a heathen goddess rationalized) in which the eminences of Heaven are imagined at an everlasting wassail:

I'd like to have the men of Heaven
In my own house
With vats of good cheer
Laid out before them.

I'd like to have the three Marys,
Their fame is so great.
I'd like to have people
From every corner of Heaven.

I'd like them to be cheerful
In their drinking.
I'd like to have Jesus too,
Here amongst them.

I'd like to have a great lake of beer
For the King of Kings.
I'd love to be watching the family of Heaven
Drinking it through all eternity.

The midwinter carolling custom is very ancient. We know it existed in ancient Greece. And today from western Europe to the Balkans it still persists, whether the songs have pagan or Christian words, and whether the singers are in disguise or not. Quite often the carols, text or tune, resemble each other over a wide stretch of the continent. For instance, as Lajos Vargyas[17] has noticed, the first part of a French luck-visit song from Bas Poitu is more or less the same as a *regös* song of similar purpose in Hungary:

I somm's de pau-vres gens,Bon-ne gent, Qui ne sont guè-re ri – ches,
I cher-chons de l'ar-gent,Bon-ne gent, Pour nour-rir nos fa-mi – lles.

(a)

Por-ka ha-vak 'e-se-dëz-nek, de hó, re-me ró-ma.
Nyu-lak, ró-kák ja-tzsa-doz-nak, de hó, re-me ró-ma.

(b)

Many readers will remark that the tune is known in England too, likewise attached to the luck-visit custom. In fact, in its sundry variants, it is our commonest melody for *quête* songs, and has been sung extensively at various seasons of the year, with secular or Christian words. A variant of it comprises the first part of the well-known "God rest ye merry, gentlemen" carol (the second strain of the tune, both in French and English forms, seems to be a later addition). Another variant is sung to the words of the May Day carol, "The moon shines bright". As a wassail-tune, with one strain or two, it crops up over and again. Here is a version that lies close to the continental sets, though whereas the French and Hungarian words correspond in many details, being compounded of good wishes, roistering and begging, the English words in this instance are religious in content but at least one verse offers good wishes for New Year. The old singer who gave the song to Sharp remembered bands of youths tramping through the village singing it at Christmastime for money.

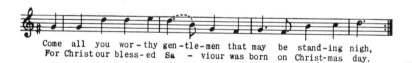

Come all you wor-thy gen-tle-men that may be stand-ing nigh,
For Christ our bless-ed Sa – viour was born on Christ-mas day.

Similar tunes for *quête* songs are known in Sweden and Bulgaria. More than half a century ago, Lucy Broadwood drew attention to the Scandinavian song "Och jungfrun", remarking on its close resemblance to the "God rest you merry" branch of the tune. It begins:

To this, more surprisingly, we may add a Bulgarian New Year song that also lies very close to our tune, barely concealing its outline under a piquant *aksak* rhythm:

How does it happen that our dominant luck-visit melody corresponds to airs of identical purpose far scattered across the continent? Has it spread out from medieval France, as would seem likely, or do its roots extend much further, as Vargyas suggests, to some old Mediterranean heritage brought westward by Greek colonists, but acquired by the Hungarians in their ancient resting-place on the shores of the Sea of Azov, through contact with the Greeks of Asia Minor? If so, we presumably acquired the tune during its secondary diffusion from France, perhaps late in the Middle Ages. Certainly it was well-established here by the sixteenth century, and Giles Farnaby wrote at least one set of variations on it, called "The flatt pavan" (*Fitzwilliam Virginal Book*, No. CCLXXXIV).

Mention of May Day carols reminds us that the great Labour festival of the modern proletariat is but the continuation, on a new plane, of the springtime processions and revels of working people in ancient times. Nor has the old sense of ceremonial orgy quite faded; in some continental countries, May Day is

D*

at least as boozy and unbuttoned as any Durham Big Meeting Day. The ribaldry persists, though the old sacred reasons no longer apply. Formerly the peasantry were strong in the belief that the fertilization of plants involved the sexual participation of the grower, and that at seed-time licentiousness is not only permitted but demanded. The monkish chronicle of Lanercost tells of John, priest of Inverkeithing, who at Easter 1282 'revived the profane rites of Priapus, collecting young girls from the village and compelling them to dance in circles in honour of Father Liber. When he had these females in a troop, out of sheer wantonness he led the dance, carrying in front on a pole a representation of the human organs of reproduction, and singing and dancing himself, like a mime, he reviewed them all and stirred them to lust by filthy language.'[18] Like Priapus, Father Liber, the equivalent of Dionysus comes into this account somewhat fancifully; the indignant chronicler is merely exercising his classical education. The Scots girls dancing with the ribald priest no doubt had other, less lofty, more domestic gods in mind.

Bawdiness and sexuality, loose talk, obscene gesture, priapic dance, are the starting points for many ceremonial dramas of springtime. The seeds are in the ground, and in the peasant mind they have to be helped or accompanied in the process of germination. At such times, whatever is done in common will have the best results, and so the critical season of the germination of plants is accompanied by ritual orgies, especially on the part of the young, the sexually most vital, in the conviction that, by example, the regeneration of nature is being aided. It was an idea that faded only slowly in England, and in some parts of Europe has still by no means disappeared, though the vague gods departed long ago.

The tone of the monk's report is echoed in a later account of spring ritual, from vinegary Phillip Stubbs, who in a famous passage from his *Anatomie of Abuses* (1583) offers this view of merrie England in Shakespeare's time:

'Against May, Whitsonday, or other time, all the yung men and maides, olde men and wives, run gadding over night to the woods, groves, hils, and mountains, where they spend all the night in pleasant pastimes; and in the morning they return, bringing with them birch and branches of trees, to deck their assemblies withall . . . But the chiefest jewel they bring from thence is their May-pole, which they have bring home with great veneration . . . They have twentie or fortie yoke of oxen, every oxe having a sweet nose-gay of flouers placed on the tip of his hornes, and these oxen drawe home this May-pole (this stinkyng ydol, rather), which is covered all over with floures and hearbs, bound round about with strings, from the top to the bottome, and sometime painted with variable coulours, with two or three hundred men, women and children following it with great devotion. And thus beeing reared up . . . then fall they to daunce about it, like as the heathen people did at the dedication of the Idols, whereof this is a perfect pattern, or rather the thing itself. I have heard it credibly reported (and that *viva voce*) by men of great gravitie and reputation, that of fortie, threescore, or a hundred maides going to the wood over night, there have scarcely the third part of them returned home againe undefiled.'

Commenting on Stubbs' last sentence, Violet Alford remarks: 'If this was true, and, allowing for some exaggeration, it seems to have been, it was a confirmation of firmly seated use at this time of the year and belonged, not to lack of moral sense, but to an earlier stage of culture.'

The mayers would return from the woods in the night or early on May morning, with big bunches of May or garlanded poles. They had their special May songs to sing at every door and, as usual, they expected their ritualistic reward of a bit to eat or the price of a pint. Here are characteristic verses of a May carol with its intimation of the 'everlasting circle' (plant nourishes man nourishes soil nourishes plant) that intimately links human life to the life of nature.

> Oh, I've been rambling all this night
> And some part of this day,
> I'm now returning back again,
> I've brought you a garland gay.

A garland gay I've brought you here
And at your door it stands.
It's nothing but a sprout but it's well spreaded out
By the work of our poor hands.

And when you're dead and in your grave
And covered with clay so cold,
The worms shall eat your flesh, dear man,
And your bones turn to good mould.

The life of man is but a span,
He's cut down like the grass,
But here's to the green leaf of the tree
As long as life shall last.

Why don't you do as we have done,
The very first day of May,
And from our parents we have come
To roam the woods so gay.

And now our song is almost done
And we can no longer stay,
So bless you all both great and small
And we wish you a joyful May.

Hoppy Flack of Fowlmere near Cambridge was well in the tradition of spring carollers when he and a friend went out one May eve, singing through the darkness and being given drinks at each house they sang by. At last Hoppy could stand no more and fell into a ditch. His friend went on, and there Hoppy lay, his head buzzing like a hive of bees, listening to the May carol being sung outside cottage after cottage through the still spring darkness to the break of day. He recounted this raffish and magical experience to Vaughan Williams who bore it in mind when writing the music that begins the second act of *Hugh the Drover*.[19]

Hoppy, no less than the Chaucerian Mrs. Overd, Sharp's dancing-partner, recalls for us the perennial English 'peasant' of the kind that has been with us at least since the time when, at the break-up of the feudal manor, the country was changing from being a producer of wool into a producer of cloth. A new class of townsfolk was emerging then, of complicated structure, with merchants on the one hand and artisans, especially stone-masons and weavers, on the other; though in the early stages, trader and craftsman were one and the same. The merchants organized themselves into gilds, to be strong to get and hold. And often in opposition to the merchants the craftsmen formed their gilds too and battened on the journeymen. And what could the journeymen do but form their gilds in turn, even though in the face of intimidation they often had, like early trade unionists, to combine in secret? To this day, in some trades, initiations survive from the time when the craft was a mystery and its practitioners were virtually members of a secret society. So for amiable example the young coopers of the Bass-Worthington yard at Burton-on-Trent, at the end of their apprenticeship, are rolled round the workshop in a hot barrel, having been drenched from head to toe in a mixture of beer, soot, and sawdust before they are 'reborn' as full-fledged participants in the mystery of coopering. A few of the songs associated with these rites have survived, but garbled and in shards.

The shifting attitude of the Church towards the music of the folk is relevant to our story. We know the common people were singing, dancing and playing their instruments without being much troubled either by theoretical argument or pulpit denunciation. It was not only the pagan customs of the folk that upset the Church. All those improper gestures and dis-guises, the crossdressed men-women, the 'man drunkards' covered in animal skins or wearing bestial masks, the ram-dancers, horse-dancers and the rest who careered through the villages especially during the magical Twelve Days, were a regular target of ecclesiastical anathema. But besides that, any kind of instrumental music was deplored as devil's work, perhaps because so many of the instruments used had been spread in the first instance by wandering Greco-Roman *joculatores* and so were associated with tribal paganism, slave-holding and the excesses of a degenerate Roman aristocracy. It has been suggested more than once that in fact, in so far as the

Church in the early Middle Ages was a force bringing new moral standards, some economic security, a new perspective for art and learning, their puritanical decrees against minstrels had at first some elements of progressiveness.

The harrying of instrumental musicians became much less during the twelfth and thirteenth centuries, though by then musical activities outside the Church were increasing rapidly. The folk had been busy with their secular music all the time. The professional minstrels had been regaling their audiences, aristocratic, artisan or peasant, with whatever kind of music they wished to hear. By the eleventh century, for the first time members of the upper class began to make vocal music for themselves, even if they generally left the instrumental accompaniment to their minstrels. And instrumental music was 'the cheerful accompaniment of the growth of the new burgher class'.[20]

For all that, the clergy for a while muffled their thunder against instrumental music and the reasons are not hard to seek. From the time of the Norman invasion, for the next two hundred years or so, feudalism in England was firm and almost complete, and the Church, the greatest feudal landowner, felt strong, stable and secure, willing to some extent to compromise with the blandishments of popular music.

However, the compromise was but temporary. By the end of the thirteenth century the old order was on the decline. The Church felt its power seriously challenged by the rising merchant class and by the increasing demands of the masses for greater freedom and economic independence. On the one hand the minstrels, particularly those who had lost their employment as domestic staffs were cut down on the manors, became severe critics of the established order. On the other hand, not only were the folk songs likewise taking on a note of protest, but pagan customs and observances were temporarily on the increase, not simply out of ancient awe and affection for the banished mythology, but also because, as the historian Michelet says, with Church and State in league against the commoners, 'the medieval peasant would have burst but for his hope in the Devil', that is in the genial horned deity who survived in twentieth century England as the Derby Ram.

So in the fourteenth century, all over western Europe the Church fiercely intensified its war against paganism, and as a parallel process, once again and even more furiously resumed its denunciations of instrumental music and itinerant musicians, who comprised the great majority of professional performers by the end of the Middle Ages. The upholders of pagan belief and ritual in the villages were denounced as witches, and the witch-groups and the minstrels were seen as powerful purveyors of sedition. The figure of the minstrel as he is commonly shown is misleading. The languid lute-player in the *Swan Lake* suit was not the representative of his craft in the fourteenth century; rather we should think of the sly jester of, say, the Shakespeare plays, sardonic, irreverent, plebeian-oriented, outrageously subversive. Now that so many manors were broken up and their households discharged, the minstrel found himself on the road, facing a new audience and a new set of patrons, the peasantry. The effect on folk song was enormous, and a relatively modern parallel allows us to see what happened, for with certain inessential differences, the same thing occurred, five hundred years later, at the other end of Europe. In Rumania, serfdom was abolished in the mid-nineteenth century and at the same time the gipsy musicians, feudally bound to the monasteries or the courts of the petty nobility, were emancipated. They left the estates and settled in nearby villages or, less commonly, became wanderers. Their living now came in the main from playing at village dances and singing at festive parties, weddings and such. Even the sentimental, often trivial part of their repertory became to a large extent folklorized because their livelihood demanded it, and because they were now in contact with a different level of art anyway. But if they were affected by rural song, the village repertory was also affected by them, for they brought a shapeliness, a supple agility, a light lyrical fantasy, sometimes a touch of urban briskness that had been in short supply among the serf shepherds and ploughmen whose music ran deeper but on a meandering course. Something similar happened in England at the end of the Middle Ages and from this synthesis of peasant and minstrel, amateur and professional, private and public-entertainment music grew the kind of song that remained dominant in the lower-class repertory for the next five hundred years, in short, folk song as we most readily recognize it today.

Towards the end of the fifteenth century new worlds were being discovered, new trade rivalries were sharpening; the towns not the courts were now the centre of intellectual life. In the villages the distinction between performer and listener had always been vague, but now in bourgeois households passive listeners were becoming active makers, and whereas hitherto formal compositions had mainly been dedicated to the Church, by the end of the fifteenth century this was no longer the case. We know from Chaucer that, for a good hundred years already, new themes with finer nuances had been daily entering the songs of both the middle and lower classes, and peasants were singing about the beauty of nature, the joy of love, the pleasure of dancing, the pride of such trades as the blacksmith's, as well as of the rigours of the ploughman's life and the pity of war and death. Such themes brought a fresh spirit, a new realistic content into European song that clashed with the stately impassive abstract music of the Church. The magic of those mysterious Latin syllables intoned in the twilight of lofty cathedrals began to lose its suggestive and intimidating power as the old medieval order declined. C. G. Coulton, in his *Social Life in Britain from the Conquest to the Reformation* quotes a document that seems to illustrate this (anyway the anecdote has charm):

'Ther was a preste that trowid he was a passand gude singer, nothwithstanding he was not so. So on a day ther was a gentylwoman that sat behind him and hard him sing, and sho began to wepe; and he, trowing that sho wepid for swettnes of his voice, began to sing lowder than he did tofor; and aye the higher sho hard him sing, the faster wepid sho. Than this preste askid her why sho wepid so as sho did, and sho answered him agayn and said: "Sir, I am a pure gentylwoman, and the laste day I had no calfe bud one, and the wulfe come and had it away fro me, and ever when that I here you sing, anon I remember me how that my calfe and ye cried alike." '

Town and country both were contributing to the fund of popular dance and song melody that had become the dominant and representative culture of the time, to the dismay of churchmen, one of whom wrote in disgust: 'My dear friend, wild and wanton women in my country, when they go in the ring, among many other songs that are little worth the singing, so say they thus:

> At the wrestling my leman I chose,
> And at the stone-casting I did him lose.'

Exactly what 'stone-casting' was we are not sure; probably a sport is meant, though some say it signifies the heaping of stones on a funeral cairn, a heathen ritual. 'Fair ladies in rings, knights in carollings, both dances and sings', wrote Sir Richard Holland in 1450, but we may be sure the milkmaids and stonecutters were still lustier in their round-dances and musical revels. Folk songs and folk dance melodies were so much in the air that they broke down the doors of the Church itself. A Worcestershire priest was kept awake all night by villagers dancing in his churchyard, singing a song with the refrain: 'Swete lemman, thine ore' (Sweetheart, have pity). The prelate could not get the song out of his head, it seems, and next morning at mass, instead of intoning the *Dominus vobiscum*, he sung 'Swete Lemman, thine ore'. Gerald of Wales reports it as a scandal, but before long the clergy had become so accustomed to the idea of ecclesiastical and secular tunes being combined that folk dances became models for motets and love songs were used as the *cantus firmus* for parts of the mass. A famous piece used in this way by Taverner and others is "The western wind", whose words have survived as a fragment in a song-book of the first decade of the sixteenth century:

> Western wind, when wilt thou blow,
> The small rain down can rain?
> Christ, if my lover were in my arms
> And I in my bed again!*

* This is always printed as a stray verse from a lost poem. But among H. E. D. Hammond's manuscripts is a night-visit song collected at Puddletown, Dorset, in

It is characteristic of the time that the earliest printed publications of religious songs, the little booklets of Christmas carols that began to appear early in the sixteenth century ('kesmes corals' as the Oxford bookseller John Dorne wrote in his ledger in 1520) were likely to contain as many saucy songs as sacred, the amorous enterprise of parsons and monks being favourite. So for instance in Kele's *Christmas Carolles newly Inprinted*, issued some time before 1546, besides such pieces as:

> Mary mother, come and see,
> Thy son is nailed on a tree.
> Hand and foot he may not go,
> His body is wrapped all in woe,

we find also:

> The nunne she walked on her prayer,
> *Inducas, inducas,*
> There came a friar and met with her,
> *In temptationibus,*

and so on with the tale of the high-handed cleric.

It is from Kele that we have the exquisite carol beginning 'Oh my heart is woe' that we quote a few pages hence. Only a single page in the little booklet separates this poignant piece from:

> Sing dillum, dillum, dillum, dillum,
> I can tell you and I will
> Of my lady's water-mill.

Kele's roughly-printed chapbook gives us a glimpse of the thought and taste of common people in the mid-sixteenth

1905, which may represent the complete form of the piece. It is a version of the familiar ballad of the cock that crew too soon and made the lover turn out of his sweetheart's warm bed into the cold windy night. The identifying verse runs: 'The wind it did blow and the cock it did crow / As I tripped o'er the plain, so very plain, so very plain / And I wished myself back in my true love's arms / And she in her bed again.'

century, and the casual attitude to religious matters did not change much over the centuries to the time when Mrs. Leather was recording her hop-picking, carol-singing gipsies, and Vaughan Williams and Ivor Gatty, one snowy afternoon in the uplands of Derbyshire were noting from old Mr. Hall the carol on which scholars have tacked the title: "Corpus Christi":

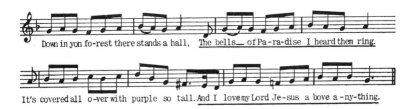

Down in yon fo-rest there stands a hall,   The bells__ of Pa-ra-dise I heard them ring.
It's covered all o-ver with purple so tall. And I love my Lord Je-sus a bove a-ny-thing.

Down in yon forest there stands a hall,
The bells of paradise I heard them ring,
It's covered all over with purple so tall,
And I love my Lord Jesus above any thing.

In that hall there stands a bed,
It's covered all over with scarlet so red.

At the bedside there lies a stone,
Which the sweet Virgin Mary knelt upon.

Under that bed there runs a river,
The one half runs water, the other runs blood.

At the foot of the bed there grows a thorn,
Which ever blows blossom since He was born.

Over that bed the moon shines bright,
The bells of paradise I heard them ring,
Denoting our Saviour was born this night,
And I love my Lord Jesus above any thing.

Mr. Hall's carol is a slightly come-down version of a strange hooded song, very different from Mendelssohn's "Hark, the herald angels" or those other amiable author-made pieces that giggling boys sing through the letter-boxes or brass bands blurt at street corners nowadays around Christmas time. The older song has a knight on the bed, whose wounds bleed by night and day, and a hound at the foot of the bed, 'licking the blood as it daily runs down'. The Derbyshire singer swore his song was 'as old as Jesus Christ'. That is pitching it rather high, but we know it to be more than four hundred and fifty years old.

Early in the sixteenth century a former London grocer's apprentice elevated to mayor, named Richard Hill, kept a commonplace book in which he noted tales and poems, dates of fairs and notes on horse-breaking, and recipes including one titled: A good medycyne for a Cutt, which begins 'Take a pynte of good ale'. He also wrote down a number of popular carols of his time, among them a version of the "Corpus Christi" song. Ever since Hill's notebook was found about a hundred years ago lodged behind a cupboard, scholars have cudgelled their brains to reach the meaning of the carol. There has been talk of Mithraic ritual and Grail legend; the Couch of the Maimed King is knowingly mentioned, the diligent hound has been identified with Joseph of Arimathea at the sepulchre with his vessel, and the blossoming bush has brought to mind the 'miraculous' thorn at Glastonbury. But as usual with folk song, how much is direct symbolism and how much is simply the picturesque fantasy of common people would be hard to say. Certainly the country singers who used the carol were not troubled to interpret it but they were impressed by its mystery or they would not have preserved it in such relatively full shape.

Another carol that the grocer's apprentice had copied in his notebook has lived on to our day in the countryside. That is the curious "Joys of Mary", very popular also in Mediterranean Europe. In Tudor England the number of joys was seven, but over the years, they were added to, and in the nineteenth century, towards Christmas time, some tattered poet of Seven Dials was encouraged to push his beer-mug aside and scrawl some new joys for the Mother of God, increasing them to twelve. Here is a set of Mary's elations to a tune obtained from a group of 'traveller' children in the Ashdown Forest:

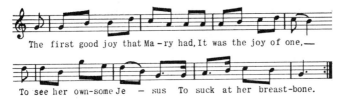

The first good joy that Ma - ry had, It was the joy of one, —
To see her own-some Je — sus   To suck at her breast-bone.

The first good joy that Mary had,
It was the joy of one,
To see her ownsome Jesus
To suck at her breast-bone.
    To suck at her breast-bone, good man,
    And happy may you be,
    O Father, Son and Holy Ghost,
    And all eternity.

The second joy that Mary had,
It was the joy of two,
To see her ownsome Jesus
To make the lame to go.

The third joy that Mary had,
It was the joy of three,
To see her ownsome Jesus
As made the blind to see.

The next good joy that Mary had,
It was the joy of five,
To see her ownsome Jesus
As raised the dead to life.

The next good joy that Mary had,
It was the joy of six,
To see her ownsome Jesus
To bear the crucifix.

The next good joy that Mary had,
It was the joy of seven,
To see her ownsome Jesus
To wear the crown of Heaven.

The next good joy that Mary had,
It was the joy of ten,
To see her ownsome Jesus
To write with a golden pen.
   To write with a golden pen, good man,
   And happy may you be,
   O Father, Son and Holy Ghost,
   And all eternity.

To carol, we are told, meant originally to dance in a ring, and it is usually thought that the origins of carolling lie in the pagan round-dances that people performed, especially at midwinter to ensure the re-birth of the sun. If that is so, then our Christian carols have arisen out of the Church's action to capture and baptize the old gods and to take over rituals that it could not abolish. Perhaps it was as a survival of more primitive custom that a number of bawdy songs found their way into early printed carol books. However, the bawdy carol seems to have died in the countryside, and likewise the idea of the carol as a dance song has been lost sight of by those who sing carols traditionally. But the old pagan custom of the luck-visit, is obstinately kept to. Even today, here and there, groups of carollers go their rounds dressed in a travesty of rags, and carrying brooms to sweep away evil spirits. A favourite carol of some guisers is "The moon shines bright", a song once sung on May Day more often than in midwinter, but nowadays only heard as a Christmas carol:

The moon shines bright and the stars give their light,
And a little before it's day.
Our Lord our God he called on us
And bid us awake and pray.

Awake, awake, good people all,
Awake and you shall hear
Our Lord our God died on the cross
For you he loved so dear.

The life of man it's but a span.
He flourishes like a flower.
He's here today and tomorrow he's gone
And he's dead all in an hour.

And when you're dead and in your grave
And covered over with clay,
The worms shall eat your flesh, good man,
And your bones shall mould away.

And the trees shall be green as the grass can grow,
For from his glorious seat,
Our Lord our God will water them
With the heavenly dew so sweet.

If there are pagan relics in that song, there is also an echo of
medieval scholastic argument, and perhaps too, behind the
sombre morality, a trace of a foxy grin rather like that on the
famous portrait of John Donne in his winding sheet. More truly
popular are those vivid carols based on picturesque Bible
legends, especially the legends found in the apocryphal gospels.
Some of our best ballad-carols must have been made up under
the influence of constant dramatic visualization, in the market
square mystery plays, of the Annunciation, the Nativity, the
misdeeds of Herod. Sometimes the mystery stage would be set
up next to the gallows, which must have made the scourging
and crucifixion scenes all the more impressive. In the fifteenth
century Coventry play called *The Miraculous Birth and the
Midwives*, Mary and Joseph are on their way to Bethlehem.
By the roadside, Mary sees a tree, and the following dialogue
takes place:

Mary: Ah, my sweet husband, would you tell to me
         What tree is yon, standing upon the hill?

Joseph: Forsooth, Mary, it is called a cherry-tree.
         In time of year, you'd feed thereon your fill.

Mary: Turn again, husband, and behold yon tree,
         How that it bloometh now so sweetly.

Joseph: Come on, Mary, that we were at the city,
        Or else we may be blamed, I tell you truly.

Mary: Now my spouse, I pray you to behold
        How the cherries growen upon yon tree.
        For to have of them, of right fain I would,
        An it please you to labour so much for me.

Joseph: Oh, to pluck of those cherries would be a work wild!
        For the tree is so high. It will not be lightly.
        Therefore let him pluck you the cherries that got you
            with child.

Mary: Now good Lord, I pray thee, grant me this boon:
        To have of these cherries, an it be Your will,
        Now I thank it God, this tree boweth to me down,
        I may now gather enough and eat my fill.

This lively little scene is based on a legend in the Gospel of Pseudo-Matthew—concerning a date-palm, by the way, and not a cherry-tree (in Ireland, as in Provence, it is an apple-tree). The medieval playwright has added a point of peasant wit by coupling Joseph's ill-humour to a suggestion of infidelity on Mary's part. And the anonymous balladeer, who apparently knew the play and made his carol on the strength of it, has added his imaginative touch, for in the song the unborn child speaks out from within his mother, to bring about the miracle that is a rebuke to rude Joseph.

> Now Joseph was an old man,
> And an old man was he,
> And Joseph married his cousin,
> The Queen of Galilee.

> Joseph and Mary
> Walked through an orchard good,
> Where there was cherries and berries
> As red as any blood.

Up then spoke Mary
With words so meek and mild:
Pluck me a cherry, Joseph,
For I am with child.

Up then spoke old Joseph
In answer rude and wild,
Let him gather thee cherries, Mary,
That put thee with child.

Up then spoke the baby
All in its mother's womb:
Bow down, bow down, you cherry-tree,
That my mother may have some.

Oh, then bowed down the highest tree
Unto his mother's hand,
And so she cried: See, Joseph,
I've cherries at command.

Then Mary plucked a cherry
As red as any blood,
And she did travel onward
All with her heavy load.

It is a reflection of the "Cherry Tree's" popularity, and one of the reasons for its persistence, that like "The joys of Mary", it was often printed in penny carol books and on broadsides during the eighteenth and nineteenth centuries. Indeed, the dissemination of our folk carols reminds us again that oral means are by no means the only way in which our traditional balladry has been passed on. In the case of the folk carol, the part played by the popular printing presses of the towns seems to have been specially important. Incidentally, a popular carol book printed in 1722 contains perhaps the earliest forerunner of the television advertising jingle, a *Christmas Carol on Pekoe Tea*, beginning:

Now Christ was in a manger born,
And God dwelt in a bush of thorn,
Which bush of thorn appears to me
The same that yields best Pekoe tea.

The ballad of "The carnal and the crane" is another that
owes some of its persistence to its appearance on a fairground
leaflet in the mid-eighteenth century. In it a crow ('carnal' is
the French *corneille*) is instructed by a well-informed crane
on various events in the childhood of Christ. Herod's con-
ference with the Three Kings is mentioned, which ended with
the tyrant's roast chicken sprouting feathers and crowing from
its dish. The flight into Egypt is described, and the miraculous
harvest when Jesus turned the sower's seed into ripe sheaves,
thereby throwing his pursuers off the track, for, so the legend
goes, Herod's horsemen questioned the sower, who truthfully
said that the Holy Family had passed that way just as he was
sowing his seed, but now he was reaping his harvest; the
horsemen presumed that too long had elapsed since their
quarry passed that way, and they abandoned the chase.
Here is a version of the carol taken by Lucy Broadwood from
three gipsies in Surrey. The medieval literary convention of
the knowing birds has dropped out of the folk-singer's mind,
the action is very much condensed, and, gipsy-like, in place of
Herod appears King Pharaoh, or rather, Pharim.

King Pharim sat a-musing,
A-musing all alone,
There came a blessed Saviour,
And all to him unknown.

'Oh, if you come out of Egypt, man,
One thing I fain to know,
Whether a blessed Virgin
Sprung from a Holy Ghost?'

'If this is true, is true, good man,
That you've been telling to me,
That the roasted cock do crow three times
In the place where we do stand.'

Oh, its straightway the cock did fetch
And feathered to their hand.
Three times that roasted cock did crow
On the place where they did stand.

Joseph, Jesus and Mary
Were travelling for the West,
When Mary grew a-tired,
She might sit down and rest.

They travelled further and further,
The weather being so warm,
Till they came to some husbandman
A-sowing of his corn.

'Come, husbandman,' cried Jesus,
'Throw all your seed aside,
And carry home your ripened corn
That you've been sowing this day.

(If anyone should ask you
Whether Jesus has passed by,
You can tell them Jesus did pass by
Just as your seeds were sown.'

King Pharaoh said to his armed men:
'Your labour and mine's in vain,
It's full three-quarters of a year
Since these here seeds were sown.')

For to keep your wife and family
From sorrow, grief and pain,
Keep Christ in your remembrance
Till the time comes round again.

Of all our folk carols, perhaps "The bitter withy" is the most
delightful. No early printed version is known, so its age has to
be guessed. It too is based on a jumble of apocryphal legends

transformed into a scene that fits the English landscape perfectly. The carol ends with Mary spanking her little son like any dutiful village mother. This incident is said to be shown on a fresco at Lucca, though when the surrealist artist Max Ernst painted a similar scene some years ago, his picture was impounded in France, as a blasphemy. "The bitter withy" has had great appeal for common folk, partly because in it, the haughty young lords are sternly put in their place. It is easy to imagine what such a song meant in villages under the shadow of squire and parson at the time, say, of the Enclosures.

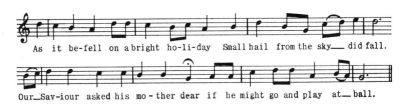

As it be-fell on a bright ho-li-day Small hail from the sky— did fall.
Our— Sav-iour asked his mo - ther dear if he might go and play at— ball.

As it befell on a bright holiday
Small hail from the sky did fall.
Our Saviour asked his mother dear
If he might go and play at ball.

'At ball, at ball, my own dear son,
It's time that you were gone,
But don't let me hear of any mischief
At night when you come home.'

So up the hill and down the hill
Our sweet young Saviour run,
Until he met three rich young lords—
'Good morning' to each one.

'Good morn, good morn, good morn,' said they,
'Good morning', then said he,
'And which of you three rich young lords
Will play at ball with me?'

'We are all lords and ladies' sons,
Born in our bower and hall,
And you are nothing but a poor maid's child,
Born in an ox's stall.'

'It's if I'm nothing but a poor maid's child,
Born in an ox's stall,
I'll make you believe in your latter end
I'm an angel above you all.'

So he made him a bridge of the beams of the sun,
And over the water run he.
The rich young lords chased after him,
And drowned they were all three.

So up the hill and down the hill
Three rich young mothers run,
Crying: 'Mary mild, fetch home your child,
For ours he's drowned each one.'

So Mary mild fetched home her child,
And laid him across her knee,
And with a handful of willow twigs
She gave him slashes three.

'Ah bitter withy, ah bitter withy,
You have caused me to smart,
And the willow shall be the very first tree
To perish at the heart.'

Some folk carols, like "The bitter withy", have survived
only in the mouths of country singers, and there is no early
printed trace of them. Others that do appear in the old song-
books have fallen out of use or at least have not been found by
folk song collectors. A handsome example is "O my heart is
woe" from Richard Kele's little book already referred to. What
would we give to know the tune of this sweet song?

Oh, my heart is woe, Mary did say so,
For to see my dear son die, saying I have no mo.

When that my sweet son was thirty winter old,
Then the traitor Judas he became wondrous bold.
For thirty plates of money his Master has he sold,
And when I wist of that, Lord, my heart was cold.

On a Shere Thursday truly then thus it was,
On my dear son's death that Judas did compass.
Many were the Jews that followed him by trace,
And before them all he kissed my son's face.
Oh, my heart is woe.

My son before Pilate straightway brought was he,
And Peter said three times he knew him not, pardye.
Pilate said to the Jews: Now then what say ye?
And they cried all with one voice: Crucifige, crucify.
Oh, my heart is woe.

It was on Good Friday at the Mount of Calvary,
My son was on the cross and nailed with nails three.
But all the friends he had, never one could he see
But gentle John Evangelist that still did stand him by.
Oh, my heart is woe.

That I sorrowful were, no man have no wonder,
For how it was the earth quaked and horrible was the thunder
I looked on my sweet son, the cross as I stood under,
Longeus came with a long spear and clave his heart asunder.

Oh, my heart is woe, Mary did say so,
For to see my dear son die, saying: I have no mo.

Another fine Passion carol that has regrettably dropped out
of the folk repertory is "Suddenly afraid, half-waking, half-
sleeping". Made in the fifteenth century, perhaps a little
earlier, it conveys the sort of thorny anguish one sees in those

Grünewald pictures where Mary has the face of a weeping peasant and the Son of God resembles a rustic rebel done to death.

> Suddenly afraid, half-waking, half-sleeping,
> And greatly dismayed, a woman sat weeping,
> With favour in her face far passing my reason,
> And of her sore weeping this was the occasion:
> Her son in her lap lay; she said, slain by treason.
> 'Jesu', so she sobbed, so her son was bobbed (*beaten*)
> And of his life robbed.
>> Saying these words as I say to thee:
>> 'Who cannot weep, come learn at me.'

Generally the crucifixion carols have not lasted among the singers so well as the nativity ones, perhaps because they were less profitable. Villagers would be more generous in their donation to carol-singers at Christmas than at Easter-time. However, an excellent Passion song has survived until today, chiefly among gipsies, who have proved over the last half-century or so to be the preservers of several of our best folk carols. "The seven virgins" has not the emotional intensity of "Oh, my heart is woe" or "Suddenly afraid", but it attracts the singers' imagination by its mysterious opening, virgins amid the foliage of the Tree of Life, that most powerful, most universal of all vegetal symbols known to popular piety. The opening recalls the dazzlingly beautiful illuminations in the Arundel Psalter. This psalter, in the British Museum, shows the Tree of Death very sombrely, with dismal birds in its branches. The Tree of Life is gleaming gold, with iridescent vine-shaped leaves. On the boughs are discs inscribed with the Seven Virtues, and in the shade of the leaves, four of these Virtues stand as handsome girls. Perhaps the unknown maker of the carol had this piece of fourteenth century symbolism in mind. A version was obtained by Cecil Sharp in 1923 from a gipsy named Samson Price. We have filled it out with some phrases from a version that Vaughan Williams got from two gipsy women hop-picking in Herefordshire.

Oh, it's under those leaves and the leaves of life,
Our eyes spied the maidens of seven,
And one of those was Mary mild,
What was our gentle Mother of Heaven.

She did ask me what I was looking for
All under the leaves of life.
'I'm looking for sweet Jesus Christ
To be our heavenly guide.'

'Go you down, go you down, to yonder town,
As far as you can see,
And there you'll find sweet Jesus Christ
With his body nailed to a tree.'

'Dear mother, dear mother, don't weep for me.
Your weeping does me some harm,
But let John be a comfort to you
When I am dead and gone.'

'Oh no, dear son, that never can be,
That I should love young John
As well as my own son Jesus
From my own body was born.'

Here's the rose and the rose and the gentle rose,
The fern that grows so green,
May the Lord give us grace in every place
To pray till our ending day.

In architecture, the pelican is used as an emblem of the
Church. And half a century ago an old man in the Southampton
workhouse sang to George Gardiner a curious symbolic carol
called "The pelican", about the bird that feeds its young with
blood from its own breast.

As I was a-walking down by a wilderness,
There I was assaulted by many wild beasts,
And there I did hear a bird making her moan,
That her young ones had fled and gone far from their home.

Then she followed me down to the yonder green grove,
And searched for the young'uns all gone from their home,
And when she had found them, how sad were they,
And cold was the harbour wherein they did lay.

Then she took them safe home all at her own breast,
And she fed them on dillon and food of the best,
And she spared them some blood from her own breast did pour
And she bade them drink freely and leave home no more.

"The pelican" reminds us of Thomas Dekker's little penitential book about the birds of Christendom, written as a potboiler at a time when London's theatres were closed by the plague. Another carol that has survived in the West Country bears on a disaster in sixteenth century London. An earthquake occurred in 1580, which brought down part of St. Paul's. The long-winded Elizabethan balladeer Thomas Deloney wrote a song about it, which was sold on the streets. And somehow, Deloney's ballad, with its threats of awful judgement, lived on into our own time, in altered and shortened form, among Herefordshire carollers, who tramped from house to house of a winter night, singing their doleful warning at the windows. Vaughan Williams noted this version, to yet another variant of our most persistent *quête* tune:

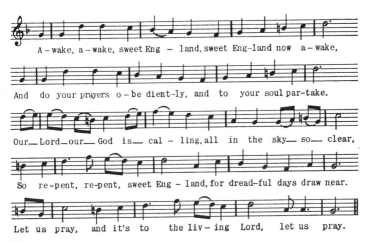

A-wake, a-wake, sweet Eng - land, sweet Eng-land now a-wake,

And do your prayers o-be-dient-ly, and to your soul par-take.

Our— Lord— our— God is— cal - ling, all in the sky— so— clear,

So re-pent, re-pent, sweet Eng - land, for dread-ful days draw near.

Let us pray, and it's to the liv - ing Lord, let us pray.

E

Awake, awake, sweet England, sweet England now awake,
And do your prayers obediently and to your soul partake.
The Lord our God is calling all in the sky so clear,
So repent, repent, sweet England, for dreadful days draw near.
Let us pray, and it's to the living Lord, let us pray.

It's woe unto the woman that big with child do go,
Likewise their silly nurses as they give suck also,
For there's never any man so stout nor woman looks so gay
But worms will eat your flesh and your bones will waste away,
Let us pray, etc.

Today you may be alive, good man, with many a thousand
   pound.
Tomorrow you may be dead and gone, and your body underground,
With one stone at your head, dear man, and another at your
   feet
And your good deeds and your wicked ones together they will
   meet,
Let us pray, etc.

God bless the ruler of this house and send him long to reign,
And all the sons and daughters, kind heaven to obtain.
But we'll shake all shame and sorrow, put on our best array,
So I wish you all Good morrow and God send us a happy day,
Let us pray, etc.

Students of the carol have remarked that the high time for
creating religious folk song was 'during the two centuries and
a half between the death of Chaucer in 1400 and the ejection of
the Reverend Robert Herrick from his parish by Oliver
Cromwell's men in 1647',[21] that is, between the flowering of
lyricism at the end of the Middle Ages and the spread of
Dissent that accompanied the ascendancy of the sober burgess.
With the growth of bourgeois Nonconformism, the old-style
religious folk song receded. First the Puritans Sternhold and
Hopkins, then, following the Glorious Revolution, Tate and
Brady exerted their influence on the sacred songs of the poor

in village as well as town, with such powerful masters as Watts and Wesley hot on their heels. The new nativity carols were of the hymnbook kind of "While shepherds watched" and "Hark, the herald angels sing". The old carols became submerged, living a near-clandestine life in the mouths of a dwindling number of folk singers. Their practice had so waned by the middle of the eighteenth century that Goldsmith wrote as if it were a curiosity that the vicar of Wakefield's parishioners 'kept up the Christmas carol'. A century later, W. H. Husk reported that carols had become rare on broadsides because the street-ballad printers 'find the taste of their customers rather incline towards hymns, mostly those in use among dissenting congregations, rather than to the genuine Christmas carol'. The performance of folk carols might linger on, but the creation of new ones ceased early. Indeed, of all important categories of lyrical folk song, the carols seem to have been the first to wither at the root. Among the reasons for this, we may bear in mind that at any time between 1660 and 1860, a good proportion of gifted lower-class 'musicianers' would be found playing or singing in the church gallery of a Sunday, much affected by the prestige of printed music and the poems of 'official' hymnwriters.

True, for a time during the exuberant revivals of the late eighteenth and early nineteenth centuries, folk tunes or folk-style tunes enjoyed a lively vogue among Primitive Methodists and other such Evangelicals, but the texts they carried were mostly formal ones of the Watts, Wesley, Newton, Cennick kind, though in some cases lightly 'folklorized' by the addition of refrains. Thus, Cennick's "Children of the heavenly king" was sung at Midland camp-meetings as:

> Children of the heavenly king,
>> When we get to heaven we'll part no more,
> As ye journey sweetly sing:
>> When we get to heaven we'll part no more.
> Lord, obediently we go;
>> When we get to heaven we'll part no more.
> Gladly leaving all below;
>> When we get to heaven we'll part no more.

A rare late production, perhaps the last English folk carol to be composed*, is "Christ was born in Bethlehem", of which about half a dozen versions have turned up in Lancashire and the Midlands though none so far published, I believe. The carol seems to have arisen quite early in the nineteenth century, perhaps in the years between 1816 and 1818 when revival excitement was at its peak in the Midlands. At these meetings enthusiasm abounded and hymnbooks were few, and as we see from the Cennick example above even the sacred songs of learned authors might be turned into 'primitive' form by the obsessive repetition of interpolated refrains. So in structure "Christ was born in Bethlehem" seems as rudimentary as many Negro or backwoods-white spirituals though in fact it is no more primitive than some earlier pieces such as "I saw three ships come sailing by". In 1906, Percy Grainger heard the carol sung to the following tune at Scotter, North Lincolnshire (his informant began at the third verse):

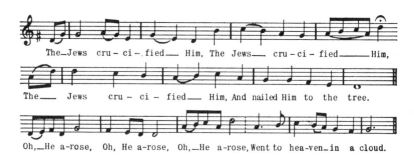

The Jews cru-ci-fied Him, The Jews cru-ci-fied Him,
The Jews cru-ci-fied Him, And nailed Him to the tree.
Oh, He a-rose, Oh, He a-rose, Oh, He a-rose, Went to hea-ven in a cloud.

---

* If it *is* English. George Pullen Jackson, the American revival-hymn specialist, notes that a version of the text was printed in *The Christian Songster* (Dayton, Ohio, 1858) and one stanza with tune in the 1859 edition of the Georgia *Sacred Harp*. So America has strong claim on the piece though not a clear title; the traffic in old Baptist and Methodist revival stuff moved both ways between Britain and the United States. Versions from oral tradition are reported from North Carolina (by Cecil Sharp) and Tennessee (by Mellinger E. Henry). John Meredith recorded a set (unpublished) in Teralba, New South Wales. The English tunes, from Wigan, Macclesfield and Evesham as well as Scotter, are distinct from the American and Australian versions.

Christ was born in Bethlehem,
Christ was born in Bethlehem,
Christ was born in Bethlehem
And in a manger laid.
    Oh, he arose, oh, he arose,
    Oh, he arose, went to heaven in a cloud.

Judas he betrayed him
And sold him to the Jews.

The Jews they crucified him
And nailed him to a tree.

So Joseph begged his body
And hid it in a tomb.

So Mary she came weeping
And rolled away the stone.

(So go and tell each nation
And preach to honest men
    That he arose, oh, he arose,
    Oh, he arose, went to heaven in a cloud.)

Grainger's singer, Mr. Spencer, was not very clear with his words, and lacking other reference to the carol the collector transcribed the final verse as: 'So don't you feel it's reason A-feelin' on 'is wind, And we are o (or: all), so we are o, so we are o, when to 'eaven in a cloud.' The versions collected subsequently show us the way out of this tangle.

If the carols were among the first folk songs to lose ground among the poor, they were also the first to enter on a 'second existence' following their revival among educated people. Just as they seemed to be dying out in the villages, the nativity songs at least were being recovered from both oral and broadside sources for such publications as Davies Gilbert's *Collection of Christmas Carols* (1822), William Sandys' *Christmas Carols Ancient and Modern* (1833), the small but valuable anonymous compilation published at Dudley in 1847 called *A Good Christ-mas Box*, and W. H. Husk's *Songs of the Nativity* (1868). The first effect of these publications was to take a number of dying folk carols from the villages and back streets of towns and restore them to life in novel surroundings of church, guild and women's institute. Eventually certain of these pieces passed back into something like general currency with "The holly and the ivy" and "God rest ye merry, gentlemen" taking their place indifferently alongside author-made hymns such as Nahum Tate's "While shepherds watched", the American J. H. Hopkins's "Kings of Orient", and J. M. Neale's doggerel "Good King Wenceslas" which is neither carol nor hymn nor has it anything to do with Christmas. The revival of a number of traditional carols at the end of the nineteenth century and their re-emergence into 'natural' use by bands of street-corner singers or by hoarse boys chanting on door-steps in the ancient hope of reward was the first amiable evidence that moribund folk song might return to vigorous life despite a certain change of function and setting. In some respects, the resurrection of the carol announced the 'impossible probability' of the urban revival of general traditional song.

III

THE BIG BALLADS

'Ballads are the unquestioned aristocrats of the folk song world.'
That is the scholar's view, seldom the folk singer's. The singer is
more democratic, tending to cherish alike big ballads, love
lyrics, bawdy bits, nonsense songs, without much concern for
high or low—unless the folklorist has got at him, of course.
The scholar, his head full of aesthetic value judgements, is
often at a loss to know why the folk singer may attach more
importance to a seemingly banal and humble song than to the
ace and deuce of Eng. Lit. masterpieces. But in any case the
statement is too sweeping. If we are using the term 'ballad' to
describe the generality of our longer narrative songs, why then,
only a small proportion has clear title to nobility.

Most English songs are narrative in that, to say what they
have to, they pose a situation ('As I walked out on a May
morning') and provide a setting ('down by a riverside') for an
encounter (' 'twas there I met a bold fisherman come floating
on the tide'). Sometimes, with shorter songs, the device is
merely a semblance of narrative animating a gratuitous lyrical
expression of mood: the song starts off like a story, but before
it has gone any distance the narrative has given way to the
description of an emotion, as often as not the regret of lost love.
It is the properly narrative songs of substantial length and
strong story-line that we call 'ballads', and they are of many
kinds and qualities, enthralling or tedious in plot, of glorious or
banal poetry, with tunes that may pull down the stars or never
get off the ground. The matter of 'unquestioned aristocracy'
can only refer to a limited selection of ballads, if at all. And
whatever the literature dons might think, not all these nobles
are in Francis J. Child's *English and Scottish Popular Ballads*, nor
can all the items in that great compilation be numbered among
the peers of the folk song realm. The majority of Child's
selection represents but one stage of the ballad, a middle stage
lying between the old form of epic song and the newer form of
domestic ballad, journalistic ballad, street song and the like,
such as began to show itself with the invention of printing, and

had become dominant by the end of the eighteenth century (most powerfully with the 'come-all-ye' type beloved of latter-day narrative singers).

Generally speaking our folk song has not been much illuminated by learned comment. Some studious starlight falls on the carol, but most kinds of English traditional poetry and music remain in the darkness of a night pierced here and there by the hand-torch of the *Folk Song Journal*. But if the greater part of the field is pallidly lit, the sun of scholarship has turned the full force of its one-eyed glare on the ballad. Neglecting other folk songs, generations of students commented on the ballads devoutly but inequitably, for in their absorption with the texts they had left the tunes in the cold. There is sadness in the thought of Child, the 'prince of ballad students', labouring all those years on the poetry of the songs with hardly a thought for the music that brought the words to life. Phillips Barry, with his great experience among singers, saw the deficiency: 'The field-worker knows that the ballad is a living organism, tune and text together, the spirit and the body. When the spirit is gone, what is left is a dead thing.'[22] To him, bare ballad texts preserved in print were like the bones of prehistoric creatures caught in tar-pits. For the reading student, Robert Frost put the matter neatly: 'Voice and ear are at a loss what to do with the ballad until supplied with the tune it was written to go with. Unsung, it stays half-lacking.' In fact, not only voice and ear are left at a loss, but heart as well.

The blunder of treating the ballads solely as literature, of considering the tunes, if at all, as poor relatives of the words, so that all speculation concentrates on the poetry, has led scholars to pose a number of pseudo-problems, notably about the way the ballads were created. Arguments as to whether or not they sprang up through communal composition by a dancing throng or working gang seem rather dusty now. The notions of the communalists, romantic to a point near mysticism, were based on the consideration of ballad words only, and perhaps if they had known more about the music they might have thought differently.* We hear of Balkan

* And yet the communalist cause, seemingly long discredited, is not quite lost. A contemporary champion, the musical ethnographer André Schaeffner, speaking

frontier-guards, American loggers, Australian drovers, pooling their ideas in guard-post, shanty or camp to construct ballads 'by committee', but such cases are the exception. Nowadays it is generally conceded that most of the ballads were made by individuals and subsequently re-shaped to some extent by the mass of people in the course of being handed on. That is, the collectivity enters not in their creation but in their diffusion. Only in that practical sense can they be spoken of as 'the spontaneous expression of the collective soul of the people' (to use the vaporous terminology of romantic ballad scholarship).

If the ballad students have until recently taken little note of the music, they have paid still less attention to the folk who carried the songs. Yet two important questions pose themselves at the outset of any ballad study: What did people want from life at the time they made this song? To what extent does the song reflect the realities of time past and present?

Early enthusiasts loved the sport of tracing ballad stories to some literal historical source. So "The dowie dens of Yarrow" was supposed to refer to a duel fought between John Scott of Tushielaw and Walter Scott of Thirlestane early in the seventeenth century. "Young but growing" was thought to reflect the marriage between the juvenile Lord of Craigton and a girl some years his senior in 1631. On slender evidence the lady who ran off with the three (or was it seven?) draggletailed gipsies has been identified as the Earl of Cassilis' wife who died in the same year as young Craigton was married. Even "The two brothers" with its primeval story of fratricide and its vast international diffusion becomes associated in some dry-stick minds with a banal occurrence near Edinburgh in 1589, and the quest for the historical Robin Hood still follows a meandering river of ink.

The fact is, well substantiated or ill, this kind of historical attribution tells us nothing essential about the ballads. Many of their personages are real-life characters, but what of that?

from deep experience in Africa, has remarked, rather testily: 'The possibility of collective creation has nearly always been denied. . . . The only reason I can see for this prejudice is a lack of contact with every living kind of music, our own no less than that of the primitives.' (*Journal de Psychologie Normale et Pathologique*, Paris, 1951, 44ᵉ, Annee Nos. 1–2, p. 249.)

E*

That the ballads have, all of them, an historical basis is sure, but in a subtler way than the old students thought. There is a reflection of an historical reality even in the most fantastic ballads; specific social ideas are mirrored even in the least 'factual', most magical and miraculous of ballad themes.

Ballads differ in function and content, and they range themselves in groups that probably represent different stages of historical development. In Britain, and notably in England, our array of ballad-categories has shrunk; as our society developed in more complex forms, some earlier kinds of ballad dropped out of the repertory. In countries where ancient social organizations lingered and continued to exert their power till recent times, we find a far broader folklore horizon. In eastern Europe, particularly in parts of Albania, Jugoslavia and Rumania, in a single village, in the repertory of a single performer even, the folklorist may find an assembly of ballads whose various themes lay their tracks not merely through centuries but through millennia. The Russian specialist V. I. Propp suggests that the oldest epic ballad subjects concern the search for a wife and the struggle to obtain her. Almost as ancient are those magical narratives of fantastic journeys whose ritual function is to instruct the dead how to find their way from this world to the next, 'from the land of pity to the land of no pity', or those cosmogonic epics such as the ballad of the sun's amorous pursuit of his sister the moon, which attempt to supply answers to riddles of the natural universe. Also archaic is the theme of heroic fights against dragons and like monsters. These, and all the songs in which heroism and magic go hand in hand relate to an ancient pre-feudal era; where they survive, they are ideological remnants of a tribal stage of society. In a whimsical but well-defined passage in his *Contribution to the Critique of Political Economy*, Karl Marx has noted how the invention of the printing press, the locomotive and the telegraph had disposed of the pre-requisites for making and singing epic balladry. In fact, the lays of our pre-feudal heroes such as Beowulf and Hereward had fallen out of the folk singers' memory a good five hundred years ago; but though Iovan the Rumanian dragon-killer, the Greek Digenis Akritas, the South Slav heroes of Kossovo, are all long dead, the songs celebrating their deeds are still vigorously alive in the villages of south-east Europe where the heroic sense of life has not yet faded. At a Balkan wedding-feast or corn-husking bee one may still meet the lawful heirs of Homer, who perform—and in some cases make part of their living by performing—epic songs that may last for hours, just the one song, telling of marvels, and adventures no less fantastic than those that faced Odysseus and his men, and provided a long night's entertainment for the farmer-colonists of Asia Minor in ancient times. Listening to the Balkan 'singers of tales' we may guess at some of the riches now lost from our English treasury of ballads.

The road of the ballad runs from the magical to the heroic to the domestic. What was once a kind of narrative incantation becomes a complex tale in recitative form whose aim is to encourage and inspire, and finally the sung narrative becomes a romance with little more purpose than to divert and enter-tain. The idea at the heart of each ballad depends on the kind of society that makes it. Tribal societies, clan societies grappling with little-understood forces of nature, create and make use of ballads full of magic, and the magic only slowly fades out of ballads made for subsequent societies. The world of the primi-tive hero is full of dragons, harpies, women who change men to stone at a glance or kill with a kiss, and the hero himself is a giant riding a horse that only he can master, wielding weapons no other warrior can lift. Towards feudal times, the hero becomes more realistic, the landscape through which he moves, though idealized, is recognizable as our own. The enemies are no longer dragons and demons but men whose daring and ferocity is only slightly larger than life. Charac-teristic of the genuine ballads of late feudalism are the songs telling the exploits of forest outlaws whose heroism is directed not against supernatural beings but against harsh authorities. Finally, as feudal society gives way to capitalism, the epic spirit falters and yields to something less broadly heroic, something smaller and more lyrical; the ancient recitative melodies are replaced by song-tunes, the 'solid block' narrative is broken up into regular strophes; the ballad as we know it best is born, but if its build is neater and its features more gracious than those of its ancestors, it has nonetheless inherited a number of wild traits from the past that will take centuries to eradicate. Now the hero is no more than man-sized and his deeds, bold as they are, are performed in a world familiar to us, where wonders may be explained and mysteries are capable of solution. Yet in many of our ballads, domestic as they seem on the surface, ideological strata are found from all the savage and heroic ages that the ballad-idea has travelled through. Their form, in regular verses set to a lyrical songlike tune (a curious form for sung narrative; surely the old recitative style such as is still found in south-east Europe is more apt for singing a tale?), is relatively modern, but the content may be extremely archaic in essence.

The bride-stealing ballads of the sort of "Bonny Baby Livingstone", "Eppie Morrie", "Walter Lesley" are light romances far removed from the desperate air of the old epics of marriage by rape, yet in fact they preserve well the manners of a barbarous past that lingered on, in Scotland at any rate, into the eighteenth century.* The well-known "Lyke-Wake Dirge", collected from oral tradition by curious John Aubrey in the seventeenth century, seems to be a fragment of one of those funeral ritual songs that are among the most archaic poems still surviving in parts of Europe, notably in the Balkans where they are sung around the coffin by chosen women with the aim of instructing the dead person how to make the hazardous journey from this world to the next and how to behave in order to become properly incorporated among the residents of the land of the dead (the idea is to prevent the dead person from becoming restless and returning as a ghost to plague the living). So also in "Thomas Rhymer" the verses that describe the young man's dark journey into Elfland across the roaring river of blood, the alternative roads, narrow and thorny, broad and bonny, that face him, the ceremonial meal of bread or apple and water or wine that he receives from the hand of the

---

* Not only in Scotland, of course. Among others, the French folk song tradition abounds in specimens of the survival of tribal notions of marriage by capture. An excellent pioneer study of this was made in 1886 by Karl Marx's son-in-law, Paul Lafargue, in 'Les chansons et les cérémonies populaires du mariage (Études sur les origines du famille)' reprinted in Paul Lafargue: *Critiques Littéraires*, ed. Jean Freville (Paris, 1936).

fairy queen, his 'psychopomp' or soul-guide, are paralleled closely in Rumanian ritual songs for the dead,[23] and may well have been transplanted into the Scots lyrical ballad from some earlier funeral-ceremonial of general European currency that died out in these islands with the fading of paganism.

In the outlaw ballad of "Johnnie Cock", the setting is feudal enough and Johnnie's camouflage-suit is the familiar 'Lincoln twine' of all forest runagates at the close of the Middle Ages. Nevertheless when the outlaw, with his back to an oak and his legs struck off at the knee, fights the seven foresters on the stumps of his limbs, and when he addresses his bow of yew and his fingers five, and calls on them for help as if they had a will of their own, a breath from earlier shaggier hero epics blows through the song; so too the forest bird of starling size that is to dip its wing in the wan water and stroke it on Johnnie's brow before carrying the news of his death to his mother's window-stone is but the reincarnation in miniature of the eagle that spread its wings to shield from the sun the maimed hero of the old tribal epics, or carried water in its beak to the parched and dying Young Stoyan, or acted as messenger for Digenis Akritas and earlier warriors a good thousand years before the time of Johnnie Cock. In making the transit from epic to romance, our folk singers cast many a nostalgic glance backward along the arduous highway.

The ballads of heroism are the poetic illustration of a community's heroic ideal, and a means of forming and sustaining a way of life based on that ideal.[24] From them, the listeners learned how to comport themselves in the face of adversity and dilemma; that is the social and artistic purpose of the songs, and to achieve it the old epics went far beyond current reality and presented heroic values and actions in high relief by means of hyperbole. We have mentioned Digenis. He was a champion of Byzantium, brave as Achilles, strong as Hercules, glorious as Alexander. The cycle of ballads describing his deeds arose out of the wars against nomads of the Syro-Arabian desert on the frontiers of the Eastern Empire, and they are sung to this day, notably in Crete, Cyprus and the Dodecanese. In 1953 a Cypriot farmer was recorded singing the following description of the giant hero whose name, Digenis, was taken as a *nom de guerre* by General Grivas in his fight against British imperialism:

> On his head a thousand windmills turned.
> On his back a thousand oxen ploughed.
> Mares were stabled in his nostrils.
> Partridges cooed under his finger-nails.
> The crawling creatures of the earth did not draw near
> but hounds chased hares across the palms of his hands.

How could this exuberant hero, the dream of a remote past of club and lance, inspire the modern partisan who can strip down a complicated machine-gun blindfold? How can a singer in twentieth century Canada of automobiles and Coca Cola feel himself involved literally to the hilt in a sword-fight between two semi-feudal Scottish chieftains? W. Roy Mackenzie gives us a vivid instance. He was noting a version of "Sir Niel and M'Van" from an old cobbler, Bob Langille, in Nova Scotia. The ballad tells how the generous Sir Niel is forced against his will to fight and kill M'Van, his sweetheart's brother. No sooner done, Glengyle, his rival in love, taunts him to a second duel. Sir Niel tries to reason with him.

> While talking thus, he quit his guard.
> Glengyle in haste advanced,
> And pierced his generous manly heart.
> The sword right through him glanced.

Mackenzie says: 'The ballad was suddenly interrupted at this point by a howl of rage from the singer. "O God!" shouted Bob, "why ain't I standin' right behind that Glengyle with a sword in me hand? Wouldn't I drive it right through he's treacherous body!" '[25] Many folklorists, in their fieldwork, have similar experience of performers whose emotions are flooded by the heroic and pathetic sense of what they are singing. In V. I. Propp's view the main and decisive characteristic of the epic is its heroic content. This is relevant to the Western narrative songs too. The ballad shows whom the people consider as heroes, and for what qualities. To define the character and meaning of the heroic personage is the main task of ballad study.[26] The content is struggle, whether of champion against dragon, outlaw against forester, ploughboy against the rich girl's parents who would have him press-ganged, miner against mine-owner. In different epochs, the source of the struggle is different. We can hardly hope to understand our ballads fully if we do not try to define what the struggle is about.

The outlaw ballads comprise a class-conscious category in the wake of the hero-epics. Class-conscious? Well, yes, in the sense that whereas the old epics were the product of a society more or less of a piece, when the vital interests of leader and led, chieftain and henchmen, were substantially identical, the outlaw songs grew in a society divided, poor against rich, villein and small freeholder against landlord, gentry and higher clergy. The heroes on the dodge among the green leaves of the forest represent a kind of dream of the zenith of bow and arrow culture. They are champions of the downtrodden against the haughty, their weapons pointed towards the dragon of social injustice, and it is to be expected that the songs celebrating them should first appear in force in the latter half of the fourteenth century, after the Black Death had devastated the country, making labour scarce, speeding the decline of the feudal system and helping to set ablaze the smouldering class antagonisms of the countryside.

Johnnie Cock, Adam Bell, William of Cloudesly (whom some mythopoeic scholars tried to make into a sun-god) and the many popular heroes who combine to make up the synthetic figure of Robin Hood have social struggle as the motive force of their adventures. The plane on which that struggle is waged is a realistic one, only slightly idealized. The forty or so ballads of Robin Hood—and he is the only character who appears in a considerable number of songs; in that respect he is by far our most popular ballad-hero—unroll their adventure-stories in terms of everyday life with all its contradictions. Ever since the study of folklore began, learned fantasy has identified Robin Hood with Wotan or Mithras, with the horned god of the witches or a vegetation sprite, or alternatively with this or that real-life nobleman mentioned in manorial rolls. All in vain.

Mythology and historicity, both are irrelevant. Whether he wore the rags of an old god out of favour, or the stained velvet of an earl on the run, what does that tell us? The Robin Hood of the ballads is simply an artistic generalization, a hero conceived as ideal by the common people at a given moment in history, the stressful time of the break-up of feudalism. Nor is it important whether his songs were made by peasant amateurs or by the new class of yeoman minstrel. That they were not made by courtier poets is clear enough, and we know that as the big landowners inclined to cease the direct cultivation of their fields and to hand them over to leaseholders, a sizeable yeoman class was growing up prosperous enough to offer patronage to minstrels who would make songs on themes congenial to folk of lower social grade, instead of setting all their attention on romances of chivalry. Written and printed copies of the Robin Hood ballads passed from hand to hand from early times and now it would be hard to distinguish purely oral versions from those that have been affected by 'the calamity of print'. In the form in which most of the ballads have come down to us, the style of the professional minstrel shows clearly, both in the *incipits*, the opening formulas, and in the rather humdrum poetry of many versions, which generally lack the strokes of delightful surprise so often experienced in orally-diffused amateur composition. E. K. Chambers notes a characteristically sly 'pro' touch in the opening of the *Gest of Robyn Hode*, a piecing-together of a number of outlaw ballads into a long poem (456 verses) that was already in print in the opening years of the sixteenth century, and may have originated even earlier than 1400. The *Gest* begins:

> Lythe (that is: Hark) and listin, gentilmen,
> That be of frebore blode;
> I shall you tel of a gode yeman,
> His name was Robin Hode.

Chambers remarks: 'There is courtesy here, for some at least of the audience must have been of villein descent'.[27] That is, presuming the *Gest* was ever sung or recited. It may have existed simply as a written compilation. Of the extensive cycle of Robin Hood ballads that were sung, only seven* have survived in the mouths of English and Scots singers in the twentieth century (three more in North America), but the hero who so early 'won his way to the mythical' still haunts the popular imagination and re-appears over and again in boys' comic-papers, cinema-epics, television serials and the like. 'Many men speak of Robin Hood that never bent his bow' was already a proverb by 1400. Walter Bower, in the fifteenth century *Chronica Gentis Scotorum* remarks that even in Scotland the 'rough commoners' have great admiration for the ballads of the English Midland outlaw, 'and are delighted to hear the jesters and bards sing them, above all other romances'. In another chronicle of the period, John Mairs reports: 'The feats of this Robin are told in song all over Britain. He would allow no woman to suffer injustice nor would he rob the poor, but rather enriched them from the plunder taken from abbots. The robberies of this man I condemn, but of all thieves he was the prince and the most gentle thief.' In short, he belongs to that line of popular champions that runs from Hereward the Saxon to Pretty Boy Floyd. Like the modern cinema stereotype of the 'long-tailed heroes of the revolver', he was taken as a model for generosity, gallantry, and fidelity to a code of freedom. But the medieval outlaw is the child of his time. A certain nostalgia for the older social order and an idyllic notion of the free life of the greenwood gives him a romantic rather primitive air that brings him near the epic hero. Though the role of the songs is to sustain a spirit of resistance to oppressive authority, the lack of any clear political direction— and who could expect that?—prevents the ballad-outlaw from being a revolutionary; he remains simply a champion of insubordination, and that is already much.

Of historical ballads proper, the songs based on the chronicles of great events and big battles, most seem to have remained more interesting to the scholars than to the folk. Such ballads are few, nor did they last well in the singers' mouths. Generally we know them from early print not later recording. Sir Philip

* Numbers 125, 126, 131, 132, 138, 140, 144 in F. J. Child: *The English and Scottish Popular Ballads*, 5 vols. (Boston, 1882–98; New York, 1965).

Sidney's heart may have been more moved with "Chevy Chase" than with a trumpet, but though it was reprinted over and again as a reading-piece, the singers let it die long ago; we have no trace of it from oral sources. So with others, "Durham Field", "The Rose of England" (celebrating the battle of Bosworth that gave Henry VII the throne in 1485), "The Rising in the North" (concerning the fortunes of the earls of Northumberland and Westmorland who led a Catholic rebellion against Elizabeth in 1569) and their kind, long factual pieces resembling versified newspaper accounts, often short on characterization and heroic detail, usually vacillating in the face of the political events related. Probably such ballads were always more esteemed in the hall than the cottage-kitchen. The high affairs of state rarely caught the imagination of lower-class singers and their listeners because such affairs were seldom in their interest. Where is the folk ballad of Magna Carta? Or of Agincourt for the matter of that? It was celebrated in upper-class poetry and song but did not engage the attention, or failed to hold the interest, of the folk. Clearly too there were certain dangers in making topical ballads closely related to fact and interpreted in the light of lower-class experience. 'Whosoever shall follow truth too near the heels, it may haply strike out his teeth.'

Raleigh's warning on the writing of contemporary history applied sternly to the ballad-maker. As a rule then the historical chronicle ballads, though often well-known from print, have generally been short-lived and only weakly diffused among the folk. What seems at first sight a curious exception is offered by the 'survival' of the song about the important battle of Harlaw. The engagement took place in 1411 and a song about it was current in the sixteenth century. A ballad describing its course exists in tradition today particularly, though not exclusively, among Scottish travelling folk (called 'tinkers' by some who should know better), but there is no sign that the present ballad is old. The text may have originated early in the nineteenth century, at the hand of an enthusiastic antiquarian. If so, his sense of style was keen enough for his product to be taken up by folk singers.

If a ballad was to have an historical theme or treat of the

great personages of the land, the poor preferred to draw its substance not from official chronicles but from the unofficial legends and traditions floating through the villages and back-streets of the towns. As with the carols so with the ballads, the apocrypha were found more attractive than the authoritative accounts. Jane Seymour bore the son of Henry VIII in a natural way though she died a couple of weeks later, but the songmakers, hotshot eager for romance, would have it that she died in childbirth in poignant circumstances; and the makers of the celebrated Charles Laughton picture, *The Private Life of Henry VIII*, followed the same fiction. Picturesque and sentimental detail has kept the ballad green, and in Dorset (as elsewhere) in the twentieth century the circumstances of Edward VI's birth were still being sung as:

Queen Jane lay in labour full nine days or more,
Till the women were so tired, they could stay no longer there.

'Good women, good women, good women as ye be,
Do open my right side and find my baby.'

'Oh no', said the women, 'that never may be.
We will send for King Henry and hear what he say.'

'King Henry, King Henry, will you do one thing for me?
That's to open my right side and find my baby.'

'Oh no' says King Henry, 'that's a thing I'll never do.
If I lose the flower of England I shall lose the branch too.'

Then they gave her some cordial which put her in a swound,
And her right side was opened and her baby was found.

The sly old ballad of "Queen Eleanor's Confession" seems as delightful to the blue-jeaned and pony-tailed youngsters in modern folk song clubs as it did to the crowds round the broad-side seller on a seventeenth century fairground. The Eleanor concerned is of Aquitaine, who divorced Louis VII of France and a few weeks later married Henry Plantagenet. That was in 1152, when she was thirty and Henry nineteen years old. Within a short time he was ruler of England and the richer half of France, and the most powerful monarch in Western Europe. In history, no special scandal attaches to this opportunistic lady (if so she was) but in legend she is a prime villainess, and the ballad has her unmasked by an amusing trick, worked over and again in medieval joke-tales. The queen is sick and sends for two friars. The king proposes to his Earl Marshal that they two should disguise themselves as monks and administer to her. The Earl Marshal is terrified of the consequences of tricking the queen, but the king promises him protection. So off they go to hear the queen's confession, which reveals the Earl Marshal as the father of her bastard son. The ballad, which appeared in print in the seventeenth century was still in fair circulation at the beginning of the nineteenth (it was one of the favourite songs of blind Jamie Rankin, Buchan's main informant) but by the twentieth century it seems to have practically disappeared. For all Gavin Greig's searching in the best ballad-singing area, only the redoubtable Miss Bell Robertson (of course!) could sing him a version of it. However, thanks to its piquant narrative, the ballad was too charming to be allowed to sink without trace, and at present, aptly set to a new-made tune, it is enjoying a lively 'second existence' in the urban folk song clubs of England.

Ballads such as those of Queen Jane and Queen Eleanor hardly count as historical. They deal with real persons but in terms of uncertain tradition not firm fact. Though, as Alexander Keith maintains, pieces of this sort are likely to have been based either on actual, if trivial, occurrences or on general gossip, and though 'the dovetailing of truth and fiction is so compact throughout these ballads with a smattering of history and an appearance of empirical origin', their place is alongside the romantic novelistic songs that make up the greater part of the ballad repertory as it has survived into the twentieth century.

Who made the big ballads? Educated men, poets of culture and artistic power, say many scholars, notably Alexander Keith.[28] Others, more wary, have noticed how little ballad stuff derives from the medieval literature of court and mansion, hardly anything from high romance or satire, and only scraps from the metrical *fabliaux*, ribald and seemingly 'folky' as these often were. Against Keith's view, McEdward Leach notes: 'There is little in the English and Scottish ballads that suggests material from the portfolio of the professional poets of the Middle Ages.' Most likely, in the case of our earlier romantic ballads at least, the repertory is of mixed origin, with a fair proportion made by members of the upper class, and just as many made by commoners in town or country. The old novelistic ballads were sung by aristocrats, by professionals of high grade or low, and by cottagers and cattle-herders too. The audiences were not only the country folk and casual crowds at fairs and hangings or on pilgrimages, but also knights and ladies in hall, and gatherings of students or parties of young people of the urban nobility or merchant class. Sometimes the ballads would be more or less identical in style regardless of which social circle they were sung in, but any good collection of narrative song shows artificial pieces alongside simple ones, and pieces of aristocratic atmosphere alongside those of authentic peasant ambiance. On this account Walter Wiora suggests that though the traditional ballads were mainly diffused by oral means, it is sheer prejudice to think of them simply as *folk* ballads; they were a form not so much of folk music as of 'general' music, common to all layers of society, at least in the period towards the end of feudalism and in early capitalist times. Be that as it may, even the high-toned ballads became mainly confined to the lower classes in general, and eventually to the rural lower class almost exclusively. Whether made in cottage or manor, for most of their centuries-long life the big ballads circulated in the main among small farmers and graziers, country labourers, shepherds, tinkers and tradesmen, nursemaids, dairymaids, and the like. For centuries, the vagrant hawkers of broadsides, along with drovers, carters, itinerant harvest hands, pedlars, gipsies, soldiers too, were the main instruments for spreading the ballads across the shires and through the streets. When we are considering our big 'classical' ballads, for instance the most prized pieces in the Child compilation, we have to think of them not simply as educated products nor merely as peasant compositions, but as a general oral form of narrative song that originally flourished both within and outside the orbit of folklore proper, but for which, in later time, folk tradition became the main source.

How vague our terminology is! 'Ballad' may mean the "Odyssey", "The wife of Usher's well", "The Sheffield apprentice", a composition by Chopin, a sentimental lyrical product of Tin Pan Alley. In our consideration above, we mean the kind of ballad that represents a middle stage between the archaic and the relatively modern, between the old form of epic and the recent form of broadside song, that is to say, compositions like "The outlandish knight", "Little Musgrave and Lady Barnard", "The grey cock", "The broomfield hill". Only a small proportion of such ballads are firmly localized. In many cases, in its transit from singer to singer, district to district, the same song takes on the local colour and associations of a score of localities. 'What county does that song come from?' is a question commonly put by innocent amateurs. They inquire in vain. Sundry versions of "Barbara Allen" give the young lady's dwelling-place as Scarlet Town, London town, Quelick town (wherever that may be), as Reading, Newbury, Newry, Dublin, and as far afield as Lexington, Virginia, no doubt with a view to making the ballad interesting in whatever locality it is sung. Even such an apparently pin-pointable ballad as "Edom o' Gordon" has an English, a Lanarkshire and an Aberdeen setting.

And where did the ballad-makers draw their themes, if not from cultured literature? Clearly enough they drew on oral tales, folk legends local or international, the tragedies and comedies of real life, and also on their own artistic imagination and fantasy. In part they were actual stories of recent events involving contemporary personalities. In other instances the ballad stories have come to us from remote times and far-away places. Just how ancient and outlandish they may be, we are only starting to discover. Take as example the ballad that scholars, but not folk singers, call "Lady Isabel and the Elf Knight". 'Of all ballads', says Child, 'this has perhaps obtained the widest circulation'. At least 150 variants of it have been collected in the English-speaking world, and its relatives are well-known from Portugal to Poland, from Scandinavia to the Balkans. More than 250 versions are reported from

Germany, 80 from Poland, 60-odd from France and French Canada, about 50 from Hungary. Of the big ballads it is perhaps the commonest still to be heard in the English countryside: that is, if one finds a country singer with any of the older ballads in his repertory, he is likely to know this one.

As we have it in England, the ballad usually tells this story: A foreign deceiver persuades a young woman to rob her parents and elope with him. They ride to the water's edge, and he asks her to alight. He tells her he has drowned a number of women here (her six sisters, in some versions; in others, nine or eleven king's daughters) and she is to be his latest victim. The girl tricks him (sometimes by asking him to modestly turn his back while she takes off her valuable dress) and after a struggle she contrives to kill him in her stead. She rides home, and is questioned by her father's inquisitive parrot. She promises the bird a cage of ivory and gold if it will be silent about her escapade, and the bird accepts the bargain.

The story is conventional enough, apart from the witty detail of the parrot, which is merely a rationalization of the magical talking birds of ancient folklore. But what lies behind the story? A real event, a dream, a legend, a myth? In Ayrshire a rocky promontory called Gamesloup has been pointed to as the spot where the outlandish knight was in the habit of drowning his victims, and where he met his deserved end. Such innocent notions often occur when a ballad or tale so strikes the common imagination that people want to make the piece their own by giving it a local setting. No less quaintly, scholars have tried to attach the ballad to historical accounts of notorious murderers, notably the Breton Gilles de Laval early in the fifteenth century. In Dutch versions the heroine cuts off the false knight's head and brings it home to display proudly to her father as he sits at table; on that account the Danish ballad-student Sophus Bugge, a great one for Biblical parallels, believed the ballad derived from the story of Judith and Holofernes, and so suggested the Netherlands versions were the original ones, and many who might have known better* have followed this shot in the dark. Others have vaguely, but perhaps more plausibly, suggested a connection with the large

---

* Including W. J. Entwistle in his *European Balladry* (Oxford, 1939).

class of Bluebeard tales. Two further interpretations, reflecting intellectual preoccupations of the nineteenth century and our own time, seem too clever by half. To Leon Pineau the ballad was clearly a solar myth, the villain was the spirit of night and winter, the murdered maidens were the months of the year, the triumphant girl represented the summer sun that puts darkness to rout. Nowadays we smile at the foggy notions of the old solar mythologists, but what are we to say to Paul de Keyser's psychoanalytical interpretation,[29] suggesting that in the singer's subconscious mind the murderer is the brother of the beguiled maiden and his beheading at the girl's hand symbolizes castration, the punishment for the singer's own suppressed incestuous desires?

Medieval Scandinavian and German origins have been sought for the ballad, and from Finland, following Bugge, comes the theory that it was composed by a Dutch minstrel some time in the twelfth century; but the recent researches of a Hungarian scholar, Lajos Vargyas, take us much further eastward and far longer back in time.[30] In many versions, a curious detail stands out. The eloping couple come to a tree, and the man persuades the girl to dismount. He begs her not to look in the tree, and lays his head in her lap so that she may de-louse him. While she is at this friendly task, he falls asleep, and she, glancing upward sees either his victims or his blood-stained weapons hanging from the tree. Generally in British tradition this vivid scene is lost, though its shadow remains in one Scottish version:

> 'O sit down a while, lay your head on my knee,
> That we may hae some rest before that I die.'
>
> She stroak'd him sae fast, the nearer he did creep,
> Wi a sma charm she lulld him fast asleep.

Now, in certain medieval churches of Hungary and Slovakia, one may see frescoes showing St. Ladislas, an early king of Hungary and a redoubtable champion of Christendom, lying with his head in a woman's lap while she fingers his hair. The couple are under a tree from which the champion's weapons and helmet hang. Some frescoes show not Ladislas but a Cumanian or Tartar warrior. The motif turns out to be an ancient one, for a gold-plated sword-scabbard ornament in the Hermitage collection in Leningrad shows that, as long ago as 300 B.C., the imagination of Siberian craftsmen had been struck by precisely the same scene. There in this handsome piece of early goldsmithing, the obliging lady is seen searching in the recumbent warrior's hair under a nine-branched tree decked with weapons, with two saddle-horses standing by. The tree, the attitudes, the entire composition are almost identical with the medieval church frescoes painted seventeen hundred years later. Where did the ancient goldsmith draw his inspiration from? The researches of Russian scholars show that even in modern times the magical nine-branched Tree of Life and the maiden under it with her insecticidal fingernails still survive in old Siberian and Altaic epic songs. Radlov among the Kirgiz, Potanin among the western Mongols, collected heroic ballads and tales, savage intricate narratives telling the adventures of, say, the hero's sister abducted by a foreign warrior or demon, or of brother and sister pursued by a bloody invader who has already killed and plundered the rest of the family. In several of these epics from the Central Asian uplands the de-lousing scene, the magical tree—also the wonderful horses—crop up at the critical moment, the turning-point of the narrative, the instant before the heroine's great struggle with the outlandish warrior.

Vargyas's notion is that this stuff from Asia was brought into Central Europe by the migration and settlement of the Magyars, a people partly of Eastern Turkic—that is, Central Asian—origin. From Hungary, he suggests, it spread like ripples on a pond, across the face of Europe. Whatever the case, it is clear that the narrative song of the murderous stranger and the resourceful girl, known to English country singers under such various titles as "The false-hearted knight" and "If I take off my silken stays", is a product of that process well-described by Menendez Pidal, by which certain elements and incidents in a complex hero-saga become detached, condensed, and re-worked into a short lyrical ballad. If Vargyas is right, at least some vital motifs of our common European ballad derive from imaginings vastly remote from us in time and space, from the anxious dreams of prehistoric herdsmen on the wild steppes between the Tienshan and the Altai Mountains of western Mongolia.

How many English ballads are based, wholly or in part, on such venerable and far-travelled stuff? Till now, the study of our ballad origins has not gone deep enough to allow a clear answer. What ancient shamanistic duel suggested the theme of the amorous metamorphoses of man and maid, wizard and witch, known in Britain through the rare ballad called "The two magicians" and, in attenuated form, through the lyrical song of "Hares on the mountains"? The story of the young woman pursued by a hero, often a blacksmith, who changes herself first into one form then another, dove, duck, hare, horse, rose in the garden, oak in the wood, full-dressed ship on the ocean, and is outwitted each time because her pursuer can cap every change she makes, is known throughout Europe in a variety of forms, rough or graceful. A glow of this fantasy is in the ballad of "Tam Lin" (still to be heard in Scottish raspberry-picking camps in the 1950's), in which a resolute girl holds fast to her bewitched lover though he is changed into a bear, a lion, a snake, a burning coal. Perhaps one day we shall determine the diffusion-limits of this theme which, in many cases, embraces the Bronze Age notion of the smith as an essentially superhuman being, a triumphant wonder-worker, the magical master of the Earth-Mother in whose belly metals grow. In most of its European forms, notably in France and Rumania, the metamorphosis ballad has become so prettily lyrical, so harmless, so genteel, that few would suspect its savage ancestry; yet the chances are the story was already old before it appeared in the ancient world as the cosmogonic transformations of Yajnavalkya, the Hindu Adam, and his wife, or as Peleus's rape of Thetis, who changed herself into fire, water, a lion, a serpent and an ink-squirting cuttlefish before yielding to his determined embrace (Peleus was no blacksmith, but it will be remembered that he possessed a magic sword forged by the mastersmith Daedalus, who was instructed in his art by Athene herself).

The ballad of "Molly Bawn", "Polly Vaughan" or "The

shooting of his dear", despised by Jamieson (who thought it 'one of the very lowest descriptions of vulgar modern English ballads') and rejected by Child but still much loved by singers in Ireland and the eastern counties of England, concerns a young man out hunting at dusk, who mistakenly shoots his sweetheart as she shelters from a shower; he is tried for her murder, but the girl's ghost appears in court and explains that she had thrown her apron over her head and so the hunter had taken her for a swan. It seems clear enough that the story is a come-down relic of the same myth that, long before Ovid's time, became attached to the figures of Cephalus and Procris. Procris, an enthusiastic huntress, had a dog that never failed to catch its quarry and a dart that never missed its mark (she obtained them from Minos in return for bed-favours). She gave both dog and dart to her husband Cephalus. He went out hunting in the dusk, and Procris, suspecting he was visiting a mistress, put on a camouflage robe and stole out after him. As she hid in a thicket, the dog detected her, and Cephalus, mistaking her for a deer, cast his unerring dart and killed her. He was banished for her murder and haunted by her ghost.

Several commentators, including Annie Gilchrist and Phillips Barry, have identified the girl under the apron as a descendant either of a swan maiden or an enchanted doe. There is even the suggestion, rather far-fetched, that in their title for the song, singers have been confused between 'dear' and 'deer' 'Vaughan' and 'fawn'. In any case the magical maiden who is a woman by day and a beast by night, and fatally hunted by her brother as like as not, is as familiar a figure in folklore as the swans and other birds flying by night, who are thought to be souls in bird form. So the modern-seeming ballad of Molly-Polly Bawn-Vaughan, that Jamieson thought so paltry, in fact reaches far back beyond the time of classical mythology. The song that the most experienced Irish folk song collector, Patrick Joyce, thought 'obviously commemorates a tragedy in real life', turns out to be connected with the fantasies of primitive hunting societies such as produced the ballad of the magic deer that Rumanian peasants still sing as a mid-winter ceremonial piece, and that Béla Bartók immortalized in his superb *Cantata Profana*.

"Polly Vaughan", the incest song of "Lucy Wan" (out of which grew the famous piece dismally named "Edward"), the sprightly "Broomfield Hill", concerning the girl who for a bet makes a rendezvous with a knight in the broomfield and yet contrives to return a maid (having put her importuner to sleep by magical means), these and dozens more ballads clearly have their relatives in the remote past, and to trace their lineage should not be fruitless work. From the Horsham shoemaker and bell-ringer Henry Burstow, Vaughan Williams notated the ballad called "The devil and the ploughman" or "The farmer's curst wife". This tale of the shrewish wife carried off by the devil, who terrifies even the demons of hell so that they are glad to send her back to earth again has its Hindu avatars in the sixth century fable collection called *Panchatantra*. Another ballad, the well-known "Grey cock", tells of the lover who returns from the dead to visit his sweetheart. They must part at cockcrow, and they seek to bribe the cock to delay his dawn signal:

'Then O cock, O cock, O handsome cockerel,
I pray you not crow until it is day,
For your wings I'll make of the very first beaten gold,
And your comb I'll make of the silver grey.'

But the cock it crew, and it crew so fully,
It crew three hours before it was day.
And before it was day, my love had to go away,
Not by the light of the moon or the light of day.

The cock in our ballad is a descendant of the legendary fowls of Oriental folklore, with feathers of gold and diamond beak and ruby claws. A sweet Indian miniature of the early eighteenth century illustrates an incident in the old tale of "Rati and Kamadeva". On a couch under the fading stars we see the two lovers, she asleep, he sitting up and furiously aiming an arrow at the implacable cock perched on the wall and about to crow. The tale seems to have spread from the East, through Byzantium and across Europe as far as Ireland, being turned into a song ballad on the way.

Other ballads have origins more obscure. What ancient saga of trickery and revenge lurks behind the favourite joking song of "Our goodman", "Five nights drunk", "The old farmer and his young wife"? Known all over Europe, it tells of a man returning home to find another man's horse, sword, cloak etc., where his own should be. Like an epic hero he asks in formula fashion: Whose horse is this? Whose sword? Whose cloak? Each time the adulterous wife insists that his eyes deceive him, and that the objects are really a cow, a spit, a bed-sheet etc. In the ballad, the husband's rival appears only at the very end of the song and then merely as a head on the pillow. No struggle takes place, there is no retribution; the ribaldry of the situation has seemed sufficient for modern singers. Yet somehow, in the form as well as the atmosphere of the song, there is the sense of something far more than a rough joke, something larger than life, something to suggest that important things have happened before the song begins, and that weighty and perhaps terrible events will occur after the song ends. In his studies of the medieval folk ballad, Lajos Vargyas makes a fleeting reference to "Our goodman" in connection with what seems on the surface to be a separate and distinct song, namely the ballad, known in Hungary as "Barcsai", with parallels in the Balkans, France and Spain, of the couple surprised in adultery by the returning husband, who kills his rival, daubs his wife with pitch or gunpowder and burns her. In 1879, the Russian explorer Potanin found an epic version of this theme in north-western Mongolia, in "The tale of Tonchi Mergan". But more research is needed before we may surely link our drunken cuckold to the mighty Mongol hero, or identify the strange head on the pillow as belonging to a foreign warrior, or declare that the cheating wife is the lineal descendant of that bygone adultress who was trampled to death by eighty mares on the steppes of Tannu Tuva.

Let us not be confused by this talk of great age and remote territories. A song as we know it may be nothing like so old as the story it tells. The matter of beginnings is plaguy. In one sense a ballad version may be no older than the day on which it was last recorded, since voluntarily or not singers habitually alter details of their performance each time they sing, unless they are so far gone on the road to stylization that the song is firmly and inflexibly fixed in their mind, word for word, note for note, nuance for nuance. In another sense, a version may be far older than its first appearance in print or manuscript. We have suggested that, just as the recitative epic songs emerged in their grand form in the declining years of primitive communism, so the strophic ballad as we know it began to show itself—in England at least—towards the end of feudal times. If we rely entirely on printed evidence to support this suggestion, we are at a loss. In the whole great collection of Child, embracing 305 ballads in as many varying forms as came to his hand, only eleven texts can be dated before 1600. The first recorded versions of ballads taken from tradition in Scotland go back no further than 1700. True, in Barbour's *Complaynt of Scotland* (1594) there is mention of shepherds entertaining themselves with songs of 'quhon the king of est mure land mareit the kyngis dochtir of vest mure land', or 'the yong tamlene', of "Brume brume on hil" and "The frog cam to the myl dure", and it is a fair guess that these may be identified as "King Estmere", "Tam Lin", "The broomfield hill" and perhaps "The wedding of the frog and mouse": but we have no such early records of the texts and tunes. The earliest-known set of "Hind Horn", our only important ballad based on medieval romance, is no older than the nineteenth century, though it must have been circulating among folk singers for centuries before Motherwell first wrote it out in the 1820s or the rowdy Irish brothers Andy and Tommy Hearn carried it about the countryside as they followed the harvests through England with their fiddle and jew's harp.

Facing the problem of 'periodization', Alexander Keith takes as evidence the sixty-nine Child ballads centred on real events and historical persons, on the ground that at least we know these ballads did not precede the happenings and figures they describe. Thirteen of these ballads refer to occurrences before 1500. Six of them treat of incidents and characters of the period between 1500 and 1550. Only two of the remaining fifty concern actual episodes later than 1700. The inference is that the art of the ballad-maker and -singer was only just emerging before 1550, and that the ballad heyday lay between the middle of the sixteenth century and the end of the seventeenth. Well, that holds for the pieces that most interested Child and other literary editors, but not for the sort of ballads that folk communities held in at least equal regard, namely those appearing on broadsides or composed in broadside style, whose high time was rather in the years between 1750 and 1850. Generally, the fortunes of the ballad follow the rise, stability and decline of English folk song in general. For three centuries before 1550 our ballads were evolving from some early shape. For two and a half centuries after 1550 they were in a state of fair stability, being produced in a steady flow (even if they were growing progressively shorter and more matter-of-fact). Subsequently, their creation and, finally, their performance dwindled before the advance of agricultural and industrial capitalism with its pitiless dampening of the spirit and its gross exploitation of people's leisure pursuits.

The ballads have been widespread over the English-speaking part of these islands, from Somerset to the Moray Firth, from Norfolk to Leitrim. Four important centres for their composition and singing are known to us—the north-east of Scotland, the Border country, the English Midlands, and the West Country. Probably the majority of ballad versions that have been recovered in England in this century were noted in Devon and Somerset, but that may simply be due to collectors' chance, to the fact that industrious searchers such as Baring-Gould and Cecil Sharp worked there. The Midlands have yielded far less, but they were the home of a large number of forest outlaw and, later, highwayman ballads. The bare rolling stretch of country from the North Tyne and Cheviots to the Scottish southern uplands was for a long time the territory of men who spoke English but had the outlook of Afghan tribesmen; they prized a poem almost as much as plunder, and produced such an impressive assembly of local narrative songs that some people used to label all our greater folk poems as 'Border ballads'. But the territory just north of Aberdeen turned out to be the best ground for ballads to survive on, as we see from Gavin Greig's experience, who collected 2,500 ballad texts and 2,300 tunes, mostly in the decade 1904–1914, and principally in a single parish, the parish of New Deer.

London must have been an important receiving centre for ballad motifs—and melodies—from France, Italy, Germany and elsewhere, but it is likely that much of our best 'classic' ballad stuff that is not purely local in origin drifted across to us from Scandinavia by way of the Scottish north-east. In the Middle Ages, there were close political ties between Scotland and 'Norrowa o'er the fame', that were prolonged in the commercial connections of the early capitalist time (for example, by the mid-seventeenth century there was a sizeable Aberdeen colony in Bergen that included the forbears of Edvard Grieg the composer), and cultural exchanges, including the swapping of poetry and music, were of the liveliest. And let no one imagine that the late Scandinavian ballad heritage was an affair of Nordic gloom. In contrast with the narrow sombre bloodshot sagas of earlier times, Scandinavian ballad and tale literature towards the end of the Middle Ages was the most coloured and cosmopolitan in Europe, affected by the spiritual treasures brought home by countless Viking expansionists who roamed through Ireland, France, Sicily and Byzantium, or by way of the Scandinavian settlements throughout Russia—where, it is said, a Norseman could speak his own language freely from the Gulf of Finland to the Caspian Sea— and so to Arabia, Persia and beyond. The travellers, knowing what an eager audience awaited their landing at home, would return with chivalrous romances from the Latin countries, bits of Celtic fairy lore, voluptuous Oriental love-stories, elaborate wonder-tales from India, any of which would be likely to combine with local narratives about trolls and heroes to form the kind of ballad, at once deeply national and broadly international, characteristic of western Europe. It was this many-coloured stuff that the Scottish north-east received from across the North Sea, and that gradually spread southward to mingle with the feuding ballads typical of the border country, the characteristic peasant outlaw recitals of the English midlands, and the lyrical pieces of the agricultural south. Not that Aberdeen was the only port of entry for such stuff, by any means; but it was surely a busy one and many of the goods it received are still stored in fine condition in its countryside.

Like all poetry and music, the ballads reflect the time and place from which they sprang, or rather the epoch and locality in which they crystallized into the form we know. But that reflection is not direct, not without distortion. On the surface the songs may show a rich highly-coloured society, but under the surface the thought is determined by a way of life that may be as poor, wild and rough as that of any snot-nosed moss-trooper who stravaged the robber-valleys of Redesdale and the North Tyne in the seventeenth century. The reflection of social reality provided by the ballads is often blurred because so many ghosts of so many pasts are looking back out of the mirror. Variants of the same song may show the spirit of the rough democracy of clan times, or of the incipient class division between aristocrat and underling, or the full high-horsed lording of master over man, according to the district's cultural development and the singers' conception of life at the time when the variant became more or less fixed. Most of the ballads are made of the stuff that moved the humble people and mirrored their idealized view of a world they knew to be hard-grained, cruel, even barbarous. If, over and again in the ballads, hands are lilywhite, seams are silken, cloaks are of crimson velvet, and the personages are noble earls and proud king's daughters, this is no sign that the texts were made by aristocrats. Who are more likely to be impressed by the notion of a milkwhite skin than men and women whose complexion is darkened by work in the fields? Who would be more entranced by the vision of a bird-cage of ivory and gold than those who live in a smoke-stained cottage and sleep under sacking? Poor people's songs are full of riches because deprived men and women take special delight in the 'conception of the impossible', in imagining a world of wonders where ships may have sails of silk and masts of gold, and fifty-nine silver bells hang at every lock of the mane of the Queen of Elfland's horse, and a heroine can be imagined in a smock of lilies, with marigold stays, a camomile petticoat and clover gloves. The magnificence of the classic ballads is often merely a reflection of the poverty of the ballad-singer and his audience, and a sign of their eagerness to create for themselves an atmosphere of magic, conjuring up an idealized world governed by its own laws and logic.

Not that the idealized world remains unchanging, any more than the world of reality. The very character of fantasy alters as society itself is transformed. The ballads created by a primitive freebooting folk will differ in many ways from those dreamed up among farm-workers in fat-stock country, because whereas the one society idealizes because it is weak in the face of nature, the other may idealize because it is weak in the face of the masters. The conflict between man and nature is replaced by the conflict between man and society, and the songs change in expression and content accordingly, but the aim of the singers, consciously or not, remains similar; it is to impose an illusion on reality, in order to get the better of it. Vain hope, some would say. Yet the ploughman plunged into the fantasy of a ballad of heroism, nobility and passion displayed in a cruel world is likely to return to reality with a little more confidence and self-esteem, and thus be better equipped to grapple with what faces him. Even the saddest ballads where all ends in tears, smoke and desolation have within them the temper of victory. Over and again, and not only in the ballads evolved among the feuding families of the border lands, the message is repeated: be wily, brave, and loyal to your own.

Professors of literature have constantly lamented the decline of poetic force in the ballads. The old ballads had such grandeur and intensity and their poetry flashed like a knife-blade; whereas in the latter products much of the terror and pity had drained away, the ample heroic gestures became more modest, the epic wind tempered to a lyrical breeze. The big ballads were being reduced in stature and were turning into middling songs, and (in the critics' view) the song-makers were losing their creative power because they no longer made new ballads of the sort of "Clerk Saunders" and "Child Waters". Well, the process is all part of the logical disappearance of the epic. A people living on meagre soil, far from authority, eking out their existence by raids on their neighbours' cattle, lead lives subject to sudden bloody triumphs and disasters, and the psychological and artistic climate of their songs is affected by that. With the appearance of new modes of living, feudal, capitalist, the development of the old hero epic becomes an anachronism because the common people now look for other forms in which to express the changed reality of their lives. They may go on singing certain of the old songs, gradually modifying them as they pass them on; but when it comes to making their own new songs they make them in a manner that corresponds to their way of life. The massive hero-epics of the remote warrior past recede before the more lyrical, yet still bloodshot, ballads of the late-feudal, early-bourgeois time. And these in turn tend to fade and fall away as economic and social life alters with the discovery of new ways of working the soil, new cares for stock-breeding, new developments of industry, new relations between man and man. The old 'we' song gradually changes to 'I' song, 'classic' ballad is replaced by the broadside ballad and, in the historical conditions of the bourgeois age, the song-proper, the short lyrical arioso type of composition, becomes increasingly the most important vehicle for expressing the ideas and hopes of ordinary folk. And just as in the Middle Ages single episodes became detached from complex epic narratives to form complete ballads on their own, so in more recent times single lyrical details have become detached from ballads to lead an individual life as short songs. For instance, several epic accounts from ancient Greece, the Orient and Viking Iceland include among their chain of adventures the detail of an amorous battle of wits between a hero and a princess; the man wins the girl through the riddles he sets or solves. Detached from all its surrounding exploits, this episode became the substance of at least three English ballads—a supernatural one that Child calls "The elfin knight", a homilectic one sometimes titled "The Devil's nine questions", and an amatory one known as "Captain Wedderburn's courtship" or in slightly different shape as "Scarborough Fair". Probably the oldest form is the story in which one must guess riddles in order to avoid being carried off by a fairy; the change from paganism to Christianity is reflected in the versions in which the girl puts the Devil out of countenance by answering his riddles and thus demonstrating that she is God's and none of his; finally the change from homily to romance comes with those ballads in which the answering of the riddles wins a spouse for the astute solver of puzzles. The latter form seems to have come fairly late to England, and the change from sober parable to lovers' jest may have occurred during the seventeenth century within the lifetime of Henry Playford and Thomas Durfey, who included in their *Pills to Purge Melancholy* a rather good version, with the famous refrain of 'Lay the bent to the bonny broom' (a phrase of 'physiological significance'— 'bent' = 'horn'—says Miss Margaret Dean-Smith who has a sharp sense for euphemism). At some time, the riddles became detached from the story and formed into a short lyrical song, a sentimental piece of seemingly unassailable popularity usually bearing as first line: 'I gave my love a cherry without a stone', that is surely one of the widest known of all folk songs in urban circulation today. It has had a long life, starting out in the fifteenth century and establishing its ascendancy only as the mass of folk composers lost their great zest for creating the longer-winded ballads and placed their affection on the short song-proper, a process that grew more powerful as and where feudalism faded and capitalism came to dominate, and the working people looked for other forms to express the changed reality of their lives.

The transit from epic to ballad and from ballad to song, from the complicated exploits of the "Spendthrift Knight" to "The heir of Linne" and from "The heir of Linne" to "Wild rover", is no indication that the common people are losing their talent and their creative force, but rather that their social and economic life has outstripped the older kinds of song and demands a new poetry and melody, a different spirit, a fresh tone of voice. The process is logical and necessary. The conception of nature and society in the remote past called for intense heroism and magic, and the way of life allowed audiences to listen to single epics lasting for hours or even days on end. The disorders of the feudal age are reflected in the wolfish ferocity of many of our lyrical ballads, but there is something else, a splendour and shapeliness and tinge of romance that presages a new time; moreover a certain conciseness became the order of the day in songs to be listened to by ploughmen, smiths and stable-hands whose leisure was to an extent limited by the demands of the master. Finally the 'classic' ballad itself declines as it is outdated by the very content of a society that takes on the character of capitalism with its new tempo, outlook and demands. The singer becomes more immediately aware of his audience and the need to win it, a need that had hardly existed in a close-knit and homogeneous society, but which becomes urgent in the heterogeneous and looser-knit one of more modern times. In this milieu the typical function of epic and 'middle stage' ballad is assumed by songs that make their point more succinctly, more directly, often with a strong tinge of social revindication. So, in the old ballad of "Glasgerion", the high-born feudal lady, consumed with chagrin that a low-class youngster has tricked his way into her bed, stabs herself; in the later, more 'democratic' analogue of this ballad, the fo'c'sle song called "Do me ama" or "Jack the jolly tar", the bourgeois lady is delighted with the sailor who so cheekily smuggled himself into her arms in place of the squire.

The broadsides of the capitalist age show another amiable democratic feature in the profusion of dauntless lower-class heroines. Lovely Joan the milkmaid is a true descendant of those witty highborn ladies who fooled their would-be seducers by the power of magic or their coaxing tongue in "The broomfield hill" or "The baffled knight". The wind of epic, faint perhaps but still having some edge, blows through the dashing narrative of "Sovay the female highwayman", and the one about the servant girl who, having left her job, saunters along the lanes with her box on her head, quite nonchalantly leaving a trail of dead robbers in her wake. And something of the old heroic breeze still stirs even in such melodramatic broadsides of the nineteenth century as the ballad of Mary, the farmer's daughter on the banks of sweet Dundee, plotted against by her wicked uncle and the local squire.

He clasped his arms around her and tried to throw her
    down.
Two pistols and a sword she spied beneath his morning
    gown.
Young Mary took the pistols and the sword he used so
    free,
And she did fire and shot the squire on the banks of sweet
    Dundee.

Her uncle overheard the noise and hastened to the ground.
'Oh, since you've killed the squire, I'll give you your death-
    wound!'
'Stand off, stand off!' young Mary said, 'Undaunted I will be'.
The trigger drew and her uncle slew on the banks of sweet
    Dundee.

Great girls they are, worthy to walk in company with the
bold butcher Johnson, celebrated in "Three worthy butchers",
who fought ten highwaymen and killed eight before a treacherous woman, stark naked as it happened, gave him his
death-blow from behind, or with modest Jack the sailor (in
"The saucy bold robber") who slugged it out with a giant
villain 'full seven foot high, in proportion as strong' and slew
him barehanded at the ninety-seventh encounter, or with John
Morrissey, last of the really grandiose mythological heroes to
be sung about in these islands, who wielded his fist like Thor's
hammer in that long battle with the foreign champion in the
Land of Fire (this great Irish hero was a real-life pugilist, later
a senator of New York State, who died aged forty-seven in
1878; no trace of his celebrated fight with the Russian sailor
in Tierra del Fuego is found in the sporting handbooks).

We have seen that folk tradition is not static, that 'authentic' folklore changes constantly. If, as the Russian folklorists
say, the content of ballads has always been struggle, then
through various historical epochs the basis of the struggle
alters, and accordingly the style, ambience and climate of the
songs change with the times.

The process of change in the creation and content of folk
song is gradual, of course; as a rule it does not march in step
with social change but proceeds at rather slower tempo.
Moreover, like other forms of art, the best old songs keep their
grip on the audience long after the conditions that gave rise
to them have disappeared; they become accepted as a valuable
part of the cultural patrimony of past ages (every field-worker
knows what reverence folk singers attach to songs believed to
be old, irrespective of the type of song) and only gradually do
these pieces lapse into obsolescence and finally disappear from
living folklore. They go on being a source of enjoyment though

songmakers may long have ceased to compose according to their model. 'New epochs demand new songs', and as capitalism develops the demand becomes more and more frequent, the disappearance of the 'classic' big ballads is accelerated, and not only the big ballads of course, for ultimately the broadside ballads and lyrical folk songs too wither in the mouths of their poor old bearers, and the whole range of folk songs lies moribund. And yet all is not over, for the pieces show a miraculous aptitude for resurrection, and many of them enter on a 'second existence' not simply as museum specimens and study-objects, but as an active factor of popular urban culture, in Britain and America at least, performed in novel ways, with text and tune streamlined to various degrees, in the sundry tones of voice that modern society approves of. The stereotype of today's singer of folk songs as a shaggy young urbanite in jeans, humping a guitar in a canvas case, is often not far off the mark, and we smile or frown at the image, according to our temper, and it slips our mind that in fact the folk songs he carries in his head and retails to his comrades in the upstairs room of a pub comprise a whole education in pride and courage and love, conveyed through characters and situations that have been found typical by generations of common people through the changing scenes of time. But we are running ahead too far: we have some way to go yet before we take our course through a modern industrial landscape. In our story, we are at a time when people were to all intents freed from their medieval trance, ready to rejoice in a countryside gradually growing fatter, moving towards mercantile expansion (hurra-ed on by the image of the bold sea dogs) and with the fire of the spirit not yet damped under the sooty mass of industrialism. It is the age of growing capitalism, the age when the song-proper becomes the most characteristic lyrical form through which the common people express their fantasies, their codes, their aspirations. Let us consider the destiny of this most typical, most numerous, most powerful part of our musical folklore, the relatively short lyrical arioso type of song, whose various sub-species—pastoral, love, occupational, convivial, sea, crime, army, etc.—denote the aspects of life covered rather than the distinct artistic forms used (a song celebrating a ploughboy's life may be expressed in the same kind of melody and poetry as one setting out a highwayman's defiance or a seaman's love complaint). By virtue of its broad horizon of ideas and sentiments, by the extreme suppleness and sensitivity with which it adapts itself to the constant changes, social and psychological, of everyday life, and by the way in which, in the best instances, it concentrates and refines its message, this kind of folksongproper is the summit of popular lyrical creation. Far more than the ceremonial and functional songs, more than the ballads even, the short lyrical folk song comprises a fascinating point of contact between country and town, class and class, epoch and epoch, word of mouth and word of book, peasant amateur and professional musician, collective and individual. It is a vine with roots gnarled in the soil of tradition and tendrils constantly renewing themselves in the changing atmosphere of everyday life, a good old growth that started to wither when the soil turned sour, and now is in process of being re-planted in novel conditions. Whether it will take, and what its mutations may be, it is too early to say.

IV

THE LYRICAL SONGS AND
LATER BALLADS

Too often we think of folk traditions as being like 'constant marble stone', changing very slowly, if at all, under the snail-bite of erosion rather than through any sharply-defined action of history. If that is the view from the library, experience in the field teaches otherwise. The recent arrival of Indian elephant-drivers in some African logging districts is already transforming the local melody. In the inter-War years, the opening of the bus service and the introduction of artificial fertilizer helped to broaden the life and alter the singing style of a group of Transylvanian villages, bringing an ornate lyricism to what was formerly dour and bitter.[31] A living tradition is not a stone column but a plant, hardy but sensitive to climate change.

If casual or obliquely operating events can affect a people's songs, it is small wonder that such a powerful movement of history as the rise of the English middle class after 1500 should work its transformation not only on the music of the gardens and drawing rooms of higher society but on the melodies of village green and kitchen as well. Nor need we be surprised that, at a later date, with great change overtaking the life of many country workers towards the end of the eighteenth century, the folk tradition took one of those famous qualitative leaps and, within a dramatically short time (it seems) the songs presented a new face in which some of the old features were recognizable but the expression was much altered.

If we were Hungarians we might show it by computer. But a general impression may be got by simpler means if one picks at random, say, a hundred traditional tunes recorded before 1750—such as we find among the examples in Claude M. Simpson's *British Broadside Ballad and its Music* (New Brunswick, New Jersey, 1966)—and contrasts these with a similarly haphazard choice of English folk tunes recorded during the nineteenth century and after. Remarkable and at first sight bewildering differences may be found. In general the earlier melodies are more vigorous, squarer, franker in cast, their harmonic structure dominated by the common chord. The newer versions tend rather to be dominated by the fourth, their rhythm is elastic, they incline to hover and take unexpected directions; their formal structure is well-enough defined but their intonations may be so surprising as to baffle the unaccustomed listener. True, some of the later melodies will be seen to carry on the bluff earlier tradition, but others are distinct in form and spirit, more mysterious and searching, less sure and outward-looking than the songs of the older world. Compared with most of the pre-1750 airs we know from song-book and ballad opera, the versions of more recent collection often seem strange in intonation, secret in emotion. A Liverpool schoolteacher reports a pupil's remark: 'The trouble with folk song, it sounds so Chinky.'

Our first presumption is that the differences are so because the older melodies are not adequately notated. Where the conventions of folk music were at variance with the prevailing conventions of fine art music, the editors of former time would sometimes set themselves to the task of 'correction' with more zeal than tact, to produce versions as they felt they ought to be. 'We cannot, therefore, without discrimination, accept as genuine folk products the so-called folk tunes which were collected and printed in the eighteenth, seventeenth and earlier centuries', says Cecil Sharp. Just so. Neither should we, without discrimination, push them aside. In the first place, a number of tunes survived in recent tradition pretty much as they appeared in early print. Moreover not all the old editors were gross. Some of them altered no more than Oswald, for example, whose Scots versions usually seem convincing. And if others tampered with the airs that came their way, the tune-skeletons still remain serviceable as equipment for demonstration. For instance, if ever we came to making a proper statistical comparison, we might expect a fair answer to the question: How many ABBA tunes (first line, second line, second line repeated, first line repeated) do we find before 1800 and how many after? In the old collections we would find the form hardly exists—6 examples out of *c.* 400 in Chappell's *Popular*

Music of the Olden Time;* in the later collections it is so abundant —about 20 per cent in Broadwood's *English County Songs*—that we may take it as the characteristic shape for nineteenth century folk melodies.

An analysis of tune outline, harmonic structure and phrase formation alone—disregarding the subject-matter of the texts—would probably confirm that while English folk song is unitary, two stages are nonetheless perceptible. We may call these stages the 'early tradition' and the 'late tradition'. Put roughly, the flourishing time of the early tradition falls between, say, 1550 and the middle of the eighteenth century. During the later years of the century it begins to give way to a new style of song that persists vigorously for a hundred years or so before its springs start to run dry in the second half of the nineteenth century. But let us not make too much of this; the hypothesis remains to be scientifically tested. The line we are tracing is crude, and it runs on too far. Later, we shall briefly return to the matter, in a more proper place. Let us first look at the musicians who created and carried our 'early tradition', which itself seems to show two distinct kinds of tune, a robust emotional 'Elizabethan' type (as "Joan's ale is new", "The keeper"), and a more airy elegant softer 'eighteenth century' type—already showing itself in Restoration times, in fact— that in its latterday forms (for example, "The Berkshire tragedy", "Searching for lambs", "Strawberry Fair") makes a bridge between the early and the later traditions, exemplified by the countless avatars of the "Green bushes", "Dives and Lazarus", "Banks of sweet Dundee" tunes.

Our lyrical folk song, then, owes part of its style and re-pertory to the peculiar years of the sixteenth century and shortly after. It was a time when town and country, class and class, had firmer effect on each other than ever before, in cultural as well as practical matters. Between town and country the traffic in music and dance went busily in both directions. The upper classes profited by the vigorous art of the masses, and commoners in turn took into their music and dance some of the graces flowing from above, though as ever receiving less

* Only 3 out of 600, for that matter, in *The Scots Musical Museum*, where one would expect to find more.

than they gave. The matter can be overstated: a golden picture is given of a time when unity reigned and all interests were common and a lute hung in every barber shop for the carmen and cobblers to try out the latest court pavan while waiting their turn; but the student of folk music, looking from below, observes a less idyllic view. The rosy tales of 'common interest between highest and lowest' have no more substance than the myth of the lute and barber shop (how many poor townsmen ever went to barber shops, particularly those fine enough to keep the relatively expensive bourgeois and courtly instruments as part of the furniture?).

True, there was some unity of emotional life between the middle and lower classes, at least over part of the social spectrum. Small merchants and artisans were hardly distinguishable, socially or culturally. And since many of the rising merchant nobility came from quite low down among the middle class, to be sure they took with them into their new mansions the tunes they had grown up with in humbler streets. However, by the time those tunes reached the drawing room their character was rather altered, just as the appearance of the sturdy burgesses was changed, who had carried the tunes through layers of society. During Elizabeth's time and for a while after, the new high-art music that had grown up mainly as a secularization of church music absorbed a great deal of folk song and popular dance melody into itself. That is clear from *The Fitzwilliam Virginal Book* (probably put together in the first quarter of the seventeenth century) which contains among its 297 pieces a good number of folk tunes made into variations or fantasias, or adapted and harmonized as they stood. Even such sophisticated composers as Dowland availed themselves of folk tunes, and at weekend parties in the grand country houses, the guests might be expected to take their part in singing rounds and catches based, for instance, on a stringing-together of the musical cries of street traders. Commentators tell us that all this is due to Elizabeth's success in uniting the nation, first by rallying all classes in the face of the Spanish threat, secondly by an improvement in living standards through her patronage of colonial expansion and her encouragement of industrial development. This social and political unity, it is suggested, is reflected in the musical life of the time. Look, we are invited, folk song and art song, one and the same; there's glory for you!

The fact is, the times worked their effect on folk song in more oblique fashion than that rosy view would suggest. There was a wider gulf between the music of the classes than shows at first sight of the printed stave. The lutenists, keyboard composers, writers of ayres, borrowed folk tunes all right, but transformed them to suit the taste of a class residing in, or aspiring to, gentility. The adaptations of folk melodies they produced bore the same relation to the lower-class originals that the court Morris dances bore to the springtime agricultural rites of the village green. Consider the mood of the "Greensleeves" tune in its settings by Dowland or in the aristocratic vocal arrangement with those ghastly 'Alas, my love, you do me wrong' words; contrast these with the atmosphere of versions surviving in lower-class tradition, such as the set of "O shepherd, O shepherd, will you come home?" obtained by H. E. D. Hammond near Dorchester some sixty years ago and reprinted in *The Penguin Book of English Folk Songs*. The skeleton is the same, but the stately refinement of the Dowland pieces and the droop of the genteel vocal version are in the fashion of quite another world than that of folk song. In their aristocratic or high bourgeois adaptations, such pieces would have been hardly recognizable to the commoners who created them, so great is the transformation a tune may undergo on its passage from kitchen to hall, even in a time of reputed cultural unity.

If, in Elizabeth's time, the gentry were using folk song in their compositions, that is not necessarily a sign of class alliance, any more than the contemporary fashion for Irish tunes showed solidarity with the sons of Grania Uaile. It amused the composers to make variations on Irish airs, it amused the court to dance to Irish melodies, it amused everyone to sing garbled Gaelic phrases such as 'Callino casturame' (in William Byrd's orthography; Shakespeare spells it differently; the Gaelic is probably *Cailin ó chois tSiúire mé*—'I'm a girl from beside the Suir'), just at a time when England was waging a ferocious and repressive war, accompanied by famine and followed by confiscation, that reduced large tracts of Ireland to a wilderness, and broke the back of the ancient Gaelic culture that had produced the tunes. There is something melancholy in the image of a Tudor gentleman amiably beating time as his wife at the virginals plays the fashionable keyboard setting of the lament called "The Irish ho-hoane"[32] at the moment when, in Edmund Spenser's description, the Irish patriots and their fine musicians 'were brought to such wretchedness as that any stony heart would have rued the same. Out of every corner of the woods and glens they came creeping forth upon their hands for their legs could not bear them; they looked like anatomies of death; they spoke like ghosts crying out of their graves; they did eat the dead carrions, happy where they could find them: yea, and one another soon after, inasmuch as the very carcases they spared not to scrape out of their graves . . . that in a short space of time they were none almost left, and a most populous and plentiful country suddenly left void of man and beast.' We are told that Elizabeth would hum Irish melodies along the corridors of her palace at Greenwich. So, as I write, might President Johnson whistle a lively Vietnamese air (if he knew one) as he settled to his work in the White House.

The historians of art music have over-simplified the relationship between learned and lower-class composition, because they have generally ignored the filters through which folk music flowed in its transit from one social stratum to another, seeping up to the topmost layer and percolating down again through the realms of merchant, artisan, labourer, to the crypts and hedgerows of the vagabonds (of whom there were a great number in those golden days). The sixteenth century was a time when a host of humble professional musicians, full-time or part-time, were making it possible for the twin currents of town popular music and countryside folk song to merge. The floating population in and out of the cities contained a great many musicians, playing a jumble of urban and rural stuff like the 'unprofitable pipers and fiddlers' of whom Gosson wrote in 1586, 'London is so full . . . that a man can no sooner enter a tavern than two or three cast of them hang at his heels to give him a dance before he departs'. In this exchange of town and country music none was more effective than the part-time professionals, the weekend minstrels. They might be urban-dwellers, tailors, shoemakers and such; or they might be country labourers, ploughmen, shepherds. On Sundays and holidays, at weddings and other festivities, they would supplement their earnings by playing for the amusement of villagers or people in the poorer quarters of the town, on bagpipe, reed-pipe, flute, or perhaps a battered viol played upright on the knee with the bow held underhand.

Understandably, the established professional popular musicians, whether independent minstrels or town waits employed by the municipality, resented the competition of the part-timers, and those that were organized often laid complaint against the weekend players through their fraternities, their 'trade unions'. Nearly every town had its waits—wind-players as like as not, though the Norwich waits could double on violin and 'a whole noise of recorders' as well as playing their customary oboe-like shawms. Their job was to play for official visits, for the mayor on feast- and market-days, for the aldermen at their ceremonial beef-breakfasts, and of a summer evening from the guildhall roof or a roadside scaffolding to blow and scrape for an hour or so 'to the rejoicing and comfort of the hearers', just like any modern band in the park. It was also the waits' duty to act as a perambulating watch for fires and loiterers at night, and in Coventry for instance they played softly at various corners of the city for five days a week between midnight and 4 a.m. for the reassurance of citizens. They ranked as respectable craftsmen, and their salary would keep them comfortably by lower middle-class standards. Now and then, the more popular groups of waits took engagements to play in other towns, and sometimes went on quite lengthy tours, not always with the permission of their paymasters. Thus in Chester in 1613, Master George Cayley petitioned that he and his fellow musicians be appointed town waits instead of 'the waits now absent'; the corporation deferred its answer until it could discover what had become of the old waits.

The greater part of the waits' repertory consisted of adapted folk song, popular dance tunes, and theatre music. Among the common pieces played by them at the end of the sixteenth century we find "Dargason", a dance tune carrying many texts, the putative grandfather of the American "Skip to my Lou", "When Joan's ale was new" which leads a vigorous life in present day folk song clubs, and the enormously influential "Quadrant pavan", sometimes called "Gregory Walker". According to Thomas Morley, the tune was given its nickname 'in derision . . . because it walketh among barbers and fiddlers more common than any other'. It is distinguished by its peculiar harmony structure, its ground (I IV I V, I IV I–V I) forming the basis of many pieces composed around 1600, also of a sizeable group of folk song and dance melodies.* In Elizabethan popular music its harmonic sequence seems to have been established in the player's mind as firmly as the blues sequence nowadays under the thatch of the pop singer, and melodies improvized on its ground were heard on all sides, in town and country, seemingly not always with skill, for Morley, in his *Plaine and Easy Introduction to Practicall Musicke* says sharply to his pupil: 'Nay, you sing you know not what, it should seeme you came latelie from a barbers shop, where you had Gregory Walker plaide in the new proportions by them latelie found out.'

Few towns could support more than two or three waits permanently on the municipal payroll. We must remember that urban populations were small in Elizabeth's time. Around 1580, London had some 120,000 inhabitants, and Norwich, in population the second city, only 17,000. York had 10,000 and Bristol, probably the fourth largest, but 6,000. But if the towns supported few waits, the number of full-time freelance popular musicians was large. Some of these were organized into craft fraternities with proper rules regarding apprenticeship, examinations, professional conduct etc. The story of these fraternities makes an absorbing chapter in the early history of trade unionism in Britain.[33] Within the fraternities, competition was controlled, and no musician might canvass for a wedding or

* Well-known tunes using this harmonic background include "John, come kiss me now", the Playford dance melody "Paul's Wharf", the set of "My lodging is in the cold ground" from which Moore made "Believe me if all those endearing young charms", and the Yorkshire version of "Mary across the wild moor" collected by Kidson. A familiar American example is the commonest set of "On top of Old Smoky".

other engagement that he knew a 'Brother' had already applied for, nor was he permitted to play in a colleague's territory unless invited. In some towns, musicians with no fraternity of their own joined the local barbers' and surgeons' guild.

Both town waits and independent musicians were affected by the uncontrolled competition of the part-time musicians who were artisans and labourers during the week and fiddlers and pipers at weekends. Some of these dressed in the coloured cloaks of 'fraternity' musicians, to give themselves airs and perhaps to command higher fees. Enquiry commissions of the sixteenth century mention that 'many unskilled rustics and artificers pretending that they are our own minstrels by their livery, deceitfully collect and receive great exactions of money from our lieges. And although they are by no means skilled and expert in that art, and practice divers labours on working days and thence amply obtain their living, nevertheless on festal days they run about from place to place and entirely win that gain whereby our minstrels, not practising any other labours, ought to live.'

If in the towns some impostors were able to pass as accredited 'fraternity' musicians, in the country the rustic part-timers would likely be playing in their own or neighbouring villages where they were too well-known to be taken for full-fledged professionals. But though the pickings in the villages were probably to be counted rather in farthings than shillings (if, indeed, the players were not being paid in beans and firewood), the organized musicians felt it worth while to restrict the working area of the part-timers by such regulations as that drawn up at Beverley in 1555, directing that 'no shepherd or husbandman or man of other occupation playing upon pipe or other instrument, shall sue any wedding or other thing that appertaineth to the said science, except it be within the parish wherein he dwelleth'.

However, to established popular musicians, far more irksome than the part-timers were the rough unorganized freelance ballad-singers and street instrumentalists, many of them petty criminals or associates of criminals, young delinquents like the Reading trio, Wheler, Jackson and Jones, described as 'idle boys professing themselves musicians, living basely and of themselves without masters in this town', and sturdy rogues like Robert Craundon, 'sometimes a weaver, sometimes a surgeon, sometimes a minstrel, sometimes . . . a bullard running from place to place with a bull or two', who was hauled up at the Wiltshire quarter sessions in 1605 for his 'marvellous ill life and conversation'. In his *Micro-cosmographie* (1628) Bishop John Earle gives his portrait of the two-string fiddler of the time: 'A good feast shall draw him five miles by the nose and you shall track him again by the scent. His other pilgrimages are fairs, and good houses where his devotion is great to the Christmas: and no man loves good times better. He is in league with the tapsters for the worshipful of the inn, whom he torments next morning with his art, and has their names more perfect than their men. A new song is better to him than a new jacket: especially if bawdy. . . . A country wedding and Whitsun-ale are the two main places he domineers in, where he goes for a musician and overlooks the bagpipe. The rest of him is drunk and in the stocks.'

Between them, the independent usually unorganized musicians of the towns, the Sunday fiddlers and pipers from tailor shop or sheepfold, and the roguing ballad-singers, made the greater part of music heard by working people, whether urban or rural. Apart, that is, from the music they made for themselves at the cradle, the loom, the last or the plough. We have a good notion of the repertory of these various musicians: old country folk tunes, new town popular tunes, minstrel compositions of the kind of "Constance of Cleveland" and the effusions of Martin Parker and Deloney set sometimes to complex and handsome airs, some scraps of foreign melody especially dance-tunes from Italy, and a certain number of pieces by the leading composers of the day: all these to varying extents synthetized, hybridized in style, and, especially among the part-time musicians, 'folklorized' and (for all their novelty) made apt for incorporation into the body of the folk song tradition. So, around 1600, at the climactic moment when art music was regularizing itself, melodically and rhythmically, in the interests of harmony and architecture, the old medieval lyrical kind of folk song, while retaining some of its meandering freedom, nevertheless took a leap into modernity, not only as regards poetry and melody, but, increasingly, in psychological ambiance too.

If, however superficially, the musical cultures of rich and poor seemed fairly close in Elizabethan times, they were soon to move decisively along different roads. The great part of our surviving lyrical folk song is the product of capitalist times, formed in the years when feudalism lay far behind, when Spain the rival was defeated, when the burgesses had their 'Glorious Revolution', when an Empire was being gained with beads and bayonets, and when the rumble of industry was reaching the pitch of thunder. It was a time when men of affairs felt like lords of creation, with a Mr. By-ends' vision of themselves walking 'in golden slippers, in the sunshine, with applause'. The musical accompaniment to their promenade was written by Purcell, Handel, Arne, and the Bishops, Balfes, Sterndale Bennetts and others who came after them, not so much lacking in talent as in opportunity to develop it; in any case composers whose music, in character and content, had moved further and further away from the selfmade songs of working men.

Now, because we are dealing with relatively modern times and circumstances, and with songs evolved out of experience of often quite novel relations between man and man, it is both possible and necessary to make our terms clear. Throughout our argument, we have been speaking of folk song as 'lower-class' song, which is certainly not to condemn but to interpret. What do we mean by 'class'? E. P. Thompson's definition is handier than most: 'Class happens when some men, as a result of common experiences (inherited or shared), feel and articulate the identity of their interests as between themselves, and as against other men whose interests are different from (and usually opposed to) theirs.'[34]

The folk songs are lower-class songs specifically in so far as they arise from the common experience of labouring people and express the identity of interest of those people, very often in opposition to the interests of the masters. In the folk songs of any period, behind the recitals of lost love and violent death, of hanged robbers and sweethearts pressed to sea, of the beauty of a country spring and the hardness of country labour, of transported poachers and colliers on strike, something more is to be heard: the longing for a better life. Sometimes, especially in the later, industrial era of folk song creation, that longing expresses itself directly, actively by the description of bitter times and hard masters, and by exhortation to do something about it, as in the Yorkshire machine-wrecking song:

> Come all you croppers stout and bold,
> Let your faith grow stronger still,
> For the cropper lads in the county of York
> Have broke the shears at Foster's Mill,

or rather wistfully in the lament of Lancashire handloom weavers:

> Our Margit declares if hoo'd clothes to put on,
> Hoo'd go up to Lunnon to see the great man,
> An' if things didn't alter when there hoo had been,
> Hoo says hoo'd begin an' fight, blood up to th'een,

or resolutely, as in the song of the striking miners of Framwell-gate Moor, Durham, in the 1830's (in style, their ballad looks forward to the political mass songs of a later age):

> For ten years or more we've been regular slaves,
> Bound down by our masters, the greatest of knaves,
> But no longer we'll bear it, for now we are free,
> And right will beat might, that the masters will see.

It will be complained that these are not among the masterpieces of the common muse, nor even characteristic of her, and the complaint is just. Generally the folk song makers chose to express their longing by transposing the world on to an imaginative plane, not trying to escape from it, but colouring it with fantasy, turning bitter even brutal facts of life into something beautiful, tragic, honourable, so that when singer and listeners return to reality at the end of the song, the environment is not changed but they are better fitted to grapple with it. How many country girls through the centuries, left with a bastard baby, have been heartened to face the sorrow of their plight and the scorn of their neighbours by the sweet nobility of the following song (it exists in many versions, some as rough as a chaff-bag; this one, got in Woodbridge, Suffolk in 1937 is the best I know):

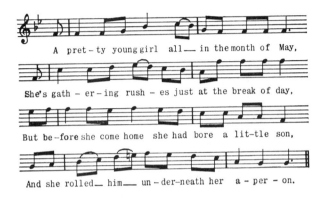

A pretty young girl all in the month of May,
She's gathering rushes just at the break of day,
But before she come home she had bore a little son,
And she rolled him underneath her aperon.

Well, she cried on the threshold and she come in at the door,
And she folded in her aperon that pretty babe she bore,
Says her father: 'Where you been, my pretty daughter Jane,
And what's that you got underneath your aperon?'

'Father, dear father, it's nothing,' then says she,
'It's only my new gown and that's too long for me,
And I was afraid it would draggle in the dew,
So I rolled it underneath my aperon.'

In the dead of the night when all were fast asleep,
This pretty little baby, oh, it begin to weep.
He says: 'What little dicky bird is crying out so shrill
In the bedroom among the pretty maidens?'

'O father, dear father, it's nothing then,' says she.
It's a sweet little dicky bird that fluttered to my knee,
And I'll lay it to my breast and I'll build for it a nest,
So it don't wake too early in the May morning.'

In the third part of the night, when all were fast asleep,
This pretty little baby, oh, it begin to weep.
'Oh, what's that baby that's crying out so clear
In the bedroom among the pretty maidens?'

'O father, dear father, it's nothing then,' says she.
'It's just a pretty baby that someone give to me.
Let it lie, let it sleep this night along o' me,
And I'll tell you its daddy in the May morning.'

'Oh, was it by a black man or was it by a brown,
Or was it by a ploughing-boy a-ploughing up and down,
That give you the stranger to wear with your new gown,
That you rolled up underneath your aperon?'

'It's neither by a black man, it's neither by a brown.
I got it from a sailor boy that ploughs the watery main.
It was him give me the stranger to wear with my new gown,
That I rolled it underneath my aperon.'

'Oh, was it in the kitchen got, or was it in the hall?
Was it in the cow-shed or up again the wall?
I wish I had a firebrand to burn the building down
Where you met with him on a May morning.'

'It wasn't in the kitchen got, it wasn't in the hall.
It wasn't in the cow-shed nor up again the wall.
It was down by yonder spring where them little birds do sing
That I met him in the dew on a May morning.'

Consolation is one of the most powerful functions of folk song
anywhere, and the solace and encouragement has not merely

to do with the subject of the poem that is being sung. For instance, songs of lovers' separation and betrayal abound, but to sing them and listen to them has given comfort not only to lonely and deserted sweethearts but also to the casual labourer worried where the next job is to come from now the hay-field is mowed, or to his wife facing prosecution for stealing wood from the master's hedge on a frosty February day. The lost-love songs may be poignant, sometimes wild with grief and apprehension, but often, at the last, the oppression lifts, some kind of peace of mind is recovered. So with the familiar "Seeds of love" song, which delicately contains an almost explosive emotion of disappointment, and holds it all in tight, and then at the end gently and wryly allows of hope because, well, if life is hard, people can still be tough and resilient in face of it. The comment of the listeners would probably be: 'If that young woman in the song can surmount her sorrow, then surely I can overcome mine.' Here is a version got in Sussex by Iolo Williams:

I sowed the seeds of love
That blossom in the spring,
In April, May and likewise June
When the small birds do sweetly sing.

My garden was well-provided
With flowers everywhere,
But I had not the liberty to choose for myself
The flower that I would wear.

The gardener was standing by
I asked him to choose for me.
He chose me the lily with the violet and pink,
But I did refuse all three.

The lily I first forsook
Because it fades so soon.
And the violet and the pink I both overlooked,
And I vowed I would wait till June.

For in June there's a red rose bud,
And that is the flower for me;
But I oftentimes have snatched at the red rose-bud
And gained but the willow-tree.

Oh, the willow-tree will twist,
And the willow-tree will twine,
And I wish I were in that young man's arms,
Where he once had the heart of mine.

Come all you sorryfoot (sorrowful) lovers
That learn for to chipper and to change.
The grass oftentimes has been trodden underfoot,
But in time it will rise again.

Are such songs made by women? They put the woman's point of view, but that is no sure sign of the author's sex. We know from Burns, for instance, that men may convincingly and with pleasure make erotic poems in which they speak as women. Certainly "The seeds of love" has often been sung by men. After all, wasn't it from a Somerset gardener, the aptly-named John England, that Sharp took down his famous version, the very first folk song that he collected? Generally, though, the men's songs of the kind incline to harsher passion or to an ironic shrug; they rarely take the matter so to heart, perhaps because for them not so much is at stake, though such pieces as "The false bride" show there are exceptions. In this connection it is interesting to recall that towards the end of his life, Béla Bartók had started on a psychological analysis of some two thousand Rumanian song-texts, to see, among other things, wherein the women's lyrics differ from the men's. Alas, he did not live to finish the study, but in a letter to József Szigeti at the end of January 1944, he wrote: 'I believe this collection will show some interesting things. Thus, for instance, to be abandoned by a lover is a far worse misfortune for a girl than for a young man. We knew this before, but with these texts we can prove it in black and white, according to statistical data. And then the girls (or married women) are much more violent and hot-tempered than the men. The maledictory songs against unfaithful lovers are addressed in far greater number to men than women. And these texts are among the strangest, and their authors show an imagination worthy of Shakespeare.' He quotes some examples of elaborate curses expressed in song: 'May thirteen chemists' shops be emptied for you!' 'May nine waggonloads of chaff and straw rot in your bed!' 'May your hand-towel throw flames, and the water you wash in turn to blood!' English women's songs contain few imprecations of the kind (Scots and Irish have more, especially in Gaelic) and perhaps there's scope for psychologists in that, too.

But if the women's love songs can affect the bearers and listeners far beyond the emotions surrounding the subject of the piece, so too can the men's, not as a rule in any quality of consolation, but rather by their resolve. As example, the handsome "One night as I lay on my bed" that Hammond notated (from a woman, as it happened) at Upwey, in Dorset, in 1907. It is one of the huge and ancient class of night-visit songs, and again it carries in itself the power to leave its listeners a bit better able to grapple with life, for it begins in disquiet, continues in resolution, and ends in an iridescent blaze of triumph whose lift is all the more glorious for its terse economy. The words are charming on their own, but they only spring to full vigorous life when impelled by the grand tune with its springing seventh leaps.

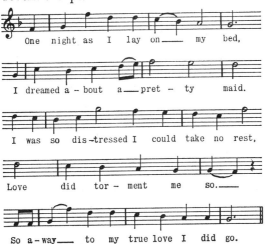

One night as I lay on my bed,

I dreamed a-bout a pret-ty maid.

I was so dis-tressed I could take no rest,

Love did tor-ment me so.

So a-way to my true love I did go.

One night as I lay on my bed,
I dreamed about a pretty maid.
I was so distressed, I could take no rest,
Love did torment me so.
So away to my true love I did go.

But when I came to my love's window,
I boldly called her by her name,
Saying: 'It was for your sake I'm come here so late
Through this bitter frost and snow.
So it's open the window, my love, do.'

'My mum and dad they are both awake,
And they will sure for to hear us speak.
There'll be no excuse then but sore abuse,
Many a bitter word and blow.
So begone from my window, my love, do.'

'Your mum and dad they are both asleep,
And they are sure not to hear us speak,
For they're sleeping sound on their bed of down
And they draw their breath so low.
So open the window, my love, do!'

My love arose and she opened the door,
And just like an angel she stood on the floor.
Her eyes shone bright like the stars at night,
And no diamonds could shine so.
So in with my true love I did go.

Distantly related to this piece by a chain of intermediate
versions is an extraordinary song presenting the circumstances
of the night-visit with subtle irony. Baring-Gould heard it from
a blacksmith, 'Ginger Jack' Woodrich of Thrushelton, Devon.
Not fully appreciating what he was faced with, the parson
chose to re-write the words (in his *Songs of the West* it is called
"Come to my window") and so took the savour out of the song.
As Ginger Jack had it, it was part of a tale. A young woman
had two suitors, one old and rich, the other young and poor.

She married the rich old man; the other became her lover and she had a child by him. One night, mistakenly thinking the old man is away from home, the lover comes tapping at her window. Fearing lest her husband should discover him, the adultress rocks the cradle and begins to sing an improvized lullaby that is, in fact, addressed not to the child but to her lover, to warn him that the old man is at home.

> Begone, begone, my Willy, my Billy,
> Begone, my love and my dear.
> Oh, the wind is in the west
> And the cuckoo's in his nest,
> And you cannot have a lodging here.

> Begone, begone, my Willy, my Billy,
> Begone, my love and my dear.
> Oh, the wind and oh, the rain,
> They have sent him back again,
> And you cannot have a lodging here.

And still the lover keeps tapping, till at last the exasperated woman sings:

> Begone, begone, my Willy, you silly,
> Begone, my fool and my dear.
> Oh, the devil's in the man
> That he cannot understan'
> That he cannot get a lodging here!

The song goes back to the sixteenth century at least. Substantially the same tune as Ginger Jack's appears in the *Fitzwilliam Virginal Book* under the title "Goe from my window" in arrangements by Morley and John Munday, while snatches of the text appear in Beaumont and Fletcher's *Knight of the Burning Pestle* (1613). Fletcher was evidently taken with the song, for he used it again in two other plays, *Monsieur Thomas* and *The Woman's Prize*.

The origin of this subtle and amusing piece is not clear, but it is well-known in northern and central Spain, where it exists as an actual lullaby. In a lecture given in Havana in 1930, the poet García Lorca quoted a number of Spanish versions that provide an interesting gloss to Ginger Jack's song. The Asturian text is at once blunt and artful, for it frightens the child by suggesting a mysterious man at the door, reassures him by reminding him of the presence of the father, and yet all this is pretence, for in fact it is a message to the lover in the most direct of codes:

> El que está en la puerta
> que non entre agora,
> que está el padre en casa
> del neñu que llora.
> > Ea, mi neñín, agora non,
> > ea, mi neñín, que está el papón.

> El que está en la puerta
> que vuelva mañana,
> que el padre del neñu
> está en la montaña.
> > Ea, mi neñín, agora non,
> > ea, mi neñín, que está el papón.

(The man at the door, let him not come in now, for the crying baby's father is at home. Ea, my baby, not now. Ea, my baby, daddy is here. The man at the door, let him come back tomorrow when the baby's father is up in the mountain. Ea, my baby, not now. Ea, my baby, daddy is here.)

As sung in Salamanca it is more lyrical and the sentiment, as Lorca remarks, is more veiled:

> Palomita blanca
> que andas a deshora,
> el padre está en casa
> del niño que llora.

> Palomita negra
> de los vuelos blancos,
> está el padre en casa
> del niño que canta.

(Little white dove, you come at a bad time. The father's at home and the baby is crying. Little black dove with the white wings. The father's at home and the baby sings.)

The Burgos variant is particularly close to Ginger Jack's last verse:

> Qué majo que eres,
> qué mal que lo entiendes,
> que está el padre en casa
> y el niño no duerma.
> Al mú mú, al mú mú del alma
> que te vayas tú!

(Spruce as you are, can't you understand, the baby won't sleep and its father's at hand. Al mu mu, al mu mu, darling, won't you go away!)

Lorca comments: 'This is the only lullaby in which the child is of no importance at all. It is a pretext and no more. I do not mean to say that every woman who sings it is an adultress; all the same, without realizing it, she is entering the ambit of adultery.' For, as he reminds us, that mysterious man at the door is the man with the tilted hat-brim and shadowy face of whom every real woman dreams.

In England, the song also has an industrial setting. A version reported from Liverpool in the mid-nineteenth century presents the cuckold husband as a miner on night-shift. Unexpectedly, bad weather keeps him from the pit, and when the lover comes tapping, the woman sings—ostensibly to her child—

> The wind is in the west,
> And the cuckoo's in his nest,
> And the coal-pit is tomorrow,
> *Uz, uz, uz, uz.*

Still the tapping continues. The wife sings of how the wind and the rain have driven her husband home again, and stresses that 'the coal-pit is *tomorrow*'. But the lover will not take the hint and persists in rapping, and at last she cries in exasperation:

> And is the foo' so fond
> That he cannot understand
> That the coal-pit is *tomorrow*,
> *Uz, uz, uz, uz.*

We have suggested that the majority of English songs tell a story or at least purport to. But there are also songs that are simply expressions of mood and nothing more. They are not numerous but they are confusing in their variety because they make use of a stock of symbolic or epigrammatic verses that are combined and re-combined in song after song, so that often it is hard to tell one piece from another. This stock of commonplace lyrical 'floaters' (so called because they float with ease from one song to another) is relatively restricted, comprising perhaps not many more than fifty tropes in all, but through the centuries singers have delighted in selecting them, matching them up, stringing them together as girls might string beads of various colours bought off a cheapjack's tray. The verses are usually concerned with love, especially love betrayed or denied, and a repertory of such verses provides a handy kit for making countless songs almost at will. Here are a few of these lyrical floaters that readers will recognize as cropping up in song after song:

> Must I go bound and he go free?
> Must I love a man that never loved me?
> Why should I act such a childish part
> As to love a young man who would break my heart?

> I wish, I wish, but it's all in vain,
> I wish I was a maid again.
> A maid again I'll never be
> Till apples grow on an orange tree.

I put my back against an oak,
Thinking it was some trusty tree,
But first it bent and then it broke,
And so did my false love to me.

I put my hand into a bush,
Thinking some sweetest flower to find.
I pricked my finger to the bone,
Leaving that sweetest flower behind.

When my apron strings hung low,
He'd follow me through frost and snow.
Now my apron strings won't pin,
He'll pass my door and not come in.

Oh, meeting is a pleasure
And parting is a grief,
But an unconstant lover
Is worse than any thief.

A thief he will but rob you
And take all that you have
But an unconstant lover
Will bring you to the grave.

The grave it will decay you,
And turn you unto dust.
There's not a man in a thousand
That a poor girl can trust.

They'll kiss you and they'll court you
And tell to you more lies
As the hairs upon your head, love,
Or the stars in the skies.

Come all you pretty maidens,
A warning take by me.
Don't you place your sweet affection
On a green willow tree.

> For the leaves they will wither,
> The branches decay,
> And all your poor love
> It'll soon fall away.

Over and again the turtle dove sits on top of the tree, mourning for her own true love (as I shall do for thee). Time after time a cloudy morning brings forth a shining day. In song upon song the lover protests he'll be true until the sea runs dry and the rocks melt in the sun. And still the girls may have the last word with some such metaphor as:

> He gave me honey all mixed with gall.
> He gave me words and vows withal.
> He gave me a delicate gown to wear,
> All stitched with sorrow and hemmed with fear.

Fluid as the use of these floating stanzas may be, sets of them sometimes show signs of crystallizing into specific songs. A certain sequence may be considered as typical of "The water is wide", another of "Died for love", "The cuckoo", or "The waggoner lad". But as often as not they appear more or less at random, as they come into the singer's head. It is not hard to arrange such floaters into a reasonably logical sequence, as poor John Clare did in poems such as "A faithless shepherd" which he made out of lyrical scraps he had learnt from the last village cowherd in his native Helpstone, when he was a youngster tending geese and sheep on the common before, to his sad regret, the village was enclosed in 1809.

Few of these floating lyrics are datable. They are the product of some sentimental flowering of the spirit, but whether they were all produced at the same period or represent the accretion of centuries would be hard to say. Narrative songs may show their age in the way that deeds, persons, customs, beliefs are spoken of; language and form may also help us to imagine what period-costume the actors are wearing. But the floating lyrics can rarely be referred to such and such an epoch: their concepts are universal, their ways of expression general, they offer too little detail to give clues as to their origin. Occasionally we have a wisp of information. For instance, there is a relatively commonplace stanza (though it occurs more often in America than in England):

> How hard is the fortune of all womankind!
> They're always in fetters, they're always confined;
> Bound down by their parents until they're made wives,
> Then slaves to their husbands the rest of their lives.

We know that this floater occurs in a stage song of 1734, "The ladies' case", with words credited to Henry Carey, who wrote "Sally in our Alley", but even so, we may not be sure whether the folk took it from the stage or whether it entered the playhouse by way of the cottage.

As a specimen of the inconsequential way in which these movable motifs may be strung together, here is a nineteenth century broadside text published by T. Birt of Seven Dials, London. The song is a version of a present day favourite in urban folk song clubs, but in this case the night-visit narrative (ordinarily, it is a variant of "The grey cock") is promptly discarded after the first two lines in favour of a random sequence of floaters. On the stall-sheet it is titled: "I'm often drunk and seldom sober."

> Many cold winter nights I've travelled
> Until my locks were wet with dew,
> And can you think that I'm to blame
> For changing of old love for new?
> *Chorus:*
> I'm often drunk and seldom sober,
> I am a rover in every degree;
> When I'm drinking, I'm often thinking
> How I shall gain my love's company.

> The seas are deep, I cannot wade them,
> Neither have I wings to fly;
> I wish I had some little boat
> To carry over my love and I.

I leaned my back against an oak,
Thinking it had been some trusty tree;
At first it bent and then it broke,
So false my lover proved to me.

In London city the girls are pretty,
The streets are paved with marble stone;
And my love she's as clever a woman
As ever trod on England's ground.

I wish I was in Dublin city,
As far as e'er my eyes could see,
Or else across the briny ocean
Where no false love could follow me.

Yes, love is handsome and love is pretty,
And love is charming while it's new;
So as love grows older it does grow colder
And fades away like the morning dew.

There are two nags in my father's stable.
They prick their ears when they hear the hound.
And my true love is as clever a woman
As ever trod on England's ground.

I'm often drunk and seldom sober,
I am a rover in every degree;
When I'm drinking, I'm often thinking
How I shall gain my love's company.

Not every folk song is a masterpiece, and among the love
lyrics as with other kinds, there are many crude sentimental
narratives as conventional as any girls' magazine story, in
which the wish for a better life shows itself in easy day-dreams,
as in "The green mossy banks of the Lea", for instance, where
a young man makes overtures to a country girl, and is rebuffed
with scorn; but he is so taken with the maiden's modesty that

he offers marriage on the spot, and is accepted, and then, to her delight and the admiration of the neighbourhood, it turns out that he has a fortune of ten thousand a year. Less banal, but still as conventionalized as a cheap Victorian engraving is "Fair Phoebe and her dark-eyed sailor", a song on the theme of "Hind Horn", with parted lovers, a shared token in the form of a broken ring, the man's return unrecognized and the woman's fidelity put to test. The piece had enormous success after 1836 or so, when it was printed by Catnach, and it has turned up over again in tradition in the present century with the words always ultimately learnt off the Catnach broadside. Too well known to be worth quoting, it probably owes some of its success to its good tune, variants of which had been circulating for a good hundred years before Catnach's unnamed pot poet scribbled his verses.

A great deal of attention has been paid to such harmless pieces by commentators to whom the chief merit of folk song is its quaintness. But these, and the recitals of bumpkin affection between the pretty ploughboy and his lass, and the laments of betrayal, are by no means all the chapter of our amatory songs. There is another kind, often of beauty and power, of great significance as folklore, and occupying an important place in the repertory of many localities, namely the explicitly sexual-erotic songs. The outsider would hardly guess it. Until quite recently, in the printed collections of traditional song—including the *Folk Song Journal*, meant for the eyes of specialists—there has been an almost complete expurgation of erotic detail, resulting in false suppositions and sour recrimination with a rearguard of dear souls defending the notion that all folk song is as sweet as lavender against the onslaught of raw young militants convinced that a rich treasure of pornographic balladry is being kept from us by a folklorists' conspiracy.

Why did the English collectors habitually modify the texts of erotic songs before committing them to print? Sometimes they wanted to protect polite people from being offended by the notions of rougher men and women. Then too, working without support or subsidy, they had to rely on popular publication and concert performance if they were to get even a meagre financial return for their labours in the field. Most important, certainly in Sharp's case, was the need to tread carefully in the presence of the Establishment, if one was going to get folk song accepted officially and returned to the mass of people. Sixty years ago, few men of property and power were ready to believe that the lower class had anything valuable to offer by way of cultural goods. Sharp knew well that if educators were to be persuaded that folk song was worth taking up, they had to be approached with caution, bearing in mind the prevalent sensitivity and hypocrisy about sex matters in particular. So, while as a good folklorist Sharp usually transcribed faithfully into his notebooks whatever came his way, rough stuff or smooth, as a good popularizer he compromised where he had to, however regretfully, feeling that if certain excellent songs were to appear in public at all, they had to be made milder, until in some time of greater tolerance the unabashed originals could be published.

In his preface to *Folksongs from Somerset*, Sharp put the matter as clearly as he could: 'In a few instances the sentiment of the song has been softened, because the conventions of our less delicate and more dishonest time demand such treatment, but indication has been given, and we plead compulsion and not desire, on these alterations.' What alternative had he? In England we have never made the life of folklorists easy.

So prudence finished what prudery began. Between them, they caused a not very extensive body of important songs to remain unpublished, a small number to appear with hopelessly mangled texts, and a rather larger group to be made known in versions less pointed than the original. Let us distinguish, if etymology allows, between the bawdy and the pornographic. Of that famous storehouse of traditional pornography awaiting its 'Open sesame' there is no clear sign, not in the main body of song tradition at least. It is true that on the margin of tradition, in the world of half-grown students and uprooted men-without-women such as soldiers and sailors (and prisoners? we haven't found out), and also among middle-class 'outsiders' like those fops at the fag-end of the seventeenth century who provided the more sniggering items for Playford and Durfey's *Pills to Purge Melancholy*, or the bourgeois bucks of the Crochallan Fencibles drinking club who made such poor company for

Burns when *The Merry Muses* was being assembled, a high proportion of pornographic folklore may be found, with an excess of graphic sexual or scatological detail and a shortage of affection. Much of this is crude, hateful, gruelling to listen to, and terribly different from the erotic folklore of the soil. The latter, with its clean joy and acceptance of the realities of virginity and desire, passion and pregnancy, belongs to a country people living an integrated deeply-communal life, in tune with natural events, with the cycle of the seasons, seed-time and harvest, a people who 'experience cherries as cherries', and for whom all nature is sexualized and the closest relation exists between the fertility of seeds, beasts, and humans. For them, a love affair is not simply established within the couple, nor even between the couple and the community, but extends beyond that to the whole natural environment as an echo, however faint, of an ancient ritualistic way of looking at the world. Nowhere does this intimate consonance with nature show clearer than in the erotic folk songs. Their symbols are of germination and fruitfulness, while those of the pornographic song are generally of lovelessness and sterility. With misplaced sympathy, modern city writers have remarked on the 'disconcerting ease' with which young women in the folk songs become pregnant, forgetting that for balanced rural societies the arrival of children is vital and joyous because among other things it means more hands to help with the work. The notion of trying out a girl before marriage, in order to be sure of her fecundity, was common enough in a society where pregnancy was only unwelcome if the girl was deserted, and not always then. In the old agricultural societies the whole notion of the sacred was the notion of increase; that was the sense of the ceremonies, the rituals, the dances and songs.

Even in the twentieth century, songs have still survived expressing the old idea that all natural phenomena are interdependent, that there is an intimate sympathy between the germination of seeds of wheat and the amorous encounters of men and women. So more than once our great collectors heard "The wanton seed" or "The chiefest grain" sung in Dorset and West Country village pubs, but considered it too crude for publication, though nowadays it seems gentle enough.

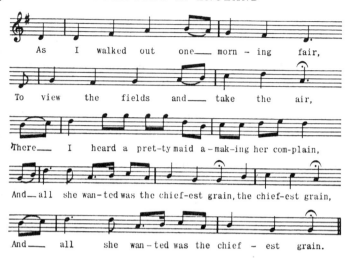

As I walked out one spring morning fair,
To view the fields and take the air,
There I heard a pretty maid making her complain,
And all she wanted was the chiefest grain, the chiefest grain,
And all she wanted was the chiefest grain.
I said to her: 'My pretty maid,
Come tell me what you stand in need.'
'Oh yes, kind sir, you're the man to do my deed,
For to sow my meadow with the wanton seed, the wanton seed,
For to sow my meadow with the wanton seed.'

Then I sowed high and I sowed low,
And under the bush the seed did grow.
It sprang up so accidentally without any weed,
And she always remembered the wanton seed, the wanton seed,
And she always remembered the wanton seed.

'Eros, who was a god for the ancients, is a problem for the moderns. The god was winged, charming, and secondary: the problem is serious, complex and cumbersome.' Thus, Denis de Rougemont in his *Myths of Love*. The problem has indeed been cumbersome for the great folk song collectors, particularly for the cranky squire-parson Sabine Baring-Gould who was sometimes so startled by the casual way in which country singers treated sundry aspects of sex that he presumed they couldn't possibly know what they were singing about. Over and again he took his pruning-knife to the songs he heard, to such effect that the poor things were completely emasculated. "Strawberry Fair", for instance, as he first heard it, was not the mawkish thing of buttercups and daisies that has wearied generations of primary school children for the last half-century. When it was sung to him in a Devon pub, he liked the tune, but said later: 'The text is unsuitable and I've been constrained to re-write it. The words turn on a *double entendre* that is quite lost—fortunately so—on half the old fellows who sing the song.' And what was this daring *double entendre* (whose significance wasn't lost on the parson, by the way)? What was this contaminating folk metaphor against which the folk themselves had to be protected by their vigilant pastor? Nothing less obscene than the old lock-and-key image that has persisted gaily from Roman times at least, through Herrick's "Corinna's going a-maying", up to the 1930s and the days of Eddie Cantor's film hit-song "What a perfect combination". Here is the kind of verse that drove Baring-Gould to re-write the song and make it fit for infants and concert singers:

> Oh, I have a lock that doth lack a key,
>   Ri tol, ri tol, riddle tol de lido,
> I have a lock that doth lack a key,
>   Tol de dee,
> I have a lock sir, she did say,
> And if you got the key then come this way.
>   Ri tol, ri tol, riddle tol de lido.

It is well known that our amatory folk songs are rich in euphemism and metaphor. Plough and pegging-awl, flower garden and cuckoo's nest, may have erotic sense to country singers, likewise the dew on the rose, the bird in the bush, the scythe in the grass. Soil and womb, farm work and sex act are

common, ancient, even sacred identifications. Oedipus 'dared
to sow seed in the sacred furrow where he himself was formed,
and plant there a bloody branch', according to Aeschylus.
A twelfth century hymn praises the Virgin Mary as 'un-
ploughed earth who yet bore fruit' (*terra non arabilis quae
fructum parturiit*). Of Caesar and Cleopatra, Shakespeare says
'He ploughed her, and she cropped'. With that kind of metaphor in which sexuality and husbandry combine, the makers
of folk song are very much at home. Ploughing, sowing, reaping,
mowing are simple vivid symbols in a sizeable number of
verses that set out a woman's body in terms of a landscape.
The well-known song that country singers usually call "The
Mower" (though it has sundry other titles on at least half a
dozen broadsides) has in its best versions a moral grain, a
didactic quality if you like, treating delicately of a problem
seldom aired in 'educated' poetry—or in folk song either, for
the matter of that. The maiden invites and her kind offer is
accepted but then, when it comes to it, she has her difficulties.
The young man deals with the situation resolutely, with understanding and good humour and we leave them ready to
bravely try again, without any sense of blame, guilt or in-
adequacy; a lesson to us all, not merely to simple country
lovers. As usual, the broadside versions of this song quite fail
to match the oral sets.

As— I   was   a - walk ing on—the four-teenth of___ Ju-ly
I__ met a maid and I asked her__ age, and she gave me this re-ply:
I have a__ lit-tle mea – dow I've__ keeped for you___ in store,
And it's on-ly due I should tell you true, he ne-ver was mowed be-fore.

As I was a-walking on the fourteenth of July,
I met a maid and I asked her age, she made me this reply:
'I have a little meadow I've keeped for you in store,
And it's only due I should tell you true, he never was mowed
    before.'

She said: 'My handsome young man, if a mower that you be,
I'll give you good employment if you'll come along with me.'
So it was my good employment to wander up and down
With my taring scythe all to contrive to mow her meadow
    down.

With my courage undaunted, I stepped out on the ground.
With my taring scythe I then did strive to mow her meadow
    down.
I mowed from nine to dinner-time, it was far beyond my skill,
I was 'bliged to yield and quit the field, and her grass was
    growing still.

Oh, the more she kissed and did protest, this fair maid being
    young,
Her little eyes did glitter like to the rising sun.
She says: 'I'll strive to sharp your scythe, so set it in my hand,
And then perhaps you will return again to mow my meadow-
    land.'

This theme too has its foreign cousins, among them the
Spanish ballad of "Doña Inés y el segador", reported from
oral tradition in the Santander region, in which the bastard
daughter of the emperor of Rome, a lady much courted by
dukes and earls, invites a young reaper with an impressive
sickle to come and cut her barley and rye.

Among a profusion of these women-as-landscape songs, a
handsome specimen is "The furze field" heard by Gardiner in
Hampshire in 1907. Here the sexual allusions are jubilantly
made in terms of sport: the angler at the fish-pond, the ferret
in the burrow, and at the outset the sporting gun. To identify

sex relations with ordnance displays is an old joke. Cupid with his bow and arrows is but the forerunner of those sailors in so many ballads of Jack ashore who fire their cannon and hole their girl amidships and fall asleep with an empty shot-locker, or of those sportsmen rambling in the shrubbery, shotgun at the ready, confident of success, as in the fine song with the punning title of "The bonny black hare":

> The birds they were singing on the bushes and trees,
> And the song that they sang was: 'Oh, she's easy to please.'
> And I felt her heart quiver and I knew what I'd done.
> Says I: 'Have you had enough of my old sporting gun?'

> The answer she gave me, oh, her answer was: 'Nay,
> It's not often, young sportsman, that you come this way,
> But if your powder is good and your bullets are fair,
> Why don't you keep firing at the bonny black hare?'

It has been remarked that "The furze field" is in the form of an invitation offered by a woman, but that is no evidence that the song was made by one, or necessarily meant to be sung by females. The sporting interest is masculine and the song is of the kind that generally pleases men more than women. In many parts of the world one finds erotic folk songs that are ostensibly from the woman's viewpoint without really being so. To men, singers and listeners, such songs are all the funnier for being put that way, and rather reassuring too.

> I have got a furze field, my own dearest jewel,
> Where all my fine pheasants do fly,
> And if you comes a-shooting when shooting's in season,
> I'll tell you, love, how to proceed.
> You bring your dog with you, your gun in your hand,
> All loaded and primed all at your command,
> When the pheasants take fright, you must take sight,
> You shoot the next moment, you're sure to be right.

I have got a fishpond, my own dearest jewel,
Where all my fine fishes do play,
And if you comes a-fishing when fishing's in season,
I'll tell you, love, how to proceed.
You bring your nets with you, your rod in your hand,
Your hooks and your angles all at your command.
When you throws in, all the fishes will play.
It's down to the bottom and that's the right way.

I have goi   a   furze field, my   own dear – est jew – el,
And if   you comes a shoot – ing when shoot-ing's in sea – son,

Where   all   my   fine   phea – sants___   do   fly,
I'll   tell   you,   love,   how   to ___   pro – ceed.

You bring your dog   with you, your   gun   in   your hand,

All   load – ed   and primed___   all   at   your   com – mand,

When the phea – sants   take fright,   you___ must take___ sight.

You   shoot   the   next   mo – ment, you're sure   to   be right.

I have got a warren, my own dearest jewel,
Where all my fine rabbits do play,
And if you comes a-ferreting when ferreting's in season,
I'll tell you, love, how to proceed.
You bring your dog with you, your ferret in your hand,
Your spade and your nets all at your command.
And the ferret will bolt and the rabbits will play,
For it's down to the bottom and that's the right way.

I have got a park, my own dearest jewel,
Where all my fine deers I do keep,
And if you comes a-hunting, when hunting's in season,
I'll tell you, love, how to proceed.
You bring your dog with you, your nag in your hand,
All saddled and bridled at your command,
When the deers they will prowl and the dogs they will bawl,
It's 'Gee up, then Dobbin', and back they will fall.

Beside more serious songs of sexual encounter—usually in the open-air—such as "The wanton seed", "The mower", the familiar and often singularly sensual "Bird in the bush", and lighter brisker pieces of the kind of "The stone-cutter (bricklayer) boy", "With my cattle-smock (navvy boots, pit boots) on", and the ubiquitous and seemingly indestructible "Rosemary Lane", there are also a number of country songs of sexual humour of a kind that seems crude enough to us, yet has remained an inexhaustible source of laughter for common people throughout the centuries and over a vast area of the globe. "The crab-fish" is one of these, still often to be heard in barrack-rooms, on building sites and in city as well as country pubs (the last version I heard was from a film technician on location with John Huston); it has been flying around Europe, from Italy to Iceland, for the last five hundred years or more. Another old and widely-travelled piece of erotic whimsy, not so well-known but far commoner than one might guess from its rare appearance in print is "The trooper's horse". A version appeared early in the eighteenth century in *Pills to Purge Melancholy*, and in 1907 George B. Gardiner recorded a set from a Basingstoke woman, Mrs. Goodyear (this version was published in 1965 in *Marrowbones: English Folk Songs from the Hammond and Gardiner Mss.*) Another version, more vivid, concerning a sailor, circulates in north-east Scotland. The blunt humour has a quality familiar from medieval jest-books drawn from international sources and perhaps it is no surprise to find the same joke reported from as far away as Russia, where the great nineteenth century folk-tale collector Afanasyev found at least two story-versions (one more or less identical with ours but concerning a coachman and his mistress, the other, slightly removed, in which the trickster exploits the euphemisms of prison and dungeon, applied by the priest to the sexual parts of his wife and daughter, to win a wager from the priest as well as to have his will of the two women). The Russian versions are printed in the first volume of *Kryptadia* (Paris, 1883). The following set was obtained near Leiston, Suffolk in 1941.

It's a landlady's daughter and her name was Nelly,
    And it's green o green the leaves do grow,
And she took sick with a fever in her belly,
    And it's ha, young man, do you tell me so?

It was a bold trooper rode up to the inn,
He's perishing cold and wet to the skin.

The landlady put 'em in the bed together,
To see if the one couldn't cure the tother.

'Oh, what's this here, and what's it called?'
'It's my fine nag and they call him Bald.'

'Oh, what's this here and what's it called?'
'It's my little well where you can water old Bald.'

'Suppose my nag he should slip in?'
'Just catch on the grass that grows around the brim.'

'How can you tell when he's had his fill?'
'He'll hang down his head, turn away from the well.'

'How can you tell when your nag wants more?'
  And it's green o green the leaves do grow.
'He'll rear up his head and go pawing round the door.'
  And it's ha, young man, do you tell me so?

We know very little about the ceremonial music formerly attached to peasant weddings in England. A few traces survive, or so we think, in songs accompanying children's games (always the last resort of the rituals of dead gods). But it is precisely the kind of erotic songs concerning us at the moment, some delicately allusive, others as obvious as a slap from a bull-pizzle, that are sung today at special moments of country weddings in those parts of Europe where folk ceremonial remains most in evidence—in Hungary, for instance. Kodály has remarked that on such occasions licentiousness is not merely tolerated but expected; some sort of occult meaning becomes attached to words and gestures not ordinarily used in public life. He reminds us that in parts of China, a bride may sit for hours in the bridal chamber while the groom's friends, whose behaviour towards women is normally bound by strict convention, drift through the room, telling dirty stories, singing bawdy songs, and behaving in a generally ribald manner. And when the men have done, it would be the turn of the women to come and sing their lessons—cautionary or instructive, serious or comic, lamentation or paean—on the physical aspects of marriage.[36] From Byzantium at the end of the fourth century, similar customs were reported by St. John Chrysostom, who described how the wedding guests 'sing of lewdness, adultery, forbidden love-making, licentious coition and other shameful things on that day. After so much baseness, having got drunk, they escort the bride in a festive procession reciting obscene verses to her in public.' Sober Henry Bullinger, writing at the beginning of the sixteenth century, found English wedding customs past praying for. 'After supper . . . though the young persons, being weary of the babbling noise and inconvenience, come once toward their rest, yet can they have no quietness. For a man shall find unmannerly and restless people that will first go to their chamber door and there sing vicious and naughty ballads that the devil may have his triumph now to the uttermost.' The ritual sense of the custom may have been declining into horseplay by Henry VII's time; in any case the good burgess Bullinger would never have admitted any other motive than diabolical to such a pagan observance. We do not know what vicious and naughty ballads he heard, but we may well imagine songs like "The husband with no courage" being used for such a wryly humorous ceremonial purpose. Wherever it has turned up (it is sparsely scattered from South-west England to North-east Scotland) it has been sung in fun; but as often happens with songs of sexual content, behind the joke there is a problem and a fear. Again, it is interesting to speculate whether the song was first made by a man or a woman.

As I walked out one summer's day
To view the fields, and the leaves were springing,
I heard two birds upon a bough,
Changing their note and sweetly singing;
And all of their conversation was:
'My husband's got no courage in him.
O dear O, O dear O.
My husband's got no courage in him.
O dear O.

Seven long years I've made his bed,
And six of 'em I've lain agin him,
And this morn I arose with my maidenhead.
That shows he's got no courage in him.
O dear O, O dear O,
That shows he's got no courage in him.
O dear O.

All sorts of meat I do preserve,
All sorts of drink that's fitten for him.
Both oyster-pies and rhubarb too,
But that don't put no courage in him.
O dear O, O dear O.
That don't put no courage in him.
O dear O.

Come all pretty maids where'er you be,
Don't marry a man before you try him,
Or else you'll sing a song like me:
My husband's got no courage in him,
O dear O, O dear O.
My husband's got no courage in him.
O dear O.

I wish to the Lord that he was dead,
And in his grave I'd quickly lay him,
And I would try another one
That got a bit of courage in him.
O dear O, O dear O,
That got a bit of courage in him,
O dear O.'

In folklore, the sexualization of the world does not stop
at the mystique of nature and agriculture, it extends to the
kingdom of things and tools made by man, and the trades
associated with those tools. Mircea Eliade is prominent among
those who have illustrated the close relationship between

mining, metal-working, sex and obstetrics in the mythology of
the Iron Age. Metals were believed to grow in the womb of the
earth; miners were those who penetrated the cavern-matrix,
and smelters and smiths were obstetricians assisting the birth
of the metals. Sexual taboos and rites still surround the miner's
calling and the blacksmith's trade in many parts of the world,
and their tools—picks, hammers, anvils and such—are rendered
'living' by being sexualized, their functions considered parallel
to the human generative act.[37] So in Africa, among the
Bakitara, a new anvil is treated like a bride, and the men
bringing it to the forge sing as though in a wedding procession. Among the BaNyankole, the smith has sexual intercourse
with his wife as soon as he gets a new hammer, in order that it
will work well. Not dissimilar beliefs extend to pottery, weaving,
and other activities of the kind.

By a familiar process of folklore, what was solemnly ritualistic
in origin lives on to become a comedy as the magic and sanctity
leaks out of it. So we have a profusion of humorous songs whose
erotic metaphors concern the miller's grinding stones, the
weaver's shuttle (and its to-and-fro as he works at the loom
the young woman carries beneath her apron), the blocking-iron
of the priapic jolly tinker ('She brought me through the kitchen
and she brought me through the hall, And the servants cried:
The devil, are you going to block us all?'), or the cobbler's
awl, as in this song recorded in 1954 from Harry Cox, the
Norfolk singer, by Peter Kennedy:[38]

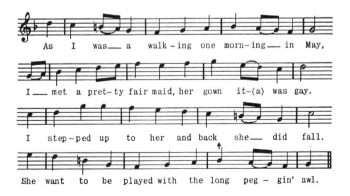

As I was— a walk-ing one morn-ing— in May,
I— met a pret-ty fair maid, her gown it-(a) was gay.
I step-ped up to her and back she— did fall.
She want to be played with the long peg-gin' awl.

As I was a-walking one morning in May,
I met a pretty fair maid, her gown it was gay.
I stepped up to her and back she did fall.
She want to be played with the long peggin' awl.

I said: 'Pretty fair maid, will you travel with me,
Unto foreign countries, strange things for to see?
And I will protect you whate'er may befall,
And follow your love with his long peggin' awl?'

Then home to her parents she then went straightway,
And unto her mother these words she did say:
'I'll follow my true love whate'er may befall.
I'll follow my love with his long peggin' awl.'

'O daughter, O daughter, how can you say so?
For young men are false as you very well know.
They'll tell you fine things and the devil and all,
And leave you big-bellied with the long peggin' awl.'

'O mother, O mother, now do not say so.
Before you were sixteen, you very well know,
There was father and mother and baby and all.
You followed my dad for his long peggin' awl.'

If we have lingered rather long on the topic of amatory songs, it is because these interesting pieces, often looking back to sacred intuitions of primitive man, have been unfairly neglected or deliberately suppressed in the past, and have only recently begun to make their public appearance in print (or reappearance, for a good number are to be found on broadsides). Commenting on the exclusion of sex from the great folklore collections in Britain, the liveliest and most learned of our neophallic crusaders, Gershon Legman, remarks that while ballad compilations such as Child's offer us a welter of killings, drownings, stabbings, poisonings, beheadings, and any amount of hatred, cruelty, intolerance and treachery, the simple normality of sex has to be apologized for or silently omitted, and he suggests that it is 'time to stop begging for fair play for sexual intercourse as though it were no worse, really, than murder'.

Before we quit the subject, here are two further pieces, hitherto unpublished. They are from the papers of a fine and unjustly neglected pioneer collector of the songs of the English north-east, a region rich in peculiar folklore. John Bell was born in Newcastle in 1783 and already in his boyhood he was a passionate collector of curiosities. In 1803 he opened a secondhand bookshop on the Newcastle Quay but he could never bear to sell any item of interest that came his way, and his home was a magpie's nest crammed with curios, coins, archaeological oddities, and great stacks of broadsides, hand-bills and manuscripts relating to ceremonials, prizefights, crimes, scandals, disasters. His passion extended to song gathering, and his *Rhymes of the Northern Bards*, published in a small edition in 1812, was a sizeable collection (334 pages) of Northumbrian songs and local poems. For several years after its publication he continued to collect songs, obtaining copies from friends or notating them himself (his hefty tune-book is a painstakingly written affair, very clear to read, with an elegant hand-lettered title-page drawn with rather boyish care and fantasy). To Bell's collecting we owe some of the best-known north-eastern pieces such as "Buy broom buzzems", "Bonny at morn", and "A U hinny burd". Frank Rutherford, the leading student of the region's folk song, contends that Bell's work was 'the main source for at any rate the songs as distinct from the ballads and pipe tunes' in the *Northumbrian Minstrelsy*, though the editors of that famous compilation gave him precious little credit.

A considerable number of songs not published either in the *Rhymes* or the *Minstrelsy* remain among Bell's papers in New-castle (texts in King's College Library, tunes in the library of the Society of Antiquaries). One of these, written on paper watermarked 1811, comprises a series of erotic metaphors threaded together like a set of lyrical floaters to make an aromatic, in places pungent, garland very characteristic of its time and locality. It is titled "The pitman's lovesong" though there is little enough to connect it with colliers.

Aw wish my lover she was a cherry
Growing upon yon cherry tree,
And aw mysel a bonny blackbird;
How aw would peck that cherry cherree.

Aw wish my lover she was a red rose
Growing upon yon garden wa',
And aw mysel was a butterflee;
O on that red rosie aw wad fa'.

Aw wish my lover she was a fish
Sooming doon in the saut sea,
And aw mysel was a fisher lad;
O aw wad catch her reet cunningly.

Aw wish my love was in a kist
And aw mysel to carry the key.
Then aw wad gan tin her when aw had list,
And bear my hinny good company.

Aw wish my love she was a grey ewe
Grazing by yonder river side,
And aw mysel a bonny black tup;
O on that ewie how aw wad ride.

O she's bonny, she's wondrous canny,
O she's well far'd for to see,
For the mair aw think on my love's on upon her,
And under her apron fain wad aw be.

Aw wish my lover she was a bee skep,
And aw mysel a bumble bee,
That aw might be a lodger within her;
She's sweeter than honey or honeycombe tea.

Aw wish my lover was a ripe turd,
Smoking doon in yon dyke side,
And aw mysel was a shitten flee;
Aw'd sook her all up before she was dried.

> O my hinny, my bonny hinny,
> O my hinny, my bonny hinnee;
> The mair aw think on her, my heart's set upon her.
> She's fairer than ever she used to be.

Another song among Bell's papers is the earliest-known copy of the familiar and controversial "Foggy dew", about whose title-image ink has flowed and typewriter ribbons grown faint. What is the mysterious 'foggy dew' that so frightens the girl in the song? 'Foggy', we're told, is Middle English for 'coarse rank marsh grass' and so may stand for maidenhead (why?); 'dew' is a familiar folk symbol for chastity (and many things besides); there is a suggestion that the expression is merely a clumsy Anglicization of Irish 'orocedhu' meaning 'darkness, black night', and Robert Graves, always ready to make a bold dash into folklore matters, takes this Irish notion further with the suggestion that the blackness relates to the Black Death which may have been raging at the time of the song's inception (though so far we've no grounds for dating it before the closing years of the eighteenth century) and to the black dress of nuns. So there we are: the girl is not terrified of her coarse rank virginity; she is hammering on a convent door begging the nuns to save her from the plague. The version that Bell received early in the nineteenth century offers another, less spectacular but more convincing explanation. He calls it "The bogle bo", meaning 'ghost', of course:

> When I was in my prenticeship and learning of my trade,
> I courted my master's daughter, which made my heart right glad.
> I courted her both summer days and winter nights also,
> But I could never her favour win till I hired the Bogle bo.

> Day being gone and night coming on, my neighbour he took a sheet,
> And straight into her room he went just like a wandering spirit.
> She running up and down, not knowing where to go,
> But right into my bed she went for fear of the Bogle bo.

So my true love and me both fell fast asleep,
But ere the morn at fair daylight, sore sore did she weep.
Sore sore did she weep, sore sore did she mourn,
But ere she rose and put on her clothes, the Bogle bo was gone.

You've done the thing to me last night, the thing you cannot
  shun
You've taen from me my maidenhead, and I am quite undone.
You've taen from me my maidenhead, and brought my body
  low,
But, kind sir, if you'll marry me, I will be your jo.

Now he's married her and taen her hame and it was but his
  part.
She's proved to him a loving wife and joy of all his heart.
He never told her of the joke, nor ne'er intends to do,
But aye when his wife smiles on him, he minds the Bogle bo.

Even "The foggy dew/Bogle bo/Bugaboo", mild as it is, had
to wait long before any set of it was printed in full, apart from
the broadsides. Where love songs were concerned, the collectors
and publishers gave all their preference to the kind of sentimental idylls whose creation flourished particularly towards
the middle years of the eighteenth century.

The time has been pictured as a Golden Age of the English
village, though the Hammonds remind us that 'no reader of
Fielding or Richardson would fall into this mistake, or persuade
himself that this community was a society of free and equal
men, in which tyranny was impossible. The old village was
under the shadow of the squire and the parson, and there were
many ways in which these powers controlled and hampered
its pleasures and habits.'[39] Golden or not for the labourers, for
men of substance it was an age of great complacency. What
Defoe called the Middle Station of life had every reason for
self-satisfaction. If the money for investment was to hand, fortunes were for the making. There were war contracts, the
colonial empire was expanding, India lay open to plunder,
foreign trade was increasing, the landlord class had more
capital and credit to devote to agricultural improvement and

was impatient to put into operation the large ideas of the new type of farm-improvers, muddy-booted patricians such as 'Turnip' Townsend, and, later, Coke of Holkham. To them it seemed that prosperity had come to stay, that all was stable and assured after the disarray of the previous century. To match this stability and balance, the fashionable arts were classical, their emotion precisely ordered. Merchant and squire sat plump with their long churchwarden pipes, surveying the life of the common people with amusement and indulgence. It was a great time for the sentimental travesty of lower-class life, with poems and paintings of idealized orange-girls, romantic cottage scenes, gentle shepherds and coy shepherdesses named Colin and Phillida, lolling on Flora's carpet under a sun called Phoebus.

Songs reflecting this mild idyllic view entered the lower class repertory either from the stage, as with the famous "Sheepshearing Song" ('Here's the rose-bud in June'),* or through town-made broadsides, or were created by the villagers themselves by simple contagion from the prevailing fashion. So at this period a large number of pieces of conventional charm became current among folk singers, of the kind that were later to dominate the popular collections prepared for print by Baring-Gould, Lucy Broadwood, Sharp, Kidson and others because the tunes are sweet and the words gentle or quaint and there is no darkness or offence in them. Such compositions as the ubiquitous "Pleasant and delightful", the even more famous but far less common "Searching for lambs", and "The banks of the sweet primroses", are good specimens of this kind. One less-known than it deserves to be, although Vaughan Williams made a fine choral setting of part of it, is "Lovely on the water", with a glorious placid tune and words as prettily stylized as the woodcuts of rustic or nautical scenes that decorated the idyllic broadsides; but in the concluding verses a shade of sterner reality comes over the sunny scene. The Norfolk singer who gave the song to Vaughan Williams could not recall all the words, but the sense is clear. In fuller form, the text contained the familiar motif of the girl volunteering to sail with her sweetheart and being dis-

* Sung in *Country Lasses, or the Custom of the Manor* (1715), music by J. Barrett.

suaded (women did sometimes sail in the battleships, as late as
Nelson's time; one, from Leith, gave birth to a child in the
'tween-decks at the height of the battle of the Nile).

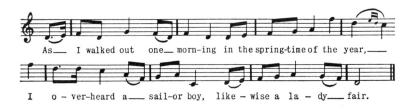

As— I walked out   one— morn-ing in the spring-time of the year,—
I   o - ver-heard a— sail-or boy,   like - wise a   la - dy— fair.

As I walked out one morning in the springtime of the year,
I overheard a sailor boy, likewise a lady fair.

They sang a song together, made the valleys for to ring,
While the birds on spray and the meadows gay that proclaimed
    the lovely spring.

Said Henry to Nancy: 'We soon must sail away,
For it's lovely on the water to hear the music play'. . . .

Poor Nancy fell and fainted, and soon they brought her to.
They both shook hands together, and took a fond adieu. . . .

For Tower Hill is crowded with mothers weeping sore,
For their sons are gone to face the foe where the cannon loudly
    roar.

Perhaps the most famous piece of the idyllic kind is the often-
printed "Lark in the morning", with its pretty evocation of a
spring morning and its affirmation that 'there's no life like the
ploughboy's all in the month of May' (and to demonstrate this,
the oral and broadside versions continue the eclogue rather
more coarsely than one would gather from the truncated sets
generally published in the folk song books). But of course, the
romantic idealization of labouring life in the countryside was
by no means the only theme of eighteenth century folk song.

There was another side to the picture, a side shown better by Hogarth than by Morland, the side of Gin Lane, the *Newgate Calender*, the *Beggar's Opera*. Highwaymen cantered on the heaths, pirates scudded over the high seas, dashing heroes in folk legend if shabby enough in life. 'Streetpacing harlots', pickpockets, coiners, forgers, swarmed in the back-alleys of towns, sheep-stealers roamed the moonlit downs, thimble-riggers and other tricksters bawled their patter on the fairgrounds, while smugglers, whole communities of them, united in the coastal villages ready to fight bloody battles with authority if need be. Throughout the century the law grew more repressive till, as Goldsmith remarked, the paltriest possessions of the men of property were hung about with gibbets. Parliament was energetic in increasing the number of capital offences for crimes against property till finally it stood at well over two hundred—sixty-three of them added in the half-century between 1760 and 1810. Death might be prescribed for the most trivial offences. A man could be hanged for sheep-stealing, for shoplifting over five shillingsworth, for picking a pocket even if the booty were only a handkerchief. In *The Making of the English Working Class*, E. P. Thompson says: 'The procession to Tyburn . . . was a central ceremonial of eighteenth century London. The condemned in carts—the men in gaudy attire, the women in white with baskets of flowers and oranges which they threw to the crowds—the ballad-singers and hawkers, with their 'last speeches' (which were sold even before the victims had given the sign of the dropped handkerchief to the hangman to do his work): all the symbolism of "Tyburn Fair" was the ritual at the heart of London's popular culture.'

About the middle of the century, the novelist Henry Fielding and his blind half-brother John, both prominent London magistrates, established an office in Bow Street for their 'runners', the predecessors of the Metropolitan Police. "The flash lad", a song of the time has led a brisk raffish life ever since, turning up repeatedly in the present century in various parts of England, Ireland (it was known there before 1840, when Bunting published a set of it) and the United States. Among many good versions is this one, whose tune was recorded in Somerset by Cecil Sharp:

When I was eighteen I took a wife,
I loved her dearly as I loved my life;
And to maintain her both fine and gay,
I went a-robbing, I went a-robbing on the king's highway.

I never robbed any poor man yet,
And I was never in a tradesman's debt,
But I robbed the lords and the ladies gay
And carried home the gold, and carried home the gold to my
    love straightway.

To Cupid's Garden* I did away,
To Cupid's Garden for to see the play.
Lord Fielding's gang there did me pursue,
And I was taken, and I was taken by the cursed crew.

My father cried: 'O darling son!'
My wife she wept and cried: 'I am undone!'
My mother tore her white locks and cried:
'Oh, in his cradle, oh, in his cradle he should have died!'

---

* Cupid's Garden: a corruption of 'Cuper's Gardens', a pleasure-ground on
the south side of the Thames, opposite Somerset House. It was finally closed in
1753, 'in consequence of the dissoluteness of its visitors', according to some
reports.

And when I am dead and go to my grave,
A flashy funeral let me have.
Let none but bold robbers follow me.
Give them good broad swords, give them good broad swords
    and liberty.

May six pretty maidens bear up my pall,
And let them have white gloves and ribbons all,
That they may say when they speak the truth:
'There goes a wild youth, there goes a wild and a wicked youth!'

We know very little about the psychology of folk singers and
can only speculate why some features of melody remain constant and satisfactory to them while others are subject to perpetual alteration, why some verses of a ballad have an insecure
hold on the singers' memory while others, on the face of it less
vital to the narrative, are utterly memorable and turn up in
more or less identical shape in version after version, nor why
certain songs go on gaily blossoming in the repertory when
almost all else has withered. Nearly every surviving traditional
singer in England with anything like a decent repertory knows
a version of "The flash lad", and it is not easy to account for
the extreme vigour the song still shows after two hundred years
or so of life. Two centuries is no great time in the life of a folk
song, it is true, but this particular piece, picturesque as it is,
is hardly of the kind whose roots lie very deep in the psyche,
one would think. Yet not only does it survive well, but it has
powerful relatives too. The air quoted above is not the only
one to which the song is sung, (sometimes it goes to that
favourite tune for songs of disaffection that carries such texts
as "The croppy boy" and "McCafferty"), but thousands of
folk song club enthusiasts will recognize it, with its jimp
doubletting of the first half of the final phrase, as a variant of a
familiar tune to "Sovay, the female highwayman", another
eighteenth century piece, that has come back to life in our
towns in recent years. Moreover, the text of "The flash lad"
recalls a still hardier song, for the 'Tyburn Fair' aspect with
its ordering of a ceremonial funeral connects the dashing
young blade to the soldier dying of wounds received not on

the battlefield but in Venus's train, who demands to go down with more than military honours, as described in the ballad called "The unfortunate rake":

> Get six of my comrades to carry my coffin,
> Six girls of the city to bear me on,
> And each of them carry a bunch of red roses,
> So they don't smell me as they walk along.
>
> And muffle your drums, and play your fifes lowly,
> Play the dead march as you carry me on,
> And fire your bright muskets all over my coffin,
> Saying: 'There goes an unfortunate rake to his doom!'

The song was heard in Dublin in the 1790s, and a version of the tune was printed in London in 1808, but the first full text of it appeared only on a Such broadside of the 1860s, though the piece was probably a good century old by then (oddly enough, a broadside of it had appeared in Czech before it emerged in print on the London streets). As is known, this favourite homily gave rise to a number of widely accepted songs. "The bad girl's lament" was re-created from it, and in America "The cowboy's lament" (or "The streets of Laredo") and "The wild lumberjack" were made on its model, military funeral and all. Finally its protean hero reappears as a Negro gambler demanding his colourful obsequies in the blues-ballad of "Saint James Infirmary". Usually under some such title as "The whores of the city", the song of the rakish soldier has survived in unbroken tradition in both countryside and town in Britain, and it emerged as the unofficial 'regimental anthem' of the Royal Marine Commandos during the Second World War. It would be hard to find a ballad more supple in its adaptation to social and geographic change.

Ever since the Middle Ages the sympathy of the poor has inclined towards the outlaw, the man living in a state of perpetual war with authority. From one end of Europe to the other, in the popular imagination the forest bandit, haiduk, klepht, bandolero is a symbol of freedom, a righter of wrongs, a friend to the poor. In America the notion has even been extended to such louts as Jesse James and Pretty Boy Floyd, and in Australia to Ben Hall and the half-baked hothead Ned Kelly. However, both in their ballads and in their mythological stature, these heroes mark the successive decline, the falling graph that runs from the song-cycles of the organized bands of upland partisans and medieval forest outlaws, through the broadside ballads of individual highwaymen, to the short often barely coherent songs of poor nineteenth century poachers. Perhaps it was only because, in the minds of humble people on foot, the highwayman, bad man and bushranger cut a dashing figure on horseback that some of the attributes of folk hero ever clung to them. The burglar, pickpocket, footpad were never in the same class. So in the engaging song called "The saucy bold robber" it is the gallant sailor not the giant thief who is the admired one. The song does not seem to have appeared on any broadside. Its tune is our Example on p. 46. The moral is Brechtian: It is folly to rob the poor when one can so much more profitably plunder the rich.

Oh come all you good people that go out a-tippling,
Pray pay attention and listen to my song.
I'll sing you a ditty of a jolly bold robber,
Stood seven foot high, in proportion quite strong.

He robbed lawyer Morgan and old Lady Dawkins;
Five hundred bright guineas from each one of them;
And as he was a-strolling he met a young sailor,
And bold as a lion he slewed up to him.

'Hand over your money, you saucy young sailor.
You've plenty of bulk in your pocket, I know.'
'Oh aye', says the sailor, 'I have got a bit of money,
And I'm damned if I see why I should give it to you.

I've just left my ship, give the press-gang the slip,
And I'm bound up to London my sweetheart to see.
I've four bright sovereigns for to pay our sweet lodgings,
So I pray you, jolly robber, please leave it to me.'

Then the robber caught hold of that gallant young sailor;
With a blow like a pole-axe felled him to the ground.
'Oh aye,' says the sailor, 'You have struck me quite heavy,
And now I'll endeavour to repay you in kind.'

It was then, boys, they stripped and like tigers they skipped,
And they fought blow for blow like to soldiers in the field.
At the ninety-seventh meeting it was the completing,
For this gallant young sailor the bold robber he killed.

Then the sailor looked down on the bloodstained bold robber.
'I hope you'll forgive me, old fellow,' says he,
'But if I had just lifted a thousand bright guineas,
I'm damned if I'd have stopped a poor sailor like me.'

The tatters of some bygone epic hero still seem to flutter
round the shoulders of that plucky sailor. By his good nature
and boldness he is first cousin to opportunistic Jack in "Do me
ama", the tarry sailor who made his way into the fine lady's
bed in place of the squire, and had some success there (an
amiable dream of class revenge). Such were the folk heroes of
the period; of champions in direct and open opposition to the
master there is little trace in the earlier part of the eighteenth
century, perhaps because though the customary definitions of
men's relations to the agrarian means of production were
already being eroded, the process had not reached any dramatic
proportions.

If the romantic idealization of labouring life amused the
gentry, and if at least the more paternalistic among eighteenth
century landowners took a kindly and indulgent view of their
peasants while they were properly humble, amiability and
lenience soon gave way to displeasure and severity if the farm-
hand was seen to give himself airs above his station. For folk
songs made in the period shortly before the great enclosures no
theme is more characteristic than of the ploughboy who falls
in love with the rich man's daughter and is pressed to sea by
the girl's indignant father, or is falsely accused of robbery and
sentenced to transportation. Sometimes the parents' determination costs the youngster his life, and the broken-hearted girl

dies too, by her own hand as like as not. In these ballads—and
there are upwards of fifty of them on the same topic—family
opposition is invariably based on social considerations; the
poor boy is a sterling character, the rich parent curmudgeonly;
all sympathy is with the lovers. Romantic as it is, this pre-
sentation of the opposition between the classes is one of the
great themes of democratic tendency among our latterday
rural lyrics. Repeatedly we find songs whose narrative begins
like "The bonny labouring boy":

Young Johnny was my true love's name as you may plainly see.
My parents did employ him their labouring boy to be,
To harrow, reap, and sow the seed, and plough my father's land,
And soon I fell in love with him as you may understand.

My father stepped up one morning and he seized me by the
    hand.
He swore he'd send young Johnny unto some foreign land.
He locked me in my bedroom, my comfort to annoy,
And to keep me there to weep and mourn for my bonny
    labouring boy.

With the very first wave of "The rolling main" we are
plunged waist-deep in tragedy:

Come all ye bold wanderers that range round the globe,
I'll tell you of young Henry, young Henry my love.
I will tell you of young Henry, a ploughboy was he,
When my cruel father pressed my Henry to sea.
    He was lost on the rolling main.

Likewise in "*The Nightingale*", the farm-boy woos the
gentleman's daughter but, conventionally enough, her father
will have none of it:

My cruel father made it so
That he from me was forced to go;
The press-gang sent, which did not fail
To press my love on the *Nightingale*.

The *Nightingale* founders and the boy's dripping ghost appears
to the girl. The song ends in double tragedy, as does "The Isle
of Cloy", where, in similar circumstances the serving-boy is
shanghaied aboard the *Tiger* man-o'-war and is soon killed in
battle. Then, we are told:

> The very same night this young man was slain,
> Close to her father's bedside she came,
> All weeping sore for her own true love,
> She hanged herself from the beam above.
>
> The squire's servants they stood around.
> They viewed this lady and cut her down,
> And in her bosom a note unsealed:
> A girl of sorrow it revealed.
>
> 'My father is one of the best of men,
> But he's drove me to this disgraceful end,
> And of this vain world pray a warning take:
> I died a maid for my true love's sake.'

With its melodrama and its passivity, "The Isle of Cloy"
bears the inky thumbprint of broadside writing. Perhaps more
characteristic of true folk creation are those mettlesome
versions of the theme in which the plucky girl refuses to accept
her parents' hardhearted behaviour and sets off to sea in search
of her love, like the daughter of the 'old London merchant of
honour and fame', who turned down three squire courtiers in
favour of her lower-class sweetheart:

> They walked and they talked both night and day.
> They walked and they talked and fixed the wedding day.
> The old man overheard it and these words he did say:
> 'He shan't marry my daughter. I'll press him to sea.'
>
> As they was a-walking toward the church door,
> The press-gang overtook him and from her side tore.
> They pressed this young fellow all on the salt sea.
> Instead of getting married, he sorrowed for she.

She cut off her hair and she altered her clothes,
And to the press-master she immediately goes,
Saying: 'Press-master, press-master, do you want a man?
I'm willing and ready to do all I can.'

Then she shipped on board of the very same ship.
Her true-love for a mess-mate so quickly she take.
True-love for a mess-mate you quickly shall hear;
She sleep by his side for full half of a year.

The young man tells his 'messmate' how his sweetheart's cruel father had him pressed to sea and how, if he cannot have his love, he will 'soon end his days in a watery grave'. Then follows an engaging detail:

She says: 'Now, kind sir, I can act up to my pen.
An astrologer's part I can take just now and then.
Come tell me your age and I'll cast up your lot,
To see whether you be free to have her or not.'

He told her his age and the day of his birth.
She showed him his fortune, a great deal of worth.
She showed him his fortune, she said: 'This is your lot.
And I am your true love though you knew it not.'

The detail of the girl spending half a year in a ship without her sex being discovered seems far-fetched, yet in the seventeenth and eighteenth century were several cases of women joining either army or navy and serving for a period dressed in men's clothes. The renowned Mrs. Christian Welsh enlisted twice (the first time in search of her kidnapped husband, the second because she was fascinated by army life). She fought with distinction in Marlborough's army, was wounded at Ramillies, and her imposture was discovered as a consequence. She ended her days as a Chelsea pensioner and was accorded a military funeral. Hannah Snell was another bold Amazon, who served for years as a marine in the East Indies, and being

wounded she extracted the bullet from herself to avoid being
unmasked as a woman. She became a Chelsea outpensioner,
took a public house in Wapping and wore trousers for the rest
of her puff. Even these shining heroines of the folk are somewhat eclipsed by the dashing Mary Read, who had served as
both soldier and sailor before she became notorious as the
Female Pirate. The theme of the female warrior constantly
occurs in seventeenth and eighteenth century song, not only
because it was sometimes played in real life, but because the
dream that one of their companions might be a girl dressed
as a boy is an inevitable fantasy for lonely men in barrack bunk
or fo'c'sle hammock. Among many sprightly songs such as
"Jack Munro" and "The handsome cabin boy", a piece of the
period, "The female drummer boy", comes to mind:

In pulling off my britches, to myself I often smiled,
To think I lay with a hundred men and a maiden all the while.

Of course, the girls did not necessarily have to enlist in
order to go in quest of their sweethearts. Probably the favourite
of all songs of labouring-class lovers pressed to sea is "The brisk
young ploughing boy" that Harry Cox recorded on a gramophone record in the 1930s:

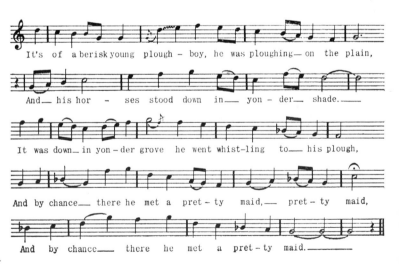

It's of a brisk young plough-boy, he was ploughing— on the plain,

And— his hor - ses stood down in— yon - der— shade.—

It was down— in yon-der grove he went whist-ling to— his plough,

And by chance— there he met a pret-ty maid,— pret-ty maid,

And by chance— there he met a pret-ty maid.—

It's of a brisk young ploughing boy, he was ploughing on the
    plain,
And his horses stood down in yonder shade,
It was down in yonder grove he went whistling to his plough,
And by chance there he met a pretty maid, a pretty maid,
And by chance there he met a pretty maid.

So when the aged parents they come for to know
That her love he was ploughing on the plain,
They sent for the press-gang and pressed her love away,
And they sent him to the wars to be slain.

So she sailed till she came to the ship her love was in,
And unto the captain did complain.
She said: 'I've come in search for my pretty ploughing-boy,
Who was sent into these wars to be slain.

So four hundred bright guineas she then did lay down,
And so carefully he told them all o'er,
Until she had her pretty ploughboy all in her arms,
And she hugged him till she got him safe on shore.

She set those bells to ring, and so sweetly she did sing,
Just because she'd saved the lad that she adore, she adore,
Just because she'd saved the lad that she adore.

Fortunate ploughboy, to have a sweetheart who is not only
fond and resolute but also rich as well! Fantasies of the kind
were very consoling for the poor cottager with a tiny holding,
running a few geese on the common waste, and living mainly
on bread and cheese, some vegetables, and ale. Such a man was
likely to be the most characteristic bearer of folk song in the
period immediately before the maximum enclosures. It was an
important period, of vital and terrible consequence to many
aspects of labouring life, and among other things to the destiny
of our folk song tradition. Let us be clear who were, and who
were not, the folk singers at this time. A normal village would
have its lord of the manor, its yeomen farmers whether their
property was great or small, and its tenant farmers some of

whom occasionally worked as labourers for others. Then there were those who, though they might farm a little patch of commonland on their own behalf nevertheless lived mainly as hired labourers, namely the cottagers, the squatters who had built themselves huts in a clearing on the commons or in the woods (in some parts the right was established if the squatter could build his hut in a single night and show a smoking chimney in the morning), and finally the farm-servants—ploughmen, shepherd and the teenage hands, often the children of cottagers and small farmers, who did the milking and the odd jobs and lived in the hay-loft, sometimes happily sometimes not, depending on the master. The casual day-labourer without land or common rights was rare at this time, though he was soon to become familiar enough.

With this in mind, it will readily be seen that village culture was far from uniform. The lord of the manor and the richer farmers would be book-readers relying chiefly on the culture of the provincial towns, the Gloucester gentry, if they so fancied, driving into Bath to hear the new Handel oratorio while their Yorkshire cousins rode topbooted to the pretty theatre in Richmond to see the fashionably garbled version of *Lear* with its happy ending. Such notables, even if they were rough and raucous as Squire Western himself, were well outside the orbit of unwritten tales and songs, though in exceptional cases they might show some benevolent curiosity about the odd stuff their servants narrated or sang. The middling farmers would likely be at the crossroads between educated and oral culture, but by their pretensions moving away from the arts of the illiterate towards something more fashionable, impelled particularly by their daughters we may be sure. The folk singers and makers of folk song would be found mainly among the small farmers, cottagers and farm-servants. And even here the repertory would not be all of a piece, for some songs and singing styles would be associated with beggars, gipsies and folk at the poorest ends of the village, and the small farmers, artisans and others with pretensions to respectability would be likely to deplore these items and manners as rude and ignorant. Below a certain economic level it is hard to make clear distinction between the various classes in the village, and perhaps the best dividing line can be drawn between those who made their living mainly as farmers and those who made their living mainly as labourers. An enquiring folk song searcher of the time, such as peppery old Joseph Ritson, moving among countryfolk living close to or just above that dividing line would be more likely to hear idyllic broadside ballads sung in plain measured fashion, than poaching songs or ritual pieces sung in the rambling, more decorated style of those on the margin of society. Yeomen do not sing in the same fashion as tinkers. We may ask: why should the very poor sing in freer, more capricious manner than other people? Is it because they have less regard for form and order? Or because, having nothing to lose, they are ready to bring a more venturesome, less inhibited treatment to their songs, regardless of criticism?

At this stage, let us return to the hypothesis offered a few pages back, suggesting that during the course of the eighteenth century certain changes took place and new features became prominent in the general style of English folk song. A fair number of tunes persisted in the square robust common-chord-based manner of the 'older tradition' as depicted by the examples in early tune-books, ballad operas and such; but an increasing number of melodies were being created in a different shape and spirit, in the more circuitous, tentative manner of the 'newer tradition', with the fourth as the important interval rather than the third and fifth, with gapped intervals abounding and plenty of scope for loose decoration—melodies that, for all their shapeliness, seem sometimes to wander along with no clear idea of which direction to take, a kind of melodies the older song books do not show, but the collections of the nineteenth century and after display in abundance.

Why should English folk melody, in part at least, so change its nature? For the discrepancies between the older and newer records are not to be explained away simply on the ground that the early editors notated the tunes as they felt they ought to be, not as they heard them (though this was often the case). Our tradition is elusive, uncorseted, slippery as Thetis, and it is notoriously hard to characterize its styles except in the most general terms. What we are dealing with is nothing as clear-cut and definable as the 'old style', 'new style' and 'mixed style' of Hungarian song so neatly pinned down by Bartók. It has been suggested, by Francesca Allinson[40] and others, that our folk song qualitatively altered in style because it became saturated with Irish melody, and indeed notably from the eighteenth century onward—but the process began much earlier—a huge repertory of Anglo-Irish melody evolved, though it is not always clear on which side of the Irish Channel its various components were forged. Partisans of the Irish invasion may feel their cause is supported by the suggestions of Samuel P. Bayard,[41] who contrasts the English and the Irish melody-styles in these terms: 'The English style is characterized by a certain solidity of melodic build—and emphasis throughout the tune of the strong notes of the mode, like the tonic or dominant tones—and by a preference for the sort of melodic movement which "gets somewhere", which is not held up by hesitating progression or undue overlay of ornamental features. . . . The English singer's leaning to relatively straightforward and simple melodic lines is counteracted in Irish tradition by a love of ornament, of multiplying notes, of varying rhythmic patterns by this sort of multiplication.' This same ornamental tendency gives to Irish music a 'wavering and unemphatic' movement that is further contributed to by the habit of lingering on certain notes or tones, 'repeating them before going on to another tone, thus almost impeding the onward course of the melody from time to time'. Another feature noted by Bayard is the tendency to emphasize and dwell on inconclusive or indecisive scale-tones, 'the ones that do not contribute to resolution or finality in the entire phrase or musical utterance, but rather to easy flow and facile continuity'. Bayard concludes that these qualities give to many Irish airs a graceful softness of outline that often seems 'on the point of slipping into diffuse weakness'.

Bayard's description of the 'English' style is neatly apt for the tunes of our older tradition, but our later tradition shows a great, perhaps preponderant number of melodies that fit his 'Irish' characterization. Are we to take it that this is due solely to the effect of Irish immigration into our villages and towns? The explanation seems too simple. May it not be that something happened in the lives of our song-carriers that caused them to favour a looser, vaguer, less sure and confident style of melody? If indeed the style was affected by models brought in by Irish labourers, what pyschological factors disposed the English singers to adopt these enchanting hesitancies, these hovering mysteries that pervade so much of our countryside lyric as the later collectors found it?

Consider what was happening to rural England. The comfortable stability that Stubbs reflects in his pictures of fat horses and fine pastures, a stability echoed in certain idyllic folk songs, was in some measure deceptive. In fact a transformation in land ownership and farming methods was already taking place, that was eventually to change the form and character of rural life. For many country labourers, the great advances of capitalist agriculture in the latter part of the eighteenth century meant pauperization, shame and angry bewilderment. Their relation to the master they worked for, the neighbours they lived beside, the very soil they tramped over, became utterly altered, the traditional elements of their old peasant society, for long almost imperceptibly eroded, began dramatically to fall away. Their plight had its effect on what they sang, not merely on the kind of words they uttered but also on the way they expressed their tunes. If this is indeed so, then the hovering, meandering qualities of so many of our handsomest tunes, with the unstable tonalities, the profusion of labile passages susceptible to infinite variation, the secrets concealed within so many unexpected intonations and rhythms, may be seen as the product of social and emotional disarray, and as a sign of impending decadence. Sad glories, if so.

At the start of the eighteenth century England had been mainly a land of village commons, common meadowlands, common fields. The common fields were divided into strips, some peasants farming many strips, others few; the common meadowland was divided by lot among the owners of the strips; the village common itself was there for the people to graze their cow or run their geese or gather their firewood. It was an ancient system by which even the poor man could farm a bit of land for himself or at least pasture a few animals and get fuel; his life might be thin and sordid and far from merrie, but he had some rights, some independence, some pride. For centuries, almost imperceptibly, the common lands were being encroached on, enclosed, turned into private properties; but with the development of capitalist agriculture the process was swiftly intensified as tracts over which the villagers had traditionally held petty rights were annexed by the squirearchy and joined to large compact estates working a relatively scientific kind of mixed farming. The new ways of stockbreeding and crop-growing vastly increased England's resources, but the manner in which they were effected meant bitter hardship for the village labourer; the great landowners who led the agricultural revolution were making seven-league strides forward, but the way of their progress was destroying the traditional village economy, culture, morality even. The rich grew richer, the peasants became pauperized, the classes angrily estranged. Even in the lower reaches of rural society there was dissension, small men against poor men, the one lot like hard-fisted peasants anywhere, pushing for enclosure because it might mean another acre added to the three or four they held already, the other lot pushing hard against it because by enclosure they would lose all. Such rifts, weakening the fabric of the rural community, were likewise not without effect on the health of the folk song tradition. It was not so much the pioneers of the new farming, heroes of the turnip, horse-hoe and rotation, as the imperious squires and their pen-and-ink men of the farm offices and country banks who dug the grave of rural song.

For it was precisely the folk singing part of the country community that was most affected by rationalized farming and enclosure. The gradual reorganization of agriculture, which had already begun by the end of the seventeenth century, made itself bitterly felt towards the end of the eighteenth, and many small farmers and cottagers had either to move to the new industrial towns, to go as pick and spade men on the canals (the 'navigation', hence 'navvy'), to emigrate or—and this was particularly the fate of men with families—to become landless day-labourers, which in the long run was likely to mean throwing themselves and their children on the parish, status lost, community destroyed, morality adrift.

In the old days, farm servants and labourers tended to save and marry late, so as to have a little place of their own. But as the frame of capitalist agriculture expanded and the enclosures greatly spread, the labourer's hope of a small farm shrank. 'The practice of consolidating farms operates as a check to matrimony and tends to licentiousness', we read in Duncombe's *Herefordshire*, and in Young's *Suffolk* (1797): 'In the last ten years we see a high price of corn and a great multiplication of unlawful births as the labourer has no advancement to hope.' With small farms powerless against the competition of the big estates, and with no common land to help out, a large number of yeomen, cottagers, squatters were flung on to the country labour market, many of them with little hope of regular employment. The lucky ones became farm servants hired by the year, but this was a shrinking class, as agriculture became more rationalized. Others might become part of the odd-job labour force that was 'independent' but likely to obtain employment on the larger farms more or less throughout the year. The rest became casual labourers, working on piece rates, at the worst, vying with the migratory Irish labourers at haymaking, harvest and potato-lifting time, and with the gipsies and 'travellers' at the fruit- or hop-picking. And when the work failed, the labourer and his family could go on the parish. Then they might be sent from farm to farm by the Poor Law authorities until someone gave them work at any price, or their labour might be put up for auction, notably for the benefit of the mill-owners in the growing industrial towns, whose smoking stacks the father of the family might see as he broke stones on the upland roads. A Suffolk workhouse master advertised: 'We have numbers of small families, such as man and wife, willing, if you could engage them together, say man at 8s., woman at 4s.' In many villages the greater part of the labour force was drawn from those on poor relief. Labourers would be employed for a day or two and then when the job was done, or bad weather intervened, they would be sent back to the parish officer. E. P. Thompson reports one workhouse master as saying: 'If there comes a frost, they discharge them. When the season opens they come to me and take 'em back again. The farmers make my house what we call in our trade a house of call.' And a labourer, interviewed by the Poor Law Commissioners declared: 'It would be better for us to be slaves at once than to work under such a system . . . when a man has his spirit broken, what is he good for?' Finally, from the *Annals of Agriculture:* 'Go to an ale-house kitchen of an old enclosed country, and there you will see the origin of poverty and poor-rates. For whom are they to be sober? For whom are they to save? For the parish? If I am diligent, shall I have leave to build a cottage? If I am sober, shall I have land for a cow? If I am frugal, shall I have half an acre of potatoes? You offer no motives: you have nothing but a parish officer and a workhouse! Bring me another pot—.'

The effects of the social upheavals of the revolution in agriculture and subsequently, industry, upheavals that meant such a rapid erosion of the traditional ways, pastimes (not all agreeable, it is true) and culture of the villages, were intensified by a run of bad harvests from 1789 to 1802, and by wars, on a scale never known before, that raged from 1793 to 1815. The country labourer got to know more about poverty, starvation and crime than his father had ever dreamed of. All signs of the old idyll had gone, and for the first time the ballad of desperate crime (for some time a phenomenon of the towns) became one of the most characteristic kinds of country folk song.

Let us be clear: the mid-eighteenth century was not the only period when ploughmen and blacksmiths composed rustic idylls, nor was the end of the century and the start of the nineteenth unique in the production of desperate murder ballads. For example, "The merry haymakers", recorded from the Sussex singers Bob and Ron Copper in the 1950s, with such characteristic verses as:

We called for a dance and we tripped it along,
We danced all round the haycocks till the rising of the sun,
When the sun did shine such a glorious light and the harmless birds did sing,
Each lad he took his lass in hand and went back to his haymaking.

was already printed on a Bates broadside in 1695. Likewise perhaps the most important and widest-accepted of the murder songs carried across the country by broadside pedlars and street singers, known as "The miller's apprentice", "The prentice boy", "The Oxford miller", "The Wexford miller" (in Ireland), and (in Scotland) "The butcher boy", had appeared in print on a London broadside very early in the eighteenth century, when it was called: "The Berkshire tragedy or the Wittam miller, with an account of his murdering his sweetheart" (Wytham is just outside the city of Oxford but falls within the Berkshire county boundary). But our point is that just as the songs with firm tunes and idyllic words occupied a particularly prominent part in the country repertory during the time of stability, so the vogue for meandering ballads of desperation, violence and disaffection assumed special importance during the time of upheaval. Thus, the printed records tell us, "The miller's apprentice" remained uneventfully in circulation until near the close of the eighteenth century; but then suddenly it begins to show signs of great activity, being recomposed time and again, appearing in one form or another on broadsides from nearly every stall-ballad publisher in business between 1780 and 1850, and serving as a model for a large number of pieces of musical journalism relating to murder cases. We have printed a tune of this firm favourite on p. 79. Here is a text as Hammond obtained it in 1905 from an old fisherman, Joseph Elliott of Todber, who learned most of his songs from other Dorset men while fishing on the Grand Banks of Newfoundland nearly half a century earlier.

Oh, once I was a prentice boy, to the miller did agree.
I served my master for seven long years, no longer could I stay;
Till I fell courting a pretty girl; 'twas a little now and then,
For I been shamed to marry her, for I was so young a man.

I went unto her sister's house at eight o'clock at night,
And little did she think that I owed her any spite.
I took her to the fields so green and to the meadows gay,
And then we sat and talked a while for to fix the wedding day.

I took a stick all from the hedge, I laid her body down,
Then the blood of innocence came raining from the wound;
When she on bended knees did fall and loud for mercy cry,
Crying: 'Jimmy dear, don't murder me, for I'm not fit to die!'

I took her by the curly locks, I dragged her through the groves
   so green,
Until I came to some riverside, and there I throwed her in;
And with the blood of innocence my hands and clothes was
   stained.
Instead of being a pitiless corpse, oh, she ought to have been
   my bride!

I went unto my master's house at twelve o'clock at night,
He quickly came to let me in, and he quickly struck a light.
When the master begin for to question me what stain my hands
   and clothes,
The answer that I had for him, 'twas the bleeding of my nose.

'Bout a nine weeks after, oh, this pretty girl was found,
Down the river floating clear not far from Ensmore town.
When the judges and the jury they do so well agree,
For the murdering of my own sweetheart, oh, a-hanged I must
   be.

With the brighter sparks of the village gone to work in the
new mills or else off to America with their box of tools and
their mouthful of songs (for it seems that a good proportion of
the ballads and lyrics that Cecil Sharp found in the Appalachians must have been taken there from England just at the
end of the eighteenth century and in the early years of the
nineteenth), their neighbours were left behind to scramble for
the few jobs available as full-time farm servants or else to lapse
into the huge pauper army of casual workers, an uneconomic
labour force, for men burning with grievance over lost rights,
frustrated, disorientated, discouraged, easily become scroun-
gers, lead-swingers, pilferers of turnips. Of them all, probably
those who were prepared to risk the savage punishments
handed out to sheepstealers and poachers were the most

spirited. Sheep-stealing songs are relatively few but they reflect a mood of the time. This one still circulates in the southern counties, at least among gipsies and 'travellers'; a set was recorded by Ewan MacColl as recently as 1964. The present version, obtained by Hammond in Lackington, Dorset, goes to a favourite tune whose relatives have carried many ballad and carol texts, including "Geordie", "The truth sent from above", and "The holy well".

I am a brisk lad but my fortune is bad, And I am most wonderful poor.
Oh, indeed I intend my life for to mend, And to build a house down on the moor, my brave boys,
And to build a house down on the moor.

I am a brisk lad but my fortune is bad,
And I am most wonderful poor,
Oh, indeed I intend my life for to mend,
And to build a house down on the moor, my brave boys,
And to build a house down on the moor.

My father* he do keep fat oxen and sheep,
And a neat little nag on the downs.
In the middle of the night when the moon do shine bright,
There's a number of work to be done, my brave boys,
There's a number of work to be done.

Then I'll ride* all around in another man's ground,
And I'll take a fat sheep for my own.
Oh, I'll end his life by the aid of my knife,
And then I will carry him home, my brave boys,
And then I will carry him home.

* Other versions have 'The farmer', and 'then I'll roam'.

My children they will pull the skin from the ewe,
And I'll be in a place where there's none.
When the constable do come, I'll stand with my gun,
And swear all I have is my own, my brave boys,
And swear all I have is my own.

The sheep-stealer might be a defiant fellow, but his crime
was not admired by his neighbours. The poacher, however,
was likely to stand well in the opinion of a tidy section of his
community, rather as the forest outlaw once did, and for
reasons that were not dissimilar. Villagers traditionally
accustomed to taking a rabbit or a bird or two off the common
waste and woodland naturally begrudged having to give up
this right, and the more sullenly reluctant they were to keep
out of the woods, the more vindictive became the measures
employed by the squires in defence of their game and the
privacy of their 'plantations'. Armed keepers, spring-guns,
man-traps, and after 1816 harsh sentences of transportation
(for being found at night with a rabbit-net: seven years in Van
Diemen's Land; hungry family no excuse) failed to curb the
poachers, in whose nightly activities there was now a strong
element of class revenge. Especially in the midlands, the centre
of forest outlawry in the past, the enmity between poachers and
game-keepers, hated representatives of the squirearchy,
assumed the character of a war without truce. Frequently,
the nearer the property was to an industrial town, the more
harshly determined the squire would be to protect his privileges
and preserves. Of a spring evening a traditional excursion for
girls was to go nutting in the woods, but many squires forbade
even this and we read that the streets of Sheffield in Maytime
were posted with notices warning the red-skirted young
buffers of the cutlery works that nutters would be prosecuted
for trespass, with all the ferocious penalties that such a charge
was likely to involve. From the Sheffield district comes one of
the earliest and most powerful of the poacher ballads, with
special prestige among singers in the Midlands and South
Yorkshire. The village of Brightside was enclosed about 1760,
and in 1769 in a fight with gamekeepers a local hero, William
Brown, was killed. Two broadside songs appeared, telling of

his unhappy death. Here is the one that lasted best, obtained by Frank Kidson from a singer in Goole, Yorkshire, a burning vengeful piece that held a tight grip on audiences for more than a century.

Ye gen-tle men both great and small, Game-keep-ers, poach - ers, sports - men all,

Come, lis-ten to a sim - ple clown, I'll sing you the death__ of poor__ Bill Brown.

Come, lis-ten to__ a sim - ple clown, I'll sing you the death of Bill Brown.__

Ye gentlemen, both great and small,
Gamekeepers, poachers, sportsmen all,
Come listen to a simple clown.
I'll sing you the death of poor Bill Brown,
I'll sing you the death of poor Bill Brown.

One stormy night as you shall hear,
It was in the season of the year,
We went to the woods to catch a buck,
But ah, that night we had sad luck:
Bill Brown was shot and his dog was stuck.

When we got to the woods our sport begun,
But I saw the keeper present his gun.
I called on Bill to climb the gate,
To drop the buck, but it was too late,
For there he met his untimely fate.

Then dying he lay upon the ground,
And in that state poor Bill I found.
And when he saw me, he did cry:
'Revenge my death!' 'I will', said I,
'For many a hare we've caught hard by.'

I know the man that shot Bill Brown.
I know him well and could tell the clown;
And to describe him in my song—
Black jacket he had and red waistcoat on.
I know him well, and they call him Tom.

I dressed myself up next night in time,
I got to the woods and the clock struck nine;
The reason was, and I'll tell you why,
To find the gamekeeper I'll go try,
Who shot my friend, and he shall die.

I ranged the wood all over, and then
I looked at my watch and it was just ten.
I heard a footstep on the green,
I laid myself down for fear of being seen,
For I plainly saw that it was Tom Green.

Then I took my piece fast in my hand,
Resolved to fire if Tom did stand.
Tom heard the noise and turned him round.
I fired, and brought him to the ground.
My hand gave him his deep death wound.

Now revenge, you see, my hopes have crowned.
I've shot the man that shot Bill Brown.
Poor Bill no more these eyes will see.
Farewell, dear friend, farewell to ye,
For I've crowned his hopes and his memory.

Another Midland ballad of the sort, that has lasted well among country singers to this day, is the epic story of a night's poaching usually called "Thornymoor Woods". Thornhagh is a village in Nottinghamshire. Its common or 'moor-field', with about a thousand acres of woodland that formed an extension of Sherwood Forest, was enclosed in 1799 to the indignation of the villagers. The ballad was made thirty years after that, and it offers an example of the rapidity with which certain songs spread about the countryside. The Rev. John

Broadwood found it current in the Weald of Surrey and Sussex some time before 1843. James Henry Dixon met with it in South Yorkshire before 1846. Around the middle of the century W. Armstrong of Liverpool and Henry Such of London issued stall-ballad sheets of it, and sets of it subsequently turned up in Hertfordshire, Worcestershire and elsewhere. It tells of three young men on a poaching expedition. One of their dogs is wounded by a keeper, and the owner vows vengeance:

> 'I'll take my pikestaff in my hand
> And search the woods till I find that man.
> I'll have his old hide right well if I can.'

Mercifully, the poacher fails to find the keeper, but he succeeds in killing a deer and sells some of the venison to 'an old woman as sold bad ale'. The woman informs on the poacher, and he and his mates are arrested, but at the trial her evidence is given in a manner so confused that 'the naughty old bugger' is laughed to scorn and the case is dismissed. The ending is mettlesome:

> Now Nottingham Sessions are gone and past,
>   Right falooral whack for ladderda,
> And us three blokes got clear at last,
>   Fol de rol dooral i day!
> Now the bucks and does shall never go free,
> And hares and rabbits they are for me,
> And a poacher I will always be,
>   Right fol de rol dooral i day!

Singers never seemed to vary the words of this one much, and when Harry Cox recorded his Norfolk version for the BBC in 1954, his text tallied almost word for word with that printed by Dixon more than a century earlier in his *Ancient Poems, Ballads and Songs of the Peasantry*, a sure sign that the folk have found the song peculiarly memorable and to their liking.

A former favourite that failed to stay the course so happily is "The poacher's fate". It circulated for several years before being published as a broadside by Shelmerdine of Manchester some time between 1815 and 1820. Within the next three decades, Forth of Pocklington (Yorks), Walker of Durham and others found it worth while to re-issue stall copies, but for some reason the ballad, which has its own peculiar points of interest, did not last well, and in the twentieth century it has only once been reported from English tradition, in a version of Yorkshire origin:

> Come all ye lads of high renown
> That love to drink strong ale that's brown
> And pull the lofty pheasant down
> With powder, shot and gun,
> > I and five more a-poaching went.
> > To get some game was our intent;
> > Our money being gone and spent,
> > We'd nothing else to try.
>
> The keeper heard us fire a gun,
> And quickly to the spot he run,
> And swore before the rising sun
> That one of us should die.
> > The bravest lad in all the lot,
> > 'Twas his misfortune to be shot.
> > His memory ne'er shall be forgot
> > Until the judgement day.
>
> For help he cried, but 'twas denied.
> He rose again to stem the tide,
> While down upon his gallant breast
> The crimson tide did flow.
> > Deep was the wound the keeper gave.
> > No mortal man his life could save.
> > He now lies sleeping in his grave
> > Until the judgement day.

The connection between poaching and the general discontent and subversiveness of the time shows in this ballad. Its metre was adopted for some of that remarkable crop of songs sympathetic to Bonaparte—such as "The grand conversation on Napoleon"—that flourished in the years following Waterloo among, says Kidson, 'that large party of Englishmen who, originally holding the opinions of Thomas Paine, drifted, themselves and their successors, into Chartists' (perhaps their fine striding tunes have helped to keep green several of these songs regretting the downfall of the bold Corsican; they still turn up in good shape, especially in the repertory of gipsies and other travelling folk). More conclusively, the opening verse of "The poacher's fate" was closely parodied in the well-known machine-wreckers' song current in the Cleckheaton–Heckmondwike–Liversedge district of Yorkshire around 1812:[42]

> Come, cropper lads of high renown,
> Who love to drink good ale that's brown,
> And strike each haughty tyrant down
> With hatchet, pike and gun!
>   Oh, the cropper lads for me,
>   The gallant lads for me,
>   Who with lusty stroke the shear-frames broke,
>   The cropper lads for me!

A final intelligence-report from the poaching war that raged for the best part of fifty years after 1780 provides a lesson in solidarity and staunchness: the hero may be lawless but he is truehearted and loyal to his comrades even in the shadow of the gallows. Old John Day, in the Hillingdon, Workhouse, Middlesex, sang a forthright version to Cecil Sharp in 1913, and more than forty years later George Maynard of Copthorne, Sussex, himself an indomitable poacher in his time, recorded for Ken Stubbs an almost identical version as far as text is concerned (the melodies of both these good singers show fanciful departures from the original tune, a favourite vehicle for murder songs at the start of the nineteenth century, whose most familiar—and most down-at-heel—relative is "Villikins and his Dinah"). John Day called it "The keepers and the poachers", but Pop Maynard's title is simply: "William Taylor".

Ye subjects of England, come listen a while.
I'll sing you a ditty that'll cause you to smile.
'Tis concerning some poachers and keepers also
That fought in those covers some winters ago.

Now, when we go in, boys, good luck to us all.
Our guns they do rattle and the pheasants do fall.
But in less than ten minutes twelve keepers we spy.
'Get you gone, you bold poachers, how dare you come nigh!'

Said one to the other: 'Now what shall we do?'
Said one to the other: 'We all will stand true.'
So they did agree for to all be as one,
And to fight those twelve keepers till the battle was won.

Now there's one William Taylor who won't run away,
When five of these keepers all on him did play.
Young Taylor being weary he sat down to rest.
Young Taylor was taken though he fought the best.

Now, judges and jury to him they did say:
'If you will confess now, your sweet life we'll save.'
'Oh no', said young Taylor, 'that won't do at all.
Now since you have got me, I'll die for them all.'

Now, there's none like young Taylor, nor never was yet.
Now, there's none like young Taylor, no, never was yet.
Now, there's none like young Taylor, you keepers all know,
That fought in those covers some winters ago!

A day labourer workless through frost, the flour-bin empty
and the children dining off boiled nettles, watching through
his cottage window the golden birds scuttling through the fern
in the very woods that only a few years before he had freely
roamed—it is easy to imagine the thoughts that would run
through his head. And if the night was dark and windy and
the trees making noise enough to cover his steps, of course he
would be ready to risk the spring-gun in the bracken, the man-
trap under the dead leaves, the keepers with club and blunder-

buss. But for wounding a keeper a man could be hanged; for taking the squire's pheasant or hare he could be transported to the penal stations of Van Diemen's Land, Norfolk Island, Botany Bay, Moreton Bay. In the three years alone between 1827 and 1830, more than 8,500 men and youths were convicted as poachers, and a high proportion of them shipped away in broad-arrowed felt suits, shackles on their ankles, in the company of swell mobsmen and pickpockets of the cities, unruly labourers and rick-burners of their own yokel sort, small boys (like the Clough brothers, aged 12 and 10 years, transported for seven years for stealing linen from a warehouse during the dinner-break), and political dissenters of sundry kinds. Marcus Clarke, who knew what he was writing about, has described the scene aboard the transport ships, and how the poacher, 'grimly thinking of his sick wife and children would start as the night-house ruffian clapped him on the shoulder and bade him with a curse to take good heart and be a man'. And on arrival he might find himself working in the iron gang on the roads of Parramatta, or yoked to a plough to cultivate the orchard-lands of Tasmania-to-be, or facing with a sigh the flogger's triangle at Toongabbie; and all for a crime that was no crime at all in the eyes of most of his countrymen.

Among the handful of surviving transportation ballads— some of which, like "Botany Bay" and "Jack Willliams", had in their time an enormous broadside circulation from such houses as Catnach, Bebbington of Manchester, and Henry Such—the most numerous, most characteristic and most impressive concern the plight of men condemned for poaching. One is the familiar "Van Diemen's Land", among the most popular of all nineteenth century ballads. Ireland and Scotland as well as England have claimed this lugubrious and passive piece, which was first published in London by Catnach some time before 1838, reprinted in the 1850s by both Harkness and Bebbington in Lancashire and by Gilbert in Newcastle, and subsequently issued over and again by Henry Such long after transportation ceased in 1853. Around the middle of the century the Irish poet William Allingham sent to George Petrie a version obtained in Donegal. The sets from north-east Scotland printed by Gavin Greig and

John Ord had been obtained about half a century later. A widely travelled, much appreciated song.

In the English versions the 'gallant poachers' are 'poor Tom Brown from Nottingham, Jack Williams and poor Joe', and 'at night they were trepanned by the keeper's hideous hand, and for fourteen years transported were unto Van Diemen's Land'. They are sold into slavery to the colonial planters, and their nights are terrorized by the wolves and tigers of Tasmania. The master marries a convict girl from Birmingham, Susan Summers, and she gives the prisoners 'good usage', but they dream sadly of their womenfolk at home, and waken 'broken-hearted upon Van Diemen's Land'. The Irish and Scottish sets follow the same story, but the cast-list bears other names—'Pat Malone from Nenagh town, Jimmy Murphy and poor Joe', and 'Poor Tom Brown from Glasgow, Jack Williams and poor Joe' (constant Joe!) while the good-usage girl is variously Peg Brophy from Nenagh and Jean Stewart from sweet Dundee.

Who made the song? Assuredly it was no transported convict; the piece is too stylized, too conventionalized to have been conceived by one who had ever walked with the chain-gang shuffle, and one hardly needs to point to the zoological howlers to clinch the matter. It is a pot poet's confection, based on hearsay, aimed with accuracy at a broad market of downtrodden people ready to take to their heart any touching song of injustice and hard treatment.

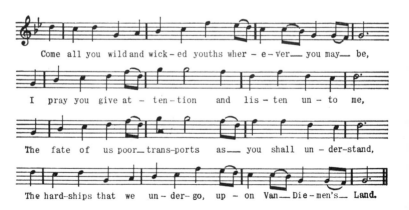

Come all you wild and wick-ed youths wher-e-ver you may be,
I pray you give at-ten-tion and lis-ten un-to me,
The fate of us poor trans-ports as you shall un-der-stand,
The hard-ships that we un-der-go, up-on Van Die-men's Land.

More convincing as a document is "Young Henry's down-fall", whose narrative follows a course closely similar to that of "Van Diemen's Land", but this time the autobiographical accent is plausible. "Young Henry" may have been the model on which, subsequently, more romantic transportation songs were based. Characteristically, it too appeared on several broadsides. Some of them set the scene of events in the neigh-bourhood of Birmingham, but the influential Bebbington (Manchester) stall leaflet has it in Lancashire.

Come all you wild and wicked youths wherever you may be,
I pray you give attention and listen unto me.
The fate of us poor transports as you shall understand,
The hardships we do undergo upon Van Diemen's Land.
　　(*Spoken*)　Young men, all now beware,
　　　　　　　Lest you're drawn into a snare.

My parents reared me tenderly, good learning gave to me,
Till with bad men I was beguiled, which proved my destiny.
I was brought up in Lancashire, near Bolton town did dwell,
My name it is Young Henry, in Chorley known full well.

I and five more we went one night into a squire's park,
Expecting there to find some game, the night being very dark,
But to our sad misfortune they trepanned us with all speed,
And sent us off to Lancaster, which caused our hearts to bleed.

It was at the March Assizes at last we did appear.
Like Job we stood with patience to hear our sentence there.
There being some old offenders, our case went bad astray:
My sentence was for fourteen years, bound to Botany Bay.

They marched us all aboard that ship, the *Speedywell* by name.
For full four month and more, my lads, we ploughed the
　　foaming main.
No land nor harbour could we see, believe me, it's no lie,
All round was one black water and above us one blue sky.

On the fifteenth of September we then did make the land.
At four o'clock we went ashore all chained hand to hand.
To see my fellow sufferers I felt I don't know how,
Some chained to a barrow and others to a plough.

No shoes nor stockings they had on, nor hat had they to wear,
But a hodden frock and linsey drawers, their head and feet was
    bare.
They yoked them up by two and two like horses in a team;
Their driver he stood over them with his Malacca cane.

The convict is fortunate enough to be taken out of the iron
gang to serve as book-keeper for a merchant; moreover he finds
a servant girl, Rosanna from Liverpool, on a fourteen year
stretch, to soften his captivity.

The narrative is likely enough. We do not find a transport
ship called *Speedywell* (*Speedwell* on some broadsides), but if
the *Speedy* is meant, the ballad must be among the oldest
transportation songs, for she was running convicts to Botany
Bay and Van Diemen's Land in the very early years between
1790 and 1810. The stall prints are later, but the song may have
been circulating for years before Bebbington, Fortey and the
rest got hold of it. It is noteworthy that "Young Henry's
downfall" is sung to a strict ABBA tune, like the commonest
versions of most transportation songs, including "Van Diemen's
Land" and "Botany Bay" (the traditional one that starts
'Come all ye men of learning', not the burlesque by Stephens
and Yardley, beginning 'Farewell to old England for ever':
that one is from a Gaiety Theatre show of 1885). The ABBA
form is particularly familiar in connection with songs of subversion, protest and disaffection, perhaps for no better reason
than that this tune-shape was soaring into popularity by 1800
just at a time when dissident melodramas were in vogue among
folk song makers, bearers and listeners, and statements of social
alienation were all the rage, for good historical reason.

Most of the transportation ballads are passive enough in
outlook; self-pity if not repentance is the mood. None of the
surviving songs of the penal settlements shows the smouldering

sense of vengefulness that characterizes the excellent "Jim Jones at Botany Bay", reported, alas, only once, in Charles Macalister's *Old Pioneering Days in the Sunny South* (Goulburn, N.S.W., 1907), a book of reminiscences, mainly of the Sydney area in the 1840s. "Jim Jones" follows the conventional pattern of arrest, sea-voyage and hard times on landing. His crime, as usual, is poaching, and his sentence, transportation for life. The judge adds a lowering postscript:

And take my tip, before you ship to join the iron gang;
Don't be too gay at Botany Bay or else you'll surely hang . . . .
You'll have no chance for mischief then; remember what I say,
They'll flog the poaching out of you, out there at Botany Bay.

The long voyage is livened by a brush with pirates, but to the convict's disappointment the pirates are driven off, and the shores of Botany Bay are reached. Then, says the song:

Night and day and irons clang, and like poor galley slaves
We toil and toil, and when we die must fill dishonoured graves.
But by and by I'll break my chains: into the bush I'll go,
And join the brave bushrangers there—Jack Donohoo and Co;

And some dark night when everything is silent in the town
I'll kill the tyrants one and all, and shoot the floggers down.
I'll give the Law a little shock; remember what I say,
They'll yet regret they sent Jim Jones in chains to Botany Bay.

"Jim Jones" stands out from the ruck of transportation songs by reason of its strong bloodshot defiance. The good Australian social historian Russel Ward observes that in the ballad 'instead of an implicit acceptance of the rules of society, there is an explicit assumption that society itself is out of joint, and even a hint that in the new land society may be remoulded nearer to the heart's desire'. If the song is to be taken literally, it must have been made up between September 1, 1828, when 'bold Jack' Donahoe first emerged as a bushranger, and the time two years later when the troopers shot him dead in the Bringelly scrub. But the date and manner of the ballad's origin is not the only mystery surrounding it; a deeper riddle is: why has such a well-made mettlesome piece failed to keep its hold on the interest of singer and audience when flabbier creations on the same theme have ostentatiously survived into our own time?

In some respects akin to the disaffection songs of poachers and transported convicts is the repertory of army-deserter ballads. The number of such songs is small; indeed the whole fund of English songs about soldiering is neither large nor generally impressive. A handful of semi-historical pieces such as "Bold General Wolfe" and "The drummer-boy of Waterloo" are more successful in their sentimental regrets than in any statement of battle glory; generally the English folk song tradition is remarkably free from the drum and trumpet view of history. Flag-waving was fine for the bourgeois song-writers, but the folk song public did not find that such gestures expressed their own desires and hopes. Nor, on the other hand, do we hear much trace of ironic or indignant opposition to army and warfare among the folk songs clearly originating in England; though there is plenty of pity and regret. For biting comment on military matters, one must look to Ireland and such splendid compositions as "Johnny, I hardly knew ye", "Mrs. McGrath", "The Kerry recruit", and "The hungry army", ostensibly comic pieces but with a grin that shows sharp teeth. The latter song, in the rather rare metre of "Glasgow Peggy", "The husband with no courage" and the old Durham satire on strikebreakers, "The tools of Shotton Moor", finds a wide choice of vital points at which to snap. A farm-worker leaves the service of his wealthy skinflint squire and 'in the rain and storm of black October' he makes his way to Dublin.

> When I arrived in Dublin town,
> I crossed the splendid Liffey river.
> In the Castle yard, a big blackguard
> Asked me to enlist, the blacks to skiver.
> I did agree, and he gave to me
> A gun, and the weight of it should have warned me;
> But I hired myself to the power of Guelph
> And went and joined the hungry army.

The sergeant flatters and cajoles him, but by the time the regiment is mustered at Chatham ready for embarkation, the coaxing is over, and the flogging starts.

> They'd said a sergeant I'd soon be made,
> But I found the rogues were giving me blarney.
> All the stripes I got were on a soft spot.
> When my back was on fire I cursed the old army.

The recruit sails off to colonial wars in a troop-ship in which the men stifle and starve.

> We were smothered to death for the want of our breath,
> And bursting with hunger, which didn't much charm me.
> We were ordered to land and make a brave stand.
> They can easy say 'Stand' to a hungry army.

In a war in which he feels no interest, the hungry soldier does his best to remove himself from spots of danger, but though he hides in the grass, too terrified to shoot lest the enemy shoots back (like the Kerry recruit at Balaklava) he is wounded, disabled, and 'Uncle Toby' (the War Office) has no further use for the spirited anti-hero.

> Unfit for service, I got my discharge.
> 'Hop it, you cripple', says Uncle Toby.
> 'A pension you'll get, or if not, you'll be let
> To stay in the workhouse till you're an old fogey.'
> If the good Lord me spares to live eighty years
> With an empty workhouse grate to warm me,
> I'll remember the day I got gunpowder tay
> When I went to enlist in the hungry army.

For all its dogged punning, the song of the hungry army penetrates to the bone of the situation of the Irish peasant forced by poverty to fight for a despised power, resenting the ill-treatment and danger he is exposed to, knowing he'll be left stranded in the end, and using in self-defence the serf's weapon, the slave's weapon, the Jew's and Negro's weapon of the double-edged joke. English singers do not seem to have made that kind of song for themselves. In the main body of our tradition, pieces mocking the army are almost as rare as pieces that glorify it. Aside from a handful of sprightly love-adventure songs such as "Jack Munro", "The female drummer boy", "Seventeen come Sunday", "The gentleman soldier", our characteristic folk lyrics of military reference are senti-mental often melancholy farewells of the kind of "The Man-chester Angel", "High Germany", "The rout came on Sunday", "The Blues"; that is, songs that neither complain nor subvert, but nevertheless offer some reasonable comment on the pity of war.

In our relative lack of songs that oppose soldiering, even (or should we surprise ourselves by saying: particularly?) the Germans put us to shame, as we see from the weighty and impressive section of soldiers' and working people's songs against recruitment and war in the eighteenth and nineteenth centuries, in the first volume of Wolfgang Steinitz's *Deutsche Volkslieder demokratischen Charakters* (Berlin 1954). Perhaps the fact that our territory has been little fought-over has something to do with it, also relations between army and the lower classes remained unimpassioned, not to say cold, until fairly recent times. Fiery denunciations of war are few; but also the deeds of Dettingen and Fontenoy, Winden and Quebec extorted only small admiration from the kind of men who made and carried the folk songs, though in a later age the 'street screamers' had some success with their broadsides of "The plains of Waterloo" and "The heights of Alma".

To all intents, the regular British army came into being during the second half of the seventeenth century, when our new accessions of Tangier and Bombay were demanding long-service garrisons, the prospect of colonial expansion was beginning to offer itself, and entire regiments of mercenaries such as the Royal Scots and the Buffs were leaving the service of Holland or Sweden now that soldiering offered a career in England. The high moral standards of Cromwell's New Model Army soon disappeared in the armies of the Restoration and after. The ranks were full of adventurous desperadoes, lumpen proletarian roughs, looters, rapers. And as the army's need for expansion grew, recruits were harder to find, because the farm-boys and drapers' clerks were far from eager to enlist unless the law was after them or they had got a young woman in trouble. Poor pay and hard treatment faced them, and in the early days the normal term of enlistment was for life. The result was a system of recruitment notable for fraud, deception and sharp practice, that contributed greatly to the wholesale desertions typical of the time.

Sergeant Kite, in Farquhar's play *The Recruiting Officer*, is the perfect model of the treacle-tongued bloody-minded humbug and bamboozler that men of his agency had to be if they were to induce recruits into the ranks (Kite's song, with its refrain: 'Over the hills and over the main, To Flanders Portugal and Spain, The queen commands and we'll obey Over the hills and far away', survived through two-and-a-half centuries among folk singers, dwindling all the time, till it seemed to be limited to the Scottish north-east, but lately a variant has come back into vigorous circulation in English cities, under the title: "Two recruiting sergeants from the Black Watch"). In Marlborough's time and after, crimpers such as Mr. Tooley of Holborn were ready to supply drugged recruits at short notice. The naval press-gang was employed also for army recruiting to such an extent that, according to Trevelyan, in 1702 a thousand men deserted to the French, saying that they had all been pressed for sea-service, mustered at the Tower, embarked blindfolded and transported to Flanders for the army. By the Mutiny Act of the same year, a pardon was to be granted to all convicted felons who would choose to enlist, and every pauper and vagrant on whom the parish beadles could lay hands was liable to be pressed into the army for at least a term of five years or the duration of a war (for each man thus enlisted the parish received the payment of one pound). Later, in 1779, another special Act authorized the forcible enlistment of all thieves, pickpockets and ruffians found in and around London, and about a thousand of these irresponsible recruits were allotted to regiments in the home counties. There was good reason for the popular prejudice against the army, which did not facilitate the recruiting of fit and uncoerced men. As for forced enlistment, the scandal grew worse as the century wore on, and in the large towns the trade of the 'gallows bitches' spread, the prostitutes whose special craft was to entice men into houses where the crimps might regale them with liquor doped with laudanum and tobacco juice; when the fuddled wretches came to, the royal shilling would be in their hand. In August 1794, a number of crimping houses in Holborn, Clerkenwell, Shoreditch were destroyed by a furious mob in three days of rioting.

In the personal account of a recruiting sergeant, written in the opening years of the nineteenth century, we read how a party from the 76th Regiment set out to beat up recruits on the fairground outside Winchester. Some of the officers dressed as grooms, some of the men as yokels, to mingle with the crowd. The disguised men would volunteer to enlist, spinning yarns of the great good fortune of their relatives and friends, such as one 'enlisted that day three years ago, now a captain in India, as rich as a nabob'. As extra bait, the recruiting sergeant would give watches as well as the bounty to each of the 'new' king's men. 'The watches usually had an astonishing effect and secured three or four fish'. One of the party, Sergeant Andrews, describes how a yokel hung back, saying he would only enlist if the recruiting sergeant made him his equal in rank. The sergeant cut three V-shaped pieces of cloth and pinned them on the man's sleeve; then he drew his sword, made the fellow kneel down, and cried: 'Rise, Sergeant Turner, in the name of St. George and the dragon.' Says Andrews: 'We had done the trick and brought in eighteen as able-bodied boobies as any in Hampshire.'

Another experienced recruiting sergeant of the same period, working the mill-towns and farmlands of the north, wrote in his memoirs: 'The best way was to make up to the man you had in your eye . . . and ask him what sort of web he was in. You might be sure it was a bad one. . . . (Tell him) weaving was going to ruin and he might soon be starving. Ploughboys had to be hooked in a different way. . . . If you see an officer pass, tell him he was only a recruit a year ago but now he's so proud he won't speak to you. . . . Don't give up the chase: tell him that where your gallant, honourable regiment is lying everything may be had almost for nothing, that the pigs and fowls are lying in the streets ready roasted, with knives and forks in them for the soldiers to eat whenever they please. . . . Keep him drinking—don't let him go to the door without one of your party with him, until he is past the doctor and attested.'

By no means all country workers were credulous bumpkins, as "Arthur McBride" shows, that most good-natured, mettlesome, and un-pacifistic of anti-militarist songs. It has been a remarkably widespread and well-favoured piece. Noble old Patrick Joyce learnt it in Limerick during his boyhood in the early 1840s, and around the same time George Petrie received a version from a Donegal correspondent. Sam Fone, the aged Dartmoor mason whom Baring-Gould found to be an inexhaustible fountain of songs, remembered it as his father's favourite in Devon in the 1830s, and he sang a good set of it to the parson in 1893. The song had made its way to the Scottish north-east during the latter half of the century, and Gavin Greig recorded a version, 'Scotticized to some extent', from Alexander Robb, his school caretaker at New Deer, Aberdeenshire. More recently, a singer from Walberswick, Suffolk, recorded it for the BBC early in 1939. In temper and action it is something of a model for songs of disaffection and protest.

I once knew a fellow named Arthur McBride,
And he and I rambled down by the sea-side,
A-looking for pleasure or what might betide,
And the weather was pleasant and charming.

So gaily and gallant we went on our tramp,
And we met Sergeant Harper and Corporal Cramp,
And the little wee fellow who roused up the camp
With his row-de-dow-dow in the morning.

'Good morning, young fellows', the sergeant he cried.
'And the same to you, sergeant', was all our reply.
There was nothing more spoken; we made to pass by
And continue our walk in the morning.

'Well now, my fine fellows, if you will enlist,
A guinea in gold I will slap in your fist,
And a crown in the bargain to kick up the dust
And drink the Queen's health in the morning.'

'Oh no, mister sergeant, we aren't for sale.
We'll make no such bargain, and your bribe won't avail.
We're not tired of our country, and don't care to sail,
Though your offer is pleasant and charming.

If we were such fools as to take your advance,
It's right bloody slender would be our poor chance,
For the Queen wouldn't scruple to send us to France
And get us all shot in the morning.'

'Ha now, you young blackguards, if you say one more word,
I swear by the herrins, I'll draw out my sword
And run through your bodies as my strength may afford;
So now, you young buggers, take warning!'

Well, we beat that bold drummer as flat as a shoe,
And we make a football of his row-de-dow-do,
And as for the others, we knocked out the two.
Oh, we were the boys in that morning!

We took the old weapons that hung by their side
And flung them as far as we could in the tide.
'May the devil go with you,' says Arthur McBride,
'For delaying our walk this fine morning!'

Throughout the whole period from the Restoration to the accession of Victoria—that is, during the liveliest time for folk song creation—the discipline of army and navy was brutal and callous, ruled by the lash. The grenadier of Corporal Trim's anecdote, whipped to such agony that he begged to be shot, was no exceptional case. The flogging triangle was a permanent fixture on the drill-square of many camps, and the cat-o'-nine-tails was everyday punishment for all offences from desertion to unsteadiness on parade. Twenty-five lashes was the minimum, fifteen hundred the maximum that could legally be awarded.

An ex-drummer wrote that for the first eight years of his service it was his duty to flog men at least three times a week. 'From this painful task there was no possibility of shrinking without the certainty of a rattan over my own shoulders from the Drum-Major, or of my being sent to the black-hole. . . . I have, immediately after the parade, run into the barrack-room, to escape from the observations of the soldiers, and to rid my clothes and person of my comrade's blood.' The floggings might be for trivial offences. In 1806, the 28th Foot went on duty to Germany. Writing some thirty years later, Sergeant Teesdale recalled: 'We had a parade to attend each morning and evening. The officers commanding companies received orders from Major B— to inspect their men closely and to turn out to the front such as they found dirty; a square was then formed for punishment and the men who had been found fault with were marched in, tried by a drumhead court-martial, and flogged to a man without reference to character. Not a lash was remitted, and I have known from ten to twenty-five fellows flogged one after another at a parade under this frivolous pretext, until it was put a stop to.' In fact, while the torment of the 28th Foot was going on, the service authorities were trying to institute a milder regime, for they had been badly shaken by the effect of the doctrines of the French Revolution on sections of the forces, and in particular by the great naval mutinies at Spithead and the Nore in 1796–7.

Desperate recruitment, barbarous treatment, low pay (fixed after the Restoration at eightpence a day for foot soldiers, and so it remained for 123 years regardless of the raised cost of living); small wonder that the country was peppered with soldiers on the run, harboured in hundreds of towns and villages though their helpers knew they faced loss of civil rights and long sentences of hard labour without trial if they were discovered. As deserters became more numerous the laws against them sharpened. At the start of the nineteenth century, a man deserting when on sentry duty or from escort in charge of a prisoner could be sentenced to death; deserting when under orders for active service entailed a thousand lashes and 'mark D'; deserting to enlist in another regiment carried eight hundred lashes and 'mark D'. 'Mark D' meant being branded with a capital D for life, on the body or the cheek. The branding was done by a jab with a bunch of saddler's needles or, after 1840, by a brass tool that projected a set of keen spikes into the skin and withdrew them again; gunpowder was rubbed into the punctures to make an indelible tattoo; the operation was carried out with much ceremony, as a preliminary to the flogging.

With the deserter such a characteristic figure of the time, the desertion ballads made a deep impression on soldiers and the working country- and townsfolk from whom they came. In general the people were firmly on the side of the deserter, and their sympathy shows in many contemporary reports as well as in several widespread and much-loved songs. The London broadside called "The new deserter" spread throughout the country, establishing itself particularly well in Yorkshire, and being carried as far north as Aberdeenshire, where Gavin Greig heard it sung by the same school caretaker who had given him "Arthur McBride". It tells of a young man wandering down the Ratcliffe Highway in Stepney. He meets a recruiting party, is treated to drinks and before he knows what is happening he is enlisted.

> But soon I deserted and set myself free,
> Being advised by my true love a deserter to be.
> I was quickly followed after and brought back with speed.
> I was handcuffed and shackled—heavy irons indeed.

> The day was appointed that flogged I must be,
> With the rest of my comrades all ranked around me.
> Our colonel laid out for three hundred and three,
> And it's oh, the Queen's duties are cruel to me.

Again the soldier deserts, but this time his 'cruel sweetheart' informs on him, and again he is brought back in irons.

> Court martial, court martial was very soon got,
> And the sentence they passed was that I should be shot.
> The guns were presented, a cruel sight to see,
> For now the Queen's duties lie heavy on me.

However, the country being at war needs every available hand on the musket, and so:

> Up rode Prince Albert in his coach and six.
> 'Bring to me that young man whose death it is fixed.
> Release him from his irons and let him go free,
> For he'll make a clever soldier for his Queen and country.'

(The song seems to belong to the eighteenth century, and Kidson, who noted several sets of it in the neighbourhood of Leeds, suggested that Prince Albert comes in only as a substitute for one of the Georges).

The idealized 'happy ending' lifts the ballad into the air of unreality and marks it as a broadside poet's product rather than a true life confession. Some would say that the subjectivity of the piece also indicates the professional hand, but in fact the sense of community had been slowly fading out of the folk songs for some time, and the isolated ego coming to the fore, first in the love lyrics, and subsequently in songs of general condition. This 'personalization' spread from town to countryside notably as rural labouring society became more fragmented and disarrayed. The fact that a great proportion of deserter songs are in the form of autobiographical accounts is not to say that they were necessarily made by disaffected soldiers. Increasingly after the mid-eighteenth century the 'I' convention for ballads of delinquency grew common and song-maker and singer came more and more to identify themselves with the miscreant. Perhaps it is a symptom of the increasing social alienation of the poorer classes who clung most doggedly to folk song in the disturbed years of the agricultural and industrial revolutions and after, that the vogue for the objective narration of songs of misdeed declined, and was replaced by a subjective account in which the singer presented himself as the outlaw, the defaulter, the doomed man: 'To keep my wife both night and day, Robbing I went on the broad highway'; 'Then I says to myself: I will desert. When the guard-room it was silent I stole out of my sentry-box And laid down my gun and bayonet'; 'It's now in chains in Newgate Gaol I lie Expecting every moment for to die.' A deserter song that Walter Ford got from a Surrey farm-worker some sixty years ago is characteristic enough in the way it expresses popular sympathy with the deserter and a general contempt for informers, but it is un-typical in that it is an observer's account, not a confessional piece.

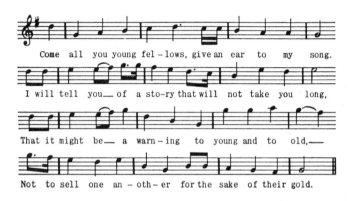

Come all you young fellows, give an ear to my song.
I will tell you of a story that will not take you long.
That it might be a warning to young and to old
Not to sell one another for the sake of their gold.

It happened about a twelve month ago.
There was two young fellows which most of us know.
Oh, one was a deserter so plainlye appear,
Came from the west o' Kent up to harvesting here.

Oh, what a deceiver he met with that year!
Both sat in an ale-house a-drinking of beer,
And all in good friendship for what he did know,
Not thinking he'd been drinking all day with the foe.

Then after a while this man went away.
He met with two soldiers that very same day.
They were after a deserter, to him they did say.
Then he swore he'd been drinking with one all the day.

Then says the soldier: 'It'll answer our plan.
One guinea we'll give you; come show us the man.'
Then 'twas: 'Come along with me,' the fellow did say,
And down to the alehouse went William straightway.

Then in went the soldiers without dread or fear.
'What cheer?' says the fellow; then: 'Give them some beer.
What regiment are you?' 'The 9th', they did say.
'What regiment are you, come tell us, we pray.'

'No regiment at all,' so bold and so gay.
'Then we'll find one for you,' the soldiers did say.
They took him and kept him in hold all that night,
Until the next morning, until it was light.

Then down to Maidstone Gaol they took him straightway.
They wrote to his regiment: 'Come fetch him away.'
    (*Two lines missing*)

And now to conclude on these few lines I've penned
May all sneaking fellows come to a bad end,
That would sell one another for the sake of their gain,
No doubt they will find just reward for their pain.

A hardy late growth among deserter ballads is "The ram-bling Royal", seemingly a genuine army product of the latter part of the nineteenth century. It is better known in Ireland than in England, for all its Liverpool setting, and need not detain us long, though it deserves a mention if only on account of its pugnacious bold-as-brass qualities. 'Royal' means 'Royal Marine'. A young Liverpool Irishman enlists in the Marines while drunk. His girl in Birkenhead is heartbroken when she hears what he has done, and promises to hide him if he should choose to desert.

It was in the Chatham depot my officer gave command
That me and two of my comrades that night on guard should
    stand.
The night being dark and wet and cold with me did not agree,
So I knocked out the guardroom corporal and I run for my
    liberty.

In the night he loses his way, and is overtaken by his pursuers. A terrible fight ensues and the lion-hearted deserter is dragged back to barracks and locked in the guard-room, 'with two men at each window and another three at the door'.

It was early the very next morning I paced that guardroom round.
I leapt out of the window and felled three of 'em to the ground.
The provost and his bullies, they was swiftly after me,
But I battled my way to Birkenhead and so gained my liberty.

I am a rambling Royal and James Cronin is my name.
I can fight as many corporals as you'll find in the Marines.
I can fight as many Orangemen as ever banged a drum,
And I'll make 'em run before me like a bullet from a gun.

In period and to some extent in flavour "The rambling Royal" resembles the most famous, most persistent and best-loved of all our army songs of disaffection, the ballad variously called "McCassery", "McCaffery", "McCafferty", though it must be said that James Cronin's snuffy temper offers strong contrast to the whingeing self-pity of the barrack-square assassin. We may take it that "McCafferty" was composed very early in the second half of the nineteenth century; if so, the mention of Strangeways crept in later, for that bleak prison was not built until the 1870s (some versions more feasibly refer to Walton Gaol, Liverpool). Again, the author was presumably an Irishman, to go by the ballad's atmosphere, its hero's name, and the fact that its tune is a variant of that favourite Irish air for unruly texts such as "The rambling boy", "Charlie Reilly the robber", and the Wexford insurgent song of 1798 called "The croppy boy" (from which the 'I have no father' motif is lifted). "McCafferty" has seldom appeared in print but there is hardly a regular soldier who does not know a version of it, and during World War II it was adopted as the anthem of a parachute commando regiment, the 2nd Special Air Service. It is said of "McCafferty", as of other dissident songs, that it was a punishable offence to sing it in the army; but that is legend. The ballad's peculiar importance has been recognized by country singers, and in the early days of the Second World War, during the Saturday night sing-song in the little pub of Eastbridge, Suffolk, with the bar-parlour crowded with soldiers stationed nearby, the good ballad-singer Jumbo Brightwell prefaced his performance with the remark: 'I will now sing "McCassery" because that's a song that'll mean a lot to these boys here." Mr. Brightwell's version ran like this:

Kind friends take warn – ing by my sad tale,
As I lay here in Strange-ways Gaol,
My thoughts, my feel-ings no — tongue can — tell,
As I am list-'ning to the pri – son bell.

Kind friends, take warning by my sad tale.
As I lay here in Strangeways Gaol,
My thoughts, my feelings no tongue can tell
As I am listening to the prison bell.

When I was seventeen year of age,
Into the army I did engage.
I did enlist with a good intent
To join the Forty Second Regiment.

To Fullwood Barracks I did go,
To serve some time at that depot.
From trouble there I never was free,
Because my captain took a dislike to me.

When I was stationed on guard one day,
Some children came near me to play.
My officer from his quarters came,
And ordered me to take their parents' name,

My officer's orders I did fulfil.
I took their name against my will.
I took one name instead of three.
'Neglect of duty' was the charge against me.

In the orderly-room next morning I did appear.
My C. O. refused my plea to hear,
And quickly he had signed my crime,
And to Fullwood Barracks I was then confined.

With a loaded rifle I did prepare
To shoot my captain on the barrack square.
It was Captain Neill that I meant to kill,
But I shot my colonel against my will.

I done the deed, I shed his blood,
And at Liverpool Assizes my trial stood.
The judge he says: McCassery,
Prepare yourself for the gallows-tree.

I have no father to take my part.
I have no mother to break her heart.
I have one friend and a girl is she,
Would lay down her life for McCassery.

In Liverpool city this young man was tried.
In Strangeways, Manchester, his body lies,
And all you young soldiers who pass by his grave
Pray: Lord have mercy on McCassery.

If, at least until Waterloo, the people looked on the soldier
as a disgrace, they regarded the sailor as a glory. The men
knew it, the songs show it. Conditions afloat were notoriously
hard: crowded quarters, weevilly food, little hygiene but
plenty of lash, and perhaps a two years' wait for wages at the
end of it all, for those who survived the dangers of battle,
shipwreck, the fall from the yards, the epidemic in the fo'c'sle.
Admiral Vernon, 'brave noble Vernon' of the Porto Bello and
Cartagena ballads, who was the sailors' friend and suffered for
it, put the matter bluntly: 'Our fleets are defrauded by in-

justice, manned by violence, and maintained by cruelty.' But at Nelson's funeral, with ten thousand soldiers marching, and the admirals showing their blazing stars, and the bishops and ministers all coffin-faced, when the forty-eight men of the *Victory* trudged by with their tarry fists and greasy pigtails the crowd cried: 'We'd rather see you lads than all the show.' And when, with the coffin under a glitter of lights in the otherwise dark cathedral, the men came forward to lay the *Victory's* ragged flag in the tomb but instead, on the spur of the moment, they took the flag and tore it up and each man put in his bosom a memorial to their commander, it was the kind of bold stroke expected of seamen. In the nation's eye they were champions of fortitude and flourish. We read of the sailor Cashman, owed five years' back pay by the Admiralty and discharged penniless in 1816; coming from a fruitless visit to the Admiralty he had a few jars with a brother seaman and went to a Radical meeting in Spa Fields; after the meeting an angry mob stormed a gunsmith's shop, and in the confusion the befuddled Cashman was arrested, and subsequently condemned. At his execution, the crowd of admirers was so vast that the scaffold had to be defended by a strong force of constables behind barricades. With groans and hisses the mob surged forward while Cashman urged them on, bawling from the scaffold: 'Hurra, my hearties in the cause! Success! Cheer up!' As the executioner approached him, the sailor cried to the crowd: 'Now, you buggers, give me three cheers when I trip'; and according to the Radical press of the time, after telling the executioner to 'let go the jib-boom', the bold seaman, like a good ballad hero, 'was cheering at the instant the fatal board fell from beneath his feet'.[43] Many of the best sailor songs have something of that same hardy swagger pregnant with sadness and a history of exploitation.

If he was a lion to the people, to the authorities the seaman was a dog. If recruitment to the army was carried out largely by fraud and cozenage, recruitment to the navy was commonly done to a large extent by the cruellest compulsion. It was a paradox of eighteenth century England that side by side with a world of seemingly quiet villages and cultured society, of urbane artists and of poets who would discuss the necessity of preserving from harm the gentle hare or the innocent fly, there could also exist a world of violence and coarseness in which authority could impose so brutal a device as the press-gang, and have it accepted as a normal way to man the fleet. Certainly, the conditions of navy life being what they were, compulsion was necessary, for few men would happily volunteer. So, bands of cutlass-armed sailors under a press-officer (a 'yellow admiral') would pile into cutters and come ashore at the ports to seize any able-bodied man they could lay hands on, whether mariner or landlubber, craftsman or ploughboy, from street-corner, tavern, 'even at the church-door whence bridegroom and congregation were sometimes carried off'. Frequently the press-gang was accompanied by a detachment of marines to stop the avenues leading out of town into the countryside. The art of dodging the press was well-developed: 'With twenty minutes' warning, five hundred men can find five hundred corners to hide themselves in as snug as a bug in a wainscoat', says a document of the time. 'Being seamen they can hang head downwards for three hours over a jakes if need be.' A ballad of about 1780, titled "A dialogue between Will and Jack", describes the general terror of the press, with people frightened to sleep in their beds, the farmers and millers sending only children and old men to the markets, the carriers and carters lying hidden in the fields 'like goats in the mountains' as the gang comes bustling along the highway. Pressing was considered difficult along the Dorset and Cornish coast because so many men had their hiding-places in the smugglers' coves, the tin mines or the stone quarries (indeed, tin-miners and quarrymen fought some famous battles with the press). Even during the Heroic Age of the Navy—or particularly then, for more men were needed than ever—the press gang was a constant dread for men and their wives or sweethearts. Nelson himself, as a junior officer, led the press about Tower Hill, Rosemary Lane and Cable Street.

In 1821, on Tyneside, the soap and vitriol manufacturer Thomas Doubleday, a fierce Radical and a devoted amateur of local folk song, heard through the open door of a farm-house kitchen a girl lilting a song that took his fancy as he sat drinking rum toddy after a wet ride:

Oh,— the wea-ry cut-ters, they've taen my lad-die fre me.

Oh,— the wea-ry cut-ters, they've taen my lad-die fre me.

They've pressed him far a-way for-eign wi' Nel-son a-yont the salt sea.

Oh,— the wea-ry cut-ters, they've taen my lad-die fre me.

> O the weary cutters, they've taen my laddie fre me,
> O the weary cutters, they've taen my laddie fre me.
> They've pressed him far away foreign
> Wi' Nelson ayont the salt sea.
> O the weary cutters, they've taen my laddie fre me.

Others verses from the same locality continue the song:

> O the weary cutters, they've taen my laddie fre me,
> O the weary cutters, they've taen my laddie fre me.
> They always come in the night,
> They never come in the day,
> They always come in the night and steal the laddies away.

> O the lousy cutters and O the weary sea!
> O the lousy cutters that stole my laddie fre me.
> I'll give the cutter a guinea;
> I'll give the cutter no more,
> I'll give the cutter a guinea to steal my laddie ashore.

It is to Doubleday that we also owe the first record of "Captain Bover", whose fine and characteristic north-eastern tune may be found in *Northumbrian Minstrelsy*. The brief words are worth quoting here, reflecting the fears of merchant seamen and fishermen to come ashore from their craft in case the press-gang seizes them for long—perhaps lifetime—service in the navy.

Where hes ti been, maw canny hinny?
Where has ti been, maw winsome man?
Aw've been ti the norrard, cruising back and forrard,
Aw've been ti the norrard, cruising sair and lang.
Aw've been ti the norrard, cruising back and forrard,
But daurna come ashore for Bover and his men.

John Bover died in 1782, and a tablet on the wall of that grimy jewel, the cathedral church of St. Nicholas in Newcastle, testifies to him 'having for several years previous filled with the highest credit the arduous situation of regulating officer of this port'.

The output of songs concerning the press-gang seems to have been particularly vigorous in the north-east, and the *Northumbrian Minstrelsy* quotes another beauty, but in truncated form. We give it here in rather fuller shape, a sweet anxious song:

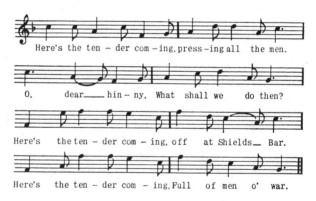

Here's the ten - der com - ing, press - ing all the men.

O, dear___ hin - ny, What shall we do then?

Here's the ten - der com - ing, off at Shields___ Bar.

Here's the ten - der com - ing, Full of men o' war.

Here's the tender coming, pressing all the men.
O, dear hinny, what shall we do then?
Here's the tender coming, off at Shields Bar.
Here's the tender coming, full of men o' war.

Here's the tender coming, stealing of my dear.
O, dear hinny, they'll ship you out of here.
They will ship you foreign, that is what it means.
Here's the tender coming, full of red marines.

Wherever the press-gang moved with their cutlasses and blackjacks, they sowed misery. Apprentices to trade were seized in the middle of their term, despite their certificates of exemption; small businesses were ruined when the tradesman, a poor spindleshanked tailor perhaps, was seized; families were broken up when the head of the household failed to come home from the harvest field because he had met a party of naval men-at-arms on the way. A song got by Vaughan Williams in Lower Beeding, Sussex, puts the woman's view of the matter in a lyric of quiet and contained grief:

> All things are quite silent, each mortal at rest,
> When me and my love got snug in one nest.
> But a bold set of ruffians they entered our cave,
> And they forced my dear jewel to plough the salt wave.
>
> I begged hard for my sailor as though I begged for life.
> They'd not listen to me, although a fond wife,
> Saying: 'The king he wants sailors; to the sea he must go'.
> And they've left me lamenting in sorrow and woe.

A masculine impression is provided by a song heard by E. J. Moeran in that nest of singing birds, the Winterton district of Norfolk. The singer was a fisherman, James Sutton, well-remembered for his large repertory of songs relating to the sea. His version of "The pressgang" relates a peaceful enough encounter between a simple-minded fellow and the press in a London street. Invited to accompany them, the cuckoo makes his innocent enquiry:

> Pray, brother shipmates, tell me true
> What sort of usage they give you,
> That I may know before I go
> On board of a man-o'-war, boys.
>
> But when I went, to my surprise
> All that they told me was shocking lies.
> There was a row and a bloody old row
> Aboard of the man-o'-war, boys.

> The first thing they did, they took me in hand;
> They flogged me with a tar of a strand,
> They flogged me till I could not stand
> On board of a man-o'-war, boys. . . .

Small wonder the song ends:

> So when I get my foot on shore
> Those Irish girls to see once more,
> I'll never go to sea any more
> On board of a man-o'-war, boys.

Musty meat and cheating pursers, the holding back of pay, the severity of discipline were all good reasons why neither bounty nor compulsion could man the fleet. A pamphleteer late in the eighteenth century made a complaint that is echoed in many ballads of the time (those composed by seamen, that is, not by the Dibdens and such): 'Whilst Gazettes are filled with encomiums of their bravery and contempt of danger, yet (the common seamen) languish under the greatest hardships and the most abject slavery, puzzled and perplexed by unnecessary trifles, hard-wrought and ill-used by almost every petty officer of but a month's standing, who, ignorant of duty whether performed right or wrong, flourishes his rattan over the head of the ablest seaman, and acts the tyrant over them without control.' And in the ballad of "Jack Tar", the once-bitten seaman, invited to volunteer rather than be pressed, refuses in terms that foreshadow the mood that raised 'the breeze at Spithead' in 1797, when the seventeen bright stars of the Channel Fleet refused to put to sea, in the middle of a war too, until their wrongs were redressed, and thus stunned the populace and threw the authorities into panic by the thunderclap of their mutiny. The ballad is contained in a late eighteenth century garland—no imprint—called *Tibbie Fowler*.

'Come, brave honest Jack Tar, once more will you venture?
Press warrants they're out; I would have you to enter.
Take some rich Spanish prize as we've done before O.'
—'Yes, and be cheated of 'em all, as we were the last war O.'

'No man that sails with me shall e'er be abused;
So Jack, come and enter and you'll be well used.
You'll be bo'sun's mate, Jack, so boldly come enter,
And not like a dog be hauled on board the tender.'

'Dear captain,' Jack says then, 'don't talk of your pressing.
It's not long ago since I gave six of 'em a dressing.'
—'I know that very well, Jack: the truth I must grant you;
You're a brave hearty fellow, and that makes me want you.'

'Dear captain,' Jack says then, 'if the truth I do tell ye,
I got so much the last war, it quite filled my belly.
For your damned rogues of officers, they use men so cruel,
That a man-o'-war's worse than hell or the devil.

There's the master a-swearing, the bo'sun a-growling,
The midshipman howling out: "Take that fore-bowling";
If you speak but one word you're a mutinous rascal,
Both your legs laid in irons and you're tried by court-martial.'

Now boys, we are pressed away from our habitation,
And we leave wife and children in grief and vexation.
We venture our sweet lives in defence of our nation,
And we get nothing for it but toil and vexation.

   As with the military ballads, historical songs about the great
sea-battles have not lasted well. Oh, any number of broadsides
survive: Firth prints about two hundred of them in the collection of *Naval Songs and Ballads* that he prepared for the Navy
Records Society, but in most cases the more important the
event the worse was the ballad; folk singers and audiences
were not interested enough in them to keep them on the go,
and very few have been found in tradition within the last
hundred years. Whether made by professional stall-ballad
writers or by the sailors themselves, the topical narrative songs
of big engagements had a short life in the pubs, and now endure
only as mummies on the dustier library shelves. Too much is
made of the journalistic function of folk song. Undeniably
there were songs that set out the news of the day, serving a

purpose similar to a modern newspaper's; but these were nearly always ephemeral, not lasting pieces. Mere reportage is not the durable stuff of folklore, and in the making of songs a string of facts was never a good substitute for imagination, though some presentday writers of 'folk-style' ballads find the lesson hard to learn. For how long were Deloney's verses sung, on the capture of the Great Galeazzo and the taking of Cadiz? Probably no longer than the ballad called "English courage display'd, or Brave news from Admiral Vernon", written by a seaman aboard the flagship *Burford* and sent home from Jamaica to find its way, rather mysteriously, into print as a slip-sheet of 1740. It is an account of the taking of Porto Bello; so many men-o'-war of so many guns, so many days of 'bumbardment', so many forts demolished and castles razed; indeed, it is rather livelier than most of its kind, with bits of colour here and there to sweeten the dry-bread account of strategy and numbers, as when Vernon's plundering seamen no sooner get ashore than 'with plenty of rum and good strong wines our men did soon get mellow, Then swore that never a house should stand in the town of Porto Bello.' But of all the ballads relating to the War of Jenkins' Ear, it is not the *Burford* seaman's composition, nor the one called "Vernon's glory" written by a sailor aboard the *Shrewsbury* and recounting all too soon the capture of Cartagena, nor any of the other doggerel documentaries of Walpole's escapade in Panama and the Caribbean that survived among the folk singers and those who loved to hear

It was one morn – ing in the spring,

I went on board to— serve my King.

I left my dear – est— dear be-hind,

Who—oft-times told me her heart was mine.

them: the song that remained green right up to our own century was the non-topical, quite un-factual, completely traditional romance of which Vaughan Williams recorded an example, from James Whitby of Tilney-All-Saints some sixty years ago, to a handsome Sol-mode tune that so interested the collector that he neglected to take more than the first verse of the text, so we have filled the narrative out from broadsides.

> It was one morning in the spring,
> I went on board to serve my king.
> I left my dearest dear behind,
> Who oftimes told me her heart was mine.
>
> When I was sailing on the sea
> I sometimes found opportunity
> To write a letter to my dear,
> But not one word from her did I hear.
>
> When we arrived off Cartagena town,
> The cannon-balls flew up and down,
> But in all the dangers that I could find,
> Her sweet young face still run in my mind.
>
> When I got back to old England's shore,
> I went straightway to my love's door.
> Her cruel old father made this reply:
> My daughter does your love deny.
> She's married a merchant for all her life,
> So you may seek some other wife.
>
> I cursed all gold and silver too.
> I cursed young women as cannot be true,
> As first make vows and then them break
> And marry a merchant for riches' sake.
>
> I wish I was back off the Panama shore
> Where thundering cannon loud do roar.
> I'd sail the ocean until I die
> Although the waves run mountains high.

If the history-book battles are generally missing from the folk singers' repertory, a few history-book heroes appear like the wispy ghosts of old mythological champions. Not that their victories counted for a great deal among the commoners, if the songs are anything to go by. 'Much blood, and is cheese any cheaper?' seems to have been a familiar enough comment on news of naval triumphs. What mattered to the folk song audience was the human interest, the poignant detail. The early eighteenth century was distinguished by the victories of Rooke and Leake, but the song that lived is the one recording Benbow's disastrous battle with the French squadron under Ducasse in 1702. Only one captain stood by the rear-admiral; the rest hung back, notably Kirby and Wade. Benbow's right leg was shattered by chain shot, and the wound was mortal, but he had Kirby and Wade hanged before he died. The folk admired the pluck of this son of the people (he was formerly a butcher's apprentice) and the balladeers made a song for him in a metre similar to the one they had used in the previous year (1701) for the hanging ballads of Jack Hall the murderous chimney-sweep and the pirate Captain William Kidd.

Bold Benbow gave the signal for to fight, for to fight.
Bold Benbow gave the signal for to fight.
The ships boxed up and down and the shots they flew around,
And the men came tumbling down. There they lie.

Admiral Benbow lost his legs by chain-shot, by chain-shot.
Admiral Benbow lost his legs by chain-shot.
And down on his stumps did fall, and so bitterly did call:
'Fight on, my noble lads, tis my lot!

And there bold Benbow lay, crying: 'Boys', crying: 'Boys',
There bold Benbow lay, crying: 'Boys,
Let's tack about once more, and we'll drive 'em on the shore,
For I value not their score, nor their noise.'

Unsupported thus he fought, nor would run, nor would run.
Unsupported thus he fought, nor would run.
Till his ship was just a wreck, and no man would him back,
For the others wouldn't slack to fire their guns.

Twas on Tuesday morning last Benbow died, Benbow died.
On Tuesday morning last Benbow died.
What a shocking thing to see Admiral Benbow carried away!
He was buried in Kingston Church; there he lies.

The folk have always been capricious in their choice of heroes
to commemorate. America, for instance, has its traditional
songs of the assassinations of Garfield and McKinley, yet no
strong folk ballad of Lincoln's death survives, nor of his deeds.
It is hard to account for Benbow's enduring fame, but his
story seems to have haunted the imagination of singers with
peculiar intensity, and his ballad remained in wider circulation
and better shape than any song commemorating more celebrated and more successful commanders, Nelson included.
Several of the most interesting folk singers of the twentieth
century had good versions of Benbow's elegy, among them
Henry Burstow of Horsham, the Lancashire ex-seaman W.
Bolton who gave such fine sea songs to Annie Gilchrist, and
Cecil Sharp's 'Captain' Lewis of Minehead.

Some folk songs of the sea were made by landsmen and are
embellished with fanciful detail that would baffle a sailor.
Others were made by seamen and they impress by the authenticity of their account of storms and wrecks and the hazards of
Cape Horn and the icy whaling grounds. But in either case,
nearly always, romance not reportage is central to the songs.
If lasting ballads of great battles are few, those of more or less
mythologized flurries with pirate ships abound, and some seem
well nigh indestructible. During the present century, there is
hardly a traditional singer of note, from Henry Burstow to
Sam Larner, who had not his good version of "Henry Martin",
a piece that has remained a favourite through many vicissi-
tudes since it was first printed (in 82 verses!) at the outset of
the seventeenth century, and sold from cheap stationers'
stalls in St. Paul's churchyard and elsewhere. Originally it
concerned the piracy, chase and capture of the Scottish merchant freebooter Sir Andrew Barton and his brothers Robert
and John, fierce men who despatched three barrels of salted
Flemish seamen's heads as a present to James IV. Henry VIII
sent ships against the pirates, and on August 2nd 1511, Barton's

ship was captured and the bold freebooter beheaded. In the course of time, passing by word of mouth from one country singer to another, the song grew shorter, the longwinded narrative pared down till only a swift account of the piracy remained. Perhaps through mis-hearing, the captain's name was altered first to Andy Bardan and then to Henry Martin. The piece remains one of the most-sung ballads of our time.

A parallel favourite is the defiant "Ward the pirate", of which Vaughan Williams recorded fine sets from a King's Lynn fisherman and from a Wiltshire pedlar, Frank Bailey, who called it 'a master song' (he won a prize for his performance of it at a travellers' singing match). John Ward, a sea-rover from Faversham in Kent, scourged the Barbary coast along with his Dutch or German comrade Dansekar (Danziger?), during the first decade of the seventeenth century. He offered his services to James I, but in reply the king sent a warship, the *Rainbow*, against the pirate. A brisk fight ensued and the pirate, crowing like a cock, was victorious.

Come on, come on, cries Captain Ward, I value you not a pin,
For if you've got brass for an outward show, I have got steel
    within.
Go home, go home, says Captain Ward, and tell your king
    from me,
If he reigns king on all the land, Ward will reign king on sea.

The first printed version of the Captain Ward ballad did not appear until some eighty years after the events it describes, perhaps because it was hazardous to sing the song openly before the Stuarts were driven off the throne in 1688. Commenting on Ward's mockery Phillips Barry remarks: 'It is only twenty years after Elizabeth, James's immediate predecessor, had won the fight with the Armada, and here is a freebooter ordering the King of England off the high seas, telling him that he has lost the sea power which was England's glory! Many of his English subjects would enjoy the mortification of their Scotch overlord under that stinging taunt, and would know the ballad when it would not be safe to be caught singing it.' We may be sure that successive generations singing the Captain Ward ballad have not been concerned in the slightest with Jacobite rights and wrongs, but were enchanted with Ward's effrontery in facing up to any high and mighty power, and it is the hero's swagger and spice that has made it a master song in their ears. In fact, during Victoria's reign, some broadside prints had the saucy pirate jeering at the queen.

"The bold *Princess Royal*", "The *Dolphin*", "The coasts of Barbary" are among favourite pirate songs that lasted well in kitchen, fo'c'sle and bar-room, as did such adventure ballads as "Rounding the Horn", "The ship in distress", "The *London steamer*" and the melodrama of the haunted murderous captain William Glen of "The New York trader". Hard powerful songs, and with many of the later chronicles of Jack ashore at the mercy of Liverpool landladies, or the doxies of the Ratcliffe Highway and the Yarmouth back-streets, they have helped to perpetuate the stereotype of the oldtime sailing ship seaman as a hairy-chested bawler, only fit to haul on tarry rope, living like a pig among straw in the fo'c'sle and roistering ashore 'like thunder: having nothing but the clap'. As usual with stereotypes, the image is one-sided. If conditions and treatment in the ships was brutish, the men were not always so. Now and then, in museums and curio shops we find sweet mermaids carved on coconuts, classical scenes scrimshawed on spermwhale teeth, a pillow-case embroidered with two hearts and an anchor, delicate fond things worked by coarse hands in the stuffy half-deck, and we are reminded that if some of the old seamen were of the ringtailed roarer kind, others were thoughtful men, masters of their vernacular culture both at work and in leisure. So too with the songs they sang. Some are as rough as a teak board, others—the majority, probably—are gentle lyrical romances spliced to tunes full of secrets. Most of these were made by landsmen, no doubt, and were widespread ashore, even far from the coast; but many of them have been recorded from old sailors or have been found scribbled in the back of ship's log-books, and there is no doubt they were much used at sea. A string of their titles is like a garland: "Farewell, my dearest Nancy", "Lovely on the water", "Just as the tide was flowing", "The dark-eyed sailor", and their poetry has an odd formal charm similar to the common representation of the sailor—ox-eyed, ringleted, with elegant white bell-bottoms and dancing pumps—on the popular engravings, or as cheap china figures of jolly Jack that decorated every other sideboard and cottage mantelpiece until a few decades ago. The words of the songs were not merely quaint: in the circumstances they had their own pathos and felicity. Men leading brutal lives in the floating wooden slums of a century-and-a-half ago felt to some extent reassured by such songs as the one in which a mother warns her daughter against sailors, and the girl replies:

> I know you would have me wed a farmer,
> And not give me my heart's delight,
> But give me the lad whose tarry trousers
> Shines to me like diamonds bright.

Of all men afloat, the oldtime whalermen led the bitterest, grossest, most tameless lives, hard work in cruel weather amid a deluge of blood, but it was a whaler who pledged his constancy in this apt and tender image:

> Now don't you weep, my pretty lass,
> Though you be left behind,
> For the rose will bloom on Greenland's ice
> Before I change my mind.

Doubtless a Scot, the maker of that verse; but English seamen sang the most famous of all whaling songs which, in some versions, begins: 'We may no longer stay ashore Since we're so deep in debt, So off to Greenland we must steer, Some money for to get.' Modest enough; but the ballad gets under way with a spirited description of the sighting of the whale, the chase, the fatal accident ('The harpoon struck, the line run out, The whale give a flurry with his tail, And he upset the boat; we lost half-a-dozen men. No more, no more Greenland for you, brave boys; And we never caught that whale.') At last, with the Arctic winter closing in, comes the forced departure from the whaling grounds, with a sombre lyrical ending to what had begun with so little resonance:

> Oh, Greenland is a dreadful place,
> It's a place that's never green,
> Where icebergs grow and the whale-fish blow,
> And daylight's seldom seen, brave boys,
> And the daylight's seldom seen.

In the half-deck and the fo'c'sle, men from the cities are cast together with men from the villages in the closest intimacy, a merchant ship is a town and country cultural relations centre *par excellence*, and urban and rural attitudes and tastes merge on more or less equal terms. More or less equal: it seems, though, that generally it was the rural style of poetry and melody that dictated the tenor of the sailor songs until the end of the eighteenth century; subsequently the seaman's lyrical creations became increasingly affected by the tone of the backstreets of the towns, not so much because the numerical balance between townsmen and countrymen in the crews was altered (though this may have been the case) as because the old 'classical' rural style of song-creation was already beginning to lose some of its force. The psychological climate of the songs as well as the character and form of the tunes became very much altered, though the older style of songs lasted well among such crews as were mainly made up of men from the coastal villages.

Old Joseph Elliott of Todber, sang to H. E. D. Hammond a song that he and his shipmates—all Dorset men—used to hearten themselves with while tossing about on the bitter cod-banks off Newfoundland, reflecting on the life of their farm-labouring friends back home, comparing lots and making the rueful best of it:

When labouring men come home at night, they tell the girls fine tales,
What they have been a-doing, all in the new cornfields.
Tis a-cutting of the grass so short is all that they can do,
While we poor jolly sailors bold ploughs on the ocean through.

Here's the night as dark as any pitch, and the wind begins to
    blow.
Our captain he commanded us: All hands turn out below!
Our captain he commanded us our goodly ship to guard:
Jump up aloft, my lively lads, and strike the t'gallant yard!

You see a storm is rising and we are all confound,
Looking out every moment that we shall all be drowned.
Cheer up! never be fainthearted; we shall see our girls again.
In spite of all our danger we'll plough the raging main.

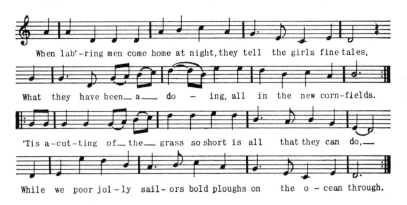

When lab'-ring men come home at night, they tell the girls fine tales,
What they have been a do - ing, all in the new corn-fields.
'Tis a-cut-ting of the grass so short is all that they can do,
While we poor jol-ly sail-ors bold ploughs on the o - cean through.

In the histories of art and literature the eighteenth century
is credited as the commonsense age and the nineteenth as the
time of romance, but this hardly holds for the folk traditions.
The formalized, marine-pastoral air of the old sailor songs
gave way to realism and irony in the later days of sail, when
capitalist competition and the need to fulfil sailing schedules
on time meant that the working of ships became more intense,
with the mate driving the men, the skipper driving the mate,
the company driving the skipper. One of the hard runs for
packet ships was the winter trip from Liverpool to New York,
through heavy seas, contrary winds, sleet and snow. The large
crews were kept busy reefing as the gales increased or piling on
canvas whenever the wind abated. The latterday favourite
song called "The Banks of Newfoundland" gives us the picture
of a bitter western ocean crossing shortly before the days of

steam. The Irish-style come-all-ye tune is of the kind that became powerful if not paramount in English folk song during the nineteenth century, and variants of it were used for "The lowlands of Holland" and the transportation song of "Van Diemen's Land". Indeed there is a very close connection between this latter piece and the "Banks of Newfoundland" and in most versions of their song the seamen have lifted whole stanzas from the convict ballad, as if they needed some model of self-pity on which to construct the story of their plight. This set, recorded in 1954 from a remarkable old sailor-singer Ted Howard of Barry, has less of "Van Diemen's Land" than usual.

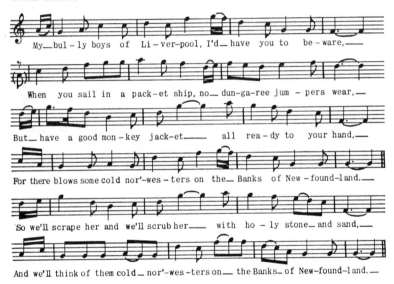

My bully boys of Liverpool, I'd have you to beware,
When you sail in a packet ship, no dungaree jumpers wear,
But have a good monkey-jacket all ready to your hand,
For there blows some cold nor'westers on the Banks of New-
    foundland.
        So we'll scrape her and we'll scrub her with holystone and
            sand,
        And we'll think of them cold nor'westers on the Banks of
            Newfoundland.

There was Jack Lynch from Ballinahinch, Jim Murphy and
    Sam Moore;
It was in the year of sixty-two those poor boys suffered sore,
For they'd pawned their clothes in Liverpool, and they sailed
    as they did stand,
And there blows some cold nor'westers on the Banks of New-
    foundland.

The mate came up on the foc'sle head and loudly he did roar:
Come rattle her in, my lively lads, we're bound for America's
    shore.
Then lay aloft and shake her out and give her all she can stand,
And there blows some cold nor'westers on the Banks of New-
    foundland.

And now it's reef and reef, my boys, with the canvas frozen hard,
And it's mount and pass, you son of a gun, on a ninety-foot
    top'sl yard,
Never mind your boots and oilskins, but haul to beat the band,
For there blows some cold nor'westers on the Banks on New-
    foundland.

And now we're off the Hook, my boys, and the land's all
    covered in snow,
With the tug-boat due ahead of us, into New York we will tow,
And as we tie up at the dock them pretty girls will stand,
Crying: 'It's snugger with me than it is at sea on the Banks of
    Newfoundland!'
      So we'll scrape her and we'll scrub her with holystone and
        sand,
      And we'll bid farewell to the Virgin Rocks and the Banks
        of Newfoundland.

One more example from the last tattered days of sail helps
to show the change that had come over the seaman's way of
expression as he became conscious of himself as an exploited
floating proletarian rather than a proud if battered sea-dog.

The song of the sailor robbed and virtually shanghaied who comes bitterly to repent his calling, emerges as a stubble-chinned red-eyed ironical report whose truth could be attested to by many seafarers particularly in the hard years of 1850–75 when competition between sailing ship lines was at its fiercest and at the same time the companies were trying to cut back their overheads, notably their outlay in crew's wages, keep and amenities, in the face of the growing threat of steam. Companies whose ships had a reputation for being hard and hungry found it difficult to man their vessels, and as a consequence this period, the third quarter of the nineteenth century, was the high era of the crimping game. The unscrupulous sailor boardinghouse master would render the seaman unconscious with drink, drug or blackjack, deliver the body to a waiting ship, and pocket his fee. Or more commonly, he might arrange for the man to be robbed, put the penniless fellow in his debt, and—in return for the seaman's advance note, loaned by the company to buy gear for the voyage—he would 'use his influence' to sign the man aboard any hard ship that was wanting hands. Among boarding-masters notorious for crimping were Paddy West of Great Howard Street, Liverpool (who has his own ballad), John da Costa, likewise of Liverpool, Shanghai Brown of San Francisco, and Thomas Moore of the Boca on Buenos Aires' waterfront. The system was so well-established that crimps would sometimes circularize those companies with manning troubles, setting out their conditions for providing crew. From that time comes the common ballad ('known to every seaman', says knowledgeable Stan Hugill), the last descendant of the raffish sailortown songs of Rosemary Lane (now Royal Mint Street) and Ratcliffe Highway in London, or Paradise Street, Liverpool (commemorated in such epics as "Maggie May" and "Blow the man down"). Ted Howard of Barry called his version: "Go to sea no more". He set the locale in Liverpool and insisted that the vengeful boardinghouse master was 'Rapper' Brown. Other texts have the seaman stranded in San Francisco at the mercy of Shanghai Brown, and this is more feasible since, by that time, the English whaling industry with hand harpoon and row-boat, had dried up. It was to re-start later, after the business had been revolutionized by the harpoon gun; but not till the twentieth century did Liverpool's Bromborough Dock become important in whaling history, whereas in the 1870s a large number of vessels were sailing out of San Francisco bound for the bowhead whaling-grounds of the Bering Sea, a trip repugnant to most seamen unless hard-pushed.

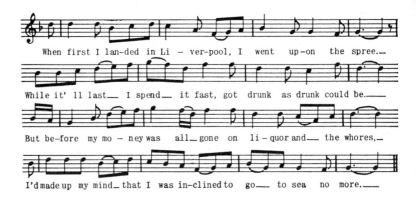

When first I landed in Liverpool, I went upon the spree.
While it'll last I spend it fast, got drunk as drunk could be.
But before my money was all gone on liquor and the whores,
I'd made up my mind that I was inclined to go to sea no more.

As I was walking down the street, I met with Angeline.
She said: Come home with me, my lad, and we'll have a cracking time.
But when I awoke, it was no joke, I found I was all alone;
My silver watch and my money too and my whole bloody gear was gone.

As I was walking down the street, I met big Rapper Brown.
I asked him if he would take me in, he looked at me with a frown.
He said: Last time you was paid off, to me you chalked no score;
But I'll take your advance and I'll give youse a chance to go to sea once more.

He shipped me aboard of a whaling ship bound for the Arctic
seas,
Where cold winds blow and the frost and snow Jamaica rum
would freeze,
And worse to bear, I'd no hard-weather gear, for I'd lost all
my dunnage ashore.
It was then I wished that I was dead so I'd go to sea no more.

Sometimes we're catching whales, my lad, but mostly we get
none,
With a twenty-foot oar in every paw from five o'clock in the
morn,
And when daylight's gone and the night coming on, you rest
upon your oar
And, oh boys, you wish that you was dead or snug with the
girls ashore.

Come all you bold seafaring lads, and listen to my song:
When you go a-big-boating I'll have youse not go wrong.
You take my tip, when you come off a trip, don't go with any
whore,
But get married, lads, have all night in, and go to sea no more.

There is discrepancy between the mood of the typical sailor
songs of the nineteenth century and the landsman's excited
view of ships with 'white sails crowding, leaning across the
bosom of the urgent West'. The sailor, sorehanded and sweating
at the long upper-topsail hauls, could have pride in his ship but
he knew her in moments when she was less than noble: he
recognized her as a vehicle hard to drive and a sorry lodging
to live in. The insurance clerk might daydream about the
brave wind in the rigging and the lovely dance of waves;
weather and sea for the sailor meant hazard, hardship and
damned little pay at the end of it all. The watcher on shore
saw the bold figurehead, the gold scroll-work, and the fine
balance of spar and sail and curving hull; he did not see the
tight sailing schedule, the mate with the belaying-pin in his
fist, the men at a giddy height above the deck, shuffling
crabwise along the footropes on a wet night. The nineteenth
century sailing ships were handsomer than ever before, but

the work was more intense because capitalist competition quite suddenly became fiercer. The effects of that competition were far-reaching, extending even into the realm of folklore, with an astonishing and paradoxical result. The modern form of capitalism that gave rise to the great shipping lines, produced at the same time the striking body of primitive folk songs that we call: sea shanties.

The shanties are very different from the kind of sea songs we have been considering. Our concern has been with songs chiefly sung for diversion and entertainment in the sailors' leisure moments. Such as those leisure moments were—working watch and watch, four hours on, four off, all round the clock, with sleep and meals to be snatched as could be, the men had little enough singing-time except perhaps during the second dog-watch from six to eight in the evening. Still, singing there would be, round the lantern in the stuffy fo'c'sle with all ports screwed down against the weather, or in warmer latitudes up on the fo'c'sle head, the crowd sprawled on the hatches and the singer sitting at ease on the iron bitts (in consequence, songs sung for fun were called 'forebitters'). In form and function, the sailors' diversionary songs, comic or tragic, nostalgic, or ironical, are hardly distinguishable from other English folk songs; but the shanties are stylistically quite different also in intent. They are specifically work songs, performed not for fun or feeling but as an aid to muscular effort. With shanties, the labour is central to the song; it is the gesture of work that provides the logic, and by chance the beauty, of the musical utterance. 'Grunt and haul' not only dictates the metre and rhythm of the song, it is also the catalyst that transmutes a raw tune and a loose chain of crude lyrics into a strident lament or an epic alleluia in the face of a hard existence.

In most people's folklore, the work songs proper (not merely songs *about* work) along with the ritual songs, usually comprise the earliest, most primitive, least altered stratum of melody, and they incline to disappear in the face of technical advance, naturally enough, because they were made to accompany hand-labour, and usually gang-labour at that, and as machines, however rudimentary, replace hands, and the single worker replaces the group, the reason goes from the old work songs, their logic drains away. A solitary Negro driving a bulldozer sings a different song from the convict gang who perhaps only a year before were working with pick and shovel on the same road. And it is not merely that his tune and lyric are different; the form of his song and its psychological climate' will be changed. In England, it seems, we once had a wealth of work songs accompanying the sweep of sickles in the wheat, the lifting of heavy stones in the quarry, the communal steeping of woollen cloth to shrink it and to fix its dye; rough songs with ramshackle words and recurring refrains, sometimes punctuated with cries. Also there were more evolved, more lyrical and coherent work songs, with rhythm and movement still dictated by labour processes, but moving firmly in the direction of the ordinary non-functional song-proper; these were attached to the rhythmical use of modest machines such as spinning-wheels or lace-bobbins, collective songs but only lightly related to the gesture of the work. All the work songs proper have a double function, to co-ordinate muscular effort and to distract the mind from the tedium of the job, but these effects reside in the songs to varying degrees; the hard-work songs are mainly shaped for the muscles, the lighter-work songs for the mind, just as with the sea shanties the *hauling* songs, for instance halyard shanties to help the heavy spasmodic pull-all-together, set more store on energetic rhythm than on word-sense, whereas the *heaving* songs, such as capstan shanties involving the use of a machine in continuous and boring effort, have a more shambling rhythm but tend to carry coherent and reasonably diverting narrative texts.

As usual with work songs proper, our nineteenth century shanties are mostly leader-chorus, solo-and-response songs. The pattern is ancient and universal. Boatmen on the Yangtse and the Niger use it in ways similar to those employed by the tarpaulin hatted johns of the Western Ocean packets. As to antiquity, the references are well-known. Brother Felix Fabri of Ulm, on a pilgrim ship from Venice to the Holy Land in the 1480s heard the seamen 'sing when work is going on because when at sea it is very heavy and only carried on by a concert between one who sings and orders and the labourers who sing in response'. And a good thousand years before, lolling on an Aegean clifftop with their mouths full of kisses and cake, the young goatherds Daphnis and Chloe watched a ship sail by below them and that 'which other Marriners used to do to elude the tediousnesse of labour, these began, and held on as they rowed along. There was one amongst them that was the Celeustes, or the hortator to ply, and he had certain nautic odes or Sea-songs: the rest like a Chorus all together strained their throats to a loud holla, and catcht his voice at certain intervals.'

We may be sure that rowing and hauling chants were raised in English ships in early times, but there is little trace of them. Probably they were in the main more in the nature of rhythmic cries than songs, those 'unnameable and unearthly howls and yells that characterize the true sailor, which are only acquired by years of sea service', such as the calls of 'How! hissa!' and 'Y how! taylia!' that the Santiago pilgrim heard aboard his medieval ship, outward bound for Vigo from Bristol; or, for the matter of that, such as the wild wavering 'sing-out' phrase with which the modern song-leader would preface his shanty while the gang was getting a firm hold on the rope. In some instances, and for certain operations, the cries might be more organized, more evolved, moving along the road towards formal compositions, with tunes of bold rhythm but vague contour, and words of firm metre though perhaps of scant sense or no sense at all. Among its several obliging references to early folk song, the mid-sixteenth century *Complaynt of Scotland* quotes such shanty scraps as:

> Haill áll and ane.
> Haill áll and ane.
> Háill him up til us.
> Háill him up til us.
>> Hou hou.
>> Pulpela pulpela.
>> Boulena boulena.
>> Darta darta.
>> Hard out strif. . . .
>>> (this for a bowline haul).

> Caupón caupóna.
> Caupón caupóna.
> Caupón holá.
> Caupón holá.
> Caupón holt.
> Caupón holt.
> Sárabossa.
> Sárabossa.

The use of scat syllables for work songs survives in our own time, for instance among Portland quarrymen who still split the stone to a hammer-song (their 'French song', they call it) that runs:

> Ee calazi,
> Calazi calenia.
> Tra la la la,
> luff, luff, luff.
> Ee calazi,
> Cazee cazenia.
> Tra la la la,
> Luff, luff, luff.
> Tra la lala la,
> Luff, luff, luff.
> Bout!

Even such rudimentary work chants seem to have died away in ocean-going vessels by the end of the seventeenth century, though they may have lingered aboard fishing craft. The small slow merchantmen of the seventeenth and eighteenth centuries carried large crews that could do all the heaving and hauling necessary without the aid of song. Also, many vessels, notably the East Indiamen, sailed under naval discipline, with no singing allowed on deck* and the hauling done to the sound of the bosun's whistle. So this venerable primitive kind of song faded fairly early from the traditional repertory of our seamen, and it seems against all laws of probability,

* The rule was not generally relaxed until the 1820s; later still in East Indiamen.

contrary to all canons of folklore, that it should revive
and flourish with such astonishing vigour in specifically
capitalist conditions, just as the main body of folk song was
starting its headlong slide towards disuse.

During the eighteenth century our merchant ships were
still sailing to farflung parts under the same six-sail rig that
Vasco da Gama had carried. They were bluff pot-bellied craft,
few of more than 300 tons, except for the big East Indiamen,
'backbone and beauty of the British Marine' but slow and
cumbersome and stubbornly conservative in design. The East
Indiamen were as much fighting vessels as merchant ships
(the *Bombay Castle*, launched in 1789, carried seventy-four
guns) and indeed there was generally but slight difference
between merchantman and man-o'-war. With the seas as
lawless as Cicero, any merchant vessel was likely also to be a
privateer or pirate; and even if owner and skipper had no
ambition beyond freight-carrying, their ship still had to be
armed for its own defence. Voyages were slow, nor was there
much incentive to speed them up, for if colonial trade was
expanding, most of the commerce was carried on by chartered
companies against which other traders were forbidden to
compete. Notably the East India Company's monopoly was a
dead hand on shipping enterprise, preventing competition,
removing any stimulus to build faster vessels. In any case,
the general theory was that fast ships would be too dear to
operate; they would have to be sleek, which meant a reduced
cargo-space, also they needed more sail, which was thought
unduly dangerous (at that time, East Indiamen, the only
vessels to carry much canvas, used to shorten sail each evening
so that if a squall came up, the ship was already snugged
down to receive it). Merchants were resigned to the slowness of
sea transport: Liverpool to Philadelphia, sixty days there, fifty
back; seventy days from Kingston, Jamaica to London; five
weeks from Liverpool to Marseilles. Small ships, big crews,
leisurely voyages, naval discipline, little scope for work-songs.

However, by the beginning of the nineteenth century,
the winds of change were blowing across the ocean. The story
has been told often enough. The end of the War of Independence had left the triumphant Americans without a navy but

with keen appetite for competition, and they applied themselves to shipbuilding with an adventurous forward-looking zest. They had plenty of natural resources for the making of good vessels, and their government was not, as the English was, hampered by obsolete laws. So, particularly in the yards close to Baltimore, they evolved a fleet of big fast frigates, brigs, schooners of novel design, flush-decked, with the point of maximum beam well for'ard, plenty of sheer from high bows to low stern, and a pronounced rake to the masts. The design had originated with pilot boats plying at the mouth of Chesapeake Bay, where competition was fierce and the first pilot to arrive alongside the incoming merchantman got the job. A little later, the model was adapted to slave-ships and privateers, vessels that needed to be able to race their pursuers and get swiftly out of cannon-range; eventually, the rakish lines were applied to ordinary merchantmen.

Meanwhile, the Industrial Revolution was bringing a novel outlook to British capitalism. The markets of the world were opening for the new machine-made goods. Business men wanted to know just when those goods could be delivered, and they wanted them delivered as quickly as possible. Also, with transatlantic trade growing fast, merchants and industrialists needed to plan business trips across the ocean, and particularly with passenger traffic the new-fangled axiom 'Time is money' was inflated to the stature of a moral principle. In 1816, Isaac Wright & Co.'s Black Ball Line began their regular run between New York and Liverpool, sailing on the first of each month, irrespective of weather or amount of cargo loaded, twenty-three days for the eastward trip, about forty coming back. The crimson swallowtail house-flag and the black ball painted on the foresail were emblems of hardship for seamen. The sailing schedules were unprecedented for tightness, the discipline was merciless, the skippers—some of them formerly hardcase commanders of privateers that harried British vessels during the war of 1812—drove ships and men with small regard for weather or weariness. The second mate was called the 'blower', the third mate the 'striker', and an early form of the halyard shanty "Blow the man down" ('blow' meaning 'knock') contains such cautionary passages as:

Now when a Black Baller is clear of the land,
   Tibby way-hay, blow the man down!
The bosun he gives out the word of command:
   Ho, gimme some time to blow the man down!
Lay aft there, my lads, to the break of the poop,
   Tibby way-hay, blow the man down!
Or I'll help you along with the toe of my boot,
   Ho, gimme some time to blow the man down!
It's larboard to starboard, on deck you will sprawl,
   Tibby way-hay, blow the man down!
For Kicking Jack Rogers commands the Black Ball.
   Ho, gimme some time to blow the man down!

On the other hand, Black Ball seamen had their special pride, and one of the most rousing of heaving shanties, with a rhythm particularly apt for work at the old-fashioned spoke-windlass such as Black Ball ships used before 1840, is a praise-song in honour of the company and its game nuggety vessels:

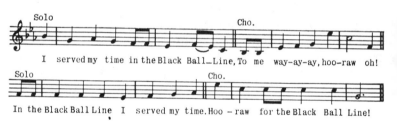

I served my time in the Black Ball Line,
   To me way-ay-ay, hooraw oh!
In the Black Ball Line I served my time.
   Hooraw for the Black Ball Line!
The Black Ball ships they make good time,
   To me way-ay-ay, hooraw oh!
With long clean runs and entrance fine.
   Hooraw for the Black Ball Line!
Oh, that's the line where you can shine,
   To me way-ay-ay, hooraw oh!
That's the line where I spent my prime,
   Hooraw for the Black Ball Line!

They'll carry you along through the ice and snow,
To me way-ay-ay, hooraw oh!
They'll take you where the winds don't blow.
Hooraw for the Black Ball Line!
                                        Etc.

Within a short time, other lines were starting, and the shippers of Manchester cottons, Bradford woollens and Birmingham nails and necklaces could rely on a Black Ball packet leaving regularly on the first day of each month, a Swallowtail packet seven days later, the second Blackballer on the sixteenth, and a Red Star flyer on the twenty-fourth. The English shipyards were sluggish in changing their ways. Initially, the great improvements in shipbuilding came from America. The packet-ships were quite small vessels, but in 1845, John Griffiths designed the first large clipper ship, the *Rainbow* of 750 tons, a big lean Baltimore-bowed vessel that many thought unseaworthy, but she made her maiden voyage round the Horn from New York to Canton and back in six-and-a-half months, to the admiration of the business world. The discovery of gold in California brought a tremendous flow of migrants to the American West Coast, mostly by ship round the Horn. American capitalists were quick to snatch the chance offered to shipowners, and within four years after 1848 nearly 160 fast vessels of the new-fangled clipper design were launched to work the run from New York to San Francisco in a hundred days or little over (incidentally, with so many seamen jumping their ship in San Francisco to try their luck on the goldfields, crews for the return journey were often hard to seek; diamond days for the crimping boarding-masters such as Shanghai Brown).

By the middle of the century, the 'principles of the inspired bagman', the *laissez-faire* notions of the merchant with un-limited goods to sell, were effecting revolutionary changes even in the conservative British shipyards. Ever since the monopoly of the East India Company was broken, the great Thamesside yards of the Green and Wigram families at Blackwall had been building good vessels for trading to the Far East, but they were mostly staid and stately 'safety first' ships, still under the influence of the old armed East Indiamen. But when, after the 'opium war', Hong Kong was annexed and five 'treaty ports' opened for the free export of British goods, and particularly when the discovery of gold in Australia in 1851 brought a sudden clamour for shipping passengers out from Europe, the Blackwall yards, affected by the American example, began to build big fast sailing ships such as the 927 ton *Kent*, swift enough to show her transom to many of the crack tea-clippers.

Now the British vessels began to move into the ascendancy. The American clippers were built of softwoods, pine and such, and under hard driving they became strained, their sailing quality soon deteriorated. The late English clippers, following the lead of the Blackwall frigates, built of hardwoods such as oak and teak, surpassed the Americans because they were stronger and, though dearer to build, were cheaper in the long run. The Clyde took over from Blackwall towards the end of the 1850s when Steele of Greenock began building the long sharp-bowed tea-clippers, light fine ships splendidly apt for the 'flying fish run' to the Orient, designed for working well to windward in the Trades, yet robust enough, if need be, for battering through the gales of the Roaring Forties on the run round Cape Horn. The star of the British clippers rose to its zenith in the 1860s, by which time the Americans were virtually out of the running. Now came the era of the famous names. Steele's built the *Taeping* in 1863, the *Ariel* two years later. Hood's of Aberdeen launched the *Thermopylae* in 1868. Scott and Linton's of Dumbarton built the swift, graceful Cape Horner *Cutty Sark* in 1869, and they went broke in doing so. The truth was, the great days of sail were already over; the noble ships were anachronisms before they left the slipway, monuments carved from snow. Steam was already putting an end to the usefulness of the sail-driven vessel. While Steele's were building the *Ariel*, in the rival yard next door Scott's were putting together the first Holt Line ships with the new compound engines. In the very year that the *Cutty Sark* was launched, the Suez Canal was opened, laying the Far East and Australia accessible to steamers that hitherto had been hindered because they could not carry bunkers enough for the long haul eastward from the Cape. The fastest clippers were taking ninety days to run from Foochow to London in good weather; much longer in bad. The new steamships could cover the distance in comfort, whatever the conditions, in sixty-five days, and make the trip pay. By 1875, the clippers were scuffling for a living; their way of working was out of date; the creative days of the sea-shanty were over.

Do we seem to take a slow boat through this short stretch of maritime history? The voyage is not in vain if we are to understand the phenomenon of the shanty. Pressed by the need to fulfil their sailing schedules if they were to compete successfully with their rivals, the shipowners were ready to try anything that might help the fast and efficient working of their vessels, especially if the aid was cheap. By the eighteen-thirties they were finding that men heaved and hauled better if they sang at work. 'A good shantyman's worth six more hands on the rope' was the saying. Some companies paid a bonus to the man who was a good leader of work songs, the man with a strong voice and a ready wit for spinning chants out of his head in a way that had his workmates toiling with a will. So the practice of shanty-singing as we know it best emerged during the American-dominated packet-ship days of, roughly, 1830-50, and it reached its peak in the British-dominated clipper-ship era of 1855-70. Forty years seems a short time for the rise and decline of such a powerful class of folk songs, but the phenomenon is not unique: in the United States, the vast category of cowboy songs has an even shorter history of barely thirty years, rising with the development of the cattle business after the Civil War, and receding as the Wild West faded, with the end of open-range grazing and the switch from longhorns to fat-stock in the 1890s. The shanties, and the cowboy songs, still hold an appeal, but their natural life is over, they are in their second existence, they haunt us but no longer reproduce their kind.

There is nothing like sea-matters for bringing out our chauvinism, and so in the popular imagination no more deeply national, heart-of-oak, true-blue British song exists than the sea shanty. An illusion. We share our heritage of marine work songs with the Americans, and if it is likely that the later, clipper-ship shanties are mostly the creation of

British seamen, it is just as probable that the majority of the earlier, packet-ship shanties were made aboard American vessels. That is not to say that the men who raised the songs aboard those ships were necessarily Americans. Every American vessel of fair tonnage was likely to carry a crew of mixed nationalities, and indeed the best historian of American square-riggers, Arthur H. Clark, suggests that the native-born seamen were not numerous, and the majority of the packet-rats sailing under the house-flags of the Black Ball, Red Star, Dramatic and Swallowtail lines were British, notably Liverpool Irish, attracted no doubt by the higher wages in U.S. ships.

Such men brought English shanties aboard American vessels, and took American shanties back into British ships. The musical accents of Liverpool and Louisiana, Cork and Cape Cod, Bethnal Green, Buckie and Baltimore went into the composition of the shanties, and the songs were all the better for the mixture. The melodies are a fine jumble of pentatonic phrases that may have derived originally from Gaelic or African culture, modal formulas from the English countryside, and modern commonplaces from stage hits of the first half of Victoria's reign. Similarly the poetic improvizations of the shantymen are incrusted with bits of traditional imagery that first sparkled in the Angle-Saxon, Celtic and Negro mind, along with tags invented by the yelping comedians of the time on both sides of the Atlantic.

Compilers of popular shanty collections in the past have been dogmatic in dividing the songs according to function: this is a capstan shanty, that a halyard shanty, the other is for the pumps, though they have not always agreed among themselves which song served what purpose. Perhaps the pedantry is there because the commentators were either landsmen or officers (the enormous gulf between bridge and fo'c'sle, and the sea of mutual ignorance that washes between them, is seldom realized). Commentators more used to working than watching, who know in their hands the feel of a big mainsail haul, exponents such as estimable Stan Hugill, warn us that tight categories are misleading; a single shanty was likely to be used for a variety of jobs, and especially with capstan work the shantyman would tend to strike up the first song that came into his head, provided the rhythm was one a man could walk to. And yet, notably in the earlier, formative years of the modern shanty, the nature of the job in hand and the gestures needed to fulfil it were important, even decisive, in shaping the melody, rhythm, metre and tempo of the songs.

Singing was handy for accompanying two kinds of shipboard work: hauling and heaving. 'Hauling' implies the hand labour required for setting and reefing sail, mostly pulling on the ropes. 'Heaving' denotes the work with machines such as windlass, capstan, pumps. As remarked, while many shanties might be used indiscriminately both for hauling and heaving jobs, others were shaped for specific uses, for long hauls or short, for hoisting yards, sweating up or bunting, for heaving on the jerky brake-windlass or smoothly shoving the capstan round.

Most primitive of the nineteenth century shanties and no doubt closest to the sea songs of the remoter past, are the sing-outs for short-hauling jobs on the sheets and braces. The sheets are ropes at the lower corner of sails for regulating the tension; the braces are ropes attached to the ends of the yards for regulating the angle of the sails to the wind. Operations such as sweating up the braces—that is, hauling them as tight as possible—call for just a few hands clustered together and reaching up to drag on the downfall of the rope. Ted Howard's favourite for this kind of work was a solo song in which the gang joined in with a grunted exhalation at the end of each short line. The simple narrative text, in which according to a well-established folklore principle the notions of hard work and sexual effort are mingled, allows for fanciful improvization, each day a fresh treatment of the same scenario, but always very brief because the job only called for a few pulls but good 'uns.

A simple form of shanty only a little more evolved than the "Miss Julia" kind was used for 'bunting up'. With the sail furled but not secured, a small number of men, standing in line aloft on the footropes, would lean over to drag the immense mass of rolled-up canvas on to the yard to bind it there. To swing the bundle up on top of the yard required a sudden tremendous heave for which all hands had to be well-prepared. So the bunt shanty would provide a lead-in of reasonable length before the big moment came. The song might be sung in unison, an all-hands affair throughout, or in leader-chorus style, or in the manner of "Miss Julia", solo with the crowd making a single shouted or grunted exclamation at the end of the phrase. In the matter of performance, the specialists report in sundry ways ('different ships, different long splices' is Hugill's comment), but all agree that the final syllable of a bunt song would be a yell just where the big pull came that would lift the heavy roll into place. The classic specimen of a bunt shanty is "Paddy Doyle's boots", one of the few work songs that shantymen seem to have confined to a single task. In fair conditions, with the canvas dry and the gang feeling good, one verse would see the job through.

Tim-my way   hay   hay__ ah.__   We'll pay Pad-dy Doyle for 'is Huh!

Shanties of this kind were sometimes called 'foresheeters' though, as remarked, they were used not merely to get an extra drag on the sheets, but were also sung at work on the braces or the bunt or when sweating up the halyards as a final touch to a long haul. Compared to the great proliferation of halyard shanties, the repertory of foresheeters—'short drag' shanties, American seamen called them—is rather limited. Musically, some are more evolved than others, but because they accompanied a task that was brutish and short, their construction is generally rudimentary, the most typical specimens having a single solo line and refrain with just the one pull, most characteristically on the last syllable, which meant that the melody-strophe ended in a shout each time round. "Boney was a warrior" is a fair specimen of this class, occupying, in respect of musical development, a midway position between rough stuff of the "Miss Julia" kind and the shapelier foresheeters such as "Johnny Boker" and "Haul away the bowline" to which we shall shortly return.

A certain number of one-pull shanties, particularly those whose accent comes at the beginning of the refrain instead of at the end, were used at the halyards, not simply for sweating up, but as full-scale hauling songs when the going was getting heavy. The great majority of halyard songs allow for two pulls within the refrain, but on the very long hauls, as the yard rose higher and the sail filled with wind and the strain increased and the men lost their freshness, the shantyman might switch to the kind of songs that take only one pull to the chorus line. In general these shanties would be sung a little faster than the double-haulers, but the tempo always depended on the circumstances of the job.

Whether they are foresheeters or halyard shanties, the one-pull songs often have a wild and desperate air. A characteristically stocky tune of great intensity goes to the shanty called "Billy Riley", associated particularly, so Miss Fox Smith and others tell us, with the frigates built at Green's Blackwall yard about the middle of the century. That so savage a melody should be raised aboard such starchy craft as the Blackwallers ('high-class ships run in high-class manner' was the company's description: 'all teak and Manila cheroots' was the seamen's) seems odd at first, but the vessels' high bulwarks and heavy sterns made them hard to drive when racing against clippers met on the high seas, though they did not shrink from taking on even such fliers as the *Taeping* and *Fiery Cross*. Heavy ships meant hard shanties, so a thickset song like "Billy Riley", with its primitive bitonal refrain just apt for hoarse yelling, well suited the desperate hauling that the Blackwallers often entailed. Hugill suggests that "Billy Riley" 'probably started life as a cotton-hoosiers' song'. Perhaps; there is no evidence of it being used by Negro stevedores in the ports of the American South, yet the air of Africa seems to blow through the tune as it does through so many one-pull shanties such as "Bring 'em down" and the (nowadays) most familiar version of "Sally Racket".

Old Bil-ly Ri-ley was a danc-ing mas-ter. Old Bil-ly Ri-ley O!

> Old Bill Riley was a dancing master.
> *Old Billy Riley O!*
> Old Billy Riley was master of a drogher.
> *Old Billy Riley O!*
> Old Billy Riley had a little daughter.
> *Old Billy Riley O!*
> Nice little daughter but I can't get at her.
> *Old Billy Riley O!*
> O Miss Riley, little Miss Riley.
> *Old Billy Riley O!*
> Screw her up and we're away, boys.
> *Old Billy Riley O!*
> One more pull and then belay, boys.
> *Old Billy Riley O!*
> > Etc.

Our examples of these one-pull shanties illustrate a whole evolution of melody-forms step by step, from the brief musical cry to the quite well-developed song-tune. The form of the shanty was likely to be important to the job in hand but it is not always clear why one song should be more effective than another. R. H. Dana, working in the Cape Horn brig *Pilgrim* in 1834, says: 'We often found a great difference in the effect of the different songs. . . . Two or three songs would be tried, one after the other, with no effect; —not an inch could be got upon the tackles—when a new song struck up seemed to hit the humour of the moment, and drove the tackles "two blocks" at once. . . . On an emergency, when we wanted a heavy "raise-the-dead" pull, which should start the beams of the ship, there was nothing like "Time for us to go", "Round the corner", or "Hurrah, hurrah, my hearty bullies".' Dana's references are some of the earliest we have to shanty singing as we know it now. Few of the songs he mentions in his book have survived, but sets of "Round the corner" have lasted well into the twentieth century in the mouths of old shellbacks such as John Short of Watchet, who gave Sharp so many fine versions of sailor songs. The expression 'round the corner' is seamen's laconism for the passage around Cape Horn. The tune has the characteristic brevity of most one-pull shanties, but it points towards the more developed, four-lined songs by its demand for an ABAB repeat, dictated by the repetition of each text-line with its refrain.

Oh, a-round the cor-ner we will go.   Round the cor-ner, Sal-ly. (2)

In a fair number of one-pull shanties, the sailor-composers have produced melodies that are just a step forward from the simple repetition of a single solo and refrain line. Characteristic of this class are sequential tunes in which the lines repeat, but at a different pitch, usually a major second down. A severe and impressive example of this major second sequence is provided, once again, by old Mr. Short, who called his song "Shallow Brown" after a shadowy figure who slinks through many shanties, in particular those connected with ships running regularly up the west coast of South America to such ports as Valparaiso, Callao and Talcahuano. Opinions differ as to the meaning of Brown's nickname. Some say it is really 'Cholo', the common Andean word for a mestizo, an Indian-European half-caste; others, less plausibly, suggest the name derives from Shiloh, Tennessee. This version illustrates the fluidity, not to say anarchy prevailing among the sea work-songs. Melodies, refrains, text-lines, all were likely to be taken as interchangeable by the shantyman faced with the problem of producing a song on the spur of the moment to suit a specific job in hand. Here, the solo tune belongs more commonly to the general-purpose shanty "Hilo, somebody Hilo", while the words are usually attached to the widespread and much-varied halyard song "Blow, boys, blow", some sets of which are associated with the Guinea Coast slave ships.

A Yankee ship came down the river. Shallow,———— Shallow Brown.

A Yankee ship came down the river. Shallow,———— Shallow Brown.

A Yankee ship came down the river.
Shallow, Shallow Brown.
A Yankee ship came down the river.
Shallow, Shallow Brown.
And who do you think was master of her?
Shallow, Shallow Brown.
And who do you think was master of her?
Shallow, Shallow Brown.
A Yankee mate and a limejuice skipper.
Shallow, Shallow Brown.
A Yankee mate and a limejuice skipper.
Shallow, Shallow, Brown.
And what do you think they had for dinner?
Shallow, Shallow Brown.
And what do you think they had for dinner?
Shallow, Shallow Brown.
A parrot's tail and monkey's liver.
Shallow, Shallow Brown.
A parrot's tail and monkey's liver.
Shallow, Shallow Brown.

Etc.

With our final specimen of a one-pull shanty we return to the class of foresheeters shaped so that the haul comes on the last syllable of the refrain, a form that sailors have found peculiarly suitable for brief jobs such as the last few pulls to haul a halyard tight or stretch a sail as taut as possible. Certain of these songs leave their rough-spun cousins behind and take us a good way along the path of lyrically evolved melody, with the solo and refrain of fair length, the solo line usually in a metre of eight stresses, four plus four, and the refrain line

basically a hexameter or octometer, but nearly always catalectic
—that is, lacking a final beat—because of the combination of
heavy emphasis and short syllable dictated by the sudden
effort of hauling that occurs just as the sailors reach the end
of their refrain. "Johnny Boker" is of this kind, and "Haul
away, Joe". A particular favourite was "Haul away the
bowline". Masefield, in *A Sailor's Garland*, says this shanty is
'certainly as old as the reign of Henry VIII', perhaps because
the bowline lost its importance as a piece of rigging during
the sixteenth century, and because the words 'Hail out the
bollene' occur—but as a command not a shanty—in *The
Complaynt of Scotland* (1549). The bowline's appearance in the
song is like Pontius Pilate's in the Creed: hardly called for.
There are no firm grounds for imagining that the shanty rose
earlier than the nineteenth century. Its tune is founded on the
widespread air best known by the corrupt Irish title "Savour-
neen deelish", though it has a dozen other names including
"The molecatcher's daughter", "Derry Brien", "The exile of
Erin", and "Miss Molly my love, I'm off". Shield used it in
his ballad opera *The Poor Soldier* in 1783, Tom Moore adapted
it for "Silent, O Moyle", and Nathaniel Gow helped to spread
it among Scottish fiddlers when he included it in his *Select
Collection of Original Dances*, published about 1815. Was it an
Irish sailor who first made a shanty of it? Perhaps, but the tune
was much in the air of England and Scotland too in the first
half of the nineteenth century, and the shanty's parentage is as
vague as its past.

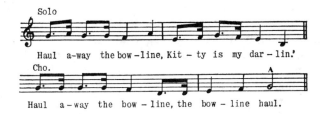

Haul away the bowline, Kitty is my darlin'.
Haul away the bowline, the bowline haul!

Haul away the bowline, the captain he's a-growlin'.
Haul away the bowline, the bowline haul!

Haul away the bowline so early in the mornin',
Haul away the bowline, the bowline haul!

The bowline, the bowline, the longtailed bowline.
Haul away the bowline, the bowline haul!

Probably the most impressive of shipboard work-songs are the hauling shanties made for the long pulls. Sails that called for hoisting were the upper topsail, the upper topgallant, and sometimes the royal at the summit of the mast (unless the ship was of the haughty sort that carried skysails). Of these, the upper topsail was the heaviest, needing the longest hardest haul. For this sail the most substantial shanties were best-suited, with a good string of ready-made verses and a strong tune whose rhythm-stresses fell right for hard pulling, and whose character would not sag under a slow tempo. Other sails, being lighter, might be set to brisker songs, but the mattter of tempo and character of the shanty chosen for the job in hand would depend on physical and psychological conditions, such as the state of the weather, the weight of the yard, the spirit of the men, the stage of the operation, the proximity of the afterguard. On a fine day, under a lively mate, with the end of the trip in view ('with the gals on the towrope', as the sailors said) and a topgallantsail to set, the singing would go briskly enough, certainly with far more verve than if the job were a mainsail haul outward bound in the wet with the mate nowhere in sight. With any sail, whatever the circumstances, the singing would become slower as the canvas filled with wind and the weight increased. Moreover, if the gang had already hoisted the fore and main topsail, their energy could have lost its edge by the time they got aft, so the last shanty, to hoist the mizzen topsail, would quite likely be of a slow draggy kind such as "Tom's gone to Hilo", described as 'the mate's anathema' because it took so long to hoist a yard to it.

Tom - my's gone and__ I'll__go too. A - way, you Hi-lo!

Tom - my's gone and__ I'll go__ too. Tom's gone to Hi-lo!

As usual with shanties, the texts sung to the "Tom's gone" tune were a loose assembly of couplets, including many 'floating' verses likely to be attached to any shanty of the same metre. For all that, two particular lines of thought seemed to catch the fancy of shantymen when singing the song. One was the conventional theme of parting and absence, usually with ironical references to the behaviour of sweethearts, as: 'His half-pay went, it went like chaff. *Away, you Hilo!* She's hanging round for the other half. *Tom's gone to Hilo!*' Just as often the shantymen would improvize an imaginary voyage to all corners of the globe for wandering Tom. As Hugill puts it: 'The game played by the shantyman was to take Tom to as many ports of three syllables as he could think of.' A few couplets that passed readymade from one song-leader to another were:

> Tommy's gone to Mobile Bay,
> Where they screw cotton by the day.
>
> Tommy's gone to the Rio Grand,
> To roll them gals in the yellow sand.
>
> Tommy's gone to Callao.
> He'll not come back from there, I know.
>
> Tommy's gone with a rolling crew.   [*rolling* =
> To Hilo town he'll see her through.   *hardworking*]
>
> Tommy's gone to Singapore.
> My Tommy's gone for evermore.

The ropes by which the yards with their canvas are hoisted are called halyards, and they pass down through various pulley-blocks until they are made fast round wooden pegs (belaying-pins) set in a perforated rail running along inside the ship's bulwarks. If a sail was to be hoist, the requisite halyard would be cast off its belaying-pin and the gang would take their places along the rope, facing the shantyman. It should be understood that the rope is rove through a leading-block fastened to the deck, so the gang have a horizontal pull, like a tug-o'-war team, whereas the shantyman standing by the downfall of the rope, grasping it with both hands high above his head, has the downhaul. So with every man ready and the rope taut, the shantyman begins his solo, then as the crowd crash in on the refrain, all hands haul, the shantyman downwards, the rest longwise. They rest on the rope while the next solo line of the song is intoned, then in comes the roaring chorus and they haul once again. By far the greater number of halyard shanties have two pulls to every refrain, such as the grand "General Taylor" that Sharp recorded from that outstanding shantyman, John Short. Mr. Short's performance displays the rather elaborate melisma (seamen called them 'hitches') that some singers liked to use particularly in the slower songs for heavy haul.

General Taylor gained the day.
Walk him along, Johnny, carry him along.
General Taylor gained the day.
Carry him to the burying ground.

O you Stormy.
Walk him along, Johnny, carry him along.
O you Stormy.
Carry him to the burying ground.

We dug his grave with a silver spade.
Walk him along, Johnny, carry him along.
His shroud of fine silk was made.
Carry him to the burying ground,
O you Stormy.
Walk him along, Johnny, carry him along.
O you Stormy.
Carry him to the burying ground.

We'll lower him down with a golden chain.
Walk him along, Johnny, carry him along.
We'll make sure he don't rise again.
Carry him to the burying ground.
O you Stormy.
Walk him along, Johnny, carry him along.
O you Stormy.
Carry him to the burying ground.

Etc.

The description of the ceremonial funeral comes from American Negro folklore, and similar imagery occurs in other shanties invoking Stormy or Stormalong, the blusterous old skipper who stands his ground alongside Davy Jones and Mother Carey among the mythological personages of the sea. Some took him to be an embodiment of the wind, others believed he was a natural man, Captain John Willis of Eyemouth, Berwickshire, skipper of the Boston ship *John Wade* in 1851, and later (as 'Old White Hat' Willis) owner of the *Cutty Sark*. General Zachary Taylor was a frontier fighter who in February 1847 gained a famous victory over the Mexican General (and President) Santa Ana at Buenavista in the course of a war that secured Texas and gained California for the United States. During that war, a number of British seamen jumped ship to enlist as mercenaries in the Mexican army, and doubtless it was sheer wishfulness that brought into being the celebrated windlass shanty usually called "Santy-anna", beginning 'Oh, Santyanna gained the day'. He seldom did, whether against 'Old Rough-and-Ready' Taylor or his fellow-general 'Fuss and Feathers' Scott, who finally brought Mexico to her knees at Molino del Rey in the September. Though no politician, Zachary Taylor became president of the United States soon after the end of the Mexican War but lived to enjoy only a brief term of office. We may presume that the shanty that celebrates the dead hero and seems to fuse his personality with that of fire-eating old Stormalong, came into being during the early years of the clipper era, perhaps not long after July 1850, when Taylor died.

Among the vast treasury of characteristic two-pull halyard shanties are such well-known pieces as "Whiskey Johnny", "Stormalong", "Blood red roses", "Blow the man down", and "Sally Brown", of which Sharp notated a vagarious version from Charles Robbins, a grand singer and seaman of lifetime experience ending his time in the Marylebone Workhouse. As shanties go, "Sally Brown" is quite an old song. The novelist Captain Marryat heard a version of it sung aboard a Western Ocean packet in 1837, but we do not know if the melody raised then was as piquant as old Mr. Robbins's, with its delicately fluctuating intervals.

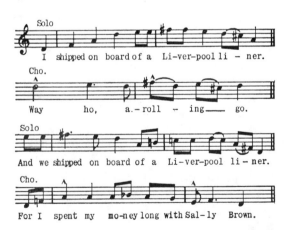

I shipped on board of a Liverpool liner.
Way ho, a-rolling go.
And we shipped on board of a Liverpool liner.
For I spent my money 'long with Sally Brown.

Now up aloft this yard must go, boys.
Way ho, a-rolling go.
Now up aloft this yard must go, boys.
For I spent my money 'long with Sally Brown.

And we spread her wings and we let her go free,
boys.
Way ho, a-rolling go.
And we spread her wings and we let her go free,
boys.
For I spent my money 'long with Sally Brown.

Etc.

'Like a bosun's chair, fit for every bum', goes the sea saying, and just so a shanty may be bent to almost any job. Songs intended for hauling were used almost as readily for heaving work, particularly in the packet ships whose winding machinery was more rudimentary than that of the later clippers. Early in the nineteenth century ships were still using spoke-windlasses of a pattern that had stayed unchanged for five hundred years or more, with a horizontal drum fitted at either end with pigeon-holes like the felloes of a wheel. In the smaller packets, four men might make a windlass gang, two at either end of the machine, each with a spoke in his hand. Two and two they would ship their bars into pigeonholes and heave downwards, pulling the bars free as their mates shoved their spoke in and heaved in turn. The movement was hard and jerky and if the gang was well in time a powerful rhythm would develop, well suited by any song of emphatic beat, such as "Billy Riley" or "Leave her Johnny, leave her" for the lighter heaving, and "Bound for the Rio Grand" or "Heave away, my Johnnies" for the heavier gait. Windlass and brake-pump (operated by a long lever with up-and-down seesaw motion) worked to a pulsating binary rhythm that many halyard shanties fitted very well, which is why so many of the earlier windlass and pump chants have a hauling-song shape.

As the ships got bigger and the working heavier, the spoke-windlass and its successor the 'up-and-down' brake windlass were replaced by the capstan, a vertical-pillared winding apparatus worked by men tramping round and round, shoving on the bars that stood out from the capstan head like the spokes of a wheel, chest-high to a man, two or three men to each bar, perhaps eighteen men to a gang. Here the rhythm of work was quite unlike that of the hauling jobs or windlass heaving. Instead of calling for well-timed intermittent effort, capstan work imposed a continuous rather shambling stamp-around. The function of all shanties is part physical, part diversionary. Synchronization of effort was the prime purpose of the hauling songs, but with the capstan songs the diversionary aspect was paramount. Capstan jobs were likely to be long and boring and the gang heaved with better will if the mind was livened by a song, but—unlike what happened with hauling—the form of the song need not be closely tied to the gesture of the work. So the capstan shanties tend to be musically more elaborate than the hauling songs, with a steadier less emphatic rhythm and more coherent texts. Being only lightly bound to assist the unison of effort, they were able to depart from the bald alternation of solo and gang-refrain that hauling imposed, and to indulge their diversionary character by the addition of so-called 'grand choruses', usually four-line refrains for all hands, that punctuated the song and helped to spin it out so that it would last the long task better, as well as aiding the gang to endure the weariness of the job. By no means all capstan songs have a grand chorus, but among the best known and most characteristic are "Yaller gals", "Whoop, jamboree", "Johnny come down to Hilo". Occasionally ballads such as "Blow ye winds" (scholars call it "The baffled knight") and "A-roving" cropped up as capstan shanties, but they are among the least typical of this class of songs. More representative are pieces like "Rio Grand", notated by H. E. Piggott from the shantyman John Perring whom Percy Grainger considered 'one of the most creatively gifted, fiery-spirited traditional singers' he had ever heard, a man who invested shanties 'with a strange blend of sea-born weirdness and human tenderness'.

I thought I heard our captain say:
Oh, Rio!
I thought I heard our captain say:
We are off to Rio Grand'.

Then away, Rio!
Away, Rio!
So fare you well, my bonny young girl,
We are off to Rio Grand'.

So heave up your anchor and let us away.
Oh, Rio!
So heave up your anchor and let us away.
We are off to Rio Grand'.

Then away, Rio!
Away, Rio!
So fare you well, my bonny young girl,
We are off to Rio Grand'.

We've a jolly good ship and a jolly good crew.
Oh, Rio!
A jolly good mate and a good captain too.
We are off to Rio Grand'.

Then away, Rio!
Away, Rio!
So fare you well, my bonny young girl,
We are off to Rio Grand'.

Etc.

Generally speaking, the capstan shanties were among the later compositions in the repertory of shipboard work songs, because the capstan did not become a common part of ship's gear until the middle of the nineteenth century. True, a familiar engraving shows men heaving at the capstan of an East Indiaman about 1830 (with a goggle-eyed Negro fiddler standing on the capstan-head, playing to the gang as they trudge round: shantying only came later aboard these ships), but East Indiamen were biggish heavy vessels, needing something more robust than the spoke- or brake-windlass that was apt enough for light packet ships. Only after the advent of the clippers did the capstan supplant the old-type windlass aboard most deepwater square-riggers.

As to the manner of singing the songs, that depended on the musical fancies of the men. Some shantymen were bawlers, others used a delicate intimate voice. Some sang their solo lines in strict tempo, others preferred a rubato that at times—as we see from Grainger's transcriptions from cylinder recordings—was quite elaborate. Whether the melody was decorated or not depended not merely on the singer's whim but also on the pace of the job in hand. The group refrains, of course, were always sung plain and in a strict *tempo giusto*. In the controversial matter of whether or not the refrains were sung in harmony, the answer seems to be: Generally no, but sometimes yes, especially if there were several Welshmen or Negroes in the crew. As to the texts, some stanzas or tags were tied to particular shanties, others were freely transferred from one song to another. Improvisation played an important part with some shantymen, and old John Perring remarked to the song-collector: 'It is so different, singing in a room. If I were on board, with all the fellows round me, I should know their names and all about them, and I was a good hand at making up little rhymes which would fit in; I should think of the next verse while they were singing the chorus.' And he explained how, like all shantymen, he would fall back on certain commonplace rhymes or jingles when he had exhausted both the stock of verses associated with the tune and his capacity for extemporizing topical tags. Among the scraps that shantymen were likely to splice into any work song they happened to sing were the following couplets:

> Haul away and pull together.
> Haul away for better weather.

> Shake her, wake her before we're gone.
> Fetch that gal with the blue dress on.

> Shake her up and away we go,
> Up aloft from down below.

> Hoist this yard from down below.
> Up to the sheave-hole she must go.

> Rock and shake her is the cry.
> This bloody topmast sheave is dry.

> Up aloft this yard must go,
> For Mister Mate has told us so.

> Sally she's a bright mulatto.
> Pretty little gal but I can't get at her.

> Jinny in the garden picking peas,
> That curly hair down to her knees.

> Sally in the garden sifting sand,
> Bosun watching with his (cap) in his hand.

Them gals of Chile they're hard to beat.
Always pulling on the old main sheet.

Them Quaker gals don't wear no frills.
They're skinny and tight as codfish gills.

Them Liverpool gals with long black hair,
They'll rob you blind and skin you bare.

The blackbird sung unto the crow:
Up aloft this yard must go.

When we get to the Blackwall docks,
Them pretty young gals come down in flocks.

One to the other you'll hear 'em say:
Here come Jack with his three years' pay.

We'll build a ship of a thousand ton
And load her up with Jamaica rum.

I thought I heard the old man say:
One more pull and then belay.

Stretch your backs and haul away.
Make your port and take your pay.

Times is hard and wages low.
Time for us to roll and go.

Spend our money in a week on shore.
Pack our bags and to sea once more.

Scraps of doggerel, rough as canvas, grainy as teak, but along with the wild or tender, impetuous or easygoing melodies, they tell us a great deal about the conditions and feelings of labouring men at sea. For a few brief years the shanties rang round the world then died away like the sound of bells under the ocean. Freak products of capitalism, mostly made by men of the sea-port towns and cities, for all their primitive character they may serve us here as a link between the songs of the rural past and those of industrial times.

V

THE INDUSTRIAL SONGS

No-one can write truly of folklore who does not know
how to recognize the spirit of the people in relation
to work, and how to use its positive characteristics
as illustrations. (Wilhelm Heinrich Riehl, 1861.)

Capitalism killed folk song, we are told: enclosure starved it,
the steam-engine put paid to it, the miseries of nineteenth
century industrialism blighted the culture of the working
people. A gloomy picture: is it just?

In the novel conditions brought by the industrial revolution
the old oral culture was in agony, but a new lower-class culture
was developing, based mainly on book not word of mouth.
As the workers' movement grew during the nineteenth century,
with its choirs and brass bands, reading circles and amateur
theatricals, the children and grandchildren of the folk singers
and storytellers were to find new forms of culture, more
educated and literary, with a new content. It was a slow dour
process, hindered by long working hours and overbearing
masters, but it meant that when the mainly unwritten culture
of the peasantry was reduced to rubble, the field was by no
means left free to 'bourgeois' culture, that is to the fine arts
and popular entertainments licensed and provided by the
established order. Particularly in the domain of song. As the
old lyric of the countryside crumbled away, a new lyric of the
industrial towns arose, frail at first but getting stronger,
reflecting the life and aspirations of a raw class in the making,
of men handling new-fashioned tools, thinking new thoughts,
standing in novel relationship to each other and to their
masters. This fresh lyric we call 'workers' song'.

If, for convenience, we consider the realm of song partitioned
into three areas—peasant folk song, bourgeois social song,
workers' song—we must bear in mind that the division is but
rough, that each of these kinds merges with and acts upon
the other (for instance there is a layer of country folk song that
is bourgeois-conditioned), and that within each handy category

are subdivisions it would be unhandy to ignore. So, within the broad region of workers' song we find an order best described as 'industrial folk songs' quite distinct from the non-folkloric labour anthems and 'literary' political mass-songs with their agitational content, elated feeling, and hymnlike style. We are speaking of a kind of folk song that, far from being destroyed by the industrial revolution, was actually created by its conditions. Miraculously enough. Jean Genet is not alone in being struck by that 'strangest of poetic phenomena: that the most terrible and dismal part of the whole world, the blackest, most burnt-out. . . . the severe naked world of factory workers, is entwined with marvels of popular song.'

An anxious query arises: 'This so-called industrial folk song, is it *authentic*?' What is authenticity? We have seen that the old classic kind of rural song is itself no thoroughbred; for centuries it was 'contaminated' by print, and influenced in sundry ways by the usages of the towns and even by borrowings from abroad. The major scale, unitary rhythm, equal verses, all had their hybridizing effect. Many forms of folk song lie close to the world of the professional arts, and the out-and-out purist might deny the label of 'folk song proper' to a great part of the traditional repertory, preferring to limit the term to a few ceremonial and functional pieces such as wassail songs and shanties—and by no means all of them! The citizenship of the home-made song of industrial workers is particularly equivocal. Some would call it stateless, and ponder whether to issue it with a passport that allows limited entry to the domain of literature but is not valid for the realm of folklore. A vain preoccupation. It is more fruitful to reflect on the aims of the creators and bearers than to fret over the pedigree of the songs themselves. The first question is: 'Who uses this song, and for what purpose?' The question: 'How was the song made?' is but secondary, though not negligible if we are to keep within reasonable bounds of definition.

By 'industrial folk song' let us understand the kind of vernacular songs made by workers themselves directly out of their own experiences, expressing their own interests and aspirations, and incidentally passed on among themselves mainly by oral means, though this is no *sine qua non*. The kind of songs created from outside by learned writers, on behalf of the working class, is not our concern here. In destination, both kinds may be similar, but in the manner of their creation and expression, as well as in dissemination and often in function too, they are distinct. In England, distinct to an unusual degree, it seems. In most European countries, although in the period of transition from handcraft to machines the workers' home-made songs hardly differed from 'classic' folk song, once industry was consolidated and large-scale workers' organizations were under way, the proletarian lyricists quickly accepted the influence of literary political hymns, and their creations came more and more to resemble fine art compositions, even if only in a half-educated way. In England, on the other hand, the folk song style persisted with peculiar stubbornness. The literary songs of Chartism and subsequent 'chants of Labour', national or international, were fairly well accepted by our organized workers, if not with the burning enthusiasm their Continental comrades showed for the anthems of revolution. But this kind of song had little influence on the sort of thing the singing miners, mill-hands and foundry-workers made for themselves. Our working class only gradually isolated itself from the peasantry to form its own culture, and if the newer tradition is generally different from the old in content, the benevolent ghosts of the fine oral culture of the past are still strongly present in some corners, to surprise the explorer with their 'melodious twang'.

Not that many song-seekers have tried these corridors so far. Till now, industrial folk song has hardly been studied at all. The great collectors, we have seen, confined their attention to the rural past and shunned the industrial present. Their concern was to rescue country lore from the onslaught of modern times, partly out of a romantic preference for rustic lanes over milltown alleys and for men of the soil over their sons in the mine, but chiefly no doubt because they were looking for beauties not documents, and they mistrusted their chance of finding much radiance among the slag-heaps. Understandable enough, but their preoccupation with country folkways allowed them only a partial view of our traditional song, for even a superficial glance shows that not only has industry a folklore of its own, but also the *creation* of folk music and poetry has, within the last hundred years or so, passed almost entirely into the hands and mouths of industrial workers. The performance of country song still goes on, though rather faintly now; but the composition of new stuff in the villages had practically ceased by the 1850s. Not so in industrial areas. Miners, textile workers and others went on making their own songs. And if this do-it-yourself song creation rather dwindled in the period between the World Wars, it has lately taken a new lease of life and flourishes quite vigorously again, for example with the new *genre* of elegies on mines being closed down by the National Coal Board ("Lament for Albert", "Farewell to 'Cotia", etc.). Early in the nineteenth century, in middle class drawing rooms and parlours, sentimental romances of the Dibdin or Haynes Bayley kind were flourishing, while in the cottages the classic folk ballads were dying and their singers falling silent before the bawling of the broadside-sellers. And at the same time starting up in the years shortly before Waterloo, we are faced with the significant appearance of the new industrial ballad, at first mainly among weavers, but rapidly spreading and growing in power among miners and other workers.

Lyrical pieces with a craft background and love songs full of occupational references had long been flourishing among handloom weavers and pitmen, and in particular the north-eastern miners had an arsenal of epigrammatic and allusive scraps that they liked to fire into their dance-tunes while jigging, at holidays, on the coaly green, or down in the pit on Christmas Eve when they and their womenfolk would dance in the newly whitewashed pony stables.

We have already referred to the fantasy, persistent in folklore since ancient times, in which working techniques are sexualized and the tools and gestures of trade are turned into erotic metaphors. Some of the earliest songs of modern industry are of this kind. While spinning, weaving, metal-working and such remained at handicraft level, the rudimentary industrial songs were close in manner to the rural tradition, but by the opening years of the nineteenth century the language was becoming noticeably different from that of the old country song, often being loaded with technical terms that gave the pieces an irresistible savour to the in-group of workers in the various trades. The songs of the textile industry were the first to show this tendency to remarkable extent. A characteristic early piece of the erotic imagery of the industrial age is "The Bury new loom", first printed on a broadside by Swindells of Manchester in 1804, and subsequently re-issued over and again by Shelmerdine (1818) and other north-western printers. For all its novel features, the song did not come out of the blue; it had its forebears, composed in earlier days when the principal makers of textile songs were itinerant weavers travelling from village to village, settling in the farmhouse kitchens to work the spun yarn and chat to the women while the menfolk were out in the fields (small wonder that so many early songs of the weaving trade tell of seduction and betrayal). "The Bury new loom" has the picaresque wit of the itinerant weaver songs, but its relish for machinery and technicalities is new.

As I walked between Bolton and Bury, 'twas on a moonshiny night,
I met with a buxom young weaver whose company gave me delight.
She says: Young fellow, come tell me if your level and rule are in tune.
Come, give me an answer correct, can you get up and square my new loom?

I said: My dear lassie, believe me, I am a good joiner by trade,
And many a good loom and shuttle before in my time I have made.
Your short lams and jacks and long lams I quickly can put them in tune.
My rule is now in good order to get up and square a new loom.

She took me and showed me her loom, the down on her warp did appear.
The lam jacks and healds put in motion, I levelled her loom to a hair.

My shuttle ran well in her lathe, my tread it worked up and
   down,
My level stood close to her breast-bone, the time I was squaring
   her loom.

The cords of my lam jacks and treadles at length they began
   to give way.
The bobbin I had in my shuttle, the weft in it no longer would
   stay.
Her lathe it went bang to and fro, my main treadle it still kept
   in tune.
My pickers went nicketty-nack all the time I was reiving her
   loom.

My shuttle it still kept in motion, her lams she worked well up
   and down.
The weight in her rods they did tremble; she said she would
   weave a new gown.
My strength now began for to fail me. I said: It's now right to a
   hair.
She turned up her eyes and said: Tommy, my loom you have
   got pretty square.

But when her foreloom post she let go, it flew out of order again
She cried: Bring your rule and your level and help me to
   square it again.
I said: My dear lassie, I'm sorry, at Bolton I must be by noon,
But when that I come back this way, I will square up your
   jerry hand-loom.

   The song requires something of a glossary. 'Lams' are the
foot-treadles that operate the jacks. The 'jacks' are levers on
the Dobbie machines, that raise the harness controlling the
warp thread. The 'heald' is a loop of cord or wire through
which the warp threads pass; a number of these make up the
harness. The 'pickers' are attachments to the upper end of
the picking-stick which impels the shuttle through the shed of
the warp threads during weaving. The 'shed' of the warp is
the V opening caused by raising or pulling down the threads.

The turn of the eighteenth and nineteenth century was a golden time for the weavers. Following the invention of the spinning jenny and water-frame, the vast output of machine yarn from the early mills meant a staggering expansion of weaving over south-east Lancashire, and every sizeable attic and even the most tumbledown barns were being fitted with looms. From the 1770s onwards, the population of the weaving districts had been soaring (Bolton doubled its population within fifteen years from 1773) and a multitude of small farmers and farm-workers were turning to the weaving trade. A commentator describing the weavers' communities at the outset of the nineteenth century gives a rhapsodic picture that is at least fair in part:

> Their dwellings and small gardens clean and neat—all the family well clad—the men with each a watch in his pocket and the women dressed to their own fancy—the church crowded to excess every Sunday—every house well furnished with a clock in elegant mahogany or fancy case—handsome tea services in Staffordshire ware. . . .[44]

The prosperity that came with the soaring output of machine yarn was short-lived. The trade fell off during the Napoleonic Wars, the manufacturers cut the weavers' prices to the bone, and when the demand returned, the manufacturers, with huge stocks of cut-rate goods on hand, were able to keep weavers' wages at the hungry level. The weavers were degraded, their status undermined, years before the power looms became so numerous as to make hand-work anachronistic. It was not until the early 1830s that the power-loom finally gained supremacy over the hand-loom, but the slow transitional period cast a shadow, that shows in a broadside from the Oldham district, a love song in which the old pride and cockiness of the hand-weaver seem to falter as he reconciles himself to the rigours of the factory:

> I am a hand-weaver to my trade.
> I fell in love with a factory maid.
> And if I could but her favour win,
> I'd stand beside her and weave by steam.

> My father to me scornful said:
> How could you fancy a factory maid,
> When you could have girls fine and gay,
> And dressed up like to the Queen of May?

The young man protests the girl's worth and his willingness to follow her even into the factory, and as he soars off into an erotic fancy, his indignant father, handicraft pride outraged, cries:

> How can you say it's a pleasant bed,
> When nowt lies there but a factory maid?
> —A factory lass although she be,
> Blest is the man that enjoys she.

The song ends on a downcast note, like the crowing of a glum rooster:

> Where are the girls? I'll tell you plain,
> The girls have gone to weave by steam,
> And if you'd find 'em, you must rise at dawn,
> And trudge to the factory in the early morn.

The situation in that song is new, but in form and language it still has something of the air of rural folk song. It was a style that faded slowly as the new forms of industrial song grew, with poetry less flowery than that of the country workers, more direct than that of the windier broadside writers. Consolation, a most powerful element of rustic lyrics, was giving way to exposition, complaint, exhortation even. In a short time, the first concern of the song-makers was no longer to create a stylized landscape as a backcloth for some emotional fantasy; rather it was to set out the facts of working men's lives in all their nudity and to appeal that something be done to set wrongs right. Often the songs gained poignancy through the use of local dialect and occupational slang. The standard themes became concerned with hard conditions, tragic events, disasters, strikes, evictions, the fight for something better.

One of the earliest exemplars of industrial protest song is the dramatic ballad variously called "The poor cotton weaver", "The hand-loom weaver", "The four-loom weaver", though its commonest title on the broadside prints is simply "Jone o' Grinfield". It belongs to the central period of the Industrial Revolution, to the years immediately after Waterloo, years of economic hardship, low wages and high prices. Weavers were working a fifteen-hour day for ten shillings a week if they were fortunate, four shillings if not; they were living on oatmeal and potatoes, onion porridge and blue milk, and hungry women roamed the moors looking for nettles to boil. Some of the indignation of the time, and some of the confusions too, are in the ballad. Judging by the number of broadside prints of it, in various breadths of Lancashire dialect, published by Shelmerdine of Manchester, Harkness of Preston and others, it remained a favourite for many years. Its anonymous author wrote his text to fit the tune of a favourite song of a few years earlier, about a simpleminded character, John of Greenfield, near Oldham, who resolved to leave his loom and join the army. The same John became the hero of a small family of ballads, whose most powerful member is the weaver's lament we are discussing. The text is from a Bebbington (Manchester) broadside of *c.*1860, after the ballad had been circulating for nearly half a century. Frank Kidson had two versions of the tune from Cheshire.

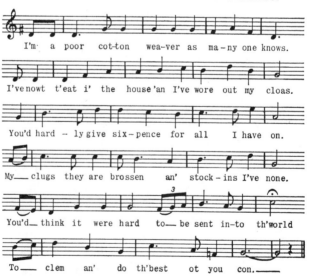

I'm a poor cotton weaver as many one knows.
I've nowt t'eat i' the house 'an I've wore out my cloas.
You'd hard-ly give six-pence for all I have on.
My— clugs they are brossen an' stock-ins I've none.
You'd— think it were hard to— be sent in-to th'world
To— clem an' do th'best ot you con.—

I'm a poor cotton weaver as many one knows.
I've nowt to eat i' th' house an' I've wore out my cloas.
You'd hardly give sixpence for all I have on.
My clugs they are brossen an' stockins I've none.
   You'd think it wur hard to be sent into th'world
    To clem an' do th'best ot you con.   [clem = starve]

Our church parson kept tellin' us long,
We should have better times if we'd but hold our tongues.
I've houden my tongue till I can hardly draw breath.
I think i' my heart he means to clem me to death.
   I know he lives weel by backbitin' the de'il,
    But he never picked o'er in his life. [picked o'er = wove]

We tarried six week an' thought every day were t'last.
We tarried an' shifted till now we're quite fast.
We lived on nettles while nettles were good,
An' Waterloo porridge were best of us food.
   I'm tellin' you true, I can find folks enew
    That er livin' no better than me.

Old Bill o' Dan's sent bailiffs one day,
For a shop score I owed him that I couldn't pay,
But he wur too late, for old Bill o' Bent
Had sent tit an' cart and taen goods for rent.
   We had nowt bur a stoo', that wur a seat for two;
    An' on it cowered Margit an' me.

The bailiffs looked round as sly as a mouse,
When they saw aw things wur taen out o' t'house.
Says one to the other: All's gone, thou may see.
Aw sed: Lads, never fret, you're welcome to me.
   They made no more ado, but nipped up t'owd stoo',
    An' we both went wack upo' t'flags.

I geet howd o' Margit, for hoo're stricken sick.   [hoo = she]
Hoo sed hoo ne'er had such a bang sin hoo wur wick.
The bailiffs scoured off wi' owd stoo' on their backs.

They would not have cared had they brokken our necks.
  They're mad at owd Bent cos he's taen goods for rent,
An' wur ready to flay us alive.

I sed to our Margit as we lay upo' t'floor:
We shall never be lower in this world, I am sure.
But if we alter, I'm sure we mun mend,
For I think i' my heart we are both at far end,
  For meat we have none, nor looms to weave on,
  Egad, they're as weel lost as found.

Then I geet up my piece, an' I took it 'em back.
I scarcely dare speak, mester lookit so black.
He said: You wur o'erpaid last time you coom.
I said: If I wur, 'twas for weavin' bout loom. [*bout* = *without*]
  In the mind as I'm in, I'll ne'er pick o'er again,
  For I've woven mysel to th'fur end.

Then aw coom out o' t'warehouse, an' left him to chew that.
When aw thought again, aw wur vext till aw sweat.
To think we mun work to keep him an' aw th'set,
All the days o' my life, an' then die in their debt!
  But I'll give o'er this trade, an' work with a spade,
  Or go an' break stones upo' th'road.

Our Margit declares if hoo'd cloas to put on,
Hoo'd go up to Lundun an' see the young Queen*,
An' if things didn't alter when hoo had been,
Hoo swears hoo would fight, blood up to th'een.
  Hoo's nought agen t'queen,*but hoo likes a fair thing,
  An' hoo says hoo can tell when hoo's hurt.

The spinners and weavers had long been famed for singing.
Already from the sixteenth century we have the charming
account by Deloney who, stretching the facts a bit, describes
the spinning-room of the clothier John Winchcomb (Jack of
Newbury), where two hundred girls sat singing like nightingales
as they worked, to the admiration of Henry VIII visiting the

  * In earlier versions, 'to see the great mon', and 'Hoo's nout agen th'king'.

factory. One of their songs was "The fair flower of Northumberland", which they sang in shanty-fashion, 'two of them singing
the ditty and all the rest bearing the burden'. And in the
nineteenth century, from the early powerloom days onward,
we hear a great deal about singing in the factories, with the
women in particular lifting their voices above the clatter of
the looms in exuberant Methodist hymns such as Perronet's
"All hail the power", to the handsome hexatonic folk tune
called "Diadem" in the hymnbooks, though country people
know it better as "The ploughboy's dream". Another favourite
in the factories was "Praise the Lord, 'tis good to praise", for
which the preferred melody was "Simeon", composed by
Samuel Stanley the evangelical publican of Birmingham.
One would have thought they had little enough to sing about,
working too many hours in the day with only a sad slum to
return to at night, bearing too many babies and seeing too
many die. A Yorkshire surgeon describes the plight of a
weaver's wife in childbirth (the period is the early 1840s):

> She is upon her feet, with a woman on each side; her arms
> are placed round their necks; and, in nature's agony, she
> almost drags her supporters to the floor; and in this state
> the birth takes place. . . . And why is this the case? The
> answer is, because there is no change of bedclothing.[45]

As to infant mortality, a Manchester survey in 1833 showed
that 40 per cent of babies born to married spinners died in very
early infancy, a heavy rate due to poor conditions and also
perhaps to the characteristic pelvic deformation in girls who
had stood all day in the mills from early childhood, making
for difficult births.

If the Methodists and Evangelicals among the women were
busy singers at the loom (sometimes keeping their hymns going
staunchly amid scenes of immorality between employers and
mill-girls that would 'put a blush to the rites of the Pagoda
girls of India and the Harem life of the most voluptuous
Ottoman'), the men seem to have sung much less at work,
though the more radical workers in particular were not

backward in making bitter songs to sing out of earshot of the masters.

One of these is "Poverty knock", recorded by A. E. Green in 1965 from an old Batley weaver, Tom Daniel, who had learnt the song some sixty years previously, at the first mill he worked in on leaving school. The old Dobbie loom, one of the early mechanical models for plain weaving, as it worked seemed to make the sound of 'poverty knock'! Hence the refrain of the song.

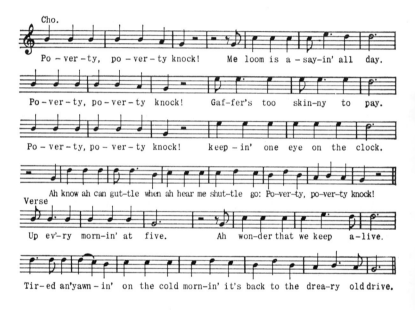

(*Refrain*)   Poverty, poverty knock!
                Me loom is a-sayin' all day.
                Poverty, poverty knock!
                Gaffer's too skinny to pay.
                Poverty, poverty knock!
                Keepin' one eye on the clock.
                Ah know ah can guttle   [*eat*]
                When ah hear me shuttle
                Go: Poverty, poverty knock!

Up every mornin' at five.
Ah wonder that we keep alive.
Tired an' yawnin' on the cold mornin',
It's back to the dreary old drive.

Oh dear, we're goin' to be late.
Gaffer is stood at the gate.
We're out o' pocket, our wages they're docket;
We'll 'a' to buy grub on the slate.

An' when our wages they'll bring,
We're often short of a string.　　　　　*[length of cloth]*
While we are fratchin' wi' gaffer for snatchin',　　*[quarrelling]*
We know to his brass he will cling.

We've got to wet our own yarn
By dippin' it into the tarn.
It's wet an' soggy an' makes us feel groggy,
An' there's mice in that dirty old barn.

Oh dear, me poor 'ead it sings.
Ah should have woven three strings,
But threads are breakin' and my back is achin'.
Oh dear, ah wish ah had wings.

Sometimes a shuttle flies out,
Gives some poor woman a clout.
Ther she lies bleedin', but nobody's 'eedin'.
Who's goin' t'carry her out?

Tuner should tackle me loom.　　*[tuner = loom-maintenance man]*
'E'd rather sit on his bum.
'E's far too busy a-courtin' our Lizzie,
An' ah cannat get 'im to come.

Lizzie is so easy led.
Ah think that 'e teks her to bed.
She allus was skinny, now look at her pinny.
It's just about time they was wed.

> Poverty, poverty knock!
> My loom is a-sayin' all day.
> Poverty, poverty knock!
> Gaffer's too skinny to pay.
> Poverty, poverty knock!
> Keepin' one eye on the clock.
> Ah know ah can guttle
> When ah hear me shuttle
> Go: Poverty, poverty knock!

Of the verse about the woman struck by the flying shuttle, Mr. Daniel explains: the point is that the weavers were on piecework, and could not afford to stop to help an injured workmate.

The proud fatalism of the old traditional ballad is no longer present in workers' folk song, but neither do we find any broad revolutionary appeal. The typical creator of industrial ballads, who made his song under a hedge perhaps, sheltering from the rain after a fruitless trudge round the mills for work, or who sat up all night by candle-light with a stub of pencil in his fist, writing an elegy on his neighbours killed in yesterday's pit-explosion, had a narrow political horizon as a rule, but he understood solidarity with his workmates, could tell when he was hurt, and more and more during the nineteenth century he realized the need for fighting and said so in his songs. Not that all the industrial folk songs are black and dour by any means. On the contrary, a good proportion, including some of the hardest-hitting, are humorously put and go to lively tunes. Such masterpieces as "The coal-owner and the pitman's wife" wear a smile that shows strong teeth.

As far as present studies take us, the miners and textile workers, who stand at the head of the British labour movement, seem to have the richest treasury of occupational songs in number, content and lyrical value. Mining, spinning and weaving had given rise to a sizeable repertory well before the industrial revolution, and workers in those industries had a good stock to build upon. Later industrial developments, steel, railways, and such, lacking an early lyrical fund seem weaker in vernacular song production; but it must be said that the resources of these industries have been little explored, and surprises may be in store for the investigator. So far, our slight researches have been concerned mainly with the mining industry, especially in the North-east, and to a less extent with the textile industry of Yorkshire and the North-west.

For centuries, English miners have possessed a vigorous song-culture relating to their work and their way of life. Indeed, throughout Europe's history, pit culture has been a powerful affair. Some of the deepest elements of folklore reside among miners, whether of coal, iron or salt. Sword-dancing,* for instance, has been associated with pitmen since very ancient times, beginning perhaps in the remote period when the use of metals was first discovered, as the ritual dance of a special caste of men who enter the Earth Mother's body and return with wonders. Even today, among the most interesting sword dance teams of continuous tradition in Europe are those associated with the coal-miners of Earsdon, North-umberland and the Grenoside iron miners in Yorkshire, while in poetry and song our coalfields can match the great areas of pit culture in the Carinthian, Saxon-Bohemian and Moravian-Silesian districts despite the early start in central Europe (already in 1531, a set of German pitmen's songbooks, the *Bergreihen*, had appeared in print).[46] Mozart himself made an ironic bow in the direction of miners' selfmade culture when he wrote his "Bergmannsmusik" in imitation of the pitmen's instrumental ensembles around Salzburg. The work greatly amused Schubert because it is full of saucy mistakes in musical grammar. But like other closed communities, miners incline to be culturally conservative, and some of what Mozart took for errors may be merely traces of an older musical system that no longer matched the conventions of the eighteenth century. Documents about the musical life of miners are much scarcer in England than in Germany, but a north-eastern poem of the earliest years of the nineteenth century gives us a picture of colliers on their brief holiday at the end of the Yearly Bond, making their way

---

* In the sense of the linked circular dance, not the warrior pantomime. The flexible metal strips used, for example, in English 'rapper' dances are probably not descended from swords but from a tool of some sort.

towards Newcastle with primroses stuck in their hats, and their girls singing "The bonny pit laddie", a song still alive in tradition that has spread, sung to various tunes and in sundry shapes, from the Tyne southward as far as Wakefield and westward to Hindley Green, Wigan. An old set of the tune is given on p. 43, and variants of the song still circulate in the Durham coalfields in several forms.

In the older stratum of pit-village lyrics, most of the surviving pieces are love-songs, such as "The waggoner", collected by John Bell at the start of the nineteenth century, but not published till more than a hundred years later It celebrates the men who used to cart coal from the pits along railed tracks to the riverside staiths in the days before William Hedley's 'Puffing Billy' did the job by steam. Nowadays the song is usually sung to a version of the pervasive "Ball o' Kirriemuir" tune:

Saw ye owt o' ma lad gannin doon the waggon-way,
Wiv his pocket full o' money and his poke full o' hay?
   Oh, ma lad's a canny lad, the canniest Aa see,
   Though he's sair frowsy-freckled an' he's blind of an ee.

There's nivor a lad like ma lad drives to the staiths on Tyne.
He's coaly black on work-days but on holidays he's fine.
   Oh, ma lad's a canny lad, the canniest Aa see,
   But he's sair frowsy-freckled an' he's blind of an ee.

Wiv his sillor in his hand and his love in his ee,
Yonder Aa see ma canny lad a-comin doon to me.
   Oh, ma lad's a canny lad, the canniest Aa see,
   And nivor an ane there is could say that black is iv his ee.

Modern colliers have made a parody of this, ribald but pithy:

Oh, my lad's a canny lad, he works down the pit.
He never comes to see us unless he wants a bit.
I asked him would he marry us, you should have seen him
   wince.
I think I've lost my canny lad; I've never seen him since.

In the early years of the nineteenth century, several compilations of north-eastern fiddle and bagpipe tunes were published, including the melodies of miners' songs and dances and also those of the keelmen who poled the coal-barges along the shallow Tyne to deeper waters where the coal-ships lay waiting. The keelmen, mostly from the poorest slums of the Tyneside towns had a reputation for fierce independence and unbiddable sharpness. Thus, in 1792, when Jacobin disaffection was rife in the north-east, when The *Rights of Man* was in the hands of every collier, waggoner and keelman who could read, and strikers were driving blacklegs naked through the town of North Shields, General Lambton was interrupted as he tried to quell the rioters by a keelman shouting: 'Have you read this little work of Tom Paine's?' 'No.' 'Then read it. We like it much. You have a great estate, General. We shall soon divide it amongst us.' The keelmen had a store of salty songs that readily mingled with the repertory of the colliers, just as readily as the keelmen themselves and their womenfolk joined with the colliers' communities in dances on the pit-village green, with the silvery-toned Northumbrian small-pipes struggling to be heard above the full shrill singing and hand-clapping of the girls giving out with such a song as "Had away to Lambton", another one that old John Bell jotted in his notebook.

> How can I be merry,
> And how can I be a wanton?
> How can I be merry
> When my lad's over at Lambton?
>> Take thy pick on thy back, hinny,
>> Take thy pick on thy back, hinny,
>> Take thy pick on thy back, hinny,
>> And had away over to Lambton.

Or this other, more original song (likewise hitherto unpublished) in which the love-lyric becomes a paean of praise for a champion worker:

Jacky in the Law Raw,
Canny hinny, bonny hinny,
Jacky in the Law Raw,
Canny hinny now.

My laddie hews twenty every day,
Canny hinny, bonny hinny,
Headways and bordways, headways away,
Canny hinny now.
My laddie hews twenty every day,
Canny hinny, bonny hinny.
Headways and bordways, had away!
Canny hinny now.

Jacky in the Law Raw,
Canny hinny, bonny hinny,
Jacky in the Law Raw,
Canny hinny now.

My laddie is a korving hewer,
Canny hinny, bonny hinny,
He hews twenty every hour,
Canny hinny now.
My laddie is a korving hewer,
Canny hinny, bonny hinny,
He hews twenty every hour,
Canny hinny now.

Jacky in the Law Raw,
Canny hinny, bonny hinny,
Jacky in the Law Raw,
Canny hinny now.
(*bordways:* at right angles to a line of cleavage)

The song is old but the mood is already distinct from that of conventional rural song. Even in the past, the miner's life differed from the country worker's in many ways. In the first place he was less rooted to a single locality. A glance at mining history since the Middle Ages shows that in many places a mine would quickly reach its peak of production and then fall off,

and the miners would have to seek work elsewhere. The social
structure of mining communities has always been affected by
mobility. At the same time, the life of those communities
is intensely communal. The men are bound together by
shared dangers, they differ from other workers by the mystery
of a trade carried on in the dark underground, and—before
the days of pithead baths, anyway—they appeared in daylight
with black faces, in queer clothes, sitting at a distance from
the world in tram or bus, a race apart. A closed community
hangs on to its traditions as a kind of defence. Moreover the
raging industrialization that, with the large-scale capitalization
of agriculture, shattered the old rural folk traditions, caused
no break in the continuity of pitmen's culture. The mines
became deeper, pit life grew more intense, relations between
master and man became spikier, but the miners were in their
element. Blackness was no novelty to them, and as for machines,
in Durham steam-engines were already in use at Washington
(still a good singing locality) before 1725. The Industrial
Revolution gave the miners something to crow about as well
as something to peck at. To the mythological figures who haunt
the pits, such as the North Country Cutty Soames, who cuts
the tow-ropes of tubs, or Bluecap who descends on the tubs in a
blue flash and helps propel them along (Yorkshire pitmen used
to leave money for him now and then) or the playful sometimes
malicious little Tommy Knockers of the Cornish tin mines, or
the Old Man with whiskers hanging low, who appears pick
in hand when trouble is impending, and who tips the mine—
and indeed the whole earth—over at midnight, to such legendary characters were added the composite epic hero known in
various localities as Temple the Big Hewer, Bob Towers the
Durham County Coal Cutter, Jackie Torr, Big Isaac Lewis.
If this superhuman worker has a hundred names and faces his
feats are described in much the same terms in South Wales,
the Midlands, the North-east. At birth he was six feet tall and
weighed eighteen stone. He was a huge eater and a prodigious
toiler who would impatiently throw aside his blunted tools
and drill with his nose and cut coal with his teeth while holding
up the roof with one hand. When the ground settles in the
mine, South Wales colliers say: 'Big Isaac's working again'.

In Durham when the timbers groan, they say: 'Bob Towers is talking to us.' This fabulous worker survives only in tales, not in songs, but something of the same epic wind that inspired the legend-makers blows through the celebrated "Colliers' rant", in which a miner, pick in hand, fights with the spirit of the mine, the *daemon subterraneus truculens* as Agricola called it, in the dark of the pit. The "Rant" is among the first English miners' songs to appear in print, being published as No. XIII in Joseph Ritson's *The Northumberland Garland or Newcastle Nightingale* (1793). By that time, it was already so old that its words had become corrupted and its story hardly coherent. But if part of the song is now lost or sunk into burlesque, some of its old epic force remains, for it has become a kind of 'national anthem' of northeastern pitmen and as such was sung by massed choirs of miners when the blue and white Coal Board flag was first raised over the nationalized pits in July 1946.

"The colliers' rant" is to be found in every significant collection of northeastern songs, except, curiously enough, the very book where one would first seek it, *The Northumbrian Minstrelsy*. But another miners' song, probably of comparable age, has been till now unjustly neglected. This is "Call the horse, marrow", printed on a broadside without date or imprint, under a cut of an old man talking to three younger ones. Like the "Rant", this song was already falling into decrepitude before it was printed, but it conveys some of the curious flavour that early distinguished miners' songs from the folk songs of other labouring men, a compound of hardness and affection, peppered with craft jargon and salted with inconsequentiality:

> Call the horse, marrow,
> For I can call nane.
> The heart of my belly
> Is hard as a stane:
> As hard as a stane
> And as round as a cup.
> Call the horse, marrow,
> Till my hewer comes up.

Me and my marrow
And Christy Crawhall
Will play with any three in the pit
At the football:
At the football
And at the coal-tram,
We'll play with any three in the pit
For twelve-pence a gam.

Hewing and putting
And keeping in the sticks,
I never (so) laboured
Since I took the picks.
I'm going to my hewer's house
On the Fell Side.
He hews his coals thick
And drives his boards wide.

The rope and the roll
And the long ower-tree,
The devil's flown o'er the heap
With them all three.
The roll hangs across the shaft;
De'il but it fall,
Twenty-four horned owl
Run away with the mill.

I'm going to my hewer
Wherever he be.
He's hipt of a buddock
And blind of an e'e.
He's blind of an e'e
And lame of a leg.
My uncle Jack Fenwick
He kissed my aunt Peg.

If oddities of that stamp were typical enough of earlier
miners' songs, those of a later time had a more categorical and
demonstrative ring. Already by the end of the eighteenth

century the militance of miners was alarming the ruling class, and a correspondent from Tyneside was writing to William Pitt: 'When I look round and see the Country covered with thousands of pitmen, keelmen, waggonmen and other labouring men, hardy fellows strongly impressed with the new doctrine of equality, and at present composed of such combustible matter that the least spark will set them in a blaze, I cannot help thinking the supineness of the Magistrates very reprehensible.' Before long—certainly by the late 1820s—the characteristic industrial ballad began to appear, in which miners and other workers expressed their grievances passionately as the masters became richer and more powerful and the exploitation grew more irksome. Of strike songs with religious-coloured texts such as we find among Central European miners, there is hardly any trace in England.* Our strike ballads have a firmly militant tone of voice from the first, and if on occasion they put their matter playfully—for humour is a peculiarly powerful ingredient of English industrial folklore—the frolic never conceals the threat. An early specimen comes from the north-eastern miners' strike of 1831. The strike, concerning security of employment, a fair wage, and safety in the pits, lasted for two months before its successful conclusion, and gave rise to a number of ballads printed by local broadside publishers such as Stephenson of Gateshead and Douglas & Kent of Newcastle. Most of these set out the colliers' complaints with painstaking clarity and little regard for poetic grace, their purpose being to instruct, not to bemuse with fantasy. The first concern of the worker-balladeers was to tell the truth about events, the truth as they saw it, and with the masters owning the newspapers, often the ballad-sheet was the only means the strikers had to state their case publicly. At least one ballad however avoids didactic doggerel and gives a grimly amused account of the blackleg hunted, stripped naked, and made to run about over the moor with only his hat to hold

* Indeed the whole of our miners' folklore is remarkably little touched by Christian myths or rituals, unlike that of German-speaking miners, for instance, from Lorraine to Silesia, where specific miners' prayers and hymns abound, as well as such oddities as the relatively recent (nineteenth century) cult of St. Barbara which has taken firm hold among the pitmen and produced its own sizeable repertory of songs.

before him. We do not know the melody of this piece, but its metre suggests some member of the vast tune-family made famous by the song of "The peeler and the goat". The broadside is titled: "The best-dressed man of Seghill, or The pitman's reward for betraying his brethren":

Come all ye miners far and near, and let us all unite O
In bands of love and unity, and stand out for our right O.
Like Israel these many years in bondage we have been O,
And if we do not still stand out, our truth will not be seen O.

Man a weak frail being is and easy to deceive O,
And by a man called black J. R. was made for to believe O.
It was on March the nineteenth day, eighteen hundred and
  thirty-one O,
A man from Earsdon Colliery his brethren did abscond O.

And to the Seghill binding he did come with all his might O;
For to deceive his brethren dear he thought it was but right O.
But when he came to Seghill town the men were standing off O,
He thought that he would then be bound and he would make a
  scoff O.

As other men were standing off, he would not do the same O,
That idle work would never do, he'd rather bear the shame O.
Black J. R. made him believe that he was in no danger O,
And to the office he might go because he was a stranger . . .

About the hour of two o'clock as I was sitting cobbling O,
A rout there came unto our house; I heard the women
  gobbling O.
Away I went with all my speed as hard as I could hie O.
To see if I could catch the hares it was my will to try O.

But there were some upon the chase long ever I got there O.
With running so I lost my breath so I could run ne mair O.
But I will tell his troubles here as he came from the binding O.
They stript him there of all his clothes and left his skin re-
  fining O.

Black J. R. was most to blame, but he lost all but his lining O;
And when he came to Hallowell his skin so bright was shining O.
They left him nothing on to hide that good old man the priest O,
But there they hung on him his hat, he was so finely dressed O.

They set him off from there with speed to an alehouse by
the way O,
And there the Earsdon men did sit a-drinking on that day O.
But of their minds I cannot tell when they did see him
coming O;
The priest he had within his hat, and he was fast a-running O.

And all the way as he went home, by many was heard to say O,
That persuaded he had been to his loss upon that day O.
The Earsdon men they set him off from there to the machine O
That stands upon the allotment hill. He there himself did
screen O.

And there under a good whin-bush his priest and he sat
lurking O.
'I'll never go back to Seghill, but I will hide in Murton O.'
And so remember, you that come unto Seghill to bind O,
You'd better think upon the man that we have tret so kind O.

If some of the agitator balladeers, such as William Johnson
of Framwellgate Moor, imitated the windy commonplaces of
broadside language, the more typical industrial songmakers
preferred something less formal and verbose. Eager to present
the bare truth of their condition and to make clear their argument for improving it, they often used a domestic, non-literary
language, full of the colour of local dialect and casually peppered with slang. After all, the early industrial ballads were
blowing no large revolutionary clarion calls, this was not yet
the time of the artistic proletarian hymns like the "Internationale", "Red flag" and such. The singers' first aim was to
describe the hard condition of life in their own locality, the
exploitation and disasters, the strikes and lock-outs affecting
their relatively small community, and to explain and

criticize the reasons to their own comrades in the clearest, most digestible way. The industrial workers' consciousness of their own interests varies, of course, and in the ballads it ranges from more or less passive lamentation over a sad plight to flaming protest against the oppressors, but it stops well short of a general call to revolt. For that, one must look to other songs. It is noteworthy, incidentally, that songs destined for a public outside the close circle of workmates and their families —for instance, accounts of pit disasters composed partly for the purpose of collecting money in the streets in aid of widows and orphans—more often used a conventional literary language than a form of dialect. Perhaps too, some themes were felt to be too tragic for any other than a ceremonious idiom. Already quite early in the nineteenth century the emerging tradition of workers' folk song showed curious and at first sight paradoxical features, arising from the position of the individual song maker within his community. The 'pure', 'authentic' folk cultures so loved by conventional folklorists reign among communities with whom conservative notions are foremost and there is but small interest in, if not downright hostility to, personal initiatives. As a society develops and its pristine collective character becomes diluted, tensions arise between the individual and the tradition and, in the creation and performance of songs as in other respects, the effect of personality makes itself increasingly felt. The affirmations of the epic 'we' begin to change to intimations of the lyrical 'I'. Naturally, this process shows itself first among the fragmented society of the large towns, and if the principle holds true for English folk song—as it seems to—then it may be said that the influence of urban broadside composition and the dilapidation of traditional rural society were among the factors that shifted the balance between collective and individual in the genesis of our later folk songs. It was always the case that the talented performer, in reproducing the songs of his group, would make certain personal suggestions which, if adopted by the community, become part of the collective inheritance, to reappear subsequently as a nameless and respected part of communally sanctioned tradition. In the past, such suggestions would be but slight, the community aspect would dominate. In more recent times, the suggestions are more drastic, the individual song-maker's personality is well to the fore. The industrial song tradition shows this development in acute form. The anonymous element has receded, we know the names and can recognize the style of several creators of the songs. In the course of being passed on among the community, quite often the pieces hardly alter at all from their original state, because they are respected as individual creations. And yet, and here is the paradox, in general the industrial songs are far more collective in expression than the more anonymous rural songs that preceded them. Indeed it may be said that, not individual emotion but solidarity and social cohesion is their great motive and message. The old dialectical struggle between communal and individual in the shaping of songs is here lifted on to a new plane.

Dialogue, an important procedure in old folk balladry, takes on a new and specifically didactic character in the workers' folk songs. Well, not so new, perhaps. The early religious ballads, such as "The devil's nine questions" and "Death and the lady" had been using dialogue to point a moral for several centuries; but now the teaching was political. So we find such pieces as the anonymous "Dialogue between Peter Fearless and Dick Freeman", likewise associated with the 1831 Durham strike. The purpose of the song is entirely to explain the strike to the less-conscious among the pitmen, to stress the justice of the miners' cause, and to plug the need for solidarity. The ballad, no masterpiece perhaps but typical, begins with a mild dig at non-militant Dick:

'Now Dicky, was thou at the meeting today?
Aw look'd, but aw saw nought o' thou by the way.
Aw hope that thou's not turnin' cowardly noo,
    Or thinkin' a gannin' doon coal-pit to hew.'

Dick rather weakly explains that he has no intention of black-legging yet but is worried at having to pawn his belongings to keep his family from starving. Peter Fearless gives an account of what transpired at the meeting, and Dick replies:

'Wey, Peter, tho knaws aw wad liked to bin there;
What wi' redcoats and bluecoats 'twad be like a fair.
But noo aw will tell thou aw've something to say:
There's things in wor bond aw think oot o' the way.'

'Things in wor bond, man? There's nought oot o' reason.
Wey, man, aw's surprised; thou talks nowt but treason.
Noo, where's there owt wrang, let's hear thou just say,
For aw think aw can prove there's nowt oot o' the way.'

'Aw'd like to hear, Peter, 'twad cheer my poor heart
If thou only could prove how the ten shilling smart
Is not far too much for the masters to pay.
This is one o' the things aw think oot o' the way.'

'Now Dicky, aw'll let thou see what all this is for.
There is bad ventilation and wantin' a door,
And a great deal more aw'll tell before aw do stop,
That the place where we hew very oft wants a prop.' . . .

So, point by blunt point, the reasons for the strikers' demands
are patiently set out till even hangdog Dicky is convinced of
their justice and the need for solidarity.

'Wey, Peter, aw begin to see things right plain,
For wor maisters they care for nowt else but gain.
Then it's only in reason worsels to protect,
And to mak them pay smartly for ony neglect.'

'Then let's keep up wor hearts, Dick. We're sure for to win.
Wor maisters, aw knaw, before lang will give in.
So let us stand fast, never stop by the way,
And Victory will shout when we win the day!'

Ballads of such crudely instructive kind were not the durable
stuff of folk poetry, though by their view from below they are
valuable documents for the historian of the working class
movement who tries to find what labouring people were feeling
at important moments. Far more intimately than pamphlets or

newspaper reports, the workers' folk songs show the temper of the men towards each other and towards the masters. Not infrequently, they do so with some wit and even grace. An impressive specimen of early strike balladry is "The coal-owner and the pitman's wife", which has entered on a lively second existence since a miner at Whiston, Lancs, unearthed it in 1951. Seemingly it was made at the time of the 1844 Durham strike by a collier, William Hornsby of Shotton Moor. It too is composed as a dialogue, but of more artful form, like a medieval French *débat pastoral*. However, in using a classical ballad form, the pitman-songmaker was not inspired by a romantic wish to revive the beauties of past folk song. In fact, no doubt involuntarily, his ballad emerges rather as a witty caricature of the lyric of former times. The tune belongs to the great family of "Henry Martin" and a score of ballads with 'derrydown' refrain:

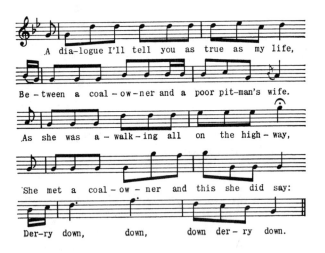

A dialogue I'll tell you as true as my life,
Between a coal-owner and a poor pitman's wife.
As she was a-walking all on the highway,
She met a coal-owner, and this she did say:
   Derry down, down, down derry down.

'Good morning, Lord Firedamp,' this woman she said,
'I'll do you no harm, sir, so don't be afraid.
If you'd been where I've been the most of my life,
You wouldn't turn pale at a poor pitman's wife.'
   Derry down, down, down derry down.

'Then where do you come from?' the owner he cries.
'I come from hell,' the poor woman replies.
'If you come from hell, then come tell me right plain,
How you contrived to get out again.'
   Derry down, down, down derry down.

'Aye, the way I got out, the truth I will tell,
They're turning the poor folk all out of hell.
This is to make room for the rich wicked race,
For there is a great number of them in that place.'
   Derry down, down down derry down.

'And the coal-owners is the next on command
To arrive in hell, as I understand,
For I heard the old devil say as I came out,
The coal-owners all had received their rout.'
   Derry down, down, down derry down.

'Then how does the old devil behave in that place?'
'O sir, he is cruel to the rich wicked race.
He's far more crueller than you could suppose.
He's like a mad bull with a ring through his nose.'
   Derry down, down, down derry down.

'If you be a coal-owner, sir, take my advice
And agree with your men and give them a fair price,
For if and you do not I know very well
You'll be in great danger of going to hell.'
   Derry down, down, down derry down.

'For all you coal-owners great fortunes has made
By those jovial men that works in the coal trade.
Now, how can you think to prosper and thrive
By wanting to starve your poor workmen alive?'
   Derry down, down, down derry down.

So come, ye poor pitmen, and join heart and hand;
For when you're off work, all trade's at a stand.
In the town of Newcastle all cry out amain:
Oh, gin the pits were at work once again!
    Derry down down, down derry down.

To judge from the industrial songs of the period that have
survived, whether on broadside or in popular memory, it
would seem that themes of strike and militance dominated
the songmakers' minds in the 1830s and '40s. Especially the
1844 Durham strike produced a host of ballads, and im-
passioned colliers seemed to find no difficulty in persuading
the broadside publishers of Newcastle, Durham, Shields and
Sunderland to issue their songs on leaflets. In this ballad
landscape the figures of certain heroic and steadfast women
stand out, forerunners of the singing women of the Kentucky
coalfields ninety years later. Their songs, moulded in the 'new-
fangled' come-all-ye form, are expressed conventionally enough
and yet allow us a glimpse of the singer's character. What do
we know, for instance, of Jane Knight? She lived in the colliery
village of Wingate, that lies between Easington and Trimdon
Grange, she may have worked in the pit (that is not clear),
and she made a ballad called "The pitmen's grievances",
published on a leaflet without imprint in 1844. For the rest, we
have but the evidence of her song, which indicates a clear-
sighted respectable woman, probably mild enough at home
but moved to indignation by injustice and treachery (how
old, by the way, is the word: blackleg?), and resolute in her
stand. Here is her ballad:

Come all kindhearted Christians and listen to my song.
Such times in Durham ne'er were known and yet to last so long.
The wives and children are turned out and camping out of doors,
Which causes us to wander and your charity implore.

'Twas on the 5th of April, that was the very day,
Our leaders had appointed our tools to bring away.
Until our wages are advanced we must work no more;
Which causes us to wander and your charity implore.

Our Masters are hard-hearted, our wages they'll not rise.
They will not hear us speak a word, our wants for to appease,
Unless our Union we will break and Roberts own no more,
Which causes us to wander and your charity implore.

Ye blacklegs of Wingate, I would have ye mind your ways.
You follow Christ for fishes and then for gold betray.
Ye have sold us all for silver, and what can ye do more?
Which causes us to wander and your charity implore.

Here's a health to Mr. Roberts, and long may he reign.
Likewise all other gentlemen who do our rights maintain.
Before our Union we will break and Roberts own no more,
We're resolved for to wander upon some distant shore.

The salutation to Roberts is almost obligatory in Durham
strike ballads of the time. William Roberts, the Chartist lawyer
who doggedly defended the miners' union cause in the law
courts, was the great hero of the time in the eyes of the pitmen
and their dependants. Another woman who proudly signed
her ballads 'Elizabeth Gair, Collier's Wife' (they were printed
on leaflets by Henderson in North Shields) begins her song,
"The colliery union", thus:

Come all ye noble colliery lads, wherever you belong.
I pray you give attention and you shall hear my song.
'Tis concerning of our Union lads, for they have proved so true,
They have stood fast, man to man, we must give them their due.
    So stick unto your Union, and mind what Roberts say.
    If you be guided by his word, you'll surely win the day.

Subsequently in the ballad, after describing the masters'
astonishment that they failed to starve the colliers into
submission, and following a scornful reference to the Scottish
and Irish blacklegs brought in to break the strike, Mrs.
Gair cries:

Success to your commander, and Roberts is his name,
Since he has proved so loyal, we'll spread about his fame.
Cheer up your hearts you colliery lads, he'll not leave you alone;
After he has eat the meat he will give them the bone.
   So stick unto your Union, and mind what Roberts say.
   If you be guided by his word, you'll surely win the day.

During the first half of the nineteenth century, not only
women but children also worked in the mines, the women often
engaged in heavy work, carrying baskets of coal up the long
ladders to the shaft, the children as 'trappers', opening the
ventilation ports for the tubs to come through, or as 'hurryers'
pushing the corves or tubs along rails from the coal face.
From the report of the *Children's Employment Commission* of 1842
come documents of interest to our theme. An eight-year-old
trapper girl, working a thirteen hour day underground, reports:
'I have to trap without a light and I'm scared. . . . Sometimes
I sing when I've light, but not in the dark; I dare not sing
then.' And an older girl, a hurryer, says: 'The bald place upon
my head is made by thrusting the corves. . . . I hurry the corves
a mile and more underground and back; they weigh 3 cwt. . . .
The getters that I work for are naked except for their caps. . . .
Sometimes they beat me, if I am not quick enough.'[47] This
last from seventeen-year-old Patience Kershaw, who longed
to work in a mill rather than in the pit, even though the mill-
work had made her sister's legs swell. Poor Patience! One
wonders if she knew the ballad of "The collier lass", printed
by Harkness of Preston, that street singers were carrying
through the Lancashire towns, just about the time she was
giving her testimony to the gentlemen of the Commission:

My name's Polly Parker, I come o'er from Worsley.
My father and mother work in the coal mine.
Our family's large, we have got seven children,
So I am obliged to work in the same mine.
   And as this is my fortune, I know you feel sorry
   That in such employment my days I shall pass,
   But I keep up my spirits, I sing and look merry
   Although I am but a poor collier lass.

By the greatest of dangers each day I'm surrounded.
I hang in the hair by a rope or a chain.
The mine may fall in, I may be killed or wounded,
May perish by damp or the fire of the train.
 And what would you do if it were not for our labour?
 In wretched starvation your days you would pass,
 While we could provide you with life's greatest blessing.
 Then do not despise the poor collier lass.

All the day long you may say we are buried,
Deprived of the light and the warmth of the sun.
And often at nights from our bed we are hurried;
The water is in, and barefoot we run.
 And though we go ragged and black are our faces,
 As kind and as free as the best we'll be found,
 And our hearts are as white as your lords in fine places.
 Although we're poor colliers that work underground.

I am now growing up fast, somehow or other.
There's a collier lad strangely runs in my mind.
And in spite of the talking of father and mother,
I think I should marry if he was inclined.
 But should he prove surly and will not befriend me,
 Another and better chance may come to pass;
 And my friends here I know, to him will recommend me,
 And I'll be no longer a collier lass.

If the conditions of work were appalling in the mines, the
miners' wages in many districts were higher than that of most
workers, perhaps because their traditional solidarity stood them
in good stead when it came to industrial action. A song,
reported quite recently from the neighbourhood of Wigan,
and current in many parts of Lancashire and Yorkshire, runs:

  My mother sent me for some water,
  For some water for my tea.
  My foot slipped and down I tumbled.
  Collier lad gat hold of me.

> Collier lads get gold and silver.
> Factory lads get nobbut brass.
> Who'd get married to a two-loom weaver
> When there's plenty of collier lads?

By the mid-nineteenth century the growth of such industries as engineering and shipbuilding adjacent to the coal-bearing areas was bringing intense urbanization. Along the Tyne and Wear, for example, pit villages were becoming first the satellites, then the suburbs of the towns. A consequence of this urbanization was the rapid growth of music hall entertainment in the coalfields. Especially in the neighbourhood of Newcastle between the 1830s and '6os, semi-professional musical performances in the mechanics' institutes and beer-halls became important to the cultural life of colliers. The audiences were mostly miners and their womenfolk, and many of the entertainers were pitmen too. In the early days of this development, the songs were frequently made around day-to-day events in the pits, and of a Saturday night in the mechanics' hall, an admired collier-comedian might clump on to the little stage and unroll over the beer-stained tables some such epic as "The Haswell cages". Big meaning for the miners; little enough for those outside the circle.

> Come all you good people and listen a while.
> I'll sing you a song that will cause you to smile.
> It is about Haswell I mean for to sing,
> Concerning the new plan we started last spring.
>   And the very first thing I will mention,
>   Without any evil intention,
>   It's concerning this new invention
>   Of winding up coals in a cage.

> It was in eighteen hundred and thirty eight,
> We began to prepare to make the shaft right.
> We put in the conductors from bottom to top,
> The materials were ready prepared at the shop.

From the top of the pit to the bottom:
One hundred and fifty-six fathom.
And the distance you do think it nothing,
You rise so quickly in the cage.

Come all you good people and listen a while,
I'll sing you a song that'll cause you to smile,
It is about Haswell I mean for to sing,
Concerning the new plan we started last spring,
And the very first thing I will mention,
Without any evil intention,
It's concerning this new invention,
Of winding up coals in a cage.

Now, considering the depth, it's surprising to say
The quantity of work we can draw in a day.
Five hundred and thirty tons of the best coal
In the space of twelve hours we can win up this hole.
 About forty-five tons in an hour.
 And, viewers, overmen and hewers,
 Our engines must have a great power
To run at such speed with the cage.

Then as soon as the tubs do come to the day,
To the weighing machine they are taken away,
Where two men are appointed there to attend
To see justice done between master and men.
 And when they leave the weighing machine, sir,
 Straightway they do go to the screen, sir,
 And the keeker does see that they're clean, sir,
 All the coals that come up in the cage.

I've wrought with the corves, I have wrought with the tubs,
I have wrought where the baskets come up by the lugs,
I have wrought by the dozen, I've wrought by the score,
But this curious contrivance I ne'er saw before.
 When we get in, they then pull the rapper.
 At the top it does make a great clatter,
 And the brakesmen they know what's the matter,
 And bring us away in a cage.

And when the bell rings and the top we approach,
It oft puts me in mind of a new railway coach.
The number of passengers I cannot tell,
But she brings a great many, I know very well.
 But I wish they may not overload her,
 And do some mischief on the road, sir.
 Too much charge makes a cannon explode, sir,
 And so will too much in a cage.

Now the young men and maids sometimes take a trip
Out to sea in fine weather aboard a steam-ship,
But if any be curious enough to engage
For a trip down below and a ride in our cage,
 It would be a fine recreation
 For to go down and view the low station.
 I wish they may meet no temptation
 When they take a trip in our cage.

Haswell is a colliery village some nine miles south of Sunderland. The song of its cages was among the earliest publications
of the Durham broadside printer George Walker when he
set up shop in 1839. The ballad is worth quoting in full because

it is such an early specimen of that painstaking factual coal-dust and cast-iron documentary manner that was to characterize so much mine, workshop and foundry poetry in later years. Typical of this kind of production is the easy glide into vaudeville commonplace in the final verse.

As opportunities grew for local professional comedians, the public entertainment repertory in the workmen's halls became less exclusively occupational. A number of colliers, made unfit for heavy work through pit-accidents, turned their talents to song-writing and public singing; but by the later 1840s and the '50s, the popular hits were concerned rather with off-work scenes—ironic, hilarious or pathetic—than with life on the job. Favourites ranged from Robert Emery's "Baggynanny" (about a group of drunken miners who go to hear Paganini, and are more impressed by his diabolism than his musicianship), through Ned Corvan's "Astrilly, or The pitman's farewell' (a wry, even sardonic song of a collier forced to emigrate to Australia through hard times in the coalfields) to Rowland Harrison's "Geordie Black" (about a modest but lion-hearted old miner, too aged to hew at the coal-face any longer, who has now to work among the children at the pit-bank, picking stones from among the cut coal). Less well-known, but enjoying something of a revival on Tyneside today, is the lamentation of the collier who lost all his wages at pitch-and-toss, called "Aw wish Pay-Friday wad come". It was written in 1870 by an Elswick miner and part-time professional comedian named Anderson, who set his poem to a much-used tune that has carried the words of "The whistling thief" and Tommy Armstrong's autobiographical "Birth of the lad" among others. These and other favourites such as "Cushie Butterfield", "Keep yor feet still, Geordie hinny", and "Geordie, haud the bairn" were reprinted over and again during the nineteenth century by publishers such as Allan of Newcastle, and some have lasted well till now, but probably the most durable of all is the song of a workers' holiday outing, "Blaydon Races", written by the collier-comedian George Ridley (1834–64), a talented song-writer who died early as a consequence of an industrial accident. "Blaydon Races" has become national property, though perhaps it is heard at its best as roared by thousands of a Saturday afternoon when Newcastle United chance to be doing well.

Productions of this stamp cannot be considered folk songs by any workable definition. They are popular songs belonging to the world of the professional stage, however humble. But they were of peculiar importance to miners and other industrial workers, and their influence was so powerful that the musical repertory of, for instance, the northeastern colliers might have become entirely urbanized, and lost what remained of its folk song character, were it not for an accident of history.

The autumn of 1845 was warm and damp, fine weather for *phtyophthora infestans*, that somehow spread its black spots and white fungus over the Irish potato crop and starved or drove into emigration the poorest third of the Irish people. They drifted over the water with heavy heart, light bundle and a mouthful of songs. Irish melody had enjoyed a certain vogue in England since the sixteenth century, at first in the world of fashion, later among the common people, and quite early in the formation of industrial folk song a small range of popular Irish tunes—and Scottish too, for that matter—were used by English workers. For instance, "The Haswell cages", quoted above, is set to the tune of "The wedding of Ballyporeen" (*Banais Baile na Poirín*). Some of these melodies were brought to England by professional composers, others by middle-class amateurs and dancing-masters, a few by migrant-workers. But towards the middle of the nineteenth century, the flow of poor Irish into our industrial districts increased greatly, and thousands of former smallholders and cottiers as well as labourers, fugitives from the Great Famine and pestilence that lasted for six years, brought into the coalfields and mill-towns a rich fund of Irish folk song far exceeding the handful of stock favourites that had hitherto circulated there. This new wave of traditional song merged with the existing pit-village repertory and helped to restore some of its folk-ish character just as that character had begun to fade. For instance, in some cases modal scales reappeared in strength, that had been losing ground rapidly to the conventional major-minor system. Even pentatonism, hitherto absent from our industrial song, began to show among the melodies used by miners. Notably, the

powerful 'come-all-ye' form* exerted great influence, with its
four-lined strophes of 14 (8 + 6) syllables, its tunes often in
6/8 time, its structure as likely as not in an inexorable ABBA
pattern (though sometimes masked by variation), with the
outer cadences on the tonic and the inner ones on dominant
or subdominant, mainly of mixolydian or dorian cast when
not in the conventional major. Probably of urban origin (from
Dublin?), the come-all-ye type, simple to compose, easy to
remember, seems to have been crystallizing during the eighteenth century. Whether its peculiar stereotyped formula, with
its almost mechanical iterations, shows a conscious attempt at
intensified artistry, or is merely a mark of decadence, of a
slack following of the line of least resistance by repeating a
familiar phrase instead of inventing or memorizing a new one,
may be argued. The fact remains that by the end of the
eighteenth century it was well-established in Irish song, and
during the nineteenth century the form spread rapidly in
rural and industrial areas throughout England; also, it flourished
among Scottish farm-workers living more or less within the
orbit of provincial towns. In fact it became the characteristic
song-form for most traditions of late growth, including those
of the loggers of the north-eastern American woods and the
pastoral workers of Australia. A characteristic example of
mid-nineteenth century come-all-ye is the elegiac "Johnny
Seddon", recorded from a collier of Irish descent in Chopwell,
Co. Durham, in 1953:

As I went out in summertime all for to take the air,
I saw a handsome maiden down by the river clear,
She wept and she lamented, and bitterly she cried,
Sayin': "My curse upon the cruel mine where Johnny Seddon
    died."

My love he was a collier lad and wrought beneath the ground.
For modest mild behaviour his equal can't be found.
His teeth as white as ivory, his cheek a rosy red,
But alas, my handsome collier lad lies numbered with the dead.

* Songs of this kind do not necessarily include the exhortation 'Come all ye
(this or that)' in the text, though they are likely to, either at the beginning of the
first verse or the last.

Last night as I lay on my bed I fell into a dream
I dreamed a voice came unto me and called me by my name,
Saying: 'Jeannie, lovely Jeannie, for me you need not mourn,
But the cruel stones do crush my bones and I'll never more
     return.

Early the very next morning my dream was clarified.
The neighbours all came running in. 'John Seddon's dead'
     they cried.
'As he was at his work last night, the roof upon him fell.'
The grief and sorrow of my heart no mortal tongue can tell.

Come all you pretty fair maids, I hope you'll lend an ear,
For the grief and sorrow of my heart is more than I can bear.
For once I loved a collier lad, and he loved me also,
But by a fatal accident, he in his grave lies low.

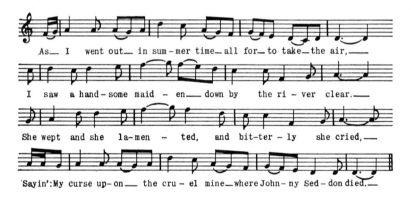

As— I   went out— in sum–mer time—all for— to take—the air,—
I   saw a hand–some maid – en—— down by   the ri – ver clear.——
She wept and she   la–men – ted, and bit–ter – ly   she cried,—
'Sayin':My curse up–on—— the cru – el mine—where John– ny Sed–don died.—

By the 1860's, the come-all-ye had become the dominant
type of songs created by miners about pit-disasters, strikes and
such. But in character and in function, the texts were changing
fast. Ballads of the kind of "Johnny Seddon" or the similarly
elegiac "Blantyre explosion"* (made on the disaster at Messrs
Dixon's colliery at High Blantyre, near Glasgow, on October
22, 1877) represent a middling stage. Both these songs, and

* Reproduced in: A. L. Lloyd (ed.). *Come All Ye Bold Miners. Ballads and Songs
of the Coalfields.* (London, 1952), p. 78.

others like them, in their attempt to express adequately a tragedy affecting a whole community, took a course that resembled and yet was already departing from the way of conventional broadside pieces. As with the stall ballads of lost love and brutal murder, the tragedy was presented in personal terms—in both the ballads named, a young woman of vague features stands by a river lamenting for her lover killed in the mine. But the listener understands this is no personal tragedy, the young woman is the symbol of all the mourning women in the stricken community. For all that, no comment is offered beyond a general curse on the cruel mine; an air of fatalism hangs over this kind of song, the hero is a fine boy but a mere toy of destiny, like the heroes of the folk ballads of earlier times.

"Johnny Seddon", conceived within the matrix of Irish rural folk song and born in a coaly landscape in the 1850's, represents the balladry of industrial disaster in its primal stage, vague in detail—not even the name of the pit is mentioned—and passive in mood, seemingly composed in calm some time after the event—if indeed it happened at all. On the other hand, "The Blantyre explosion" typifies a slightly later growth. The whole panorama is clearer, we know the name of the colliery, the number of miners who died alongside the hero is specified, the community is presented, even if only obliquely, in the mouth of the solitary riverside mourner as she describes the scene:

'The explosion was heard; all the women and children
With pale anxious faces they haste to the mine.
When the truth was made known, the hills rang with their
    mourning.
Three hundred and ten young miners were slain.'

At the same time as "The Blantyre explosion" was being made up and sung, ballads with a newer content were beginning to appear in some of the coalfields, composed hot after the occurrence, presenting the grief of the community in realistic not symbolic terms, coloured with journalistic local detail, no longer passive and fatalistic but often ready with sharp criticism of hard doing, bitter risk and owners' indifference. These ballads showed a change not merely in aspect but also in function, for they were not intended simply as gratuitous if mournful diversion; their aim was to work on the feelings of listeners so that they would give to the fund for the relief of dead miners' dependants. And ultimately, the concern of the later ballads was to tell the truth about the events as the collier and his community saw it; the more vehemently if the official account in newspapers and managerial statements seemed false. Following a mine-explosion at Donibristle, Fife, in 1901, a number of miners and rescue workers were entombed through a mistake of the management. The ensuing ballad, "The Donibristle Moss Moran disaster", in its concluding verses, exemplifies the double function of charity-appeal and comment that is characteristic of so many latterday disaster songs;

They lost their lives, God help them. Ah yes, it was a fact.
Someone put in a stopping, and they never did get back.
Was that not another blunder? My God, it was a sin.
To put a stopping where they did, it closed our heroes in.

We never shall forget them, though they have lost their lives,
So let us pay attention to their children and their wives.
It simply is our duty now, and let us all beware;
Their fathers died a noble death and left them in our care.

Raw poetry, but carrying its peculiar pathos. Later still, comment in the songs grew sharper, as in the ballad made on the disaster at Gresford, near Wrexham, in 1934, when 265 miners were killed. The song-maker provides his own journalistic comment, at once as reporter and leader-writer on the workers' behalf:

A fortnight before the explosion,
To the shotfirer Tomlinson cried:
'If you fire that shot we'll be all blown to hell',
And no-one can say that he lied.

The fireman's reports they are missing,
The records of forty-two days;
The colliery manager had them destroyed
To cover his criminal ways.

Down there in the dark they are lying.
They died for nine shillings a day.
They have worked out their shift, and now they must lie
In the darkness until Judgement Day.

The Lord Mayor of London's collecting
To help both our children and wives.
The owners have sent some white lilies
To pay for the poor colliers' lives.

We are a long way from the passive, unchallenging, personalized, lyrical lament of "Johnny Seddon". "The Gresford disaster", product of a period of large-scale union organization, is more in the nature of a public address than an intimate utterance, and perhaps, for all that it shows a certain adroitness in the way matters are put, in poignancy it falls short of the best disaster songs simply because it seems to be addressed more to the outside world than to the tight brooding community of pitmen and their families. However clumsily they may be expressed, the workers' ballads really score when they can convince that they are from the heart to the heart of a stricken community. So, more characteristic than "Gresford" is the much earlier song called "The Trimdon Grange explosion", a durable piece often heard in folk song clubs nowadays. It was made by a remarkable collier-balladeer, Tommy Armstrong (1848–1919) of Tanfield, Co. Durham, a small sharp-faced bow-legged miner with fourteen children and an indomitable thirst. Armstrong wrote a great many songs of mining life, and had them printed on leaflets to sell in the pubs at a penny a time, to provide drinking-money. 'Me dad's Muse was a mug of beer', was the comment of one of his sons. Besides these 'recreational' pieces, Armstrong's output of militant strike songs and disaster ballads was considerable, written to raise money for union funds or the relief of widows and orphans. On February 16, 1882, an explosion occurred at the Trimdon Grange colliery, killing 74 miners. Within a few days, Armstrong was singing his commemorative song in the local Mechanics' Hall. The text is rather more Victorian-sententious than is customary with him, probably because he felt his usual salty 'pitmatic' idiom was not fine enough for this kind of elegy; but he chose a good sol-mode come-all-ye tune to carry the words, and that has ensured the song's present vitality.

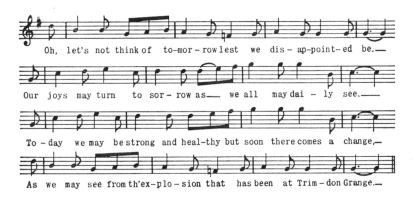

Oh, let's not think of tomorrow lest we disappointed be.
Our joys may turn to sorrow as we all may daily see.
Today we may be strong and healthy, but soon there comes a change,
As we may see from the explosion that has been at Trimdon Grange.

Men and boys left home that morning for to earn their daily bread,
Nor thought before the evening they'd be numbered with the dead.
Let's think of Mrs. Burnett, once had sons but now has none—
By the Trimdon Grange explosion, Joseph, George and James are gone.

February has left behind it what will never be forgot;
Weeping widows, helpless children may be found in many a cot.
They ask if father's left them, and the mother hangs her head,
With a weeping widow's feelings tells the child its father's dead.

God protect the lonely widow and raise each drooping head;
Be a father to the orphans, never let them cry for bread.
Death will pay us all a visit, they have only gone before.
We'll meet the Trimdon victims where explosions are no more.

Another song, of quite different type but involving mention
of a pit accident, has recently taken on a new lease of life, and
not only in the Northeast. That is the stirring "Rap 'er te
bank", collected by W. Toyn from Henry Nattress of Low
Fell, Gateshead. 'Rap her to bank!', is the cry of men at the
bottom of the shaft, waiting to come up in the cage. The
onsetter would rap, and the winding man, hearing the signal,
would draw the cage to the surface (the 'bank').

Rap her te bank, me canny lad!
Wind her away, keep tornen!
The back-shift men are gannin hyem.
We'll be back in the mornen.

Me feyther used te caal the torn
When the lang shift wes ower.
All the way ootbye, ye'd hear him cry:
'D'ye knaa it's efter fower?'

Rap her te bank, me canny lad!
Wind her away, keep tornen!
The back-shift men are gannin hyem.
We'll be back in the morning.'

And when that aaful day arrived,
The last shift for me feyther;
A faal of stones and brokken bones,
But still above the clatter, he cried:

'Rap her te bank, me canny lad!
Wind her reet slow—that's clivvor!
This poor aad lad hes tekken bad.
Aa'll be back heor nivvor.'

Finally and for good measure a heartless little jingle, suitable for ball-bouncing, to an "In and out the windows" tune, obtained in 1964 from a 13-year-old girl with the suggestive name of Barbara Allen, who learnt the elegy from her father, a collier at Denaby Main, South Yorkshire:

There was a man, they called him Len,
Got buried in t'ripping at a quarter to ten.

They tied him up so good and well,
But who it was they couldn't tell.

Up the drift then they did go.
One end was Steve and the other was Joe.

They got to the top and there stood Ben;
And Ben said to Len: 'Nay, it's not thee again?'

'Aye, it's me again', said Len to Ben.
'I got buried in t'ripping at a quarter to ten.'

Song-making proliferated among miners during the latter

half of the nineteenth century. Looking back to his boyhood, an ex-collier from West Stanley, 80 years old when he was recorded in 1952, remarked: 'Making rhymes and songs used to run through the pit like a fever. Some of 'em seemed to go daft thinking up verses. Even us young lads used to answer back in rhyme. The men would get down, take a little walk, see what the last shift had done. The man who'd been working in your place had always left his smell behind him, and we'd even make a rhyme on that. One would say: 'Whe's bin hewin in maa place in the oors sin Aa've bin gan? Aa reckon it wes aad Basher wi's lavender hair-oil on.' And another would answer: 'Whe's bin hewin in maa place? Aa reckon it wes aad Rab. He's the only man in Joycey's eats onions wi his snap'.'

Nonsense, of course, doggerel, like a good many industrial songs and a fair proportion of 'classic' ballads too. But while, to the traditionalist and the amateur of 'fragrant oldtime ditties', folk song is mostly concerned with a lovable pastoral England lost beyond hope of recovery, the songs of industry deal with pleasures, cares and tragedies that are close, sometimes terribly close, to common life today. Their creators carried in their heads a mixed musical baggage of parlour ballads, music hall songs, some hymn tunes, a few scraps of opera, a smattering of traditional song. And down in the mine with nothing to hear but the pit sounds—the drop of water, the creak of timber, the ring of the pick and the rattle of the tubs—the collier would wrestle with his muse to produce a song that might move, hearten or instruct other people just like himself, a whole community sharing his preoccupations in advance. Perhaps his intention would be strictly cautionary and didactic, as in "Jowl and listen", another song collected by W. Toyn, in which an experienced miner addresses a young one, and warns him to 'jowl', that is, strike the roof of his workplace with the haft of his pick, to sound out whether the roof is safe before he starts hewing. Jowling the coal-face itself would also be recommended to find where the coal would come away easiest, without unnecessary tearing and pulling ('rivin and tewin'). 'Tyum 'uns' or 'chummins' are empty tubs, by the way.

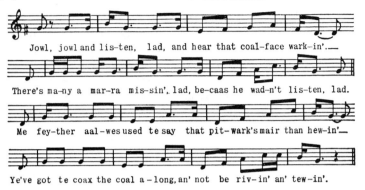

Jowl, jowl and lis-ten, lad, and hear that coal-face wark-in'.___

There's ma-ny a mar-ra mis-sin', lad, be-caas he wad-n't lis-ten, lad.

Me fey-ther aal-wes used te say that pit-wark's mair than hew-in'___

Ye've got te coax the coal a-long, an' not be riv-in' an' tew-in'.

Jowl, jowl and listen lad,
And hear that coalface workin.
There's many a marra missin, lad,
Becaas he wadn't listen, lad.

Me feyther aalwes used te say
That pit wark's mair than hewin.
Ye've got te coax the coal alang
and not be rivin and tewin.

So jowl, jowl and listen, lad,
And hear that coalface workin.
There's many a marra missin, lad,
Becaas he wadn't listen, lad.

Noo the depitty craals frae flat te flat,
While the putter rams the tyum 'uns,
But the man at the face hes te knaa his place
Like a mother knaas hor young 'uns.

So jowl, jowl and listen, lad,
And hear that coalface workin.
There's many a marra missin, lad,
Becaas he wadn't listen, lad.

A different kind of cautionary song is "The banks of the Dee", the lament of a pitman turned away from work because at fifty-six he is reckoned too old. In former times grey-haired miners were sometimes relegated to 'the colliers' second childhood', picking slate on the bank alongside little boys. The song is not only a protest against unjust treatment; it also warns young piece-workers against over-production. It was recorded in 1951 from J. White, a Houghton-le-Spring, Co. Durham miner, who explained: 'To appreciate this song, it is necessary to understand the system of wage-basing in Durham County. If the men earned more than ten per cent over the county average, the owners could and did apply for a reduction in tonnage rates and thereby ensured that wages were never high.' Conditions are changed now, but such songs as "The banks of the Dee" are slow to lose their poignancy, as Durham folk will know who ever heard the fine collier-singer Jack Elliott of Birtley handle the song before he died, so far ahead of his time, in 1966.

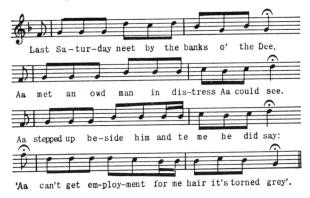

Last Saturday neet by the banks o' the Dee,
Aa met an owd man, in distress Aa could see.
Aa stepped up beside him an' te me he did say:
'Aa can't get employment, for me hair it's torned grey.

I am an owd miner aged fifty an' six.
If aa could get lots, wey, Aa'd raffle me picks.
Aa'd raffle 'em, Aa'd sell 'em, Aa'd hoy 'em awey,
For Aa can't get employment, for me hair it's torned grey.

When Aa wes a young chap Aa wes just like the rest;
Each day in the pit Aa'd do my very best.
If Aa got a good place Aa'd be hewin aal day.
Noo at fifty an' six, my hair it's torned grey.

Noo, last Wednesday neet te the reckonin Aa wint.
Te the colliery office Aa wint straight fornenst.
Aa'd got me wage-packet, Aa wes walkin awey,
When they gie us me notice, for me hair it's torned grey.

Noo, aal ye young fellers, it's ye's that's to blame.
Ye got good places, ye're daein just the same.
If ye got a good price, ye'd hew it awey,
But ye're bound te regret it when your hair it's torned grey.

For I am an owd miner aged fifty an' six.
If Aa could get lots, wey, Aa'd raffle me picks.
Aa'd raffle 'em, Aa'd sell 'em, Aa'd hoy 'em awey,
For Aa can't get employment, me hair it's torned grey.'

Another song, from the darkness of the pit itself, was collected
in 1966 by A. E. Green from a Castleford collier, William Hill,
who started work in the Yorkshire mines at the age of fifteen,
as a pony-driver. A note from Mr. Green says: 'It was then
that he learned this song, which the drivers would sing to
their ponies, sitting on the five- and seven-hundredweight
coal-tubs with their feet on the swingletree. A 'doggy' was an
overman who was responsible for maintaining the rails on
which the tubs ran; it was not unusual for tubs to go off the
'road', and it was then the doggy's job to get them back on—
if he was to be found. The 'pass-by' was a section of double
track with swing points, where tubs could pass, most of the
road being single-track. The 'standing' in verse 3 is a pony
stall. Mr. Hill says that in every pit he ever worked, the stalls
were marked with the pony's names, and the first five were
invariably as follows: TOM/KING/SHOT/DICK/TURPIN.
The business of going off the road (especially if, as here, the
pony was 'rubbing', i.e. catching its back on the low roof,
causing an unpleasant sore), was clearly very trying to a
young lad on his first job.'

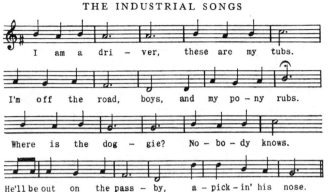

I am a driver, these are my tubs.
I'm off the road, boys, and my pony rubs.
Where is the doggy? Nobody knows.
He'll be out on the pass-by, a-pickin' his nose.

I am a driver, these are my tubs.
I'm off the road, boys, and my pony rubs.
Where is the doggy? Nobody knows.
He'll be out on the pass-by, a-pickin' his nose.

I shall be glad when this shift is done,
Then I'll be up there out in the sun.
Tha'll be dahn 'ere, boy, in this dark 'oil,
Still gruntin' and groanin', pullin' this coil.

Corn's in the manger, water's in t'trough.
Tha'll shove thee nose out when tha's 'ad enough.
I'll tek thee in t'standin' and drop off thee gears.
When I come back I know tha'll be 'ere.

It is said that folk song differs from popular song as night
from day. In a way, that is so: but the merging of night into
day is hardly perceptible, and our worker-ballad makers may
sometimes be imagined on tiptoe in the half-light, crowing for
the sunrise. Whether we call their creations folk song or
something else (but what else?), hardly matters. The main
thing is that they are created and sung by men who are
identical with their audience in standing, in occupation, in
attitude to life, and in daily experience.

From what we have seen so far, it is clear that three strata of workers' song exist, not always clearly distinguishable one from the other. There is the anonymous, orally-spread, firmly traditional kind of song made by 'insiders'. There is the author-made, print-diffused, firmly literary song made by 'outsiders'. And between these two forms, another layer interposes itself, consisting of individual creations more or less in the manner of traditional song, created by 'insiders' (or by those very close to the inside), and diffused either orally or by print or both. The anonymous oral songs were first in the field but it should not be thought that this class is made up only of creations from the earliest period of workers' songs; pieces of this traditional stamp also arose later and indeed still appear, though more rarely, in our own time. They are easy enough to fit into a pigeon-hole labelled 'folk song', just as the literary pieces made by 'outside' authors on behalf of the workers fit into a compartment of some other, non-folkloric, designation. It is the middle stratum of industrial song, of hybrid style, with known authors, the spread and perpetuation aided by print, that confuses and dismays our academic folklorists, card-indexers of the human soul. Probably this kind of song, showing a synthesis of professional and traditional folk culture, makes up the most considerable part of the industrial lyric.

If folk songs are vernacular poetical and musical statements made by working people about their specific problems, what is one to say of those mainly post-1850 industrial songs originating among stage professionals of working class origin and outlook, such as Joe Wilson's "No work"? Wilson ('me fether wes a joiner an' cabinet myeker, an' me muther a straw bonnet myeker, an' byeth natives o' the canny aud toon o' Newcassil') was a printer of cheap song-books and a humble stage comedian, who in ten brief years—he died at the age of thirty-three in 1874—established himself deeply in the affections of working-class audiences in the North through the truthful and sympathetic way in which he depicted the condition of their lives, a condition that he fully shared. "No work", characteristic in its total identification of singer with audience, was made during the slump period of the 1860s on Tyneside. Wilson set it to the well-known evergreen air of "Pretty Polly Perkins".

Aw's weary, aw's wretched, aw wander forlorn.
Aw sigh for the neet an' then wish for the morn.
For neet brings ne comfort an' morn little mair;
I' byeth mind an' body aw's worn oot an' sair.
 What wretchedness, what misery, there's ne one can tell,
 Except them that's been oot o' wark like mesel.

Aw wander te places an' try to get wark,
Where 'Call back agyen' is the foreman's remark.
Thus hopeless an' cheerless aw pass mony a day.
Though the pay-week comes roond, it brings me ne pay.

Ne wark yit! Heart-broken aw bend me ways hyem.
Ne wark yit! Te tell them aw really think shyem;
For dependence is painful, though it's on yer awn.
Though te comfort an' cheer ye they try a' they can.

There's nyen can imagine the anguish aw feel,
When aw sit doon at hyem te me poor humble meal.
Each bite seems te choke us; the day seems full lang,
An' a' that aw do, aw feel's though 'twas wrang.

Me father looks dull though he strives te look glad,
An' tells us it's nowt te the troubles he's had.
Me mother smiles kindly, though sad like the rest.
She whispers: 'Cheer up, me lad, an' hope for the best.'

It cannot last always! Aw hope before lang
Wi' wark aw'll be freed fre sad poverty's pang.
For wi'oot it, hyem's dreary; the fire's bright spark
Turns gloomy an' sad when at hyem thor's ne wark.
 What wretchedness, what misery, there's ne one can tell,
 Except them that's been oot o' wark like mesel.

Wilson, whose songs have been described as 'true photographs
in verse of Tyneside working class life', is still held in high

regard among the miners, engineers and shipyard workers of his native region, both for the wit of his songs and the sympathy he showed for working people in their struggles. Many of his compositions treat of comic domestic situations, such as "Keep yor feet still, Geordie hinny", but among his more serious works we find such songs as "The strike", written for the workers of W. Armstrong's engineering works (the firm later became well-known as Vickers Armstrongs). The song relates to the great stoppage of work in 1871 in connection with the movement for a nine-hour working day. It was the kind of song that was at once inspired by and served to inspire the worker-songmakers at the coal-face and the engineering lathe, the kind of vernacular professional—or at least semi-professional—production that impelled industrial folk song towards a new and more conscious stage of development. The melody Wilson chose for "The strike" was a folk tune he had already used for "The Gallowgate lad", the wry lament of a girl whose sweetheart, formerly a 'striker at Stivvison's factry', has joined the militia. The tune is a variant of the 'very peculiar' one used as a calling-on song for the sword dancers of Earsdon, Northumberland.

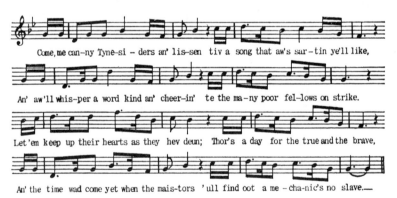

Come, me canny Tynesiders, an' lissen
Tiv a song that aw's sartin ye'll like,
An' aw'll whisper a word kind an' cheerin',
Te the many poor fellows on strike.

Let 'em keep up their hearts as they hev deun;
Thor's a day for the true an' the brave,
An' the time wad come yet when the maistors
'ull find oot a mechanic's no slave.

Is Nine Oors an unreasonable movement?
Is't not plenty te labour for men?
Let them that condemned hev a try on't,
An' see if they'll not alter the plan.
An' if lang oors industry increases,
Hev they found oot wi' the oors that *they*'ve tried?
Their capital grows through wor labour,
Wey, it's mair to their shyem, that they'll find.

But cheer up, thor's good friends that support us,
Ay, an' England depends on us a';
An' we'll prove that we're true te the Movement,
An' vict'ry shall let the world knaw
That Tynesiders'll nivor be conquered
By maistors that care nought fer them;
An' if maistors is meant te be maistors,
Let 'em find there's men meant te be men!

If the influence of the music hall was strong on the industrial
songs of the North-east, in the North-west, among the spinners
and weavers, it was much more the products of the writers
of dialect pieces for recitation that affected the way the mill and
factory songs were made up. The Yorkshire and Lancashire
weaving community, always conservative and proud where
its regional customs and traditions were concerned, nourished
a host of amateur geologists and botanists, local historians and
antiquarians, and notably recitation poets. These writers,
self-educated for the most part, tended to overstrain their
talents and run to cliché when trying to emulate the classy
literary forms, but when they kept their feet on the ground by
using local dialect, they were capable of producing work of
touching humour and real pathos, saying what they had to
freshly and astutely and in terms entirely appropriate to the
emotional problems of their audience. The line of these dialect
recitation writers runs from the eighteenth century Lancashire

poet John Collier up to Harvey Kershaw of Rochdale in our own time. Some, such as Ammon Wrigley of Saddleworth, are poets of considerable sophistication; others, like the Bradford wool-sorter Ben Preston (author of "T'poor weyver"), are close to the traditions of folk balladry, at least in its later forms. Edwin Waugh and the radical weaver Ben Brierley of Failsworth were two bright stars in the murk of the mid-century slump, but perhaps the most eloquent voice of the distressed textile workers was Sam Laycock, 'Laureate of the Cotton Panic', a power-loom weaver and cloth-looker, and librarian at the Stalybridge Mechanics' Institute. One of his telling songs is "The Shurat weaver", still—or perhaps one should say: once again—to be heard occasionally in the folk song clubs. In the 1860s, cotton was the most important British industry, and the greater part of the raw stuff spun and woven in Lancashire came from the United States. But with the outbreak of the American Civil War, and the Northern blockade of Southern ports, Lancashire experienced a severe cotton famine. Those employed found their craft pride wounded and their earnings sadly lessened by the substitution of inferior cotton, hard to work up, called 'Shurat' after the East India Company's depot near Bombay, though in fact by no means all the poor cotton came from India, some of it was Egyptian. The term 'Shurat' became applied to anything of poor quality and a Lancashire brewer took action against a customer who described his product as 'Shurat' beer.

For the workers, the famine was a tragedy, yet they remained firm in their support of the anti-slavery cause, and resisted their employers' efforts to campaign for the North to lift their blockade. After all was over, things were never the same. The historian A. L. Morton says: 'In the long run the Civil War did much to destroy the monopoly of Lancashire and to hasten the transference of the centre of gravity of British industry from Manchester to Birmingham, a transfer followed in due course by corresponding political changes.' The modest complaint of "The Shurat weaver" shows little enough awareness of large movements of history, yet it is a valuable document, and its poignant mixture of pride and pathos can still impress the listener.

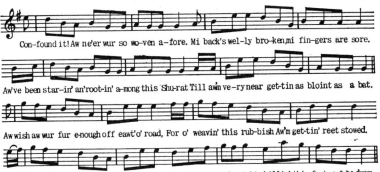

Con-found it! Aw ne'er wur so wo-ven a-fore. Mi back's wel-ly bro-ken mi fin-gers are sore.

Aw've been star-in' an'root-in' a-mong this Shu-rat Till aw'm ve-ry near get-tin as bloint as a bat.

Aw wish aw wur fur e-nough off eawt'o' road, For o' weavin' this rub-bish Aw'm get-tin' reet stowed.

Aw've nowt i' this world te lie deawn on but straw An' aw've on-ly eight shillin' this fortneet te draw.

Confound it! Aw ne'er wur so woven afore.
Mi back's welly broken, mi fingers are sore.
Aw've been starin' an' rootin' among this Shurat
Till Aw'm very near gettin' as bloint as a bat.
  Aw wish Aw wur fur enough off, eawt o' t' road,
  For o' weavin' this rubbish Aw'm getting reet stowed.
  Aw've nowt i' this world to lie deawn on but straw,
  An' Aw've only eight shillin' this fortneet to draw.

Aw haven't mi family under mi hat.
Aw've a woife an' six children to keep eawt o' that.
So Aw'm rather among it at present, ye see.
If ever a fellow wur puzzled, it's me.

If Aw turns eawt to steal, folk'll call me a thief.
Yet Aw conna the cheek on to ask for relief.
As Aw said caws houses t'other neet to mi woife,
Aw never did nowt o' this sort i' mi loife.
  Aw wish Aw wur fur enough off, eawt o' t' road,
  For o' weavin' this rubbish Aw'm gettin reet stowed.
  Aw've nowt i' this world to lie deawn on but straw,
  An' Aw've only eight shillin' this fortneet to draw.

From the same period comes a much keener-toned song,
originating among the Sheffield grinders. Throughout the
century conditions had been very hard in the cutlery trade,
and they worsened in the 1860s, when the Government was

accepting tenders for Sheffield goods, intended for army use, at prices that could only be met by employing children in large numbers in the works. The Victorian Liberal conscience suffered some twinges at the plight of the grinders' families, and enquiry commissions were set up which reported, as such commissions will, that the misery was in good part the fault of the workers themselves. The Sheffield men, who had cherished a fierce Radical tradition since the days when they were secretly making pikes for the Jacobins and Luddites, expressed their sharp criticism of grasping manufacturers and, grinding Government, and their scorn of mealy-mouthed Social Science in a number of songs of which "The grinders, or The saddle on the right horse," is a fair specimen.

> The Sheffield grinder's a terrible blade.
>> Tally hi-o, the grinder!
> He sets his little 'uns down to trade.
>> Tally hi-o, the grinder!
> He turns his baby to grind in the hull,
> Till his body is stunted and his eyes are dull,
> And the brains are dizzy and dazed in his skull.
>> Tally hi-o, the grinder!
>
> He shortens his life and he hastens his death.
>> Tally hi-o, the grinder!
> *Will* drink steel dust in every breath.
>> Tally hi-o, the grinder!
> Won't use a fan as he turns his wheel.
> Won't wash his hands ere he eats his meal.
> But dies as he lives, as hard as steel.
>> Tally hi-o, the grinder!
>
> These Sheffield grinders of whom we speak,
>> Tally hi-o, the grinder!
> Are men who earn a pound a week.
>> Tally hi-o, the grinder!
> But of Sheffield grinders another sort
> Methinks ought to be called in court,
> And that is the grinding Government Board.
>> Tally hi-o, the grinder!

At whose door lies the blacker blame?
　Tally hi-o, the grinder!
Where rests the heavier weight of shame?
　Tally hi-o, the grinder!
On the famine-price contractor's head,
Or the workman's, under-taught and -fed,
Who grinds his own bones and his child's for bread?
　Tally hi-o, the grinder!

Towards the end of the century the music-hall was reaching the height of its power; at the same time, with the organized labour movement growing fast, industrial workers were becoming familiar with labour anthems and agitational songs created on the models of high art rather than folklore. Miners and others gratefully took to the songs of a line of stage comedians leading back from Marie Lloyd and Albert Chevalier to Bobby Nunn, George Ridley and beyond, just as they accepted, for a different purpose and to a less intense degree (yet with a pioneer devotion that we must not underestimate) the sometimes rather highflown compositions of William Morris, Edward Carpenter and other heirs of the Radical songmaking tradition that is traceable back through the Chartists Ebenezer Elliott and Edward Jones to the salty Jacobin drolleries of "Pig's Meat" and "The Black Dwarf," at the start of the century.

However, for all the professional production of songs about and on behalf of the working class, industrial workers still went on making their own vernacular pieces out of their daily experience and circulating them, mainly by word of mouth, among their workmates and families. Quite often, these home-made songs were subject to the kind of variation that we consider the hallmark of folk song. On the other hand the social and economic conditions favourable to oral culture had long since been deteriorating, and as a rule the art of creative variation is one of the first victims of the decline of orality, and so it is not surprising that many pieces, even unwritten ones, circulated with only minimal alteration. In this respect, the industrial song repertory presents a picture that could just as well be the image of 'classic' folk song too:

(a) Some songs show good difference in words and tunes from one version to another; all are *variants*.

(b) Some songs formerly circulated in a number of variants, but eventually one peculiarly acceptable version emerged—not necessarily close to the original—that dominated all the rest and caused them to wither; we may call such versions, *supervariants*.

(c) Some songs survive in the singer's mouth more or less unchanged from the first laboriously handwritten or memorized version; these are *invariants*.

Our present studies suggest that invariants occupy as important a place as variants in the repertory of industrial folk song, but this impression may be due to scarcity of data; when we know more about workers' folklore we may find that some of our 'invariants' are not so unique as we had imagined. Much depends on the intensity of the song's use. For instance, some of Tommy Armstrong's songs that had long remained invariant, begin to take on a number of variant forms now that, within the last decade, they have not only spread outside their native area but also are performed more frequently.

Work-mates and family have testified to Armstrong's remarkable facility in song-making. Sixty, seventy years ago, the old practice of the bardic duel, the combat between rhyming extemporizers, still survived among Northumbrian miners. The colliers would gather in one pub or another, and the rival songmakers would draw straws ('cut kevils') to see who should have first turn at improvizing a ballad on a theme chosen by the audience. In an interview (1953), Tommy Armstrong's son, William 'Poety' Armstrong, recalled a lyrical duel fought between his father and a newcomer to the district, William McGuire, who put himself up as a song-maker. The combat took place in the Red Roe Public house in Tanfield. A few miles away, at Annfield Plain, the men of the Oakey Colliery were on strike. The owners had decided to evict strikers who were living in colliery-owned cottages, and they scoured the slums of Newcastle and Gateshead for lay-abouts and riffraff ('candymen' are rag-and-bone merchants) to help move the pitmen's furniture out into the street. 'The Oakey evictions' was chosen as the theme for the contest, after 'A pint of ale' and 'The miner's lamp' had been rejected as being too frivolous or conventional. McGuire's effusion is long since forgotten, but Armstrong's lives on, in the form subsequently polished up a bit by its maker:

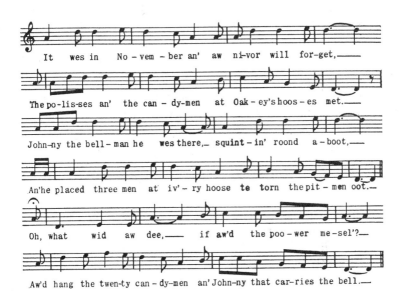

It wes in November an' aw nivor will forget,
The polises an' the candymen at Oakey's hooses met.
Johnny the bellman he wes there, squintin roond aboot,
An' he placed three men at ivory hoose te torn the pitmen oot.
    Oh, what wid aw dee, if aw'd the poower mesel?
    Aw'd hang the twenty candymen an' Johnny that carries the bell.

There they went fre hoose te hoose te pit things on the road,
But mind, they didn't hort thorsels wi' liftin heavy loads.
Some wid carry the poker oot, the fender or the rake;
If they lifted two at once it was a great mistake.

Some o' these dandy candymen wes dressed up like a clown.
Some had hats wivoot a flipe, an' some wivoot a crown.
Some had ne laps upon their coats, but there wes one chap
    warse—
Ivory time he had to stoop, it was a laughable farce.

There wes one chap had ne sleeves nor buttons upon his coat.
Another had a bairn's hippin lapped aroond his throat.
One chap wore a pair o' breeks that belang tiv a boy;
One leg wes a sort o' tweed, the tuthor was cordyroy.

Next their comes the maistors, aw think they should think
    shyem,
Deprivin wives an' families of a comfortable hyem.
But when they shift fre where they live, aw hope they'll gan
    te hell,
Alang wi' the twenty candymen an' Johnny that carries the
    bell.
    Oh, what wid aw dee, if aw'd the poower mesel?
    Aw wid hang the twenty candymen an' Johnny that carries
      the bell.

It was Armstrong's good fortune to grow up and mature
as a song-maker during the pioneer period of trade union
enthusiasm and militancy. Conscious of his standing and his
responsibility, he is recalled by his sons as saying: 'When
you're the Pitman's Poet and looked up to for it, wey, if a
disaster or a strike goes by wi'oot a song from you, they say:
What's wi' Tommy Armstrong? Has someone druv a spigot in
him an' let oot all the inspiration?' And if his creations, and
those of balladeers like him, did not find their way into the
Socialist song-books of the time, perhaps that is because the
editors, whose taste was not always that of the generality of
workers, preferred stuff of loftier tone. As to that, when Jim
Connell wrote the great Labour anthem "The red flag" in
1889, he meant it to be sung to the lively springing tune of
"The white cockade". Staider counsel in the Social Democratic

Federation threw out the folk tune in favour of the pedestrian German melody of "Tannenbaum", a tune which, as Connell scornfully said, is 'calculated to remind people of their sins and frighten them into repentance'. If "Tannenbaum" does sound more like an anthem, "The white cockade" sounds more like the kind of tune the workers were choosing for their own home-made songs. So with Tommy Armstrong's works, the majority of his texts were set to the kind of early music-hall tunes that lie close to folk song, or to familiar traditional melodies, or to newer but firmly folkloric come-all-ye airs.

Most of his songs, comic or tragic, have a strong sense of class and of social criticism, particularly the strike ballads. The last two decades of the nineteenth century were Tommy's most prolific years, and the strike songs of the time reflect the burning feelings of the period when, between 1888 and 1893 the Miners' Federation had grown from 36,000 to over 200,000 members. Not that the texts are outspokenly revolutionary. As with other industrial workers of the time, the miners' ideology was determined by bread-and-butter affairs; the ballad-maker's attention was generally on immediate practical matters rather than revolutionary perspectives. Moreover, we must remember that many strike songs, like the disaster songs, had a specific task to perform. Certainly they were intended to give information, courage, and resolution to the miners; but beyond that they were meant for singing in the streets, to collect money for the strikers' hungry families. On that account, a certain tact was needed in shaping the content of the ballads. Sentiments too fiercely revolutionary might lose sympathy among passers-by; but to protest against hard conditions, to criticize grasping owners, to set out the strikers' determination, was all in order and likely to arouse the sympathy of the working class listeners. So we find a large number of ballads ending like this one, made by Burnett O'Brien of Wigan on the big sixteen-week lock-out of 1893 (the tune prescribed by O'Brien is the much-used traditional air to which, around the middle of the century, James Ballantyne wrote the sentimental words of "Castles in the air". Coarser folk associate the melody rather with "The ball o' Kirriemuir").

Don't forget the collier lads that are trying with their might,
Enduring so much suffering to get that which is right;
And when you see his box displayed, no matter where he'll
    roam,
Think of his wife and children who are starving in their home.
    Then let us be united; we never must give way;
    Uphold the Federation, lads, and we will win the day.

Most of Armstrong's surviving strike ballads conform to the
common pattern of protest, criticism, resolve and *quête*.
During the great Durham strike and lock-out of 1892, he was
acting as 'court minstrel' to William Patterson the miners'
leader (as Burnett O'Brien did in 1893 for Sam Woods of
Wigan, the first Vice-President of the Miners' Federation),
and his ballads of that time are valuable documents for the
labour historian. The most durable of them is "The Durham
lock-out", still sung by north-eastern singers, though nowadays
to the tune of "Come all ye tramps and hawkers", and not to
the tune that Armstrong intended, which again had to be
"Castles in the air". On the ground of a fall in coal prices,
the Durham mine-owners proposed a ten per cent wage cut.
The miners rejected the proposal and were locked out. After
six weeks, with families hard-pressed, the men offered to return
to work, but now the owners demanded they should accept a
cut of thirteen-and-a-half per cent. Evidently Armstrong's
ballad was written just at this point, at the start of May 1892.
The men refused, the strike dragged on; eventually the ten
per cent reduction was agreed to.

In our Durham County I am sorry for to say,
That hunger and starvation is increasing every day.
For want of food and coals, we know not what to do,
But with your kind assistance, we will stand the battle through.

I need not state the reason why we have been brought so low.
The masters have behaved unkind, which everyone will know;
Because we won't lie down and let them treat us as they like,
To punish us, they've stopped the pits and caused the present
    strike.

The pulley-wheels have ceased to move, which went so swift
    around.
The horses and the ponies too all brought from underground.
Our work is taken from us now, they care not if we die,
For they can eat the best of food, and drink the best when dry.

The miner and his wife too, each morning have to roam
To seek for bread to feed the hungry little ones at home.
The flour barrel is empty now, their true and faithful friend,
Which makes the thousands wish today the strike was at an end.

We have done our very best as honest working men.
To let the pits commence again, we've offered to them ten.
The offer they will not accept, they firmly do demand
Thirteen and a half per cent, or let the collieries stand.

Let them stand or let them lie or do with them as they choose;
To give them thirteen and a half we ever shall refuse.
They're always willing to receive, but not inclined to give,
And very soon they won't allow a working man to live.

May every Durham colliery owner that is in the fault
Receive nine lashes with the rod, and then be rubbed with salt.
May his backside be thick with boils, so he may never sit,
And never burst until the wheels go round at every pit.

The miners of Northumberland we shall for ever praise,
For being so kind in helping us these tyrannising days.
We thank the other counties too, that they've been doing the
    same,
And every man who hears this song will know we're not to
    blame.

This text is from a broadside probably printed at Armstrong's
own instigation during the strike. The orally-transmitted
versions are not so complete, but otherwise differ only in in-
significant details. There is little enough sparkle in the poetry,
but then, there wasn't much in the situation. It is notable that,
as with many worker song-writers, Armstrong's imagination

worked freer and his language had more spring when he was
writing in dialect. Most of his songs are in the peculiar North-
eastern miners' jargon called 'pitmatic', but the disaster songs
and many of the strike ballads after 1885 were written in
literary English, as being more seemly for grave events, and
these contain rather more doggerel than radiance. They are
without the daemonic surge, the 'holy daftness', as Armstrong
himself called it, that is felt within his more eager songs.

In 1953, an anecdote was recorded from two old miners,
former work-mates of Armstrong, that shows the working of
this 'holy daftness'. Tommy had arrived at the mine one
frosty morning to find that most of the tubs he had filled the
previous day had been disallowed on the ground that they
contained too much stone. The overseer was sitting with some
cronies round a bucket fire, and Tommy swiftly drew out from
his lapel one of the 'shots' that he had prepared at home
overnight—as was the practice in those days—and threw it on
the fire, causing a lively explosion that scattered red coals on
the keeker and his friends. The owners had recently installed
a new patent cage, working in the shaft alongside the old
'breakneck' cage, and as Armstrong descended in the mine,
his thoughts about the overseer mingled with his thoughts
about the cages. That day he hacked at the coal-face in a fury.
Whenever he thought of the keeker, he had him by the throat;
whenever he thought of the cages, they were fighting together.
He imagined the new cage must surely despise the old one,
rusty, dangerous, obsolete. The old cage must detest the new
one, a showy upstart. In his fantasy, as the cages passed they
gnashed their jaws and ground their teeth, and finally came to
blows. He thought he heard the clangour of their battle ring
through the mine, and saw the blood flow from their wounds
past the weighman's cabin. In his narrow work-stall, Armstrong
made his ballad, "The row between the cages". Like most of
his compositions it is full of robust humour, but here a true
epic wind blows through the song giving it the exhilaration of a
powerful allegory of a sort rarely found in workers' balladry.
The sense of the allegory is the triumph of technical advance
and the bettering of conditions; at the same time decent respect
is shown for what is old and passing. Aptly enough, Armstrong

set his words to the same energetic traditional air that, early in the century, Alexander Rodger had used for "Robin Tamson's smiddy". In his elation, when he came to write out the song, his pitmatic spelling was curlier than usual. As a curiosity, we reproduce the song from the author's own copy; in oral tradition it circulates in rather simpler forms.

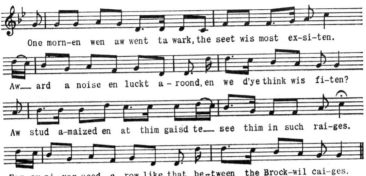

One mornen wen aw went ta wark, th' seet wis most exsiten.
Aw ard a noise en luckt aroond, en we de ye think wis fiten?
Aw stud amaisd en at thim gaisd, te see thim in such raiges,
For aw nivor seed e row like that between th' Brockwil caiges.

Wor aud caige sais: 'Cum over th' gaits, becaws it's mei intenshin
To let th' see wethor thoo or me is th' best invenshin.'
Th' neuin been raised, teuk off his clais, then at it thae went dabbin;
Th' blud wis runnen doon th' skeets an past th' weimin's cabin.

Wor aud caige sais: 'Let's heh me clais; thoo thwot thit thoo cud flae me,
But if aw'd been is young is thoo, aw's certain aw cud pae thee.'
Th' patent knockt hees ankel off, en th' buaith ad cutten fuaices.
Th' shifters rapt three for te ride, so th' buaith went te thor plaices.

Wen gannen up en doon th' shaft, th' paitint caige did threetin
For te tuaik wor audin's life if thae stopt it meeten.
Wor aud caige bawld oot is thae passt: 'Thoo nasty dorty
    paitint,
Rub thee ies eguain th' skeets—aw think too's ardly wakinit.'

Th' paitint te wor aud caige sais: 'Altho aw be e strangeor,
Aw kin work me wark is weel is thoo, an free th' men freh
    daingor.
Noo, if th' rope shud brick we me, aud skinny jaws, just watch
    us—
Thoo'l see me clag on te th' skeets, for aw's full e springs en
    catches.'

Wor aud caige te th' paitint sais: 'Aw warnd thoo think thoo's
    clivor
Becaws thi'v polished thoo we paint, but thoo'l not last for ivor.
Th' paint on thoo 'ill weer awae, en then thoo's lost thei beuty;
Th' nivor painted me at aal, en still aw've deun me deuty.'

Th' braiksmin browt thim buaith te bank, th' mischeef for te
    sattil.
Thae fit freh five o' clock te six, en th' paitint won th' battle.
It teuk th' braiksmin half e shift te clag thim up we plaistors.
Wor aud caige sent hees noatece in, but just te vex th' maistors.

As a rule, Armstrong's songs were too local in spirit or
language to spread far outside the north-eastern coalfield, but
other miners' songs have shown great mobility, turning up
alike in Midlothian, Durham, the Midlands and in the bituminous and anthracite fields of Canada and U.S.A. (seldom in
Wales, though; for generations now Welsh miners have inclined to prefer 'literary' song, perhaps because they feel the
home-made stuff is not fine enough for their grand voices).
Sometimes we can trace the route of the songs through the
wanderings of individuals; for instance, a good Scots folk
singer, Mrs. Cosgrove of Newtongrange, followed her husband
to the mines of Lanarkshire, Nova Scotia and elsewhere, and
often sang at colliers' sing-songs. Subsequently several of her
pieces were recorded from other singers along her route.
When her attention was drawn to this, she said modestly that

she seemed to have followed her songs; that she might be the carrier and planter of them did not occur to her.

One remarkable song that roamed far from its native Durham and became much altered on its travels is "The blackleg miners", a later and fiercer reflection of the kind of emotion that lay behind, for instance, the ballad of "The best-dressed man of Seghill", in which the strike-breaker is hunted like a hare on the moor and stripped of his clothes and his tools thrown down the pit shaft. Old miners still recall the dangerous practice referred to in the song, of stretching a rope across the pit-way so that, as the non-union man hurried along with his tubs of coal, he might be caught by the throat and flung backward. The great pioneer collector of American coalfields balladry, George Korson, reports a version of "The blackleg miners" from Glace Bay, Nova Scotia.[48] There, the ballad still blazes, but not so fiercely as in its English birthplace. The hard taut entirely unliterary manner of the song (first recorded in Bishop Auckland, Durham, in 1949) is in strong contrast to the rhetorical style of most official Labour anthems of the time. By a nice irony, the fierce text is set to a variant of the tune called in the North-east "The mode o' wooing".

Oh, early in the evenin', just after dark,
The blackleg miners creep te wark,
Wi' their moleskin trousers an' dorty short,
There go the backleg miners!

They take their picks an' doon they go
Te dig the coal that lies belaw,
An' there's not a woman in this toon-raw
Will look at a blackleg miner.

Oh, Delaval is a terrible place.
They rub wet clay in a blackleg's face,
An' roond the pit-heaps they run a foot-race
Wi' the dorty blackleg miners.

Now, don't go near the Seghill mine.
Across the way they stretch a line,
Te catch the throat an' break the spine
O' the dorty backleg miners.

They'll take your tools an' duds as well,
An' hoy them doon the pit o' hell.
It's doon ye go, an' fare ye well,
Ye dorty blackleg miners!

Se join the union while ye may.
Don't wait till your dyin' day,
For that may not be far away,
Ye dorty blackleg miners!

(toon-raw = town-row)

Throughout the developments of workers' folk songs, the influence of the music hall maintained its effect on some of the balladeers, especially in the coalfields. It is noteworthy that the stage songs shifted in emphasis from guffawing scenes of everyday life (1840s to 1860s) to songs of pride in the miners' calling (1870s to 1880s) and finally to sentimental, even maudlin pieces. If the first class of parlour and stage songs, such as "The fiery clock fyece", were too local for export abroad, the second and third kinds—for example, J. B. Geoghegan's "Down in a coal mine" as a song of pride, and

"Don't go down in the mine, dad" as a tear-jerker—were both in their time effective objects of transatlantic cultural exchange. "Don't go down in the mine, dad", an entirely non-folkloric piece of oracular pathos, in which a child has a premonitory dream of a pit-disaster, had almost run its course in England when in 1925 a hillbilly singer, Blind Andy Jenkins re-made it into an American hit song, "The dream of the miner's child" (some measure of its success: just one artist, Vernon Dalhart under a variety of names, recorded the song for at least fifteen different companies). In England the song is rarely sung nowadays in earnest, but certain pieces produced by amateur songmakers under the influence of the music hall stage have shown remarkable durability, more than the generality of professional productions. Of this kind, a good specimen is the favourite called "The celebrated working man", a song of American origin, welcomed and boldly adapted by Durham miners. George Korson has told the history of this song, a sly lyrical comment on the kind of workers who boast of their labour-prowess in the comfort of the bar-room. It seems that it was composed by an Irish miner in Pennsylvania, Ed Foley, who first sang it at a wedding in 1892, and it was brought to Durham by a Wobbly collier from Kentucky, Yankee Jim Roberts, some time around the period of the First World War. A comparison of Korson's Pennsylvania version[49] with the following set recorded from Jack Elliott of Birtley in 1963 shows the creative re-working of oral tradition can still be happily effective in industrial conditions in our time.

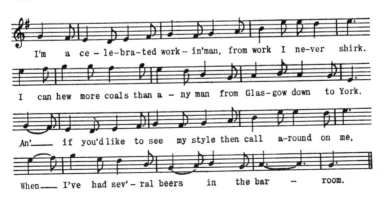

I'm a ce-le-bra-ted work-in'man, from work I ne-ver shirk.
I can hew more coals than a-ny man from Glas-gow down to York.
An'___ if you'd like to see my style then call a-round on me,
When___ I've had sev'-ral beers in the bar — room.

I'm a celebrated workin' man, from work I never shirk.
I can hew more coals than any man from Glasgow down to
York.
An' if you'd like to see my style then call around on me,
When I've had several beers in the bar-room.

Cho.:   In the bar-room, in the bar-room, that's where we
             congregate,
             To drill the holes and fill the coals and shovel back
             the slate,
             An' for to do a job of work, I am never late,
             That's provided that we do it in the bar-room.

At puttin' I'm a dandy, I hope you will agree,
An' gannin' along the gannin'-board I mak the tyum 'uns
flee.
Your Kelly sweeps an' back-ower torns they never bother me,
When I'm sittin' on the limmers in the bar-room.

I can judge a shot of powder to a sixteenth of a grain.
I can fill my eighteen tubs, though the water falls like rain.
An' if you'd like to see me in the porpendicular vein,
It's when I'm settin' timmers in the bar-room.

An' now my song is ended, perhaps we'll have another.
Now, don't you fire any shots in here, or we will surely smother.
The landlord here would sooner pull beer than go to all the
bother
To put up the ventilators in the bar-room.

Cho.:   In the bar-room, in the bar-room, that's where we
             congregate,
             To drill the holes an' fill the coals an' shovel back the
             slate,
             An' for to do a job of work, I am never late,
             That's provided that we do it in the bar-room.

    At times the newer hybridized folklore would combine
with the old in interesting ways, as we see from the nature and
function of the song called "Little Chance". Charles Bevil, a

Tow Law, Co. Durham, shotfirer, from whom the song was first obtained in 1951, remembers it as a *quête* song, 'the song we used to sing as lads at Christmas time in our pit village, whilst going from door to door with the tup, fifty years ago'. In the Tow Law area, for weeks before Christmas the boys would stand at the pit-head or drift-mouth and cadge the stubs of candles from the pitmen. On Christmas Eve they would take a pig-killing cradle (rather like a stretcher with longish handles and short legs, with a trough at either end to catch the blood), bend a wicker frame over it and set on the frame a piece of muslin rather in the manner of the hood of a covered waggon. To this vaguely bestial shape, an ambiguous head—horse or sheep?—would be attached. The candle-stubs would be set round the edge of the cradle, and the 'tup' would be paraded through the village at night by a procession of black-faced boys wearing pit clothes and carrying mining tools. Passers-by and house-dwellers would be invited to put a copper in the blood-trough for luck. Their processional anthem of "Little Chance" was originally a praise-song for a pit pony, a 'gallowa', but to it have been added a series of ironic vignettes of pit life. A collier rejoices in his fine new work-place, but the roof falls on him. Another performs prodigies in the pit but comes home exhausted and impotent. The song has elements of folklore, tags of street rhyme, bits of music hall. In it, characteristically, bitter truth alternates with mocking banalities. A fuller version than old Charles Bevil's is provided by John Elliott, a fitter at the Harriton Colliery when he recorded the song for the BBC in 1963.

Now ye gan ower the Busty fields te gan doon the pit.
Ye get yer lamp oot, ye gan inbye, an' there ye sit at the kist.
The depitty says: Thy place is holed, oo'll ha' te gan stright on.
Aw says te him: Wha's the matter wi' me own? He says:
  She canna gan on.
  Aa got sixteen oot of a jud, titty fa la, titty fa lay.
  Eh, by hell she wes good, titty fa la, titty fa lay.
  Aa cam oot te get a shaft, the timmer it gied a crack,
  And the stone fell on me back, titty fa la, titty fa lay.
  Tra la, lalalala, ower the waal's oot!

Now, ye gan o-wer the Bus-ty fields te gan doon the pit.

Ye get yer lamp oot, ye gan in-bye, an' there ye sit at the kist.

The de-pit-ty says: Thy place is holed, oo'll ha' te gan stright on.

Aa says te him: Wha's the mat-ter wi' me own? He says: She gan-na gan on.

Aa got six-teen oot of a jud,   tit-ty fa la,   tit-ty fa lay.__

Eh,   by hell she wes good,   tit-ty fa la,   tit-ty fa lay.

Aa   cam oot te get a shaft,__ The tim-mer it gied a crack,

An' the stone fell on my back, tit-ty fa la,   tit-ty fa lay.__

Tra   la,   la-la-la-la   o - wer the waal's oot!__

Ye're sure te ken me brother Bill, he's se full o' wit.
He got a job o' puttin up at 'Cotia pit.
When Bill comes home fre work, he's like a droonded rat.
Instead o' gannin upstairs te bed, he lies upon the mat.
  Now, he puts a thousand or more, titty fa la, titty fa lay.
  They pay him by the score, titty fa la, titty fa lay.
  He fills his tubs se quick, wi'oot ony delay,
  But he never can find his pick, titty fa la, titty fa lay.
  Tra la, lalalala, ower the wall's oot!

Jack an' Bill, two marrers, were in a public hoose.
The talk aboot the kevils, lads, it wadn't frighten a moose.
Jack says te Bill: By gox, she's hard.

The tops is like bell-metal, but the bottoms is not se bad.
  Aa only got ten the day, titty fa la, titty fa lay.
  Aa only got ten the day, titty fa la, titty fa lay.
  Aa wad he' gotten other fower, aa wes wishin the shift wes
    ower,
  When the putter got off the way, titty fa la, titty fa lay.
  Tra la, lalalala, ower the wall's oot!

Noo, me nyem is Jackie Robinson, me nyem aa do advance.
Aa drive a little gallowa', they call him Little Chance.
Chancy hes two greasy feet, likewise a kittley back,
An' gannin alang the gannin board, he myeks the chum 'uns
  knack.
  Aa wes comin aroond the torn, titty fa la, titty fa lay.
  Chancey wadn't haad on, titty fa la, titty fa lay.
  The tubs they gie a click, aw got off the way at the switch,
  (Ye bugger!) Aa smashed the depitty's kist, titty fa la, titty
    fa lay.
  Tra la lalalala, ower the wall's oot!

Now, me an' me wife an' me mother-in-law went doon te the
  silvery sea.
Me mother-in-law gat intiv a boat, a sailor she wad be.
She hadn't gone passin twenty yards, when suddenly there's a
  shoot.
Me mother-in-law fell inte the sea, an' there she's splashin
  aboot.
  She shoots: Help, aw cannot swim, titty fa la, titty fa lay.
  Aa says: Noo's the time te try, titty fa la, titty fa lay.
  Me wife, she says: Ye hoond, thoo's not ganna watch her
    droon?
  Aa says: No, aw'll shut me eyes, titty fa la, titty fa lay.
  Tra la lalalala, ower the wall's oot!
      (*kevil* = *stint, place of work at the face*)

Through the early years of the twentieth century the miners,
textile workers, railwaymen too (with such pieces as "Moses
of the Mail") went on making songs for their own use, but they
relied more and more on models from a music hall tradition

that was itself falling into decadence, with its old reality and truth gone and little else left but a banal stereotype of lower class life and a limited range of sickly bourgeois fantasies that the by-now powerful entertainment industry offered its audiences to suck on like a sugared rubber teat.

With the old folk tradition passing into oblivion and professional song offering only poor models, the tide of workers' home-made lyric was already at low ebb when Tommy Armstrong died in 1919. Occasionally a pit disaster might throw up a new song, but in the main the creations of 1920s and 30s were small things, often mere parodies of popular hits of the day, and just as ephemeral. Often, ironic point was given to these parodies by setting words of harsh, even coarse realism to appallingly sentimental melodies, which had the effect of radically transforming the originals and making a jeering comment on the whole stupefying genre of bourgeois popular song. A few scraps of this kind linger on, still raised in pithead baths or as pub-harmony pieces after working hours, such as the brief account of the miseries of a putter whose heavy tubs have run off the rails underground. Sardonically, his heart-cry is set to the draggy commercial tune of "Moonlight Bay".

Aa wes gannin inbye on the engine plane.
Aa could hear the putter shoutin: 'Aa'm off the way!
Ah wey, give us a lift, me arse is sair.
If aa had this tub put, aa wad put ne mair (ne mair, ne mair!)'.

Where's the sparkle of that? you may wonder. Where's the wholeness and radiance of the countless worker songs produced to fit the tune of "Keep the home fires burning" and "Bye bye, blackbird"? They sank without trace almost as soon as they appeared, unless by chance they were printed on a leaflet or duplicated in a strike songbook. For political purposes, especially during the passions of the General Strike and the slump with its hunger marches, if the workers were to sing about their own condition the repertory of international mass songs, greatly expanded since the Russian revolution, was available to them. For diversion, they had songs learnt from gramophone records and radio. The need, and the taste, for self-made songs about their own daily lives seemed to have faded, the heart had gone out of the modest vernacular balladeers, the creation of workers' folk song, even in the widest reading of the term, looked as if it was finished, not so much through any decline of creative abilities, as because talented workers, along with the rest of urban society, had moved away from the forms and diffusion-media of folklore and were now engaged at a more consciously educated and literary level. The process was not new, of course; it had been foreshadowed nearly a century earlier by such men as Joseph Mather of Sheffield, the weaver-poet Edwin Waugh, and Joseph Skipsey of Tyneside, and had been growing steadily all the while as the alert section of the proletariat aspired to a modern educated condition and worker-writers set their sights on the big London publishers. In the period between the wars, workers' folk song lost its prestige, its currency dwindled, scraps of its repertory lingered in the recesses of old men's minds, like once-prized tools that had lost their edge and purpose and now lay among the junk in the attic.

For all that the tradition seemed to have run itself out, in recent years we have seen an astonishing resurgence of the industrial songs of the past, and of new songs created from the heart of industry by individual workers, songs in something very like a traditional shape, mainly oral in transmission, liable to undergo variation, destined for—but by no means confined to—the tight community of fellow-workers, and produced under quite a new stimulus. This novel development began to show itself clearly in the mid-1950s.

It is a source of astonishment, particularly to foreigners, that side by side with folksong-like polemical songs produced mainly by intellectuals or show-biz entertainers, a kind of industrial folk song proper, produced by workers themselves, concerning the feelings of their own community about everyday events at their own workplace, should still persist in Britain, and indeed is being produced in greater volume than at any time within the past half century. The phenomenon arises from a peculiar circumstance of our musical life, from what is called the urban 'folk song revival'.

Of recent years, enthusiasm for folk song has spread among a sizeable section of young people, workers and middle class, who are searching for some less transitory satisfaction than is offered by the masters of mass entertainment, and are demanding something more relevant to their life-experience than the dim cloud-cuckoo land of the pops. At first sight it may seem paradoxical that so many find this relevance in traditional songs of the past, but there, the passions and trances of Oedipus or Juliet are more compelling than the frenzied despair of the Rolling Stones and their go-go-go successors. At the present time of writing, folk song clubs are found in practically all our urban centres, where traditional music is regularly performed in ways that vary from an imitation of old country styles through sundry adaptations to an extravagantly modernized 'pop' manner. The number of 'revival' performers is busily multiplying, new-style folk singers haunt the television screens, the gramophone companies issue a dozen folk music records for every one issued a decade ago, and the youngsters' progress from pops to folk-rock and finally to something like the genuine article is nowadays taken as quite to be expected.

What we are experiencing is the second folk song revival in England. The first one occurred some time at the beginning of the present century and inspired, and was inspired by, the great collectors such as Cecil Sharp, Vaughan Williams, Percy Grainger. It came about when educated people, mostly of liberal outlook, stumbled on the riches of poetry and music preserved by working people in the countryside, and began to make some of those treasures more widely available. The consequent revival had its greatest effect among middle-class people, musicians in search of a national idiom, educators, and others less serious with a fancy for quaintness. That first revival produced work of immense value, but despite the fact that it introduced folk song into schools it had no broad popular effect. In urban England, authentic folk song remained 'queer music' to most people.

The present revival appears under no such polite auspices. It followed the American folk song revival that began in the 1930s when many workers, notably miners in the folk singing districts of the upland South, began to accept enthusiastically the political ideas of the newly-formed and energetic Congress of Industrial Organizations. Distressed workers in backward areas took to trade unionism with a fervour similar to that with which their forefathers had embraced nonconformist religion. For them it was a powerful deliverance, to be celebrated and furthered with song. The singing organizer and the militant folk song—foreshadowed some years previously by syndicalist popular minstrels such as Joe Hill—became important to American labour during the tense times of the Depression.

At the same time, in an attempt to bolster national morale, the U.S. government was sponsoring made-work schemes that involved an exploration of the roots of the American folk tradition, and repositories such as the Folk Music Archive of the Library of Congress were enriched by thousands of field-recordings garnered by searchers subsidized from the national treasury. Much of this was made available to the public and thousands of city-dwellers became acquainted with the authentic folk music of their country for the first time. Singers were brought from remote country districts to perform the ballads of hard times in union halls and concert arenas, and enthusiastic students were neglecting their academic studies in favour of perfecting their five-string banjo technique.

The two factors of revival, the spontaneous and the state-inspired, combined to form a new consciousness of folk song in America. In this atmosphere and mainly through Radical encouragement, performers such as Josh White, Huddie Ledbetter, Woody Guthrie, Pete Seeger, came into prominence, and groups of urban singers emerged, such as the Almanacs and their successors, the Weavers, whose repertory was a mixture of traditional folk stuff and folk-style polemical song presented with absolute informality.

This kind of folk-song-with-teeth seemed to be what many British youngsters were waiting for. For some years, a handful of devoted persons such as Ewan MacColl in England, Hamish Henderson in Scotland, had been proselytizing on behalf of traditional song, but their efforts became properly fruitful only as the American example became clear. The BBC had helped to pave the way, first of all with programmes by Alastair Cooke, later with productions by D. G. Bridson presenting the leading figures of the U.S. revival. When, after World War II, American recordings became more readily available in Britain, the influence of the transatlantic folk singers spread widely. Some of the American material had an engaging impetuousness and a handy simplicity of harmonic structure, and youngsters found that with even the most rudimentary skill they could provide a passable performance. Chain-gang songs were everywhere, their Mississippi mumble further blurred by the inflections of Wigan and Walthamstow. The exploited peach-pickers of Bethnal Green and Batley consoled themselves with the "Worried man blues". The skiffle movement ran through the country like wildfire. From this exotic beginning, the British folk song revival grew.

The revival was strengthened by the enquiring minds of many young people who, searching for the roots of jazz found themselves led to American folk song and thence back to their own shores, to an interest in their native stuff and a desire to perform it. True, they incline to treat their traditional music in a variety of non-traditional ways, with voice-production, instrumentation, rhythmical treatment, etc., borrowed from the world of commercial light music. Whether the material is thereby enriched or impoverished is arguable; it is less arguable that, through new treatments, many fine folk tunes and texts are made valid for thousands of performers and listeners whose musical interests would otherwise be limited to the banalities of Denmark Street.

The folk song revival had its deep effect on ballad-makers in our industrial areas where, as we have seen, the creation of workers' song had sharply diminished in the years between the Wars. With the revival, workers' home-made song once again acquired prestige. For instance, the appearance of a collection of the folk songs and ballads of miners in 1952, at a time when the songs had almost disappeared even from the memory of ageing miners, fired some youngsters in the coal-fields to try to emulate the creations of their fathers and grandfathers, particularly as, with the emergence of folk song clubs in the mining areas, traditional-style song was becoming all the rage.

Characteristic of this new wave of creators of workers' song is John Pandrich of Newcastle, formerly a coalface worker in the Dudley and North Walbottle pits, later engaged in the survey department in a pit running some miles out under the sea. A favourite song of his making is "Farewell to the Monty", written in 1959 when the Montague Colliery at West Denton was closed by the National Coal Board, and the colliers transferred to new pits further east. The Montague was an out-of-date pit and conditions in her were bad, but she had produced a lot of coal in her time, and the colliers had affection for their old workplace on that account; moreover they were reluctant to leave her for a colliery far from their present homes. The ambivalence of sentiment gives the song unusual tension.

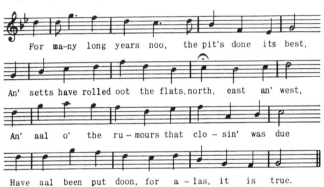

For ma-ny long years noo, the pit's done its best,
An' setts have rolled oot the flats, north, east an' west,
An' aal o' the ru-mours that clo-sin' was due
Have aal been put doon, for a-las, it is true.

For many long years noo, the pit's done its best,
An' setts have rolled oot the flats, north, east an' west,
An' all o' the rumours that closin wes due
Have aal been put doon, for alas it is true.

A meetin wes held te discuss the affair,
An' the manager said tiv us, reet then an' there:
Let's hev one last go before this pit is done,
To show a good profit on each single ton.

Noo, profits were made, but through stocks pilin high,
The Coal Board decided oor pit has te die;
An' as output gans doon we get transforred awey
Te pits te the east for the rest o' wor days.

Aa've filled in the Fan Pit, aa've cut in the seam
In the Newbiggin Beaumont since aa wes fifteen.
Aa've worked in the Sections an' in the Main Coal.
Man, it's hot doon the Monty; she's a dusty old hole.

So, farewell te ye, Monty, aa knaa yer roads well,
An' yer work hes been good an' yer work hes been hell.
Ne mair te yor dorty aad heap will aa come,
For yer coal is aal finished, an' yer life it is done.
    (*setts = groups of tubs, usually twenty*)

Songs of farewell to obsolete pits form a new category in
the stock of coalfields ballads. Sometimes the mine is seen as
a stern mother whose children can neither bear to live with
her nor to leave her. Whether grudging or not, affection and
respect prevail in these elegies. A Lancashire example is
provided by the "Lament for Albert", published on a broadside by Keith Roberts of Ashton-in-Makerfield, Wigan. A
roughly lettered note on the leaflet runs: 'December 1965
saw the closing of one of Lancashire's friendliest Pits—The
Albert Pit at Abram . . . only a small pit by most standards
but it had retained much of the atmosphere of pre-Nationalisa-
tion days. Now alas . . . owd Albert's gone ! ! !' The song
is set to the tune of an Irish lament.

Owd Albert's gone. His days are done.
His gates are shuttered fast, he lies in peace.
Through summer's warm, and winter's storm,
There's no-one to disturb his blackened sleep.

Four hundred men kept by hissen
Are gone away to work some other seam.
The tallies are hung. The knell is rung.
Lamps no longer through his darkness gleam.

No iron clogs, or proppin-logs
Move down the ramp a-shiftin to the face.
And fire-damp creeps, and water seeps,
Long held at bay but moving to their place.

Of twisted steel and broken wheels,
Owd Albert has them reckoned in his store.
Scattered around, they're all writ down,
Marked in the dusty ledger of the floor.

Closed is the door. He'll see no more
That hive of colliers workin at the coal.
A million years, ten million fears,
Sleep on inside the mine of Albert's soul.

In 1963, George Purdom, a deputy at the Harriton Colliery, Co. Durham, made a song concerning the transfer of miners from the 'Nova Scotia' pit, affectionately known as 'Cotia (it got its name through the large number of Durham colliers who returned to it earlier in the century after working in the mines of Glace Bay, Nova Scotia). The pit was antiquated and in parts of it coal was still being got by pick and shovel. During 1963–64 the men were gradually transferred away, some to South Wales, the majority to the Nottingham coalfield. Mr. Purdom explains that the reference to 'Robens' merry men' is a pun relating to the outlaws of Sherwood Forest. The song reminds the men that they are to be uprooted from their native soil, and are bound for strange places where, in order to be understood, they must modify their strong dialect, where their simple pleasures are in jeopardy (Geordies are inordinately proud of their local brown ale), and where they must forge new loyalties under an unfamiliar union banner. Regret, unease and irony inform the complaint, which is aptly carried by the dignified pentatonic air best known as "Come all ye tramps and hawkers", the same tune to which "The Durham lock-out" is sung. In its own locality the song rapidly acquired a ceremonial function, being regarded as an obligatory anthem for singing at farewell parties to groups of colliers on the eve of their transfer to distant coalfields. Jack Elliott of Birtley, an old workmate of George Purdom, always sang this piece very straight, without recourse to dialect.

Ye brave bold men of 'Cotia,
The time is drawing near.
You'll have to change your language, lads,
You'll have to change your beer.
But leave your picks behind you,
You'll ne'er need them again,
And off you go to Nottingham,
Join Robens' merry men.

Ye brave bold men of 'Cotia,
The time is drawing thus.
You'll have to change your banner, lads,
And join the exodus.
But leave your cares behind you,
Your future has been planned,
And off you go to Nottingham,
To Robens' Promised Land.

Ye brave bold men of 'Cotia,
To you I say farewell.
And somebody will some day
The 'Cotia story tell.
But leave your cares behind you,
The death-knell has been tolled.
'Cotia was a colliery.
Her men were true and bold.

Naturally, not all the present day miners' songs are so sombre. With the pop world up to the nostrils in a sea of inanity and the world of high art cultivating barren disengagement or glum cynicism, it is heartening to see that a lively pride in his craft or calling is still prominent in the working man's home-made songs. The prolific young balladeer who wrote "Farewell to the Monty" has among his most characteristic compositions a perky swaggering song named "The collier lad", that recalls the songs of professional pride that were so much in vogue among workers in the 1870s and 80s, such as "Down in a coal-mine". There is a difference in expression; the old vainglorious songs strove rather after literary tone, while today's songs are perhaps too readily content with documentary realism. The song is much liked. The North-east is a place for thunderous choruses, and the refrain of "The collier lad" has made many a pub quake between Stockton and Newcastle. Elsewhere too.

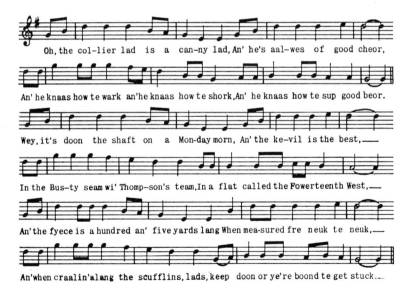

Oh, the col-lier lad is a can-ny lad, An' he's aal-wes of good cheor,

An' he knaas how te wark an'he knaas how te shork,An' he knaas how te sup good beor.

Wey, it's doon the shaft on a Mon-day morn, An' the ke-vil is the best,___

In the Bus-ty seam wi' Thomp-son's team,In a flat called the Fowerteenth West,___

An' the fyece is a hundred an' five yards lang When mea-sured fre neuk te neuk,___

An'when craalin'alang the scufflins, lads, keep doon or ye're boond te get stuck.___

Oh, the collier lad is a canny lad,
An' he's aalwes of good cheor,
An' he knaas how te wark, an' he knaas how te shork,
An' he knaas how te sup good beor.

Wey, it's doon the shaft on a Monday morn,
An' the kevil is the best,
In the Busty seam wi' Thompson's team,
In a flat called the Fowerteenth West.
An' the fyece is a hundred an' five yards lang
When measured fre neuk to neuk,
An' when craalin alang the scufflins, lads,
Keep doon or ye're boond te get stuck.

When the shots gan off, then the shovels do fly
Till the belt gets loaded full,
An' in half an oor a stone gans on,
An' the motor will not pull.
'Brokken belt!' is the cry, an' we aal creep oot,
Te the mothergate it te mend.
Geordie Hall, he's the depitty in wor flat,
Says: 'Ye'll drive us roond the bend.'

So we pull an' we strain for te fix it agyen,
An' when it's been put straight,
Tim Jones, that's the seccetary of wor Lodge,
Says: 'It's time that ye had your bait.'
So we tak worsels te a quiet spot,
Wi' a plank an' a chock for a seat,
An' the crack at last flies thick an' fast,
O' the deeins at the Club last neet.

Wey, it's very hard when ye're paid by the yard
For te tak lang ower your bait.
So we craal back on, get some timmerin done,
For the belts we can hardly wait.
For it's twenty-six inches high, me lads,
An' the wark is really grand.
An' the fillers' pay, fower quid a day,
It's the best in aal the land.

> Oh, the collier lad is a canny lad,
> An' he's aalwes of good cheor,
> An' he knaas how te work, an' he knaas how te shork,
> An' he knaas how te sup good beor.

(*neuk = end; scufflins = small coal shavings left by the cutting machines; mothergate=main tunnel; timmerin = setting props*).

From the other side of England, from the same hand that wrote the "Lament for Albert" comes a song in praise of the Lancashire miner, called "The Cage". As with John Pandrich and his "Collier lad", Keith Roberts of Wigan made up his own tune to carry the song. Like "Lament for Albert", this piece is published on a broadside.

Mon-day morn-ing, Shift Num-ber One,   Wish that the day's work was o-ver and done.

Climb   in the cage, boys, let her   roll!   We're   the war-ri-ors who   fight for the coal.

Monday morning, Shift Number One.
Wish that the day's work was over and done.
Climb in the cage, boys, let her roll!
We're the warriors who fight for the coal.

The wheels of the headgear spin around.
The cage like a stone is droppin' down.
Feel the blood in your ears pound.
Down, down into the ground.

First stop bottom, fall like a stone.
Halfway down, lads, soon be done.
There's a hell of a draught, a howlin' gale,
As the cage whistles downwards, a-tellin' its tale.

Glarin' lights, dusty floor,
Meet us there outside the cage door.
Crawl to the face, lads, sharin' a joke.
In a couple of hours you'd die for a smoke.

Sweat runs freely, matted hair,
Glistenin' bodies, black and bare.
It's damned hard work but what d'you say?
Roll on Friday when we draw our pay!

The wheels of the headgear spin around.
The cage like a stone is droppin' down.
Feel the blood in your ears pound.
Down, down into the ground.

As a tail-piece to all this, a song—from prolific Durham once again—drawing together many elements that have gone to make up the repertory of vernacular workers' song, old folklore and recent music hall, realism, irony and enduring humour. Despite the brevity of its form and its life, this little vignette, made by the collier Ned Booth of Birtley and set to a tune associated with the old revenant ballad of "The grey cock", constantly undergoes small variations as it passes from mouth to mouth. Here is one of its common forms:

Wake up, wake up, my love, we've slept the clock through.
The bus has flown, the men are gone.
And didn't he glower as he turned ower.
'You bloody fool', he said, 'its Sunday morn!'

That powerful little squib is typical of a great deal of recent industrial song in its use of a relatively un-hackneyed folk ballad air. Throughout the nineteenth century and the first half of the twentieth, there was little original tune-composition to show. Most frequently the texts were set either to known and loved melodies of stage songs ("The king of the Cannibal Islands"), sentimental parlour ballads ("In the days when we went gypsying"), and well-known traditional or *volkstümlich* songs, notably Scots and Irish ("Ball o' Kirriemuir", "There's nae luck aboot the hoose", "Rory O'Moore") because these were more widespread in print than the English folk songs, and so enjoyed broader currency in the towns. All the same a certain number of properly folkloric tunes were used (two miners of West Rainton made a sturdy ballad for the 1844 Durham Strike, to the melody of "A-nutting we will go" or "The nutgirl", and a good air for the purpose it turned out to be). However, new tunes of traditional cast were hard to seek. Two factors militated against their appearance. In the mills and factories, foundries and mines, the urge to make verse comments is more pressing than the impulse to create melodies. Also, the balladeer desiring to make a quick impression with his song would use a generally liked ready-made air to help the rapid and unhindered spread of his idea. Only in very recent times, since so many unfamiliar folk tunes have been given wide currency through the folk song clubs, have the more out-of-the-way versions of traditional tunes been widely used in workers' song, and the number of original compositions is still minimal though growing.

Where are the star-reaching beauties of workers' song to match the masterpieces of the rural folk song of the past? A fair question; yet it is fruitless to apply mechanically the *a priori* standards of classical country folklore to the spiritual productions of people leading a totally different life, with different tensions and relaxations, different relations to family and work, amid sooty brick not green grass, perhaps on shift-work that turns day into night and imposes an unnatural measure of time, a class among whom book culture is stronger than oral culture, a class at once less homogeneous and far more highly organized than the working communities that carried folk song in former times. Proletarian folklore departs from the familiar tradition in several respects, and it is precisely its novel features that make it significant to us.

It cannot be claimed that the general run of workers' songs are an artistic match for the best folk songs of the pre-industrial past. In the first place, there are fewer of them; the history of their tradition is shorter, their basis for creation is narrower, their life tends to be ephemeral because their content is often topical, made for agitational use, and their force may not endure because the flow of events may render them obsolete. In the second place, since most of the songs have been circulating only for a relatively short time and not in the best conditions for re-creation, they have not been so favoured by the paring, moulding, transforming process that successive singers may provide who live outside the orbit of book culture (a process that may smooth a song into lovely forms, but may also erode it into a shape without meaning). In the third place, in urban society, especially among half-educated folk like the majority of the nineteenth century proletariat, banal sentimental verse of bourgeois origin spreads in great force among working people, especially as entertainment became increasingly a big business affair, and this helps to inhibit or distort the home-made song creations. Then too, as a consequence of half-education, many worker song-writers wanted to work in a higher-flying and more literary fashion than their talents could support.

For all that, clumsiness and cliché are not the significant marks of industrial folklore. The point of the songs lies in their appropriateness as lyrical statements of the emotional and practical problems of the bearers. In that, many of them are singularly successful. Though so far researchers into industrial folk song in England have only feebly scratched the surface, several jewels have been unearthed, certainly enough to convince us that by systematic field-recording in industrial areas, and by a careful combing of archive and library material, broadsides, printed or cyclostyled song-books and song-sheets, local newspapers, trade union journals, workers' manuscripts and such,* a rich store of folklore native to the industrial proletariat, including material being created in our own time, may be brought to light. The matter concerns not only songs, in fact, but also tales, proverbs, customs, beliefs, craft-slang and other speechways, and oral history in the form of

---

* In Czechoslovakia, V. Karbusicky and V. Pletka found in the police files a rich crop of song-copies impounded over a long period in the past, during various strikes and demonstrations. It is doubtful whether the English police were ever as bureaucratically diligent as their old Habsburg colleagues.

personal reminiscences of great or lesser events of working class life. Properly organized and carried out, such an enterprise could produce valuable material for historians, social scientists, writers, musicians and the like, clearly enough, but its supreme importance is in its service to the working class itself, in drawing together the scattered and hidden bits of the industrial community's heritage, and in stimulating the continuation of workers' creative traditions. As yet, the working class itself is only dimly aware of the extent and value of its own home-made culture, because the thing has never been properly looked into and publicized. Workers in one area have no idea what their comrades in other areas possess in the way of folk culture. South Wales Miners are thunderstruck when by chance they are confronted with the songs made by miners in Durham. If our rural folklore is a thing of the past, our industrial folklore is still, in good part, very much of the present. The publication of one or two smallish collections of workers' folk songs, the appearance of a handful of records of industrial ballads, the circulation through the folk song clubs of a limited number of songs from the mines, mills, shipyards and foundries, have done a great deal to incite workers to resume the making of songs from the very heart of the big industries, songs that can take their place with the utmost naturalness alongside the admired stuff of the past, in the great stock of lyrics that labouring people have made for themselves, that we call our folk tradition.

Folk song in England is in a curious position; indeed it is so throughout the world, with the Rolling Stones all the rage among the switched-on youngsters of Mongolia, Somaliland flooded with samba music, and the villagers of Ardusat in the folkloristically-rich Maramureş region of Rumania choosing a composition by Dowland, no less, as one of their favourite pieces. Everywhere the old oral traditions are jeopardized by the struggle for literacy, the ceremonial repertory shrinks as the magic is no longer believed in, the flavour of feudal and other past orders is no longer palatable in the singers' mouths, and the flood of Western popular music—so easy to assimilate— is carried by radio and record to drown the local musics that once were so closely interwoven in the fabric of daily life.

These days, people may move from the Stone Age to the Atomic Age in a single leap, and what becomes of the old culture that no longer fits their new life? As Walter Wiora says in his *Vier Weltalter der Musik* (Stuttgart, 1961): 'During a transitional period, Negroes who now spend their days in factories may still devote themselves to their familiar customs of an evening, but these are mere pledges to decadence insofar as they cannot be adapted to an industrial and museum age, being given a secondary existence through the deliberate cultivation of folklore, or through the tourist industry, etc.'

The easily identified, water-pure, guaranteed authentic folk song beloved of the scholars is dying everywhere. In some parts (Germany, France, Scandinavia sooner than England perhaps) its agony had already commenced centuries ago. But in sophisticated urban surroundings it is rising again and entering on a second existence, either informally under the influence of commercial popular music as in U.S.A. or Britain, for example, or formally under the influence of concert music, as along the road from Prague to Pekin. Whether this 'second existence' is ephemeral or not, it is artificial, with the repertory at once protected as a conscious portion of 'heritage', and exposed to the winds by being shifted on to the plane of mass entertainment, divorced from its natural setting and the function it fulfilled in its former folklore milieu, so that for instance a primitive midwinter good-luck charm becomes an amiable chorus song for nuclear physics students in a university folk club, and a piece designed to console a shepherd for the loss of a beloved sheep (and perhaps meant to entice it magically from its rocky hiding-place) becomes a *Konzertstück* for a gipsy orchestra in a Balkan tourist hotel. For all that, we have to realise that many revived folk songs today, in their 'second existence', are probably enjoying a more vigorous life than they did in their first, restricted time, even if they are bent to different purposes. For instance, shanties are now sung for fun, not work, but are perhaps more often performed and better-loved and serve a wider communal end (being sung in folk clubs, on car rides, on political marches even) than they did when they were merely a work-accessory—albeit an intense one—for a small body of seamen.

Amid the disorders of death and resurrection, the show business corporations add their bit of confusion by annexing the term 'folk song' to describe certain professionally made cabaret-style products that have nothing to do with musical folklore either in the way they are created and spread, nor in formal style, psychological climate or function. Donkey and horse both have four legs and may pull carts but they are not the same beast; nor are the compositions of a Dylan or a Donovan folk songs by any workable definition. They may contain elements of alienation and protest, as certain folk songs do (though in fact the direct protest song is rare outside the radical labour tradition that began to form with the nineteenth century), but they still remain songs that firmly belong to the insubstantial world of the modern commercial hit and in no sense qualify to take their place alongside the home-made lyrics of the working people, any more than—in their different way—the literary proletarian anthems of the "Internationale" kind that are sometimes favoured with the label of 'folk song' by some in the Socialist world whose enthusiasm exceeds their common sense. If "Little boxes" and "The red flag" are folk songs, we need a new term to describe "The outlandish knight", "Searching for lambs" and "The coal-owner and the pitman's wife". In any case, no special mystical virtue attaches to the notion of folk song, grand as some folkloric creations may be. Show-business songs and labour hymns have their own qualities, and neither their mass connections nor their artistic character are satisfactorily suggested and emphasized by emotionally applying the description 'folk song' to them. Indeed, it could be argued that in some respects the term is belittling, seeing that folk song proper, modest article that it is, has neither the colossal acceptability of the commercial product nor the broad idealistic horizon of the political mass song.

It may be that the term 'folk song' is losing its meaning, just as the thing itself fades and merges into a general stream of music, into that One Music that begins to embrace not only Western high art, popular and traditional musics, but also the musics of other continents and cultures, with Japanese koto players taking to harpsichord, pop musicians experimenting with the bouzouki, a French composer writing Roman Catholic music in Indian style, and a Mongolian girl singing her horse-herding songs in conservatoire manner as if they were arias by Tchaikovsky. Almost without noticing it we are being immersed in a multistratified music aimed at all levels of appreciation and all colours of skin, while a few producers of rarefied esoteric music, such as the more introvert post-Webernians, re-nouncing all popularity or democratic spirit, fight a feeble rearguard action that may well end in silence, with a few works for reading only, not to be heard, the perfect performance all in the mind without the coarse intervention of musician or public.

With this airy perspective of a more or less unified 'classless' global music, a prospect that some find inspiring and others lowering—and which may prove to be a bit of each—we are far beyond the frontiers of our present study. Where are we at present? To what extent do the modern workers' self-made lyrical productions, scanty as they are (we imagine, without having searched very hard), to what extent do they correspond to the traditional fund of the past? For the matter of that, how closely do today's miners, mill-hands, foundry-workers and electrical engineers resemble that vague mass that in the past we called 'the folk'?

Hardly at all, many folklorists would say; the bearers of the old tradition lie under the grass of a thousand country church-yards, and we can only cherish their songs like sweet fading ghosts. And is there no continuity? May not the makers of "The Bury new loom" or "The coal-owner and the pitman's wife", and their staunch union balladeer sisters such as Jane Knight of Wingate be seen as the intermediaries between an old tradition and a new? To the folklorists of crepuscular view, Dr. Charles Seeger,[50] who has brooded over the problem longer and more wisely than any of us, gives this reply: 'Rather than say "the folk is dead" and attempt to keep folk song alive as something quaint, antique and precious, let us say "The folk is changing—and its songs with it", and then help what it is changing into—which may be the whole people welded into one by the new media of communication—not to be ashamed of its ancestors, but to select the makings of a new, more universal idiom for the more stabilized society that we may hope is coming into being, from the best materials available, whether old or new. Better than to lament the loss of ancient gold will be to try to understand its permutation into another metal which, though it may be baser, may still surprise us in the end by being nobler.'

NOTES

1. This dragon of a question is usually avoided by folklorists. It is boldly raised, and adroitly sidestepped, by Constantin Brailoiu in the course of his study, 'Le folklore musical' in *Musica Aeterna* (Zurich, Metz, 1949), vol. II, pp. 277–332.
2. Cecil J. Sharp: *English Folk-song, Some Conclusions* (London, 1907), pp. 3–4.
3. *Journal of the International Folk Music Council* ([London] 1955), vol. VII, p. 23.
4. Leslie Shepard: *The Broadside Ballad* (London, 1962), p. 52.
5. Quoted in Brailoiu, op. cit., p. 291. The phrase occurs in a letter reproduced in Julien Tiersot: *Chanson populaire et les écrivains romantiques* (Paris, 1931), pp. 160–1.
6. Rodney Gallop: *Portugal, a Book of Folk-ways* (Cambridge, 1936), p. xiv.
7. Samuel P. Bayard: 'The Principal Melodic Families' in *The Critics and the Ballad*, ed. MacEdward Leach and Tristram P. Coffin (Carbondale, Ill., 1961), p. 150.
8. A. H. Fox Strangways and Maud Karpeles: *Cecil Sharp* (London, 1933), p. 36.
9. Béla Bartók: *Hungarian Folk Music* (London, 1931), p. 2.
10. Zoltán Kodály: *Népzene és Müzene* (Budapest, 1941), quoted in Bence Szabolcsi: 'Folk Music—Art Music—History of Music' in *Studia Musicologica* (Budapest, 1965), vol. VII, pp. 172–3.
11. Szabolcsi, op. cit., pp. 178–9. Szabolcsi's essay contains the most valuable consideration to date of the *maqam* principle in folk song generally.
12. D. K. Wilgus: 'The Rationalistic Approach' in *Folksong and Folksong Scholarship: Changing Approaches and Attitudes* (Dallas, Texas, 1964), p. 31.
13. Bayard, op. cit., p. 142.
14. Walter Salmen: *Der fahrende Musiker in europäischen Mittelalter* (Kassel, 1960), p. 190.
15. Further parallels to "Le petit roysin" are provided by W. Wiora: *Europäischer Volksgesang* (Cologne, n.d.), p. 50, and W. Salmen: 'National Idiosyncrasies in Wandering Song Tunes' in *Journal of the International Folk Music Council* ([London] 1954), vol. VI, p. 55.
16. János Maróthy: *Az európai népdal születése* (Budapest, 1960). German summary, by the author, in *Beiträge zur Musikwissenschaft* (Berlin, 1962), 4 Jahrgang, Heft 1, pp. 58–70.
17. Lajos Vargyas: 'Les analogies hongroises avec les chants "Guillanneu"' in *Studia Musicologica* (Budapest, 1962), vol. III, pp. 367–78.
18. Quoted in Violet Alford: *Introduction to English Folklore* (London, 1952), pp. 8–9.
19. Ursula Vaughan Williams: *R.V.W., a Biography of Ralph Vaughan Williams* (London, 1964), p. 401.

20. Ernst Meyer: *English Chamber Music* (London, 1946), p. 18.
21. Percy Dearmer, R. Vaughan Williams, Martin Shaw: *The Oxford Book of Carols* (London, 1928), pp. xiv–xv.
22. Phillips Barry, in *Bulletin of the Folksong Society of the Northeast* (Cambridge, Mass., 1933), No. 6, p. 20.
23. Fine specimens of this kind of funeral ritual songs surviving in the twentieth century may be found in Constantin Brailoiu: *Ale mortului din Gorj* (Bucarest, 1936), translated into French by I. Voronca and J. Lassaigne as 'Chants du mort' in *Mesures* (Brussels, 1939).
24. M. Braun: *Das serbokroatische Heldenlied* (Göttingen, 1961), p. 28.
25. W. Roy Mackenzie: *The Quest of the Ballad* (Princeton, N.J., 1919), p. 28.
26. V. Y. Propp: *Russkii geroicheski epos* (Leningrad, 1955), p. 5.
27. E. K. Chambers: *English Literature at the Close of the Middle Ages* (Oxford, 1945), p. 137.
28. Alexander Keith: 'Scottish Ballads: Their Evidence of Authorship and Origin', in *Essays and Studies by Members of the English Association* (Oxford, 1926), Vol. XII, p. 117.
29. Paul de Keyser: 'Het Lied van Halewijn. Een psychoanalytisch Onderzoek' in *Nederlandsch Tijdschrift voor Volkskunde*, XXVII (1922), referred to in Holgar Olof Nygard: 'Ballad Source Study: Child Ballad No. 4 as Exemplar' in *Journal of American Folklore* (Philadelphia, Pa., 1952), vol. LXV.
30. Lajos Vargyas: 'Forschungen zur Geschichte der Volksballade im Mittelalter: II. Das Weiterleben der landnahmezeitlichen Heldenepik in den ungarischen Balladen' in *Acta Ethnographica* (Budapest, 1961), vol. X, pp. 242–94.
31. Emilia Comişel and Mariana Rodan-Kahane: 'Pe urmele lui Béla Bartók în Hunedoara' in *Muzica* (Bucarest, 1955), vol. V, No. 9.
32. J. A. Fuller Maitland and W. Barclay Squire (eds.): *The Fitzwilliam Virginal Book* (New York, 1963), vol. I, p. 87 (No. XXVI).
33. A valuable source of information about musicians' craft organizations in the sixteenth century, much drawn on by me in the relevant pages, is Walter L. Woodfill: *Musicians in English Society from Elizabeth to Charles I* (Princeton, N.J., 1953).
34. E. P. Thompson: *The Making of the English Working Class* (London, 1963), p. 9.
35. In *Journal of the English Folk Dance and Song Society*, vol. III. no. 3 (London, 1938), pp. 161–4, Anne G. Gilchrist has an interesting note on the relation of this group of songs to a sacred parody in the Wedderburn brothers' *Ane Compendious Book of Godly and Spirituall Sangis* (Edinburgh, 1567).
36. See Kodály's introduction to *A Magyar Népzene Tára* (Budapest, 1955), Vol. III: *Lakodalom*, pp. ix–x.
37. Mircea Eliade: *The Forge and the Crucible* (London, 1962), p. 57n.
38. Harry Cox's performance of this song appears on a gramophone record, *Songs of Seduction* (Caedmon TC 1143).

39. J. L. and Barbara Hammond: *The Village Labourer* (London, 1938 ed.), vol. I, pp. 26–7.

40. Francesca Allinson: 'The Irish Contribution to English Traditional Tunes' (MS. deposited in the Vaughan Williams Memorial Library, London).

41. Bayard, op. cit., pp. 139–40.

42. Reported in Frank Peel: *The Risings of the Luddites* (Heckmondwike, 1888), p. 46.

43. Quoted in Thompson, op. cit., pp. 606–7.

44. W. Radcliffe: *Origin of Power Loom Weaving* (Stockport, 1828). Quoted in Thompson, op. cit., p. 276.

45. R. Howard: *History of the Typhus of Heptonstall Slack* (Hebden Bridge, 1844). Quoted in Thompson, op. cit., p. 290.

46. Gerhard Heilfurth: *Das Bergmannslied: Wesen/Leben/Funktion* (Kassel, Basel, 1954), pp. 39–40, 766–7.

47. Thompson, op. cit., p. 334.

48. George Korson: *Coal Dust on the Fiddle* (Philadelphia, 1943), p. 334.

49. George Korson: *Minstrels of the Mine-Patch* (Philadelphia, 1938), pp. 37–8.

50. Charles Seeger: 'Folk Music in the Schools of a Highly Industrialised Society' in *Journal of the International Folk Music Council* (Cambridge, 1953), vol. V, p. 44.

SELECTED BIBLIOGRAPHY

Ashton, John. *A Century of Ballads*. London: Elliot Stock, 1887.

Ashton, John. *Modern Street Ballads*. London: Chatto and Windus, 1883.

Ashton, John. *Real Sailor Songs*. London: Leadenhall Press, 1891.

Baring-Gould, S., and H. Fleetwood Sheppard. *A Garland of Country Songs*. London: Methuen, 1895.

Baring-Gould, S. and H. Fleetwood Sheppard. *Songs of the West*. Revised edition. London: Methuen, n.d. [1905].

Barrett, William Alexander. *English Folk Songs*. London: Novello, n.d. [1891].

Barry, Phillips, Fannie Hardy Eckstorm and Mary Winslow Smyth. *British Ballads from Maine*. New Haven: Yale U. Press, 1929.

Belden, Henry Marvin. *Ballads and Songs Collected by the Missouri Folklore Society*. Columbia, Mo.: The University of Missouri, 1940.

Bell, Robert. *Ancient Poems, Ballads and Songs of the Peasantry of England*. London. John W. Parker & Sons, 1857.

Broadwood, John. *Sussex Songs*. London: Stanley Lucas and Weber, n.d. [1890].

Broadwood, Lucy E., and J. A. Fuller Maitland. *English County Songs*. London: The Leadenhall Press, 1893.

Broadwood, Lucy E. *English Traditional Songs and Carols*. London: Boosey, 1908.

Bronson, Bertrand Harris. *The Traditional Tunes of the Child Ballads*. 3 vols. *In progress*. Princeton, N.J.: Princeton U. Press, 1959, 62, 66.

Bruce, J. Collingwood and John Stokoe. *Northumbrian Minstrelsy*. Hatboro, Penna.: Folklore Associates, 1965.

Bulletin of the Folksong Society of the Northeast. Reprint (12 nos. in 1 vol.). Philadelphia: American Folklore Society, 1960.

Chappell, William. *Popular Music of the Olden Time*. 2 vols. New York: Dover Publications, 1965.

Child, Francis James. *The English and Scottish Popular Ballads*. 5 vols. New York: Dover Publications, 1965.

Christie, William. *Traditional Ballad Airs*. 2 vols. Edinburgh: Edmonston and Douglas, 1876, 1881.

Coffin, Tristram P. *The British Traditional Ballad in North America*. Philadelphia: American Folklore Society, 1950.

Colcord, Joanna. *Songs of American Sailormen*. London: Putnam, 1938.

Cox, J. H. *Folk-Songs of the South*. Cambridge, Mass.: Harvard U. Press, 1925.

Dean Smith, Margaret. *A Guide to English Folk Song Collections 1822–1952*. Liverpool: University Press of Liverpool, 1954.

Doerflinger, William Main. *Shantymen and Shantyboys: Songs of the Sailor and Lumberman*. New York: The Macmillan Co., 1951.

Entwistle, William J. *European Balladry*. Oxford: The Clarendon Press, n.d. [1951].

Firth, C. H. *Naval Songs and Ballads*. London: Navy Records Society, 1908.

Ford, Robert. *Vagabond Songs and Ballads of Scotland*. First and second series Paisley and London: Alexander Gardner, 1899, 1901.

Fox Smith, C. *A Book of Shanties*. London: Methuen, 1927.

Gardiner, George B. *Folk Songs from Hampshire*. London: Novello, 1909.*

Gerould, Gordon Hall. *The Ballad of Tradition*. Oxford: The Clarendon Press, 1932.

Gillington, Alice E. *Songs of the Open Road*. London: J. Williams, 1911.

Green, R. L. *Early English Carols*. Oxford: The Clarendon Press, 1935.

Greenleaf, Elizabeth Bristol, and Grace Yarrow Mansfield. *Ballads and Sea Songs of Newfoundland*. Cambridge, Mass.: Harvard U. Press, 1933.

Greig, Gavin. *Folk-Song of the North-East*. Hatboro, Penna.: Folklore Associates, 1963.

Greig, Gavin, and Alexander Keith. *Last Leaves of Traditional Ballads and Ballad Airs*. Aberdeen: The Buchan Club, 1925.

Hammond, H. E. D. *Folk Songs from Dorset*. London: Novello, 1908.*

Harland, John. *Ballads and Songs of Lancashire*. London: Whittaker, 1865.

Heilfurth, Gerhard. *Das Bergmannslied. Wesen, Leben, Funktion*. Kassel and Basel: Bärenreiter, 1954.

Henderson, W. *Victorian Street Ballads*. London: Country Life, 1937.

Hindley, Charles. *The Life and Times of James Catnach*. London: Reeves and Turner, 1878.

Hodgart, M. J. C. *The Ballads*. London: Hutchinson, 1950.

Hugill, Stan. *Shanties of the Seven Seas*. London: Routledge and Kegan Paul, 1961.

Ingledew, C. J. Davison. *The Ballads and Songs of Yorkshire*. London: Bill and Daldy, 1860.

Journal of the Folk-Song Society. 8 vols., 35 parts. London: The Folk-Song Society, 1899–1931.

Journal of the English Folk Dance and Song Society. In progress. London: The Folk Dance and Song Society, 1932–.

Journal of the International Folk Music Council. In progress. [London]: The International Folk Music Council, 1949–.

Joyce, Patrick Weston. *Ancient Irish Music*. Dublin: McGlashan and Gill, 1873.

Joyce, Patrick Weston. *Old Irish Folk Music and Songs*. Dublin: University Press, 1909.

Kidson, Frank, and Alfred Moffatt. *English Peasant Songs*. London: Ascherberg, Hopwood and Crew, 1929.

Kidson, Frank, and Alfred Moffatt. *Folk Songs from the North Countrie*. London: Ascherberg, Hopwood and Crew, 1927.

Kidson, Frank, and Alfred Moffatt. *A Garland of English Folk-Songs*. London: Ascherberg, Hopwood and Crew, 1926.

Kidson, Frank. *Traditional Tunes*. Oxford: Charles Taphouse, 1891.

Korson, George. *Coal Dust on the Fiddle: Songs and Stories of the Bituminous Industry*. Philadelphia: U. of Pennsylvania Press, 1943.

Korson, George. *Minstrels of the Mine Patch: Songs and Stories of the Anthracite Industry*. Philadelphia: U. of Pennsylvania Press, 1938.

Laws, G. Malcolm. *American Balladry from British Broadsides*. Philadelphia: American Folklore Society, 1957.

Lloyd, A. L. *Come All Ye Bold Miners: Ballads and Songs of the Coalfields*. London: Lawrence and Wishart, 1952.

Lloyd, A. L. *The Singing Englishman: an Introduction to Folk Song*. London: The Workers' Music Association, n.d. 1944.

Logan, W. H. *A Pedlar's Pack of Ballads and Songs*. Edinburgh: Wm. Paterson, 1869.

Mackenzie, W. Roy. *Ballads and Sea Songs from Nova Scotia*. Cambridge, Mass.: Harvard U. Press, 1928.

Mackenzie, W. Roy. *The Quest of the Ballad*. Princeton: Princeton U. Press, and London: Oxford U. Press, 1919.

Merrick, W. Percy. *Folk Songs from Sussex*. London: Novello [1912].*

O Lochlainn, Colm. *Irish Street Ballads*. Dublin: Three Candles, and London: Constable, 1939.

O Lochlainn, Colm. *More Irish Street Ballads*. Dublin: Three Candles, 1965.

Ord, John. *The Bothy Songs and Ballads of Aberdeen, Banff and Moray, Angus and the Mearns*. Paisley: Alexander Gardner, 1930.

Purslow, Frank (ed.). *Marrow Bones. English Folk Songs from the Hammond and Gardiner Mss*. London: E.F.D.S. Publications, 1965.

Reeves, James. *The Everlasting Circle. English Traditional Verse from the MSS. of S. Baring-Gould, H. E. D. Hammond, and George B. Gardiner*. London: Heinemann, 1960.

Reeves, James. *The Idiom of the People. English Traditional Verse from the MSS. of Cecil Sharp*. London: Heinemann, 1958.

Rickaby, Franz. *Ballads and Songs of the Shanty-boy*. Cambridge, Mass.: Harvard U. Press, 1926.

Routley, Erik. *The English Carol*. London: Herbert Jenkins, 1958.

Salmen, Walter. *Der fahrende Musiker im europäischen Mittelalter*. Kassel: J. P. Hinnenthal, 1960.

Sampson, J. *The Seven Seas Shanty Book*. London: Boosey, 1927.

Seeger, Peggy and Ewan MacColl. *The Singing Island*. London: Mills Music, 1960.

Sharp, Cecil J. *English Folk Carols*. London: Novello, 1911.

Sharp, Cecil J. *English Folk Chanteys*. London: Schott, 1914.

Sharp, Cecil J. *English Folk Songs, Selected Edition*. 2 parts in 1 vol. London: Novello, 1959.

Sharp, Cecil J. *English Folk Songs from Somerset*. 5 parts (parts 1–3 with C. L. Marson). Taunton: The Wessex Press, 1904–19.

Sharp, Cecil J. *English Folk Song: Some Conclusions*. London: Mercury Books, 1965.

Sharp, Cecil J. *English Folk Songs from the Southern Appalachian Mountains*. 2 vols. in 1. London: Oxford U. Press, 1960.

Sharp, Cecil J. *Folk Songs for Schools*. 9 parts. London: Novello, 1908–22.

O

Shepard, Leslie. *The Broadside Ballad*. London: Herbert Jenkins, 1962.

Simpson, Claude M. *The British Broadside Ballad and its Music*. New Brunswick, New Jersey: Rutgers U. Press, 1966.

de Sola Pinto, V., and A. E. Rodway. *The Common Muse. Popular British Ballads from the 15th to the 20th Century*. Harmondsworth: Penguin Books, 1965.

Sokolov, Yu. M. *Russian Folklore*. Hatboro, Penna.: Folklore Associates, and London: Herbert Jenkins, 1966.

Steinitz, Wolfgang. *Deutsche Volkslieder demokratischen Charakters*. 2 vols. Berlin: Akademie Verlag, 1954, 62.

Terry, R. R. *The Shanty Book*. 2 vols. London: Curwen, 1921, 26.

Vaughan Williams, R. *Folk Songs from the Eastern Counties*. London: Novello, 1908.*

Vaughan Williams, R., and A. L. Lloyd (*eds.*). *The Penguin Book of English Folk Songs*. Harmondsworth: Penguin Books, 1959.

Wells, Evelyn K. *The Ballad Tree*. New York: The Ronald Press, 1950.

Whall, W. B. *Sea Songs and Shanties*. Glasgow: James Brown, 1912.

Whittaker, W. G. *North Countrie Ballads, Songs and Pipe Tunes*. London: Curwen, 1921.

Wilgus, D. K. *Anglo-American Folksong Scholarship since 1898*. New Brunswick, New Jersey: Rutgers U. Press, 1959.

Williams, Alfred. *Folk Songs of the Upper Thames*. London: Duckworth, 1923.

Wimberly, L. C. *Folklore in the English and Scottish Ballads*. New York: Dover Publications, 1965.

Wiora, Walter. *Europäischer Volksgesang. Gemeinsame Formen in Charakteristischen Abwandlungen*. Cologne: Arno Volk Verlag, n.d.

Woodfill, Walter L. *Musicians in English Society from Elizabeth to Charles I*. Princeton, N.J.: Princeton U. Press, 1953.

* Reprinted in one volume as *English County Songs*. Edited by Cecil J. Sharp. London: Novello, 1961.

SOURCES OF MUSICALLY-NOTATED EXAMPLES

O*

105(*b*) A.L.L. (Sofia 1954). MS
115   Ivor Gatty and R.V.W. (Derbyshire 1908). FSJ IV 63
117   melody: A.G.G. (Sussex 1907). FSJ V 20
124   source untraced
129   R.V.W. (Herefordshire 1909). FSJ IV 7
132   P.G. (Lincs 1906). MS
181   A.L.L. (Suffolk 1937). MS
185   H.E.D.H. (Dorset 1907). FSJ III 78
198   H.E.D.H. (Dorset 1906). MS
200   A.L.L. (Dorset 1939). MS
204   G.B.G. (Hants 1907). MB 34
205   A.L.L. (Suffolk 1941). MS
207   melody, A.L.L. (Dorset 1939). MS. Text composite
209   transcribed from disc TC 1143-A *The Folksongs of Britain*, Vol. II Songs of
        Seduction, collected and edited by Peter Kennedy and Alan Lomax
        (Caedmon Records, New York)
216   R.V.W. (Norfolk 1908). FSJ IV 84
218   C.J.S. (Somerset). EFS II 79
226   transcribed from disc OC 87 (EFDSS)
237   H.E.D.H. (Dorset 1905). FSJ VII 87
239   F.K. (Yorks). KTT 131
246   melody, R.V.W. (Norfolk 1905). FSJ II 166
260   W. Ford (Surrey 1907). FSJ V 154
263   A.L.L. (Suffolk 1942). MS
267   T. Doubleday (Northumberland), *Blackwoods Magazine*, Nov. 1821
268   melody, *Northumbrian Minstrelsy* 126
272   melody, R.V.W. (Norfolk 1905). *Yacre* 18
280   H.E.D.H. (Dorset 1905). FSJ VII 67
281   A.L.L. (Glamorgan 1954). MS
284   A.L.L. (Glamorgan 1954). MS
297   A.L.L. (Glamorgan 1954). MS
298   generally current in some such form
301   R. R. Terry (Somerset). *Shanty Book* II 15
302   C.J.S. (Somerset), NSS Bk 262 15
303   generally current in some such form
305   source untraced (in outline, generally current)
306   C.J.S. (Somerset). NSS Bk 262 6
308   C.J.S. (London 1909). FSJ V 93
311   H. E. Piggott (Devon 1912). FSJ V 306
324   melody, FK *Garland* 94
328   A. E. Green (Yorks 1965). MS
344   A.L.L. (Lancs 1952) CAYBM 93, 131
351   melody: standard version of *The Wedding of Ballporeen*, the tune specified
        on the broadside
356   A.L.L. (Durham 1953). MS
360   A.L.L. (Durham 1952). CAYBM 78, 129
361   W. B. Toyn (Durham, 1962).
364   W. B. Toyn (Durham, 1962), as sung by Jack Elliott of Birtley
365   A.L.L. (Durham 1952). CAYBM 68, 128
367   A. E. Green (Yorks 1966). MS
370   Joe Wilson: Tyneside *Songs and Drolleries* (1872)
373   From a leaflet (n.d.) specifying the tune: *Rory O'Moore*

377 A.L.L. (Durham 1952). CAYBM 102
383 A.L.L. (Durham 1952). CAYBM 121, 131
385 A.L.L. (Durham 1952). CAYBM 99
387 A.L.L. for BBC (Durham 1963). MS
390 A.L.L. for BBC (Durham 1963). MS
397 transcribed from disc TOP 78 *Stottin' doon the Waall: Songs of mining and miners written, sung and played by Johnny Handle*
400 A.L.L. for BBC (Durham 1963). MS
401 transcribed from disc TOP 78, as above
403 from a broadside published by Keith Roberts, of Wigan
404 widely current in some such form

ABBREVIATIONS

Collectors

A.G.G.	Annie G. Gilchrist
A.L.L.	A. L. Lloyd
C.J.S.	Cecil J. Sharp
F.K.	Frank Kidson
G.B.G.	George B. Gardiner
H.E.D.H.	H. E. D. Hammond
P.G.	Percy Grainger
R.V.W.	Ralph Vaughan Williams

Publications

BECS	L. E. Broadwood: *English County Songs*, 1893
CAYBM	A. L. Lloyd: *Come All Ye Bold Miners*, 1952
ECFS	ed. C. J. Sharp: *English County Folk Songs*, 1961
EFS	C. J. Sharp: *English Folk Songs* (Centenary edition) (2 vols. in 1), 1959
FSJ	*Journal of the Folk Song Society*, 1899– in progress
Garland	Frank Kidson: *A Garland of English Folk Songs*, 1926
MB	ed. Frank Purslow: *Marrow Bones. English Folk Songs from the Hammond and Gardiner MSS.* 1965
NSS	*Novello's School Series*, 1908–36
Yacre	ed. Imogen Holst and Ursula Vaughan Williams: *A Yacre of Land. Sixteen Folk-Songs from the manuscript collection of Ralph Vaughan Williams*, 1961

GENERAL INDEX

Abbots Bromley horn dance, 97 *n*
Aelfric, *Colloquium*, 91
Aeolian (La) mode, 40, 45–6
Afanasyev, A. N., 204–5
Agricola, Georg, 336
Agricultural ceremonies, 94, 96–9
Agricultural revolution, 232, 335
  economic effects of, 232–4
Akritas, Digenis, 141, 142
Alecsandri, Vasile, *Poesii populare ale
  Românilor*, 26
Alford, Violet, 107, 412
Allinson, Francesca, 230, 414
Armstrong, Louis, 12, 64
Armstrong, Tommy (miners' song-
  writer), 83, 353, 359, 360, 376–84,
  392
Armstrong, W. (broadside publisher),
  241
Army,
  desertion, 257–62
  disaffection, 262–4
  discipline and conditions, 256–8
  popular attitude to, 250–264
  recruiting, 253–6, 257
Arne, Thomas, 179
Aubrey, John, 93 *n*, 140

Bach, Johann Sebastian, 68
Ball, John, 92
Ballad, 'classic', 135–68 *passim*
  areas of survival, 159
  b. hero as community ideal, 141, 143
  bride-stealing, 140
  changing content of, 166–8
  communal creation, 136–7
  diffusion, agents of, 149
  earliest recorded versions, 158
  epic survivals in Balkans, 138–9
  evolution of b. themes, 139
  foreign sources of themes, 150–7, 160
  funerary ritual motifs, 140–1
  heroic content, 141–5
  historical attributions, 137–8
  historical events, bs of, 145
  neglect of tunes, 136–7

medieval literature and b., 148–9
  periodization, 158–9
  reflection of society, 161–5
  scholars' view of b. as literature, 135
  strophic b., emergence of, 158
  transit from epic to lyric, 164
  vagueness of term 'b.', 150
Barbieri, Francisco, 46
Baring–Gould, Rev. Sabine, 31, 159
  186, 199, 215, 255
  Songs of the West, 186
Barry, Phillips, 22, 32, 72, 136, 155,
  276, 413
Bartók, Béla, 12, 17, 23, 47, 50, 65 *n*,
  70, 86, 89, 230, 412
  interpretation of term 'folk', 12–13
  psychological analysis of Rumanian
  songs, 184
  views on f.s. creation, 62
Barton, Sir Andrew, 275–6
Bawdiness as starting-point for spring
  ceremonies, 106
Bayard, Samuel, 18, 60, 81, 230, 412,
  414
Bebbington, John O., broadside pub-
  lisher, 27, 245, 324
Beecham, Sir Thomas, 35
Beethoven Ludwig van, 55, 78
Bell, John, 26, 211–14, 332, 333
  Rhymes of the Northern Bards, 211
Birt, T. (broadside publisher), 193
Black Ball Line, 291–3
Bluebeard tales, 152
Blues, the, 66, 89
Booth, Ned (miners' song-writer), 404
Bover, Captain John, 268
Bower, Walter, *Chronica Gentis Scotorum*,
  145
Brady, Nicholas (hymnwriter), 130
Brailoiu, Constantin, 20, 23, 47, 66,
  412, 413
Britten, Benjamin, 59
Broadside, development of, 26–31
Broadwood, Rev. John, 241
Broadwood, Lucy, 5, 31, 104, 122, 215
  English County Songs, 171
Brockman, Polk C., 75

INDEX OF SONGS MENTIONED